The Irony of Power

Studies in Peace and Scripture
Institute of Mennonite Studies

Titles in the series

Vol. 1
The Gospel of Peace: A Scriptural Message for Today's World
by Ulrich Mauser; published by Westminster John Knox (1992)
ISBN-13 978-0664253493 paperback

Vol. 2
The Meaning of Peace: Biblical Studies
edited by Perry B. Yoder and Willard M. Swartley;
1st ed. published by Westminster John Knox (1992)
ISBN-13 978-0664253127 paperback
2nd ed. with expanded bibliography published by IMS (2001)
ISBN-13 978-0936273303 paperback

Vol. 3
The Love of Enemy and Nonretaliation in the New Testament
edited by Willard M. Swartley; published by Westminster John Knox (1992)
ISBN-13 978-0664253547 paperback

Vol. 4
Violence Renounced: René Girard, Biblical Studies and Peacemaking
edited by Willard M. Swartley;
published by Pandora Press U.S. and Herald Press (2000)
ISBN-13 978-0966502152 paperback

Vol. 5
Beyond Retribution: A New Testament Vision for Justice, Crime and Punishment
by Christopher D. Marshall; published by Eerdmans (2001)
ISBN-13 978-0802847973 paperback

Vol. 6
Crowned with Glory and Honor: Human Rights in the Biblical Tradition
by Christopher D. Marshall; published by Pandora Press U.S., Herald Press, and Lime Grove House, Auckland, NZ (2002)
ISBN-13 978-1931038041 paperback

Vol. 7
Beautiful upon the Mountains: Biblical Essays on Mission, Peace, and the Reign of God
edited by Mary H. Schertz and Ivan Friesen; published by IMS and Herald Press (2003)
ISBN-13 978-0936273358 paperback
Reprint by Wipf & Stock (2008)
ISBN-13 978-1556356544 paperback

Vol. 8
The Sound of Sheer Silence and the Killing State: The Death Penalty and the Bible
by Millard Lind; published by Cascadia Publishing House and Herald Press (2004)
ISBN-13 978-1931038232 paperback

Vol. 9
Covenant of Peace: The Missing Peace in New Testament Theology and Ethics
by Willard M. Swartley; published by Eerdmans (2006)
ISBN-13 978-0802829375 paperback

Vol. 10
Atonement, Justice, and Peace: The Message of the Cross and the Mission of the Church
by Darrin W. Snyder Belousek; published by Eerdmans (2011)
ISBN-13 978-0802866424 paperback

Vol. 11
A Peaceable Hope: Contesting Violent Eschatology in New Testament Narratives
by David J. Neville;
published by Baker Academic (2013)
ISBN-13 978-0801048517 paperback; ISBN 9781441240156 e-book

Vol. 12
Struggles for Shalom: Peace and Violence across the Testaments
edited by Laura L. Brenneman and Brad D. Schantz; published by Pickwick Publications (2014)
ISBN-13 978-1-62032-622-0

The Irony of Power

The Politics of God within Matthew's Narrative

Dorothy Jean Weaver

Foreword by *David Rhoads*

☙PICKWICK *Publications* · Eugene, Oregon

THE IRONY OF POWER
The Politics of God within Matthew's Narrative

Studies in Peace and Scripture: Institute of Mennonite Studies

Copyright © 2017 Dorothy Jean Weaver. All rights reserved. Except for brief quotations in critical publications or reviews, no part of this book may be reproduced in any manner without prior written permission from the publisher. Write: Permissions, Wipf and Stock Publishers, 199 W. 8th Ave., Suite 3, Eugene, OR 97401.

Pickwick Publications
An Imprint of Wipf and Stock Publishers
199 W. 8th Ave., Suite 3
Eugene, OR 97401

www.wipfandstock.com

PAPERBACK ISBN: 978-1-62564-886-0
HARDCOVER ISBN: 978-1-4982-8855-2
EBOOK ISBN: 978-1-4982-4147-2

Cataloguing-in-Publication data:

Names: Weaver, Dorothy Jean

Title: The irony of power : the politics of God within Matthew's narrative / Dorothy Jean Weaver.

Description: Eugene, OR: Pickwick Publications, 2017 | Series: Studies in Peace and Scripture: Institute of Mennonite Studies | Includes bibliographical references and index.

Identifiers: ISBN 978-1-62564-886-0 (paperback) | ISBN 978-1-4982-8855-2 (hardcover) | ISBN 978-1-4982-4147-2 (ebook)

Subjects: LCSH: Bible. Matthew—Criticism, interpretation, etc. | Politics in the Bible. | Nonviolence—Biblical teaching. | Peace—Biblical teaching.

Classification: LCC BS2555.52 W4 2017 (print) | LCC BS2555.52 (ebook)

Manufactured in the U.S.A.   06/19/17

To Wendy,
whose sturdy friendship,
infectious sense of humor,
persistent encouragement,
and daily prayers
have gifted my life and given me energy
for my ongoing journey with the Gospel of Matthew . . .

Contents

Foreword by David Rhoads · ix

Prologue: Confessions of an Autobiographical Exegete · xiii

Acknowledgments · xxiii

Abbreviations · xxvii

Part I. Taking the Wide View: Confronting the Powers across the New Testament

1. Resistance and Nonresistance: New Testament Perspectives on Confronting the Powers · 3

Part II. Matthew and the Irony of Power: The View from the Top Down

2. Power and Powerlessness: Matthew's Use of Irony in the Portrayal of Political Leaders · 27

3. "Thus You Will Know Them by Their Fruits": The Roman Characters of the Gospel of Matthew · 44

4. "What Is That to Us? See to It Yourself": Making Atonement and the Matthean Portrait of the Jewish Chief Priests · 66

5. "They Did to Him Whatever They Pleased": The Exercise of Political Power within Matthew's Narrative · 85

Part III. Matthew and the Irony of Power: The View from the Bottom Up

6. Rewriting the Messianic Script: Matthew's Account of the Birth of Jesus · 125

7. Transforming Nonresistance: From *Lex Talionis* to "Do Not Resist the Evil One" · 137

8. The Hard Sayings of Jesus in Real-World Context: Reading Matthew 5:38–48 within the Occupied Palestinian Territories · 175

9. "As Sheep in the Midst of Wolves": Mission and Peace in the Gospel of Matthew · 199

10. "Suffering Violence" and the Kingdom of Heaven (Matt 11:12): A Matthean Manual for Life in a Time of War · 223

11. "Wherever This Good News Is Proclaimed": Women and God in the Gospel of Matthew · 248

12. Inheriting the Earth: Towards a Geotheology of Matthew's Narrative · 262

Epilogue: An Advent Meditation from Bethlehem, Christmas 2000: The God Who Is "With Us" · 285

Bibliography · 287

Author Index · 293

Scripture Index · 297

Foreword

It has been a pleasure to read this volume and a privilege to be invited to write this Foreword. There are many excellent reasons for you to experience this stellar collection of essays on the Gospel of Matthew by Dorothy Jean Weaver. Let me name some of them.

First, this study is a model of outstanding narrative analysis. Weaver plies the narrative critical craft with unusual care and acumen. She has grasped the world inside the narrative of Matthew's Gospel as a whole, and she draws us into it. She does excellent character analysis of the good and the evil figures in the story as contrasts to one another. She gives attention to the role of setting. She has an insightful understanding of the plot, especially the ironic twists and turns distinctive to Matthew. She nails the implied rhetorical impact of individual episodes and of the narrative as a whole. And she does all of this with careful attention to the significance of an accumulation of related details in the text. I for one became convinced of the integrity of Matthew's story and its literary coherence in a way I had not appreciated before. In addition, Weaver's book is remarkably clear and well-argued.

Second, her analysis of the dynamics of Matthew's story makes a significant contribution to our understanding of the relationship between early Christianity and the Roman Empire. Until recently, there had been a long-standing tendency to mistake the pacifism of early Christianity as political quietism in relation to Rome. Also, scholars have traditionally treated early Christianity as a religious conflict with Jews, while the Roman Empire provided a rather benign backdrop. All that has changed in the last several decades as scholars have turned their attention to the many ways in which early Christians critiqued and resisted the Roman hegemony and sought to create communities that manifested values and practices in direct contrast to the imperial culture. Most New Testament writings have been the object of such analyses.

Weaver's book is an important contribution to this movement. Not only does she see the Matthean Jesus enacting a political vision to renew Israel, but she is bold and innovative in addressing the "politics of God" as a way of seeing the comprehensive and ultimate vision of the kingdom of God over all authorities and powers. She correctly recognizes that Matthew is a story about power. In this regard, Weaver discerns that the conflict in the Gospel is not between Jesus and the Jews but between Jesus' movement of Judean peasants and expendables on the one hand and the authority figures on the other hand—Caesar, the Roman agents in Palestine, and the Judean leaders who act as local surrogates of Rome. As such, the conflict is between the oppressed and the oppressors, the powerless and the powerful.

In dealing with this power dynamic, Weaver lifts up Matthew's portrayal of the violence of the Roman Empire through her characterization of the two Herods, Pilate, and Caesar. Rome seems to have all the power, exercised through violent oppression and hegemony. This is especially on the minds of Matthew's late first-century audience in the shadow of the recent Roman-Judean War of 66 to 70 CE, which involved the crushing defeat of Israel and the destruction of Jerusalem and the Temple. Despite this, for Matthew, as Weaver demonstrates, God is the ultimate source, arbiter, and enactor of true power.

Third, Weaver shows how irony plays a key role in Matthew's overall treatment of the issues of power. Weaver brilliantly displays this power dynamic by untangling the pervasive irony in the Gospel to reveal that things are not what they seem. On the surface Rome and the Jewish collaborators appear to be all-powerful in their capacity to kill children, execute John, threaten any who would subvert Rome, execute Jesus, and persecute followers. Nevertheless, at a different level, the story reveals that the Romans and their agents are really powerless and ineffective in their efforts: Herod the Great's foiled strategies to kill the infant Jesus; Herod the tetrarch's efforts to stop the Jesus movement by killing John; and the efforts of Pilate and the Judean authorities to end the Jesus movement with his execution. Their ultimate powerlessness is apparent at the end of the story with the inability of Roman soldiers effectively to guard the tomb of Jesus and prevent an empty grave. Matthew does not rail directly against the Roman Empire with a prophetic rant; instead, by means of indirection, he exposes and condemns Rome by telling the story the way that he does. Rhetorically, it becomes obvious to any discerning audience what the real truth is about the Roman Empire: In the face of God's activity and those faithful to God, the authorities are ultimately powerless.

As a contrast to Roman ineffectiveness, Weaver highlights the irony of how God's kingdom belongs to the powerless. God's power on behalf of the powerless is manifested throughout the story: from the beginning of the story when the angels of God protect the infant Jesus, his father Joseph, and the Magi; throughout the story with Jesus healing and liberating people in renewing Israel; to the end of the story when there are cosmic signs at the death of Jesus and the resurrection. The politics of God benefits the powerless: Those who are crushed will be empowered; those who are grieving will be comforted; those who are meek and nonviolent will inherit the earth; those who hunger and thirst for justice will get satisfaction. Weaver lays bare the ultimate outcome of Matthew's story: While Rome is diminishing in power, God's agent Jesus is given all authority in heaven and on earth; and he sends out his followers to make disciples of "all nations."

As Weaver shows, the same ironic logic defines the conflict between Jesus and the Judean leaders. The Judean leaders are supposed to be responsible for the atonement of the people. However, they take actions that undermine that role and leave the people accepting responsibility for shedding innocent blood. Meanwhile, Jesus brings atonement for the many into a renewed community.

Fourth, Weaver shows how the powerless are empowered in the face of oppression and persecution. Weaver unpacks this in a careful and clarifying way, distinguishing resistance as retaliation from resistance as the refusal to be like the oppressor. Matthew condemns resistance as violent retaliation—a temptation from Satan to be like the oppressors. Beyond this, Matthew's Jesus promotes active resistance that expresses love for the enemy and at the same time works to create the new world of God's reign. This love of enemy is not a matter of accepting injustice. Rather, it is a proactive expression of blessing and peacemaking and goodness toward those who are evil. It is counterintuitive and countercultural to resist in such a positive way. Yet, in so doing, these actions bring dignity and power to those who are otherwise powerless; and they serve to bring transformation to the world.

Fifth, there is a fresh angle on Matthew's rhetoric. We see clearly from Weaver's comprehensive analysis *what* Matthew's ultimate purpose is and *how* the Gospel leads audiences to get there. When the audience gets to the end of the story, Matthew has led them to be aligned solidly with the Jesus movement and the reign of God and at the same time be empowered to resist the Roman Empire with positive acts of love.

Finally, it is important to say that Weaver's social location as a Mennonite female scholar committed to freedom, equality, mutuality, peace, and love profoundly enhances her insights. In particular, as several essays reveal, as a peace activist, she has spent considerable time with Christians in Israeli-occupied territory in Palestine. Her insights from these experiences have served to inform her analysis of Matthew in significant ways; and in turn, they clarify how the Gospel of Matthew continues to be a source of guidance and inspiration for those enduring oppression in our time.

These brief reflections on Weaver's collection are but a foretaste of what follows. They do not begin to do justice to the plethora of insights that await you in reading this book.

David Rhoads

Professor Emeritus of New Testament
The Lutheran School of Theology at Chicago

Prologue

Confessions of an Autobiographical Exegete

THEY SAY THAT HONEST confession is good for the soul. Well, here is my honest confession, the confession of an exegete: All exegesis, mine surely included, is autobiographical. As I see it, there is no alternative for finite human beings. This is simply the definition, both the cost and the gift, of being human. Because we are finite creatures, because we have finite vision, the "lenses" with which we view the world, and the Scriptures as well, are necessarily made up of all those experiences that have ever happened in our lives. In other words our "lenses" consist of all those things that create our unique autobiographies as human beings. And if our "lenses" are autobiographical, so also is our exegesis. This means that who we are as we read the Scriptures has, and will always have, a profound impact on how we understand the Scriptures and how we discern their message for us.

My own autobiography is one which has connected me deeply to three fundamental realities, three major M's in my life: the Mennonite community of faith, the Gospel of Matthew, and the Middle East. And it is the juxtaposition, or perhaps I should say the collision, of these three worlds within my own autobiography that has both called forth and profoundly impacted the essays within this volume.

My connections with the Mennonite community go back as far as I can remember. I grew up in the 1950s in a deeply Mennonite family in the heart of a deeply Mennonite community, Park View, a Mennonite college town later annexed to Harrisonburg, VA. And within this family and this community I learned about my Anabaptist heritage. I traced my family lines back to Switzerland: Brenneman, Lehman, Hershey, Weaver. I spent hours, even as a child, poring over the vivid stories and the graphic illustrations of sixteenth- and seventeenth-century Anabaptist martyrs in my grandfather's well-worn copy of Thieleman van Braght's *Martyrs Mirror*[1]. I devoured Elizabeth Hershberger Bauman's book, *Coals of Fire*[2], a collection of children's stories about early Anabaptists who refused to hate their enemies and responded with love instead. And I listened with avid interest as my mother read Christmas Carol Kauffman's fictional account of early Swiss Anabaptists, *Not Regina*[3], out loud to my sisters and me.

I knew deep down in my being that I belonged to a faith community where people refused all acts of violence because of the example and the command of Jesus. I knew that I belonged to a faith community where one early Anabaptist, Dirk Willems, even reached out to rescue his captor from drowning in a frozen lake. And I knew as well that I belonged to a faith community where people, Dirk Willems included, suffered to the death for their beliefs.

All of this was part of my autobiography, part of my spiritual DNA, as I grew up in Park View, within my Mennonite family and my Mennonite community. And over long years since then the impact of my Anabaptist/Mennonite heritage has only grown more powerful. There is no question that this has profoundly shaped my personal vision and the "lenses" with which I look at the world and the Scriptures.

Then there is the Gospel of Matthew, my second "M." My connections with the Gospel of Matthew surely go back all the way to my childhood, where I learned the Lord's Prayer, recited the Beatitudes, and heard the story of the Magi every year on Christmas Eve. But my deepest and most powerful connections with the Gospel of Matthew stem from that fateful moment when Dr. Jack Dean Kingsbury, my doctoral adviser at Union Theological Seminary in Virginia (now Union Presbyterian Seminary), dropped the following word into my life: "Well, if you're going to work with me, you might as well work with something that I know something about." And what Jack Dean Kingsbury knew about above all was the Gospel of Matthew. So he suggested that I consider Matthew 10, the Missionary Discourse, as a dissertation text. There were some issues to be resolved, he said. I took the bait. The outcome was *Matthew's Missionary Discourse: A Literary Critical Analysis*.[4] And the rest has been history. I'm still "tangling" with the Gospel

---

1. Van Braght. *Martyrs Mirror*.
2. Bauman. *Coals of Fire*.
3. Kauffman. *Not Regina*.
4. Weaver, *Missionary Discourse*.

of Matthew. And I doubt very much that I will ever get finished. So much for Matthew.

And then there is the Middle East, Israel/Palestine above all. This third "M" catapulted its way into my world in 1995–96, some 45 years after my entry into the Mennonite community and well after I had begun my lifelong "tangle" with the Gospel of Matthew. The Middle East that I encountered, predominantly the world of the Occupied Palestinian Territories, was a world afflicted by brutality, violence, injustice, and oppression. This was a world where powerful people were on top and powerless people were on the bottom. It was a world where things happened in seemingly illogical ways and where injustice and oppression appeared to be the rule of the day. My first semester in Israel/Palestine, Spring 1996, was a tumultuous semester for me and gut-wrenching in the extreme. But it was also a semester of deep gift. This was the semester in which I heard a call from God that has left my life profoundly changed ever since. And, some 24 Middle East tours, personal trips, and sabbatical sojourns down the road and counting, that call remains sturdy and irresistible.

So much for my "3-M" autobiography. But what about my autobiographical exegesis? What happens when "Mennonite" and "Matthew" and "Middle East" get all tangled up with each other? What follows in the pages of this volume reflects my own exegetical journey with the Gospel of Matthew over long years of study and reflection. What I have found compelling, above all else, as I have studied the Gospel of Matthew is the intense irony tucked away in Matthew's version of the "Good News." For Matthew the "good news of the kingdom" is indeed good news, but good news that unfolds in ways that we would hardly anticipate. And this good news is without question good news for a profoundly real world. Over time in my study of Matthew's Gospel, I have found myself circling around and around the same set of urgent and persistently relevant "real world" questions, namely those that concern power and powerlessness, violence and nonviolence, and the astonishing and profoundly upside-down "politics" of the reign of God (for Matthew the "kingdom of heaven") as reflected in Matthew's Gospel.

The volume presented here is one that I have, in effect, been writing and publishing one chapter at a time over long years. The central thesis of this volume lies in an essay which grew out of ongoing classroom encounters with the Gospel of Matthew early in my teaching career in a course entitled "Reading the Biblical Text." This course, in which I engaged the Gospel of Matthew narratively each year with entry-level seminary students, led me to comment regularly to the class members, "Do you *see* what Matthew is doing to the reader in this portrait of Herod the king (or Herod the tetrarch or Pilate the governor)? Do you *see* the irony here?"

So when I was invited to submit a paper for presentation to the Matthew Group of the Society of Biblical Literature at the 1992 Annual Meeting in San Francisco, CA, I took this opportunity to submit the essay "Power and Powerlessness: Matthew's Use of Irony in the Portrayal of Political Leaders," a paper subsequently published in *Treasures New and Old: Recent Contributions to Matthean* Studies, a volume of collected essays from the SBL Matthew Group.[5] In this essay I laid out what I viewed to be Matthew's persistently ironic *modus operandi* in depicting the three central Roman or Roman-affiliated political figures within his narrative: Herod the king (2:1–23), Herod the tetrarch (14:1–12), and Pilate the governor (27:1–2, 11–38, 54, 62–66; 28:11–15). And I concluded that the relentless and biting rhetoric of Matthew's narrative, while it first invests these figures with the enormous power inherent in their political roles, ultimately serves to subvert this evident power by portraying the actual powerlessness of these leaders vis-à-vis those over whom they wield their authority (Jesus for Herod the king and Pilate the governor; John the Baptist for Herod the tetrarch).

The central insight which I gleaned from this initial study of the political leaders of the Gospel of Matthew—namely Matthew's effective and ironic subversion of all standard definitions of political power precisely in order to set forth a new "God's-eye" vision of political power as reflected within the life, death, and resurrection of Jesus, Messiah and King of the Jews—is an insight which has continued to energize my ongoing studies of the Gospel of Matthew over the years since 1992. And it is this fundamental Matthean irony concerning "power and powerlessness" (along with the closely associated theme of "violence and nonviolence") which has called forth or found its way into all of my major publications focused on Matthew's Gospel.

It is this central insight which collects the essays listed below into a thematically-focused volume on "The Irony of Power," a phrase which I worked hard to identify as the theme for this volume and then, subsequently and happily and most appropriately, rediscovered verbatim in the "Concluding Observations" of my seminal essay on "Power and Powerlessness." The aim of this book is twofold: (1) to highlight the deeply "political" character of Matthew's Gospel, focused as it is on God's reign (for Matthew "the kingdom of heaven") and on Jesus Messiah, God's appointed agent to enact this reign on earth; and (2) to highlight the "politics of God," namely the profoundly ironic character of "power" as viewed from a "God's-eye" perspective within Matthew's narrative and as portrayed through the narrative rhetoric of Matthew's text. The chapters of this volume unfold as follows:

---

5. Weaver, "Power and Powerlessness," 179–96.

I. Taking the Wide View: Confronting the Powers across the New Testament

1. "Resistance and Nonresistance: New Testament Perspectives on Confronting the Powers."[6] This essay serves as a broadly-framed New Testament essay introducing the subsequent set of more narrowly-framed Matthean essays. It focuses on the twofold strategy laid out within the New Testament writings for confronting earthly and beyond-earthly powers. This strategy is reflected on the one hand in the call of James to "resistance" (Jas 4:7) and on the other hand in the call of Jesus to "nonresistance" (Matt 5:39). The first half of this essay highlights broad motifs of "resistance" vis-à-vis the cosmic powers of evil (Satan/the devil/the tempter, demons/evil spirits/unclean spirits) and their impact on human beings (temptations, demon possession, physical illness). By contrast the second half of this essay highlights the ironic and univocal declaration of New Testament writers across the canon that Jesus and those faithful to him in fact conquer the powers of evil even as they love their human enemies and suffer to the death at their hands.

II. Matthew and the Irony of Power: The View from the Top Down

2. "Power and Powerlessness: Matthew's Use of Irony in the Portrayal of Political Leaders."[7] As noted above, this essay defines and illustrates the fundamental "irony of power" underlying Matthew's narrative account of Jesus Messiah, specifically as it relates to the portraits of Herod the king, Herod the tetrarch, and Pilate the governor. While Matthew attributes power to these political figures on the "lower level" of the story through his use of public titles, designated roles, and demonstrated actions, the overall narrative rhetoric of Matthew's account paints an ironic "upper level" portrait which reveals by contrast the ultimate powerlessness of Herod the king, Herod the tetrarch, and Pilate the governor. This essay, in light of its chronological priority and its seminal impact on the remainder of my studies, clearly deserves "pride of place" at the front of the Matthean essays.

---

6. Used by permission of the publisher, from *HTS Teologiese Studies/Theological Studies*, 61, nos. 1–2 (2005) 619–38.

7. Used by permission of the publisher, from *Treasures New and Old: Recent Contributions to Matthean Studies*, ed. David R. Bauer and Mark Allan Powell, SymS 1 (Atlanta: Scholars, 1996) 179–96.

3. "'Thus You Will Know Them by Their Fruits': The Roman Characters of the Gospel of Matthew."[8] This essay reads Matthew's account of the Roman characters within the story of Jesus Messiah through the lens of Matthew's ironic rhetoric, a rhetoric which establishes the outlines of Roman imperial power on the one hand only to "unmask [its] powerful façade and reveal the true state of affairs" (p. 114, original publication) on the other. Here I discuss first of all the designated roles of the Roman characters/character groups within Matthew's narrative as Matthew portrays these roles. I then set forth Matthew's narrative portraits of the Roman characters in question vis-à-vis their designated roles. I conclude with reflections on the overall impact of Matthew's narrative rhetoric vis-à-vis the Roman characters of his Gospel.

4. "'What Is That to Us? See To It Yourself': Making Atonement and the Matthean Portrait of the Jewish Chief Priests."[9] In this essay I assess the Matthean portrait of the Jewish chief priests of Jesus' day against the Levitical backdrop which lays out their primary role within Jewish religious life, namely "making atonement" before God for the "sins" of the people. I first sketch out the Matthean portrait of the assigned role of the priestly class within Jewish religious life, connecting this Matthean portrait to its biblical antecedents. I then assess the narrative performance of the Matthean chief priests against the backdrop of their assigned role within Jewish society. The central Matthean text under consideration here is 27:3–10, the account of Judas Iscariot, who returns to the chief priests with the 30 pieces of silver which they have paid him to "hand [Jesus] over" (26:14–16) and announces to them, "*I have sinned*, because I have handed over innocent blood" (emphasis mine). This essay highlights Matthew's ironic *modus operandi* as he portrays the response of the Jewish chief priests to an Israelite who comes to them confessing his sin.

5. "'They Did to Him Whatever They Pleased': The Exercise of Political Power within Matthew's Narrative."[10] This essay extends the portrait of political power exhibited by the Roman imperial forces over the subjugated Jewish community of first-century Palestine to include the political power exhibited by the Jewish leadership in Palestine, those figures who collaborate with the Roman overlords in their authority over the Jewish people. The

---

8. Used by permission of Bloomsbury Publishing Plc., from *The Gospel of Matthew in Its Roman Imperial Context*, ed. John Riches and David C. Sim, JSNTSup 276 (New York: Continuum, 2005) 107–27.

9. Used by permission of the publisher, from *HTS Teologiese Studies/Theological Studies* 70, no. 1 (2014), Art. #2703, 8 pages. http://dx.doi.org/10.4102/hts.v70i1.2703.

10. Used by permission of the publisher, from *HTS Teologiese Studies/Theological Studies* 65, no. 1 (2009), Art. #319, 13 pages. http://dx.doi.org/10.4102/hts.v65i1.319.

essay first identifies Matthew's highly negative portrayal of these political leaders, whether Roman or Jewish, and their typical *modus operandi* in their exercise of political power. It then assesses the actual effectiveness of the power which the Roman and Jewish political leaders exhibit, concluding that this use of power is ultimately and ironically ineffective in spite of their best efforts.

III. Matthew and the Irony of Power: The View from the Bottom Up

6. "Rewriting the Messianic Script: Matthew's Account of the Birth of Jesus."[11] This essay reads the story of Jesus' birth (1:1—2:23) through the lens of Matthew's ironic rhetoric and highlights the way in which Matthew rewrites the definition of messianic identity (story of Joseph: 1:1-25), messianic character (story of Herod: 2:1-23), and messianic vocation (story of the magi: 2:1-12). In a section entitled "Concluding Reflections" the essay then follows the themes emerging from this "rewriting" of the messianic script throughout the remainder of Matthew's Gospel.

7. "Transforming Nonresistance: From *Lex Talionis* to 'Do Not Resist the Evil One.'"[12] This essay offers a detailed exegesis of Matthew 5:38-42 vis-à-vis the *lex talionis* of Deuteronomy 19:15-21, its closest biblical intertext. The essay highlights not only the ironic power inherent in the act of "not resisting the one who is evil" but also the pointed contrast with the violent Deuteronomic formula for "removing the evil one from your midst." And the essay likewise demonstrates the counter-intuitive freedom to act (rather than merely react) which emerges paradoxically from Jesus' scandalous call "not to resist the one who is evil."

8. "The Hard Sayings of Jesus in Real-World Context: Reading Matthew 5:38-48 within the Occupied Palestinian Territories."[13] This essay opens with a brief scholarly reading of Matthew 5:38-48, highlighting the ironic power inherent in the act of "not resisting the one who is evil." It then moves on to offer an existential Palestinian-Christian reading of this same text, based on personal interviews with sixteen Palestinian Christians who

---

11. Used by permission of the publisher, from *Interpretation: A Journal of Bible and Theology*, 54, no. 4 (2000) 376–85.

12. Used by permission of the publisher, from *The Love of Enemy and Nonretaliation in the New Testament*, ed. Willard M. Swartley, SPS (Louisville: Westminster John Knox, 1992) 32–71.

13. Used by permission of the publisher, from *Matthew*, ed. Nicole Wilkinson Duran and James P. Grimshaw, T@C (Minneapolis: 2013) 231–53.

reflect on their understandings of this text and its real-life implications in the world in which they live.

9. "'As Sheep in the Midst of Wolves': Mission and Peace in the Gospel of Matthew."[14] This essay lays out in parallel fashion Matthew's narrative portraits of "the prophets," John the Baptist, Jesus, and Jesus' disciples. These parallel portraits highlight (1) the respective callings of these narrative characters to peaceable vocations on behalf of the "kingdom of heaven," (2) the attendant suffering and death which come to these characters on account of their peaceable vocations, and (3) the powerful and ironic ways in which God overturns earthly verdicts and vindicates God's agents for their faithfulness.

10. "'Suffering Violence' and the Kingdom of Heaven (Matt 11:12): A Matthean Manual for Life in a Time of War."[15] This essay examines the motif of "suffering violence" (Matt 11:12) within Matthew's Gospel and analyzes the depiction of the faithful ones who "suffer violence" on account of their faithfulness to God. The essay opens with a collective portrait of the sufferings of the righteous, both as depicted narratively within Matthew's story and as predicted within the words of Jesus. The essay then sets forth Jesus' message calling the righteous to faithful response vis-à-vis their suffering. The essay concludes by employing Matthew's own narrative rhetoric to deconstruct both the power of the oppressors and the powerlessness of the faithful sufferers.

11. "'Wherever This Good News Is Proclaimed': Women and God in the Gospel of Matthew."[16] This essay first examines the overall societal portrait of women within Matthew's Gospel, a portrait which shows them to be fundamentally powerless within their social context. The essay then examines the impact of the God-dimension within the portraits of these same women, highlighting the ironic reversal of their powerless status as they engage faithfully in the story of Jesus.

12. "'Inheriting the Earth': Towards a Geotheology of Matthew's Narrative."[17] This essay discusses the ironic claim of the Matthean Jesus

---

14. Used by permission of the publisher, from *Beautiful upon the Mountains: Biblical Essays on Mission, Peace, and the Reign of God*, ed. Mary H. Schertz and Ivan Friesen, SPS (Elkhart, IN: Institute of Mennonite Studies, 2003; republished by Wipf and Stock, 2008) 123–43.

15. Used by permission of the publisher, from *HTS Teologiese Studies/Theological Studies* 67, no. 1 (2011), Art. #1011, 12 pages. http://dx.doi.org/:10.4102/hts.v67i1.1011.

16. Used by permission of the publisher, from *Interpretation: A Journal of Bible and Theology* 64, no. 4 (2010) 390–401.

17. Used by permission of the publisher, from *The Journal of Inductive Biblical Studies* 2, no. 1 (2015) 6–29, DOI: 10.7252/JOURNAL.02.2015S.02.

that "the meek"—and thus neither the powerful in general nor the Roman Empire in specific—"will inherit the earth" (5:5), a claim unique within the Canonical Gospels and one that reflects Psalm 36:11 (LXX). The essay examines Matt 5:5 alongside its biblical intertext in Psalm 36 (LXX) and also within its own Matthean context in order to assess its significance within Matthew's overall narrative. For Matthew ultimate "inheritance of the earth" clearly awaits "the renewal of all things" (19:27) and the "Parousia" of the Son of Man (24:3, 27, 37, 39). But in the meantime the Risen Jesus, with "all authority in heaven and on earth" (28:18), calls his disciples to a worldwide mission to "all the nations" (28:19–20) and thus to a proleptic "inheritance of the earth."

Epilogue: "An Advent Meditation from Bethlehem, Christmas 2000: The God Who Is 'With Us.'"[18] This Advent meditation reflects on the irony that the war-torn city of Bethlehem 2000—a city living under the opening onslaughts of the Second Intifada (or "uprising") and a city not so very different from the brutally violent Bethlehem of Matthew 2:13–23—is, by the same token, nothing other than the hometown of Jesus Emmanuel, "God with us." This meditation emerges from "my first war," the opening months of the Second Intifada, a fall semester in which I was, in the amazing providence of God, teaching a "Life of Jesus" course to Palestinian tour-guiding students in Bethlehem.[19] And this meditation reflects, perhaps better even than the major essays within this volume, the undeniably "autobiographical" character of all biblical exegesis, my own surely included.

So I conclude where I began, with the question of autobiographical exegesis. But this time the autobiography in question is Matthew's as well as my own. As I have lived over long years into the "3-M" identity which is my own autobiography as an exegete, I have become increasingly convinced of the radical—and equally autobiographical—character of the Matthean message concerning power. If I have read and interpreted Matthew's text autobiographically, through my "Mennonite" and "Middle Eastern" lenses, Matthew has likewise offered a similarly autobiographical exegesis with his own reading of the story of Jesus Messiah as found in his literary sources, presumably Mark and Q, and as viewed through the lens of his own first-century autobiography.

Matthew's Gospel, written as it is in the catastrophic aftermath of the Jewish Revolt against Rome (66–70 CE) and the cataclysmic destruction of the Jewish temple by the Romans (70 CE), clearly reflects Matthew's

---

18. Used by permission of the publisher, from *Christ for All People: Celebrating a World of Christian Art*, ed. Ron O'Grady (Maryknoll, NY: Orbis, 2001) 54.

19. The phrase "my first war" reflects the striking question posed to me by one of my tour-guiding students in Bethlehem one day before class: "Is this your first war?"

autobiographical perspectives on questions of power (cf. 21:33–46; 22:1–10). The result is the sharply ironic rhetoric which runs like a red thread throughout Matthew's narrative, from its beginnings in the stories surrounding Jesus' birth to its conclusion on a mountain in Galilee. Matthew's message is clear: All earthly appearances to the contrary, God alone is the source, the arbiter, and the enactor of true power. Always. Everywhere. Under all circumstances. Matthew clearly knows what the Psalmist also knows, that God's laughter is always the last laughter (cf. Ps 2:4). This is the "politics of God." And this is the "good news of the kingdom" (Matt 4:23; 9:35; 24:14). Let all the empires of earth throughout all ages take notice. And let all Matthew's readers understand.

Acknowledgments

IT IS MY GREAT pleasure to acknowledge a "short list" from among the countless persons who have crucially shaped both my "3-M" autobiography and, by the same token, the "autobiographical exegesis" reflected in the essays of this volume.[1] The persons listed below have, each in their own distinct fashion, enabled my scholarly efforts over long years as I have "tangled" with the Gospel of Matthew and the "irony of power" visible in Matthew's narrative:

—My grandfather, Dr. Chester K. Lehman, whose well-worn copy of the *Martyrs Mirror*[2] introduced me, even as a child, to my spiritual DNA within the Anabaptist/Mennonite family of faith and praxis and who set me a peerless and faithful example of solid biblical scholarship[3] well before I knew that I would follow in his footsteps vocationally . . .

—My mother, Miriam L. Weaver, who in countless and creative ways nurtured my faith as a child and adolescent and supported my growth into a committed disciple of Jesus Christ within the Anabaptist/Mennonite church family, a follower of Jesus who acknowledges Anabaptist/

---

1. See the Prologue above for a discussion of my "3-M" autobiography and my "confession" and contention that "All exegesis, mine surely included, is autobiographical."

2. Van Braght, *Martyrs Mirror*.

3. My grandfather taught Bible for some fifty years at Eastern Mennonite School/College/Seminary (now Eastern Mennonite University) and, at the end of his tenure, published two volumes on biblical theology. See Lehman, *Biblical Theology: Old Testament*; and Lehman, *Biblical Theology: New Testament*.

Mennonite history, theology, and "real world" praxis as my spiritual DNA . . .

—My father, Melvin H. Weaver, whom I never knew, but whose concordance of the Greek New Testament,[4] purchased for his own Greek studies as a college Bible major and signed in his own beautiful cursive script, sits within permanent arms-reach on my office bookshelf and has crucially enabled the biblical scholarship within these collected essays . . .

—Dr. Gertrude Roten, diligent and enthusiastic Greek professor at Associated Mennonite Biblical Seminaries (now Anabaptist Mennonite Biblical Seminary), who introduced me to the delights of Koine Greek and the compelling world of the Greek New Testament, who envisioned my future as a Greek teacher long before I recognized her vision as my own, who encouraged me persistently and with deep inner "knowing" toward my academic vocation as a New Testament professor, and who stood straight, tall, and gracious in front of me as a crucial female mentor . .

—Dr. Howard Charles, beloved professor of New Testament at AMBS over long years, who introduced me as a seminary student to both the rigors and the rewards of inductive Bible study, and who inspired me daily and powerfully by his personal example to spend my own life opening the Scriptures for others, just as he was opening them to us . . .

—Dr. Jack Dean Kingsbury, consummate Matthean scholar, who guided me with passion, precision, and patience through the rigors of my doctoral program at Union Theological Seminary in Virginia (now Union Presbyterian Seminary), who introduced me to the world of Matthean studies through his own ground-breaking redaction-critical[5] and narrative-critical[6] work, who drew me by example and encouragement into narrative criticism of the Gospels, and who invited me in 1992 to address the Matthew Group of the Society of Biblical Literature with a paper[7] which not only set the prominent trajectory for my ongoing Matthean studies over the following quarter century but has also, and by the same token, given rise to this volume of collected essays . . .

—Dr. George R. Brunk III, Dr. Ervin R. Stutzman, and Dr. Michael A. King, academic deans at Eastern Mennonite Seminary throughout my tenure

---

4. Wigram, *Englishman's Greek Concordance*.
5. Thus Kingsbury, *Matthew: Structure, Christology, Kingdom*.
6. Thus Kingsbury, *Matthew as Story*.
7. Weaver, "Power and Powerlessness," 179–96.

here, who have encouraged my teaching and scholarship on campus at EMS and who have likewise enabled multiple sabbatical leaves on which I have lived, learned, and frequently taught cross-culturally in wide-ranging international contexts (England, Lebanon, Syria, Israel/Palestine, Egypt, Ethiopia) and on which I have researched and written four of the essays found in this volume as well as the concluding Advent Meditation . . .

—Dr. Wendy J. Miller, erstwhile seminary student, longtime faculty colleague, and enduring soul friend, who knows and shares both the joys and the challenges of writing and publishing, who has drawn on her learnings from "Reading the Biblical Text" in her own publications,[8] and who has encouraged me lavishly and tirelessly in my scholarly and ecclesial work with the New Testament broadly and the Gospel of Matthew specifically . . .

—Thoughtful, inquisitive, and eager seminary students over long years in "Reading the Biblical Text" and "Gospel of Matthew," who have provided me ongoing opportunities for continued "tangling" with the Gospel of Matthew and who have actively and creatively engaged the world and the message of Matthew's Gospel along with me in countless class sessions . . .

—Palestinian Christian friends, who have "thought out loud" with me about the meaning and the "real world" significance of Jesus' scandalous commands "not to resist the one who is evil" but instead to "love your enemies"[9] and who live everyday lives of astonishing and courageous faithfulness in which they "refuse to be enemies" to those who harass and abuse them . . .

—The numerous and hardworking editors at the Institute of Mennonite Studies, Herald, Scholars, Continuum, Westminster/John Knox, Fortress, *HTS Teologiese Studies/Theological Studies*, *Interpretation: A Journal of Bible and Theology*, and *The Journal of Inductive Biblical Studies* who graciously accepted and edited these essays for their initial publication and who have offered generous permission for their republication . . .

—Dr. Samuel Pagan, distinguished Old Testament scholar, widely published author, and delightful academic colleague at Tantur Ecumenical Institute, Jerusalem, who offered gracious support and sturdy encouragement to my initial feelers concerning the concept and the viability of such a volume of collected essays . . .

8. Thus, for example, Miller, *Jesus, Our Spiritual Director*.
9. See the fruits of these conversations in Weaver, "Hard Sayings," 241–52.

—Dr. Willard M. Swartley, New Testament professor par excellence, generous mentor of junior scholars, and prolific writer and publisher, who has been a longtime friend and colleague across the miles and who enthusiastically supported the concept of this volume and recommended it personally to the Institute of Mennonite Studies for their "Studies in Peace and Scripture" series . . .

—Dr. David Rhoads, renowned Markan scholar, masterful practitioner of the art and theory of biblical storytelling, and pioneer in the narrative-critical study of the Gospels,[10] whose written and oral contributions to New Testament scholarship have inspired and delighted me over long years, whose friendship has gifted and encouraged me in my own scholarly efforts, and who has graciously written the "Foreword" to this volume . . .

—Dr. D. Christopher Spinks at Wipf and Stock and Dr. Laura Brenneman at Institute of Mennonite Studies, diligent, gracious, and supportive editors, who have encouraged and assisted me in many and crucial ways throughout my journey with this republication project and whose sturdy efforts have enabled this set of essays, previously published in a wide range of locations, to find a new, collective, and readily accessible home within the present volume.

To all the folks mentioned above, and to the countless others whom they represent, I offer my sincere thanks and my deepest gratitude. To borrow a well-known saying, "it takes a village" to produce a book. And you, collectively, are that village. Thank you!

Dorothy Jean Weaver

Eastern Mennonite Seminary, Harrisonburg, VA
August 2016

---

10. Thus Rhoads and Michie, *Mark as Story*, now in second edition as Rhoads, Dewey, and Michie, *Mark as Story*.

Abbreviations

AB	Anchor Bible
AThR	*Anglican Theological Review*
CBQ	*Catholic Biblical Quarterly*
CTQ	*Concordia Theological Quarterly*
CurTM	*Currents in Theology and Mission*
ExAud	*Ex Auditu*
ExpTim	*Expository Times*
FBBS	Facet Books, Biblical Series
FBESG	Forschungen und Berichte der Evangelischen Studiengemeinschaft
HNT	Handbuch zum Neuen Testament
HTR	*Harvard Theological Review*
IB	*Interpreter's Bible*
ICC	International Critical Commentary
Int	Interpretation: A Bible Commentary for Teaching and Preaching
Int	*Interpretation: A Journal of Bible and Theology*
JAAR	*Journal of the American Academy of Religion*

JIBS	*Journal of Inductive Biblical Studies*	
JSNTSup	Journal for the Study of the New Testament Supplement Series	
JSOT	*Journal for the Study of the Old Testament*	
MQR	*Mennonite Quarterly Review*	
NCB	New Century Bible	
NICOT	New International Commentary on the Old Testament	
NTD	Das Neue Testament Deutsch	
OP	Occasional Papers	
OTL	Old Testament Library	
PNTC	Pelican New Testament Commentaries	
RB	*Revue Biblique*	
RHPR	*Revue d'Histoire et de Philosophie Religieuses*	
SBL	Society of Biblical Literature	
SemeiaSup	Semeia Supplements	
SHBC	Smyth & Helwys Bible Commentary	
SNTSMS	Society for New Testament Studies Monograph Series	
SPS	Studies in Peace and Scripture	
SymS	Symposium Series	
T@C	Texts @ Contexts	
TBC	Torch Bible Commentaries	
THKNT	Theologischer Handkommentar zum Neuen Testament	
TNTC	Tyndale New Testament Commentaries	
TOTC	Tyndale Old Testament Commentaries	
TQ	*Theologische Quartalschrift*	
WBComp	Westminster Bible Companion	
WUNT	Wissenschaftliche Untersuchungen zum Neuen Testament	
ZTK	*Zeitschrift für Theologie und Kirche*	

I. Taking the Wide View

Confronting the Powers across the New Testament

1

Resistance and Nonresistance

New Testament Perspectives on Confronting the Powers

INTRODUCTION

To UNDERTAKE A TOPIC such as "The Powers in New Testament Perspective" is a task of no minor proportions. As Professor Walter Wink notes in the introduction to his book *Naming the Powers: The Language of Power in the New Testament*, "The language of power pervades the whole New Testament. No New Testament book is without the language of power."[1] This becomes clear very quickly as one begins to survey the wide range of "power" vocabulary found within the New Testament writings: *dynamis* (power), *exousia* (authority), *archē/archōn* (principality/ruler), *stoicheion* (basic element), *kyrios/kyriotēs* (lord/dominion), *onoma* (name), *Satanas* (Satan), *diabolos* (devil), *daimonion* (demon), *pneuma* (spirit), *angelos* (angel/messenger), *basileia/basileus* (kingdom/king), *christos* (messiah), to name only some of the most important terms. And even beyond specific vocabulary, the "power" motif is likewise implicit in the narrative rhetoric of the Gospels and the Book of Acts as well as in the apocalyptic rhetoric of the Book of Revelation. In short, it is hard to imagine any New Testament topic more broad and encyclopedic in its scope. Framed in "power" terminology, the entire message of the New Testament as a whole might well be summed up in the proclamation of the seventh angel of John's Apocalypse, "The king-

---

1. Wink, *Naming the Powers*, 7.

dom of the world has become the kingdom of our Lord and of his Messiah; and he will reign forever and ever" (Rev 11:15b).[2]

But there is another reason as well that this topic presents special challenges to those who address it. As Wink, puts it,

> the language of power pervades the New Testament, not so much as a consciously articulated set of doctrines but as a background belief held almost universally by the age . . . What we are dealing with here is not so much the conscious reflections of a discrete author (or even a community or set of communities) but the unconscious presuppositions and worldview of an entire era.[3]

What this means for us is that we need to scour the New Testament writings for evidence of ideas and realities which the writers understand implicitly but see little need to define or explain. And having found such evidence, we need to assess the implicit communications as well as the explicit declarations made by the writers.

Over time, as I have been rummaging around in the New Testament, working now with this question and now with that, I have stumbled across a curious anomaly with regard to New Testament language about "confronting the powers." On the one hand James exhorts the believers whom he addresses to "resist (*antistēte*) the devil and he will flee from you" (Jas 4:7; cf. 1 Pet 5:8–9), a bold and assertive stance *vis-a-vis* this quintessential "adversary" who "prowls around . . . like a lurking lion . . . looking for someone to devour" (1 Pet 5: 8). And on the other hand Jesus issues a directly contrasting command to his disciples to equip them for their encounters with human antagonists: "Do not resist (*mē antistēnai*) the one who is evil" (Matt 5:39, DJW), a stance which appears at first glance painfully, perhaps even scandalously, passive. What is striking about these contrasting commands is that they are set forth, each in its own context, as significant strategies for "confronting the powers." Until recently I had pondered this curious anomaly casually from time to time without devoting any major energy to resolving the questions that it raised. Now, with the present task in front of me, this New Testament anomaly has moved front and center in my thinking. And much to my surprise I have discovered that it has revealed a pervasive and paradoxical pattern within the New Testament texts. In the following exegetical reflections I offer the fruits of my discovery.

---

2. All biblical citations within this chapter are taken from the New Revised Standard Version unless otherwise indicated.

3. Wink, *Naming the Powers*, 7.

I. RESISTING THE DEVIL

To read the New Testament is to enter a world caught in the throes of an apocalyptic power struggle between the forces of God the Creator[4] and those of the devil or Satan, that cosmic "adversary" (1 Pet 5:8) who is the agent of death (Heb 2:14), destruction (1 Cor 5:5), and deceit.[5] The outcome of this power struggle in the ultimate triumph of God is never in question,[6] a reality which is confirmed in advance by the resurrection of Jesus from the dead.[7] But in the present moment the New Testament writers know themselves and their readers to be living in that final turbulent era just before "the end"[8] or "the consummation of the age,"[9] an era in which Satan's "wrath" is intensified precisely because he "knows that his time is short" (Rev 12:12).

Within this present era, then, Satan, who has already "[fallen] from heaven (Luke 10:18) and been "thrown down to the earth" (Rev 12:9, 13; cf. 12: 10, 12), attacks with "great wrath" (Rev 12:12) all those whom he can reach. Principal among his targets is Jesus, Son of God (Matt 4:3, 6//Luke 4:3, 9), whose mission it is to inaugurate God's reign on earth.[10] The Synoptic Gospel Writers tell us that after Jesus' baptism but before he begins his ministry in Galilee Jesus is "led" or "driven" by the Spirit into the wilderness, where he is then "tempted" by Satan/the devil (Mark 1:12-13//Matt 4:1//Luke 4:1-2). And it is in the face of this initial onslaught from Satan that we first witness Jesus actively "resisting the devil" by repudiating the seductive schemes which Satan sets forth.

Resisting Temptation.

The "temptations" which Jesus faces in the wilderness are clearly messianic in character. The devil prefaces his propositions with the telling words, "If you are the Son of God" (Matt 4:3, 6//Luke 4:3, 9), a clear pointer to the

---

4. Thus 1 Pet 4:19; cf. Mark 10:6; 13:19; Rev 3:14.

5. Thus 2 Cor 11:14-15; Eph 6:11; 2 Thess 2:9-10; Rev 12:9, 10; 20:3, 7-8.

6. References to the present/proleptic and the future/definitive defeat of Satan are spread widely throughout the New Testament. See, for example, Matt 4:10-11//Luke 4:12-13; Matt 25:41; Luke 10:18; John 12:31; Acts 26:17-18; Rom 16:20; Heb 2:14; Jas 4:7; 1 John 3:9; Rev 12:7-12; 20:1-3, 7-10.

7. Thus, for example, 1 Cor 15:20-28; Eph 1:20-23; 1 Thess 1:9-10.

8. Thus Matt 10:22; Matt 24:6//Mark 13:7; Matt 24:13//Mark 13:13; Luke 21:9.

9. Thus Matt 13:39, 40, 49; 24:3; 28:20. But see Heb 9:26, where the writer views the "consummation of the ages" to have been inaugurated already at the time of Jesus' crucifixion ("the sacrifice of himself").

10. Thus Matt 12:28//Luke11:20; Matt 11:2-6; Luke 4:16-21.

fact that it is precisely Jesus' messianic identity and mission which are at stake in the proposals which Satan is about to set forth. These messianic strategies include breadmaking (Matt 4:3//Luke 4:3; cf. John 6:15), temple acrobatics (Matt 4:5–6//Luke 4:9–11), and allegiance to Satan himself (Matt 4:8–9//Luke 4:5–7). In each case, however, Jesus firmly resists the seductive proposal, responding each time with a word of Scripture (Matt 4:4, 7, 10//Luke 4:4, 8, 12), and finally dismissing the devil from his presence altogether with the words, "Away with you, Satan!" (Matt 4:10). And Satan, who has "come" to Jesus in the first place (Matt 4:3), is now forced by Jesus' own resistance to "leave" him (Matt 4:11) or to "depart . . . until an opportune time" (Luke 4:13).

Jesus has effectively resisted the temptations of Satan; and he is now prepared to embark on the messianic mission for which he has just been ordained by God (Mark 1:10–11//Matt 3:16–17//Luke 3:21–22). But Satan's "opportune times" will return in ever-recurring fashion throughout Jesus' life and up to the very moment of his death. When Peter rebukes Jesus for speaking about the suffering and death which await him in Jerusalem (Mark 8:31–32//Matt 16:21–22), Jesus makes it very clear that Peter's words are none other than a satanic temptation to be firmly resisted: "Get behind me, Satan! You are a stumbling block to me. For you are setting your mind not on divine things but on human things" (Matt 16:23; cf. Mark 8:33). Later, in the Garden of Gethsemane, in a statement which in this context is clearly as much self-disclosure as it is exhortation, Jesus pleads with his disciples to "stay awake and pray that you may not come [into temptation]. The spirit indeed is willing; but the flesh is weak" (Matt 26:41, alt.; cf. Mark 14:38; Luke 22:40, 46). Once again Jesus actively "resists the devil," submitting himself to the "will" of his "Father" in the face of the agonizing temptation to avoid the "cup" of suffering and death which he is being called to "drink" (Mark 14:36; Matt 26:39, 42; Luke 22:42; cf. John 12:27).

Nor is this the last of Satan's temptations. In the final moments of Jesus' life, as he hangs dying on a Roman cross, Satan hurls one final messianic temptation at Jesus, the most bitter of them all, this time in the words of Jesus' human antagonists: "You who would destroy the temple and build it in three days, save yourself! If you are the Son of God, come down from the cross! . . . . He saved others. He cannot save himself. He is the King of Israel. Let him come down from the cross now, and we will believe in him! He trusts in God. Let God deliver him now, if he wants to; for he said, 'I am God's Son'" (Matt 27:40, 42–43; cf. Mark 15:29–30, 32; Luke 22:35, 37). And once again, in that final and definitive moment, Jesus actively (and paradoxically!) "resists the devil" by suffering to the death rather than saving his own life (Mark 15:37//Matt 27:50//Luke 23:46; John 19:30). As the

Writer to the Hebrews concludes, Jesus is one who has been "in every respect [tempted] as we are, yet without sin" (Heb 4:15, alt.).

But if Jesus is called to a life of resistance to the temptations of the devil, Jesus' disciples share that same calling. As part of the model prayer he offers to them early in his ministry, Jesus teaches his disciples to pray, "Lead us not into temptation" (Matt 6:13//Luke 11:4). And as they are sharing their last meal together just before they depart for the Garden of Gethsemane, Jesus offers a pointed warning to Simon Peter and to all his disciples of what lies just ahead: "Simon, Simon, listen! Satan has demanded to sift all of you [pl.] like wheat. But I have prayed for you [sg.] that your own [sg.] faith may not fail. And you [sg.], when once you [sg.] have turned back, strengthen your [sg.] brothers" (Luke 22:31–32). In the Garden of Gethsemane Jesus repeatedly rebukes the disciples for sleeping;[11] and he pleads with them to "Stay awake and pray that you may not come into [temptation]" (Matt 26:41, alt.; cf. Mark 14:38; Luke 22:40, 46). But this is a plea that goes unheeded; and as succeeding events make clear, this is a warning that turns into "bitter" reality not only for Peter (Mark 14:66–72//Matt 26:69–75//Luke 22:54–62) but for all of Jesus' disciples (Mark 14:50//Matt 26:56; Mark 14:51–52). In contrast to Jesus who has "stayed awake and prayed" and in this way been empowered to "resist the devil," the disciples have slept through the time of preparation and, in the moment of temptation, failed the test. The Gospel Writers leave their readers this brutally honest account as an ongoing word of warning.

And for the early Christians this warning is no minor matter. Faced with the awareness of Ananias' deceit in bringing money to the disciples, Peter confronts Ananias with the true significance of his actions: "Why has Satan filled your heart to lie to the Holy Spirit and to keep back part of the proceeds of the land?" (Acts 5:3). And for this crucial failure to resist the satanic temptation of money Ananias pays the ultimate price, namely, his own life and that of his wife as well (Acts 5:5, 10). In the words of 1 Timothy, "Those who want to be rich fall into temptation and are trapped by many senseless and harmful desires that plunge people into ruin and destruction" (1 Tim 6:9).[12]

For his part Paul is deeply concerned that the believers in the struggling new churches which he has planted will fall prey to temptation. To

---

11. Thus Mark 14:37//Matt 26:40//Luke 22:45–46; Mark 14:40//Matt 26:43; Mark 14:41//Matt 26:45.

12. Cf. James 1:14–15, which uses the language of personal desire to define temptation: "But one is tempted by one's own desire, being lured and enticed by it. Then, when that desire has conceived, it gives birth to sin; and that sin, when it is fully grown, gives birth to death."

the Thessalonian Christians he confesses, "I was afraid that somehow the tempter had tempted you and that our labor had been in vain" (1 Thess 3:5). In similar fashion he offers a clear word of caution to the Galatian believers as they seek to restore those in their midst who have sinned: "Take care that you yourselves are not tempted" (Gal 6:1). Paul warns Corinthian husbands and wives not to "deprive one another" indefinitely of their respective conjugal rights, "so that Satan may not tempt you because of your lack of self-control" (1 Cor 7:5). But in a later context he goes on to assure them that "No temptation has seized you except what is common to [humankind]. And God is faithful; he will not let you be tempted beyond what you can bear. But when you are tempted, he will also provide a way out so that you can stand up under it" (1 Cor 10:13, NIV, alt.).

As the New Testament writers see it, resisting the temptations of the devil is an ongoing and active task for the followers of Jesus, a task which engages them in all aspects of their everyday living: finances, charitable giving, marriage relationships, church discipline. But it is at the same time a task which Christians can ultimately carry out only by the power of God. And when they do, as James assures them, they are "blessed" and "will receive the crown of life that the Lord has promised to those who love him" (Jas 1:12).

Overcoming the Strong Man.

But for Jesus, as well as for his followers, there is much more to "resisting the devil" than repudiating the personal onslaughts and satanic seductions of the adversary. The apocalyptic resistance of the powers which is depicted in the New Testament calls for responses which reach beyond the personal to the entire surrounding community. Within Jesus' ministry this resistance means direct and ongoing confrontation with the satanic forces which inhabit,[13] bind (Luke 13:16) and oppress (Acts 10:38) the people all around him. Jesus points to his own exorcistic activities through the "finger" of God as the definitive sign that the reign of God has arrived among humans: "But if it is by the finger of God that I cast out demons, then the kingdom of God has come to you" (Luke 11:20; cf. Matt 12:28.). When people come to warn Jesus about Herod's murderous intentions, Jesus responds with an unflinching message in which he identifies his ministry as one of exorcism and healing: "Go and tell that fox for me, 'Listen, I am casting out demons and performing cures today and tomorrow, and on the third day I finish my work'" (Luke 13:32). And Jesus defines the ultimate significance of his

---

13. Thus Matt 4:24; 8:16, 28, 33; 9:32; 12:22; 15:22; Mark 1:32; 5:15, 16, 18; Luke 8:36; cf. John 10:21.

exorcistic ministry by portraying himself as a thief intent on "entering [Satan's] house" and "plundering his property": "But no one can enter a strong man's house and plunder his property without first tying up the strong man. Then indeed the house can be plundered" (Mark 3:27; cf. Matt 12:29//Luke 11:21-22). Accordingly, Jesus views his ministry in fundamental terms as a frontal attack on the forces of evil, an attack which he carries out by "tying up" Satan, the ultimate evil power, and "plundering [Satan's] property," namely the lives of all those bound and oppressed by the devil and his minions.

The implications of this statement are of crucial christological significance. If Jesus pictures his role as that of "tying up the strong man," this can only be because Jesus views himself as "the stronger one." And indeed he does so. As Luke recounts the story, Jesus clearly alludes to himself as "the stronger one": "When a strong man, fully armed, guards his castles, his property is safe. But when *one stronger than he* attacks him and [overcomes] him, he takes away his armor in which he trusted and divides his plunder" (Luke 11:21-22, alt., emphasis mine). And for their part the Gospel Writers uniformly portray Jesus as one whose "authority" (*exousia*) and "power" (*dynamis*) enable him to "attack" and "overcome" the forces of evil. As the onlookers in Capernaum proclaim in response to an exorcism by Jesus: "What kind of utterance is this? For with authority and power he commands the unclean spirits, and out they come!"(Luke 4:36; cf. Mark 1:27). The Synoptic Gospels are replete with the accounts of those from whom Jesus has exorcised "demons" and "unclean/evil spirits": a man in the synagogue at Capernaum,[14] a Gadarene demoniac(s),[15] men who are blind and/or mute,[16] the daughter of a Syrophoenician/Canaanite woman,[17] an epileptic boy,[18] Mary Magdalene,[19] and countless others.[20] And the magnitude of Jesus' "authority" over the evil spirits which he exorcises is reflected in the vivid details of the Gospel accounts. Jesus casts out the spirits "with a word" (Matt 8:16), and at a distance (Mark 7:24-30//Matt 15:21-28). He exorcises a "legion" of demons so "strong" that no one can "subdue" the man whom they possess (Mark 5:1-20) and so "fierce" that no one can "pass that way"

---

14. Thus Mark 1:23-28//Luke 4:33-37.
15. Thus Mark 5:1-20//Matt 8:28-34//Luke 8:26-39.
16. Thus Matt 9:32-34//Matt 12:22-24//Luke 11:14-15.
17. Thus Mark 7:24-30//Matt 15:21-28.
18. Thus Mark 9:14-29//Matt 17:14-20//Luke 9:37-43.
19. Thus Luke 8:1-3.
20. Thus the summary accounts of Mark 1:32-34//Matt 8:16-17; Mark 1:39; Mark 3:11-12//Luke 4:41; Matt 4:24//Luke 6:18; Luke 7:21.

(Matt 8:28–34). Jesus casts out a spirit which "convulses" an epileptic boy and leaves him "foaming at the mouth" (Mark 9:14–29; cf. Matt 17:14–20// Luke 9:37–43a). He rebukes the unclean spirits and the demons when they recognize him as Son of God; and he prohibits them from speaking out and disclosing his identity (Mark 1:34; Mark 3:11–12//Luke 4:41). In this ongoing and brutal power struggle between Jesus and the foot soldiers of Satan, "the strong man," it is clear that Jesus is indeed, and by far, "the stronger one."

Nor is this the end of the matter. Just as Jesus calls his disciples to join him in resisting the temptations of the devil, so he calls them to participate in the task of "overcoming the strong man." To equip the disciples for this task Jesus gives them the same "authority" which characterizes and empowers his own exorcistic ministry: authority "to cast out the demons" (Mark 3:15; cf. Luke 9:1), authority "over the unclean spirits" (Mark 6:7//Matt 10:1), authority "to tread on snakes and scorpions" (Luke 10:19a), and authority "over all the power of the enemy" (Luke 10:19b). And having armed the disciples with his own "authority," he commissions them and sends them out into the battlefield.[21] There they engage "the enemy" by "casting out many demons" (Mark 6:13). And when they return from their tour of duty, they report back with great amazement to Jesus on the success of their venture: "Lord, in your name even the demons submit to us!" (Luke 10:17; cf. 10:20).[22]

As Luke tells the story, the leaders of the early church continue the exorcistic ministry to which Jesus has called his disciples and for which he has empowered them. Luke recounts that the apostles in Jerusalem, and Peter in specific, are the agents through whom "those tormented by unclean spirits" are "cured" (Acts 5:12–16). In Samaria Philip exorcises unclean spirits, who come out of their victims "crying with loud shrieks" (Acts 8:4–8). In Philippi Paul orders a "spirit of divination" out of a young slave girl who is the source of revenue for her owners (Acts 16:16–19). And in Corinth as well Paul is the agent of liberation for "those who have evil spirits" (Acts 19:11–12).

---

21. Accounts of Jesus' commissioning and of the subsequent mission of the disciples are found in Mark 6:7–13, Luke 9:1–6, and Luke10:1–20 (and cf. Mark 3:13–15). Matthew 9:35–11:1 offers an account of Jesus' words of commissioning, but no mention of any subsequent mission by Jesus' disciples.

22. See also Matt 7:22 and Mark 9:38//Luke 9:49, where the Gospel Writers portray Jesus' disciples or others "casting out demons in Jesus' name." But note Mark 9:14–29// Matt 17:14–20//Luke 9:37–43, where the disciples are not successful in their attempt at exorcism and the father of the epileptic child must appeal to Jesus for assistance.

For their part the New Testament writers, each in their own fashion, exhort their readers to ongoing vigilance vis-a-vis the spirit world. John calls his readers to "test the spirits to see whether they are from God" (1 John 4:1); and he uses the incarnation of Jesus Christ as the criterion by which to carry out this assessment (1 John 4:2). Paul assures the Corinthians that God has graced the church with those whose "gift" to the body of Christ is "the discernment of spirits" (1 Cor 12:10). And Ephesians 6:10–17 offers its readers a detailed listing of "the whole armor of God" (6:11, 13)[23] which will enable them to "stand against the wiles of the devil" (6:13). This armor consists of the "belt of truth" (6:14), the "breastplate of righteousness" (6:14), shoes that "will make you ready to proclaim the gospel of peace" (6:15), the "shield of faith . . . to quench all the flaming arrows of the evil one" (6:16), the "helmet of salvation" (6:17), and the "sword of the Spirit, which is the word of God" (6:17). There is urgent need for this armor, as the writer makes clear: "For our struggle is not against enemies of blood and flesh, but against the cosmic powers of this present darkness, against the spiritual forces of evil in the heavenly places" (6:12). Such is the apocalyptic task of "overcoming the strong man."

Healing the Oppressed.

But there is still more to the task of "resisting the devil." If Jesus is the one who repudiates "the tempter" (Matt 4:3) and "overcomes the strong man" (Luke 11:22), he is also the one who "heals all those who are oppressed by the devil" (Acts 10:38). Without any question Jesus' healing activities (along with his proclamation of the "kingdom of God/heaven) lie at the very heart of his public ministry.[24] As Luke tells the story, Jesus begins his public ministry with an "inaugural address" at the synagogue in Nazareth in which he cites the words of the prophet Isaiah to claim this healing ministry, along with his ministry of proclamation, as his God-given and Spirit-empowered calling: "The Spirit of the Lord is upon me, because he has anointed me to bring good news to the poor. *He has sent me to proclaim release to the captives and recovery of sight to the blind, to let the oppressed go free,* to proclaim the year of the Lord's favor" (Luke 4:18–19, emphasis mine). In accordance

---

23. Ironically, the term *panoplia* used here for the "whole armor [of God]" is the same term as that used to describe the "armor" of the "strong man," which the "stronger one" succeeds in "taking away" from him (Luke 11:21–22).

24. So far as the gospel writers are concerned, these healing activities include Jesus' exorcisms. Throughout the Gospels and Acts the language of "healing" and the language of "casting out demons" are closely connected and regularly interwoven within the narrative accounts.

with this view of Jesus as "healer," the Gospel Writers characterize Jesus as a man endowed with "power" (*dynamis*; Luke 4:14; 5:17; 6:19; Mark 5:30// Luke 8:46; Acts 10:38). Luke tells us that Jesus returns to Galilee "filled with the power of the Spirit" in order to begin his ministry (Luke 4:14); and he prefaces one of his healing accounts with the words, ". . . and the power of the Lord was with him [i.e. Jesus] to heal" (Luke 5:17).[25] As a result Jesus is recognized on all sides, by supporters and detractors alike, for the "deeds of power" (*dynameis*) which are the hallmark of his public ministry.[26]

And, as the Gospel Writers indicate, Jesus' "powerful" healing ministry is encyclopedic in its scope, one which reaches out to "all the sick"[27] and heals "every disease and every sickness."[28] The list of those whom Jesus heals is long and widely inclusive: epileptics (Matt 4:24); paralytics (Matt 4:24; 8:5–13; Mark 2:1–12 parr.); lepers (Mark 1:40–45 parr.; Luke 17:11–19); blind people (Matt 15:30; Mark 8:22–26; 10:46–52 parr.; John 9:1–41); those who are lame (Matt 15:30; 21:14) and maimed (Matt 15:30); those who are deaf and/or mute (Matt 15:30; Mark 7:31–37); people with hemorrhages (Mark 5:25–34 parr.), withered hands (Mark 3:1–6 parr.), crippling "infirmity" (Luke 13:10–17), and dropsy (Luke 14:1–6); those who have suffered physical violence (Luke 22:50–51); and those who have died (Mark 5:21–24/35–43 parr.; Luke 7:11–17; John 11:1–44).

And, as Luke tells us, it is precisely through these "deeds of power" that Jesus "heals all who are oppressed by the devil" (Acts 10:38) and "sets people free" from the "bondage of Satan" (cf. Luke 13:16). Accordingly, Jesus' healing ministry is revealed to be none other than a profound and massive act of "resistance" against Satan and the diabolical powers with which he "binds" his victims both in spirit and in body.

And here as elsewhere Jesus shares his mission of "resistance" with his disciples. The "power" and "authority" which Jesus gives his disciples (Luke 9:1) enables them not only to "cast out unclean spirits" (Matt 10:1) but likewise to "cure every disease and every sickness" (Matt 10:1), just as Jesus himself is doing. And when Jesus sends them out, they go out through the villages "anoint[ing] with oil many who [are] sick" (Mark 6:13) and "curing diseases everywhere" (Luke 9:6). Following Pentecost and the "empowering" gift of the Holy Spirit given on that day (Luke 24:49; Acts 1:8) the early church then gains a public reputation much like that of Jesus for its "deeds

---

25. As the gospel writers indicate, this is a proactive "power" that "goes out" of Jesus and in so doing heals the sick (Mark 5:30//Luke 8:46; Luke 6:19).

26. Thus Mark 6:2, 5, 14; Matt 11:20, 21, 23; 13:54, 58; 14:2; Luke10:13; 19:37; Acts 2:22.

27. Thus Matt 4:24; 8:16; 12:15; 14:35; Mark 1:32; 3:10; 6:56.

28. Thus Matt 4:23//9:35. Cf. Mark 1:34//Matt 4:24//Luke 4:40.

of power" (Acts 4:30; 8:13; 19:11) carried out "in the name" and "through the power" of Jesus (Acts 3:12-16; 4:8-10, 30). Outside the temple Peter and John call a lame man to "stand up and walk"; and he responds by "jumping up" and entering the temple with them, "walking and leaping and praising God" (Acts 3:8). Peter is likewise the agent of an ongoing healing ministry both in Jerusalem (Acts 5:12-16) and in Lydda (Acts 9:32-35). In Samaria those who are paralyzed and lame find healing through the ministry of Philip (Acts 8:4-8). And "God [does] extraordinary deeds of power" (Acts 19:11, DJW) through Paul in Ephesus (Acts 19:11-12) and in Malta (Acts 28:7-10).

For his part Paul views "deeds of power" as one of the "signs of a true apostle" (2 Cor 12:12). But in fact these "deeds of power" are not the sole prerogative of the leadership of the church. In writing to the fledgling churches which he has planted around the Mediterranean world Paul makes it clear that "deeds of power," just as the "discernment of spirits," are none other than a "manifestation of the Spirit" for the "common good" of the body of Christ (1 Cor 12:7, 9). And he simply assumes their presence in the life of the Galatian church (Gal 3:5). The call to "heal the oppressed" through "deeds of power" is a call to the entire church of Jesus Christ.

II. NOT RESISTING THE ONE WHO IS EVIL

As the evidence makes clear, the motif of "resisting the devil" provides us with a prominent and pervasive New Testament rubric for understanding the significance of the life, ministry, death, and resurrection of Jesus and the corresponding mission of the church. But alongside this motif stands a contrasting, and at first glance contradictory, motif which is equally prominent and pervasive throughout the New Testament, the motif characterized by the command of Jesus "Do not resist the one who is evil" (Matt 5:39). This motif, which focuses attention not on cosmic powers and the spirit world but rather on antagonistic powers within human society,[29] opens strikingly different but equally important windows for us onto the significance of Jesus' mission and that of the church. And it is only as we bring these contrasting motifs together, both in tension and in correlation with each other, that we approach a comprehensive and balanced understanding of "New Testament Perspectives on Confronting the Powers." As the New Testament texts make clear in numerous ways, the task of "confronting the powers" involves at the same time and by the same token both "resistance" and "nonresistance."

29. For a detailed study of Matt 5:38-42, see Weaver, "Transforming Nonresistance," 32-71.

Handed Over to Death.

Without question the single most prominent verbal motif in the Greek New Testament which illustrates Jesus' command "not to resist the one who is evil" is that of "being handed over," the passive form of the verb *paradidōmi*, to hand someone or something over to another. Within the New Testament this motif functions predominantly as a technical term for the delivery of a prisoner into the hands of those religious or legal authorities who will put that person on trial and condemn them to death.[30] And as such this term provides a vivid image of those who, far from "resisting" the powerful forces which oppose them, instead exhibit complete vulnerability to the "evil" actions of their antagonists.

Within the Gospel accounts it is John the Baptist who leads the way in this regard. As the Synoptic Gospels relate, Jesus begins his public ministry only after John has been "handed over" (Mark 1:14//Matt 4:12; cf. Luke 3:19–20) to imprisonment[31] and ultimate death.[32] John meets this fate as a direct result of his prophetic mission, a mission which he has been carrying out not only among the Jewish people (Mark 1:2–8//Matt 3:1–12// Luke 3:1–18) but also among their leaders (Mark 6:17–18//Matt 14:3–4// Luke 3:19), the political powers of the Jewish world. Thus it is precisely as John "confronts the powers" through his prophetic rebuke of Herod that he finds himself subject to arrest, imprisonment, and death. And it is in this same context that John meets his fate in peaceable and "nonresisting" fashion, as the accounts of John's death imply through their narrative rhetoric. Within these accounts (Mark 6:14–29//Matt 14:1–12//Luke 9:7–9) the sole act attributed to John is his prophetic rebuke of Herod, while John's antagonists consistently make him the object of their cruel, cowardly, and violent actions.[33]

And then it is Jesus' turn to "be handed over." The language of "handing/being handed over" is a prominent thread woven throughout the Gospel Writers' accounts of the life, death, and even the resurrection of

---

30. The New Testament usages of *paradidōmi* are too extensive to cite within this context. And locating this verbal motif within any English-language translation is made virtually impossible by the range of terms used to translate the Greek verb. Consult a Greek concordance or an English concordance with cross-references to the Greek text.

31. Thus Mark 6:17//Matt 14:3//Luke 3:19–20; Matt 11:2 cf. Luke 7:18–19.

32. Thus Mark 6:14–29//Matt 14:1–12//Luke 9:7–9; cf. Mark 9:11–13//Matt 17:10–13.

33. For a detailed study of the narrative rhetoric within Matthew's account of the death of John the Baptist, see Weaver, "Power and Powerlessness," 179–96.

Jesus.³⁴ Already as they recount the moment in which Jesus calls his twelve disciples, the Gospel Writers put their readers on notice that one of these disciples, Judas Iscariot, is going to "hand [Jesus] over" (Mark 3:19//Matt 10:4). Throughout his ministry Jesus himself repeatedly warns his disciples that he is going to "be handed over" to the human powers within Palestine: "into human hands" (Mark 9:31//Matt 17:22//Luke 9:44); to the chief priests and scribes (Mark 10:33//Matt 20:18); to the Gentiles (Mark 10:33//Matt 20:19//Luke 18:32); "into the hands of sinners" (Mark 14:41//Matt 26:45; cf. Luke 24:7). The Gospel Writers likewise portray Jesus as not only "knowing" in advance who will hand him over (John 6:64, 71; 13:11) but also making public reference to the identity of these people: Judas Iscariot,³⁵ the chief priests and scribes,³⁶ and, by implication, Pilate himself.³⁷ And as the Gospel Writers recount the story, each of these individuals and groups in fact participates in the joint action of "handing Jesus over" to his death: Judas³⁸; the Jewish religious establishment, variously identified as the "chief priests," "elders [of the people]," "scribes," "the whole council, and "the Jews"³⁹; and Pilate himself.⁴⁰ As the Gospel Writers tell the story, Jesus' ministry is imprinted from its very inception by the reality that Jesus himself will eventually (and necessarily⁴¹) "be handed over to be crucified" (Matt 26:2).⁴²

Nor is there any question concerning the reason for Jesus' fate. As the Gospel Writers collectively bear witness, Jesus is "handed over" in the midst

34. While English translators uniformly use the term "betray" for the actions of Judas, I have "retranslated" all forms of *paradidōmi* below, which refer to Judas to correspond with those referring to the religious leaders and Pilate, who are said to "hand Jesus over."

35. Thus Mark 14:18-21//Matt 26:21-25//John 13:21-30; cf. Luke 22:21-23; Mark 14:42//Matt 26:46; Luke 22:48; cf. John 21:20.

36. Thus Mark 10:33//Matt 20:18-19 cf. Luke 18:32; John 19:11 cf. 18:30, 35.

37. Thus John 19:11; cf. 19:10, 16.

38. Thus Mark 14:10, 11, 44; Matt 26:15, 16, 48; 27:3, 4; Luke 22:4, 6, 48; John 13:2; 18:2, 5

39. Thus Mark 15:1, 10; Matt 27:2, 18; Luke 20:20; John 18:30. Cf. the designations used by other characters in the various narratives: "chief priests and leaders" (Luke 24:20); "you Israelites" (Acts 3:12-13); and "your own nation and the chief priests" (John 18:35).

40. Thus Mark 15:15//Matt 27:26//Luke 23:25//John 19:16.

41. See, for example the following texts in which Jesus refers to the divine necessity of his upcoming death: Mark 8:31-33//Matt 16:21-23; Mark 10:35-40//Matt 20:20-23 cf. Luke 12:50; Luke13:31-33; Mark 14:32-42//Matt 26:36-46//Luke 22:39-46 cf. John 12:27; Matt 26:54; John 10:17-18; John 18:11). A fuller discussion of this question lies well beyond the scope of the present paper.

42. See also 1 Cor 11:23, where Paul prefaces his account of the Last Supper with a reference to the "night when [Jesus] was handed over" (DJW).

of his ministry and in direct response to his compassionate and prophetic activities: "casting out demons and performing cures" (Luke 13:31–33); healing people on the sabbath (Mark 3:1–6//Matt 12:9–14//Luke 6:6–11); raising a man from the dead (John 11:45–57); overturning the tables of the moneychangers in the temple and challenging the very operation of the temple enterprise (Mark 11:15–19//Luke 19:45–48); and speaking prophetic parables against the religious leadership (Mark 12:1–12//Matt 21:33–46// Luke 20:9–20). Like John the Baptist before him, Jesus suffers "in the line of duty," as he is carrying out the mission which he has received from God.

And like John, Jesus "does not resist" the forces of violence and destruction arrayed against him. When one of his disciples draws a sword in the Garden of Gethsemane and strikes out in defense of his master, Jesus rebukes the disciple and firmly rejects the use of all violence on his behalf. As Luke tells the story, Jesus responds, "No more of this!"; and he heals the slave of the high priest, whose ear has been severed by the vicious blow of the sword (Luke 22:49–51). In John's account Jesus rebukes Simon Peter with the words, "Put your sword back into its sheath! Am I not to drink the cup that the Father has given me?" (John 18:10–11). In Matthew's narrative Jesus offers a third response: "Put your sword back into its place! For all who take the sword will perish by the sword. Do you think that I cannot appeal to my Father, and he will at once send me more than twelve legions of angels? But how then would the scriptures be fulfilled, which say it must happen in this way?" (Matt 26:52–54). Finally, in John's account of the interrogation by Pilate, Jesus explains the underlying reason for his "nonresisting" stance towards his own arrest: "My kingdom is not from this world. If my kingdom were from this world, my followers would be fighting to keep me from being handed over to the Jews. But as it is, my kingdom is not from here" (John 18:36). The overall picture is unambiguous. Jesus refuses all options, both earthly and heavenly, to retaliate against the "evil ones" who "hand him over" to torture and death.

And this refusal to "resist those who are evil" characterizes the narrative rhetoric of Jesus' passion just as it does that of John the Baptist. Throughout his trial Jesus takes virtually no actions, while his antagonists for their part make him the object of an ongoing and vicious barrage of mockery and violence which comes to its climax in a brutal execution.[43] Even more striking, in those agonizing moments as he hangs on a Roman cross, Jesus calls on God to forgive those who are responsible for putting him there. As Luke tells the story, Jesus' cry from the cross is "Father, forgive

---

43. For a detailed study of the narrative rhetoric of Matthew's account of the suffering and death of Jesus, see Weaver, "Power and Powerlessness," 191–95.

them! For they do not know what they are doing" (Luke 23:34). In the words of 1 Pet 2:23, "When [Christ] was abused, he did not return abuse. When he suffered, he did not threaten. But he entrusted himself to the one who judges justly."

And then it is the turn of Jesus' disciples. If John the Baptist and Jesus have been "handed over" on account of their respective ministries, Jesus' disciples can expect no less. As Matthew tells the story, Jesus warns his disciples of this sobering fact even as he first commissions them to go out in ministry:

> But beware of people. For they will hand you over to councils and flog you in their synagogues. And you will be led before rulers and kings on account of me as a witness to them and the Gentiles. But when they hand you over, do not be anxious . . . . And brother will hand over brother to death, and father the child. And children will rise up against parents and have them put them to death. And you will be hated by all people on account of my name. (Matt 10:17–19a; 21–22a [DJW]; cf Luke 12:11)

And as Jesus speaks with his disciples about the future turbulent days just before the coming of the Son of man, he repeats these same essential warnings (Mark 13:9–13//Matt 24:9–14//Luke 21:12–19; cf. John 15:21). The message is unambiguous. Those who follow Jesus into ministry will be "handed over" to trial and death on account of this ministry, just as happened with Jesus himself. And in fact Luke's account of the life and the ministry of the early church bears out Jesus' predictions in this regard. Early in Acts Saul is depicted as "ravaging the church by entering house after house, dragging off both men and woman [and handing them over] to prison" (Acts 8:3, alt.; cf. 22:4). In similar fashion King Herod later "seizes [Peter], puts him in prison, and hands him over to four squads of soldiers to guard him . . . ." (Acts 12:4). And as an intrepid missionary for the Christian cause Paul himself is "handed over" by those who do to him what he formerly did to other believers. As Paul is on his way to Jerusalem, Agabus comes to Caesarea to warn Paul of what lies ahead (Acts 21:8–10). Taking Paul's belt and binding his own hands and feet with it, he announces to Paul, "Thus says the Holy Spirit, 'This is the way the Jews in Jerusalem will bind the man who owns this belt and will hand him over to the Gentiles'" (Acts 21:11; cf. 27:1). And Paul himself, in one of his letters to the Corinthian church, reflects on the life of the apostle of Jesus in similar language:

> We are afflicted in every way, but not crushed;

> perplexed, but not driven to despair;
>
> persecuted, but not forsaken;
>
> struck down, but not destroyed;
>
> always carrying in the body the death of Jesus,
>
> so that the life of Jesus may also be made visible in our bodies.
>
> For while we live, we are always being [handed over] to death for Jesus' sake,
>
> so that the life of Jesus may be made visible in our mortal flesh. (2 Cor 4:8–11, alt.)

And just as with Jesus and John the Baptist before him, the disciples who are "handed over" for their participation in the mission of the reign of God respond by "not resisting the ones who are evil." After Peter and the apostles have been arrested, imprisoned, tried before the Sanhedrin, flogged, and finally released with a strict warning against further proclamation in the name of Jesus (Acts 5:17–40), their immediate response as they leave the Sanhedrin is to "rejoice that they were considered worthy to suffer dishonor for the sake of the name" (Acts 5:41). In a striking parallel to his account of Jesus' own passion, Luke tells his readers that Stephen's final words as he lies dying from the stones of a Jewish mob call on God's forgiveness for all those throwing the stones: "Lord, do not hold this sin against them" (Acts 7:60).

In his correspondence with the Corinthian Christians Paul reflects with vivid realism on the life of an apostle and on the "nonresistance" with which he and his fellow apostles face persecution:

> To the present hour we are hungry and thirsty,
>
> we are poorly clothed and beaten and homeless,
>
> and we grow weary from the work of our own hands.
>
> *When reviled, we bless;*
>
> *when persecuted, we endure;*
>
> *when slandered, we speak kindly.*
>
> We have become like the rubbish of the world,
>
> the dregs of all things, to this very day. (1 Cor 4:11–13, emphasis mine).

And as Paul faces his upcoming passion, instigated by those who will "hand him over to the Gentiles" (Acts 21:11), he responds to his friends and supporters, "What are you doing, weeping and breaking my heart? For I am ready not only to be bound but even to die in Jerusalem for the name of the Lord Jesus" (Acts 21:13). As the New Testament writers make clear, the disciples of Jesus not only face the same attacks from human antagonists as Jesus himself and John before him have faced; but they also offer the same striking and utterly counter-intuitive response, that of "not resisting those who are evil." And in these "nonresisting" responses the early Christians exhibit the extraordinary strategy set forth by Jesus for "confronting the powers": "But I say to you, do not resist the one who is evil" (Matt 5:39, DJW).

Conquering through Death.

A second prominent New Testament motif which undergirds Jesus' command "not to resist the one who is evil" focuses on the paradoxical idea that death at the hands of the "powers" is itself the means by which Jesus and his disciples not only confront but also conquer the forces arrayed against them. This motif is widely visible across the spectrum of New Testament texts—the Pauline letters, the Synoptic Gospels, the Gospel of John, Hebrews, the Apocalypse of John; and it is deeply embedded within the narrative rhetoric of these writings.

Within the Pauline literature, the picture is unambiguous. In the early Christian "Christ hymn" embedded in Paul's letter to the Philippians (Phil 2:5–11), it is Jesus' radical willingness to submit himself to "death on a cross" (Phil 2:8) which leads to his ultimate "exaltation" by God with a name "above every name" (Phil 2:9) and a position of preeminence over all created beings "in heaven and on earth and under the earth" (Phil 2:10). In Paul's correspondence with the Corinthians he refers to "Christ crucified" as "the power of God and the wisdom of God" (1 Cor 1: 23–24) and at the same time "foolishness [which] is wiser than human wisdom" and "weakness [which] is stronger than human strength" (1 Cor 1:25). And in his letter to the Colossians Paul points to the death of Jesus as God's specific means for defeating the "powers":

> And when you were dead in trespasses and the uncircumcision of your flesh,
>
> God made you alive together with [Christ],
>
> when he forgave us all our trespasses,
>
> erasing the record that stood against us with its legal demands.
>
> He set this aside, *nailing it to the cross.*

> *He disarmed the rulers and authorities*
>
> *and made a public example of them,*
>
> *triumphing over them in [the cross].* (Col 2:13–15, alt.; emphasis mine)

And the Writer to the Hebrews draws the same stunning and counterintuitive conclusion in regard to the actions and intentions of Jesus himself (Heb 2:14–15, emphasis mine):

> Since, therefore, the children share flesh and blood,
>
> he [that is, Jesus] himself likewise shared the same things,
>
> *so that through death*
>
> *he might destroy the one who has the power of death, that is, the devil,*
>
> *and free those who all their lives were held in slavery by the fear of death.*

And what Paul and the Writer to the Hebrews communicate explicitly in their letters to the early churches, the Passion Narratives of the four Gospels communicate implicitly through their portrayal of the words and the actions of Jesus' opponents. In profoundly ironic fashion it is precisely as Jesus is put on trial, mocked, and finally executed by his enemies that they themselves proclaim, repeatedly and to all the world, the true identity of this man whom they hold temporarily in their grasp. From the time of his arrest until the moment of his death Jesus is charged, mocked, executed, and taunted, in unbelieving fashion, with words and with symbolism which ironically proclaim his true identity: Messiah[44]; Messiah of God[45]; Chosen One[46]; King of the Jews[47]; King of Israel[48]; Son of the Blessed[49]; Son of God.[50] As a result, for the Gospel Writers as a whole Jesus' crucifixion, the apparent success of Jesus' opponents in their attempt to put him to death, is instead,

---

44. Thus Mark 14:61//Matt 26:63//Luke 22:67; Matt 26:68; 27:17, 22; Luke 23:39.

45. Thus Mark 15:32//Luke 23:35.

46. Thus Luke 23:35.

47. Thus Mark 15:2//Matt 27:11//Luke 23:3//John 18:33; cf. 18:36–37; Mark 15:9//John 18:39; Mark 15:12; Mark 15:16–20//Matt 27:28–31//John 19:1–15; Mark 15:26//Matt 27:37//Luke 23:38//John 19:19–22; Luke 23:37; cf. Luke 23:42.

48. Thus Mark 15:32//Matt 27:42.

49. Thus Mark 14:61.

50. Thus Matt 26:63//Luke 22:70; John 19:7; Matt 27:40, 43; Mark 15:39//Matt 27:54.

paradoxically, nothing less than Jesus' public "coronation" as King of the Jews and Son of God and the unmistakable pointer to his ultimate victory over the "powers" arrayed against him. The Gospel Writers then complete their collective portrayal of "crucifixion as coronation" with the depiction of cosmic signs which accompany the death of Jesus: darkness at midday (Mark 15:33 parr.); the rending of the temple curtain (Mark 15:38 parr.); and, for Matthew, a powerful earthquake which "shakes" the earth, "splits" the rocks, "opens" the tombs, and, following Jesus' own resurrection, "raises" the bodies of many "saints" (Matt 27:51–54). As the Gospel Writers see it, the "nonresisting" death of Jesus is clearly that event in which and by which Jesus both confronts and conquers the "powers" of his world.

And what the Gospels Writers as a whole portray graphically through their Passion Narratives John the Gospel Writer makes explicit through the words of Jesus himself. From the perspective of John's Gospel Jesus views the "hour" of his death as, by the same token, the moment of his "glorification" (John 12:23–25, 27–33): "The hour has come for the Son of Man *to be glorified*. Very truly, I tell you, unless a grain of wheat falls into the earth *and dies*, it remains just a single grain; but *if it dies*, it bears much fruit" (John 12:23–24, emphasis mine). And even more to the point, Jesus depicts his death not only as his "glorification" but likewise as the very event by which the powers arrayed against him meet their demise: "Now is the judgment of this world; now the ruler of this world will be driven out. And I, when I am *lifted up* from the earth, will draw all people to myself" (John 12:31–32, emphasis mine; cf. 3:14; 8:28; 12:34). In sharp contrast to Luke's Gospel, where the Risen Jesus speaks of the "necessity" for the Messiah to "suffer these things *and then enter into his glory*" (Luke 24:26, emphasis mine), the Johannine Jesus is "glorified" *precisely as he is "lifted up" on a Roman cross and exposed to the untold humiliations and agonies of death by crucifixion.*[51] Even more importantly, from the perspective of John's Gospel, Jesus' "nonresisting" death at the hands of his enemies, far from a sign of weakness or defeat, is rather the very means by which Jesus "judges," "drives out" and in this way "conquers" the powers of "the world." As Jesus says to his disciples just hours before his death on a Roman cross at the hands of the world power of the day, "In the world you face persecution. But take courage: I have conquered the world!" (John 16:33b).[52]

---

51. That John intends this reference to Jesus "being lifted up" (or "exalted"; cf. Acts 2:33; 5:31; Phil 2:9) to point to Jesus' crucifixion is made explicit by the unambiguous editorial comment that follows: "He [Jesus] said this to indicate the kind of death he was to die" (John 12:33).

52. For a more extensive study of John's perspectives on the death of Jesus, see Weaver, "Between Text and Sermon: John 18:1—19:42," 404, 406–8.

And for John the Revelator the message is the same. According to John's vision, the "Lion of the tribe of Judah," the one who has "*conquered*" and is therefore "worthy" to "open the scroll and its seven seals" (Rev 5:5), turns out to be none other than a "Lamb *standing as if it had been slaughtered*" (Rev 5:6, emphasis mine). And as John looks and listens, an astonishing hymn of praise is sung to this "slaughtered Lamb": "You are worthy to take the scroll and to open its seals, *for you were slaughtered and by your blood you ransomed for God* saints from every tribe and language and people and nation" (Rev 5:9–10; emphasis mine). As John the Revelator bears witness, it is precisely the brutal and bloody "slaughter" of the Lamb by which he "ransoms" saints for God and, as a result, "conquers" and is acclaimed "worthy" to "open the seals" and reveal the course of history and its meaning. Here, as elsewhere throughout the New Testament writings, Jesus "conquers" not by destroying others but rather by means of his own "nonresisting" death at the hands of his opponents.

And what is true for Jesus is likewise true for Jesus' disciples. In the Gospel tradition Jesus instructs his disciples that "those who want to save their life will lose it, and those who lose their life for my sake, and for the sake of the gospel, will save it" (Mark 8:35//Matt 16:25//Luke 9:24//John 12:25).

And in John's Apocalypse the victorious saints of God are those who have "come out of the great ordeal" (Rev 7:14; cf. 7:9–17) and those who have "conquered [Satan] by the blood of the Lamb and by the word of their testimony, *for they did not cling to life even in the face of death*" (Rev 12:11, emphasis mine). For Jesus' disciples, just as for Jesus himself, confrontation with "the powers" is not a matter of inflicting death on one's enemies but rather one of suffering to the death, in "nonresisting" fashion, at the hands of those same enemies. And in that "nonresisting" death, paradoxically, lies ultimate and cosmic victory over Satan, "the deceiver of the whole world" and the "accuser" of the saints of God (Rev 12:10; cf. 12:10–12).

III. RESISTANCE AND NONRESISTANCE: A PARADOXICAL STRATEGY FOR CONFRONTING THE POWERS

As the evidence shows, the New Testament texts lay out two prominent yet apparently contradictory strategies for "confronting the powers": "resisting" and "not resisting." But as a closer examination of this evidence makes clear, these strategies do not in fact contradict each other but rather create a profound and paradoxical tension within which both Jesus and his disciples are called to live out their lives and their mission. On the one hand confrontation means the call "to resist the devil" (Jas 4:7), that call to bold and powerful action which catalyzes the overall ministry of Jesus and his disciple, as they resist the seductive temptations of Satan, their cosmic enemy, break Satan's hold on the lives of others, and heal those whose bodies Satan has afflicted with disease. On the other hand confrontation means the call "not to resist the one who is evil" (Matt 5:39), that call to radical perseverance which challenges Jesus and his disciples to respond peaceably and without retaliation in the face of the persecution and suffering inflicted on them by those earthly "powers" who oppose them and their mission to proclaim the reign of God. And it is only as Jesus and his disciples live deeply and persistently into both halves of this paradoxical tension that the New Testament task of "confronting the powers" is brought to its completion.

As the New Testament witness makes abundantly clear, "confronting the powers" is a task which is neither simple nor safe for those who undertake it. But the ultimate success of the venture is assured from the outset and at the highest levels: "The kingdom of the world has [already!] become the kingdom of our Lord and of his Messiah; and he will reign forever and ever" (Rev 11:15b, alt.). Let the disciples of Jesus Christ in all ages and all places take courage.

II. Matthew and the Irony of Power

The View from the Top Down

2

Power and Powerlessness

Matthew's Use of Irony in the Portrayal of Political Leaders

IN HIS DISCUSSION OF irony in the Gospel of John[1] Paul D. Duke cites Haakon Chevalier's statement that "the best feature of every Irony is a contrast between a reality and an appearance."[2] Duke goes on to observe that "in each case the irony emerges when the appearance is corrected or exploded by the contrasting reality perceived by the ironist and perceptive audience. *Irony, then, is a leap from what seems to be to what is.*"[3] And, as Duke establishes throughout the remainder of his book, this ironic "leap from what seems to be to what is" is an act of mental gymnastics fundamental to the reading of the Gospel of John.

What proves true for the Gospel of John is true as well for the Gospel of Matthew. While no comparable attention has as yet been devoted to the use of irony within Matthew's narrative,[4] the evidence provided by the text of Matthew's Gospel would nevertheless appear to warrant such attention. Nowhere is this more evident than in the characterizations of the three political leaders who figure within Matthew's narrative: Herod the king

---

1. Duke, *Irony*.
2. Ibid., 15, cited from Chevalier, *Ironic Temper*, 42.
3. Ibid.; emphasis mine.
4. I have not succeeded in locating any major studies, whether essays or monographs, which deal with Matthew's use of irony as a literary technique. Note, by contrast, the bibliographical citations on irony in the Gospel of John as listed by Duke (ibid., 157nn3–4) in his monograph on that topic.

(2:1–23), Herod the tetrarch (14:1–12), and Pilate the governor (27:1–2, 11–38, 54, 62–66; 28:1–15). On the one hand Matthew invests each of these characters with both the title and the attributes of power. Yet on the other hand Matthew works in unmistakable fashion to subvert the very portraits of power which he himself has painted. And in this way Matthew invites the perceptive reader to make Duke's ironic "leap" from "the power that seems to be" to "the powerlessness that is."

In the following paper I will analyze the character portrayals of Herod the king, Herod the tetrarch, and Pilate the governor in order to determine Matthew's ironic methodology and to assess the impact of Matthean irony on the reader of Matthew's Gospel. I will work at this task in three stages: (1) I will identify the basic shape and qualifying characteristics of irony as a literary strategy; (2) I will work text by text with the Matthean character portrayals of the three political leaders in question; and (3) I will then offer concluding observations with reference to Matthew's use of irony.

I. TOWARDS A DEFINITION OF IRONY

In his book *The Compass of Irony* D. C. Muecke identifies irony in terms of three basic elements.[5] The first of these is what he describes as a "double-layered or two-storey phenomenon" in which "the lower level is the situation either as it appears to the victim of irony . . . or as it is deceptively presented by the ironist" and the "upper level is the situation as it appears to the observer or the ironist."[6] Between the lower and the upper levels there is, secondly, an "opposition" consisting of "contradiction, incongruity, or incompatibility," such that "what is said may be contradicted by what is meant" or "what the victim thinks may be contradicted by what the observer knows."[7] The third basic element of irony is that of "innocence," the situation in which "a victim is confidently unaware of the very possibility of there being an upper level or point of view that invalidates his own, or an ironist pretends not to be aware of it."[8]

Typologies of irony distinguish, in the broadest of terms, between verbal ironies, dramatic ironies, and situational ironies. Verbal ironies are those in which the ironist communicates the irony in his/her own voice or in the voice of an "innocent" character within the narrative itself.[9] In such

---

5. Muecke, *Compass of Irony*, 19–20. Cf. Duke, *Irony*, 13, 17.
6. Muecke, *Compass of Irony*, 19. Cf. Duke, *Irony*, 14.
7. Muecke, *Compass of Irony*, 19–20. Cf. Duke, *Irony*, 14–16.
8. Muecke, *Compass of Irony*, 20. Cf. Duke, *Irony*, 16–18.
9. Thus the first three of Muecke's four "modes" of irony (*Compass of Irony*, 61–63;

a case the ironist is "someone consciously and intentionally employing a technique."[10] Such ironies are by definition ones in which the speaker knows more than he/she appears to know.[11]

Dramatic ironies,[12] by contrast, are those in which the ironist communicates in oblique fashion, through the actions and events of the narrative itself. In this case the ironist "arranges that the characters . . . expose themselves in their ironic predicament directly to the audience or reader."[13] In such instances the irony hinges on the fact that the audience or reader has information of which the character in question is not yet aware.[14]

Situational ironies emerge, as do dramatic ironies, from the actions or events of the narrative. They distinguish themselves from dramatic ironies, however, in that their effectiveness does not depend on the foreknowledge of the audience or reader.[15] A categorization of ironic situations includes such types as irony of simply incongruity, irony of events, irony of self-betrayal, irony of dilemma, and irony of characterization.[16]

Clues to the ironic intent of a literary work can come to the audience or reader in a variety of ways. Wayne Booth, in his book *A Rhetoric of Irony*, identifies five means which an author has for communicating irony within any given literary work: (1) "straightforward warnings in the author's own voice"; (2) "known error proclaimed" within the work; (3) "conflicts of facts within the work"; (4) "clashes of style"; and (5) "conflicts of belief."[17]

There is likewise a diversity of objects which an author can target within any given literary work. As Muecke observes, "The object of irony may be a person . . . , an attitude, a belief, a social custom or institution, a philosophical system, a religion, even a whole civilization, even life itself."[18]

---

cf. Duke, *Irony*, 30–31): "impersonal irony," "self-disparaging irony," "ingénue irony."

10. Muecke, *Compass of Irony*, 42.

11. Thus Duke, *Irony*, 23.

12. These constitute the fourth of Muecke's four modes of irony (*Compass of Irony*, 61–63).

13. Ibid., 92.

14. Thus ibid., 104; Abrams, *Glossary*, 82; Duke, *Irony*, 24.

15. Thus Duke, *Irony*, 26.

16. See Muecke, *Compass of Irony*, 99–115; Duke, *Irony*, 26–27.

17. Booth, *Rhetoric*, 53–76.

18. Muecke, *Compass of Irony*, 34.

II. MATTHEW'S PORTRAYALS OF POLITICAL LEADERS

Herod the king (2:1–23).

The first political figure to appear on the scene in Matthew's narrative is Herod the king (2:1–23), who is introduced to the reader in connection with the mention of Jesus' birth: "Now when Jesus was born in Bethlehem of Judea *in the days of Herod the king* . . ." (2:1, emphasis mine).[19] This designation at first appears to be merely a historical signpost by which to date the birth of Jesus.[20] But the immediately following text makes it clear that what is at stake here is not historical dating but rather the ironic portrayal: "Now when Jesus was born in Bethlehem of Judea *in the days of Herod the king*, astrologers from the East arrived in Jerusalem, saying, 'Where is *the one who has been born king of the Jews?*'" (2:1–2a, emphasis mine).[21]

No sooner has Matthew's narrative handed the title of "king" to Herod and made Herod's "kingship" over Judea a "fact" in his narrative than he challenges that very "kingship" by characterizing the newborn Jesus as "the one who has been born *king of the Jews* (2:2a, emphasis mine). With this abrupt and pointed juxtaposition of "Herod the king [over Judea]" and "Jesus . . . king of the Jews" the narrator puts the reader formally on notice that the "fact" of Herod's "kingship" cannot be trusted as ultimate truth. Rather, it is merely an "apparent fact" which will be undercut by the "true fact" of Jesus' "kingship."[22] Accordingly, the reader is immediately alerted to the presence of two opposing levels of reality within the narrative: the lower level of apparent reality, in which Herod is "king [over Judea]," and the upper level of true reality, in which Jesus is "king of the Jews."

The lower level of the narrative, for its part, yields a comprehensible and consistent portrait of "Herod the king" as a character of enormous power. Matthew draws this portrait in both explicit and implicit fashion. While Herod is most frequently identified simply in terms of his given name (2:7, 12, 13, 15, 16, 19, 22), he is first and most prominently introduced to the reader in his role as "Herod *the king* (2:1, emphasis mine). This title

---

19. All biblical citations within this essay represent my own translations of the texts in question.

20. As, for example, Luke 1:5; 3:1–2; cf. 2:1–2.

21. Cf. the comments of Beare (*Gospel*, 77): "If [Matthew] mentions Herod, it is not for the sake of a dating, but that he may serve as the false king who trembles at the thought of the coming of the true king, and resorts to desperate measures to eliminate him as a threat to his power."

22. Cf. n21 above.

then reappears in the corresponding designations "*King* Herod (2:3, emphasis mine) and "*the king*" (2:9, emphasis mine).[23] With these references to Herod' "kingship" the narrator attributes power to Herod explicitly.

Implicit attributions of Herod's power are no less prominent throughout the narrative. Herod's reign ("the days of Herod the king," 2:1) is the political reality in relation to which other events are dated. And Herod himself is depicted as a man of enormous political clout, whose actions have immediate impact on the lives of those around him. His personal moods affect "all Jerusalem" (2:3). People both Jewish and Gentile come into Herod's presence when he calls them (2:4, 7). They answer Herod's questions when he asks them (2:5-6 cf. 2:4; 2:7). They leave when Herod sends them (2:9b cf. 2:9a). And they carry out the commands which Herod issues to them (2:9-11 cf. 2:8; 2:16-18).

In addition to his political clout Herod possesses a range of personal characteristics which, taken together, represent power put to work for evil purposes. He is astute. When he hears of the existence of "the one born king of the Jews," he recognizes immediately the political implications for himself and his own kingship (2:3 cf. 2:1-2).[24] He is decisive. When challenges arise, he takes immediate action (2:4-5; 2:7-8; 2:13 cf. 2:20; 2:16). He is cunning. He works "secretly" and deceptively to carry out his evil intentions (2:7-8, 13, 16-18, 20), all the while convincing others that his intentions are nothing but the very best (2:8). He is cynical and ruthless. It does not matter to Herod whom he deceives (2:7-8) or how many people he has to destroy (2:16-18) enroute to achieving his personal goals.

Most significant, however, with respect to the characterization of Herod, is the fact that he both possesses and wields the power of life and death over his subjects.[25] On the one hand Herod "[seeks] the child in order to destroy him" (2:13; cf. 2:20), a threat so real and so deadly that it causes

---

23. Cf. 2:22, where Archelaus is said to be "*ruling* [*basileuei*] Judea in place of his father *Herod*" (emphasis mine).

24. Cf. the comments of Patte (*Gospel*, 33): "Herod's negative reaction to the announcement of the birth of the Christ is clarified by the contrast that the text sets up between the newborn king (2:2), a phrase that means 'one who is king by right of birth,' and Herod, who is 'king' (2:1, 3), but not by right of birth. Matthew assumes, therefore, that readers would identify Herod as the Idumean usurper, indeed as a conniving and ruthless tyrant (see 2:7-8, 16). Thus one could expect that Herod would be troubled by the news of the birth of the king of the Jews. From his perspective, the Christ threatens his political authority." In a similar vein, see Beare, *Gospel*, 77.

25. As Patte indicates (*Gospel*, 36-37), "The political and human authority of Herod is based on fear, indeed terror, that his use of the power of life and death inspire in people (see 2:16). Herod's authority is exerted through the use of disruptive and destructive power or force."

Joseph to take his family and flee the country altogether (2:14–15). And on the other hand Herod proves his power over life and death in an especially vicious move, when he "[does] away with all the children in Bethlehem and the surrounding regions who [are] two years old and under" (2:16). Accordingly, by means both explicit and implicit the narrator leaves the reader in no doubt that Herod is a man of enormous political clout and personal power.

The character portrayal of Jesus, "the one who has been born king of the Jews" (2:2), presents a striking contrast to that of Herod. On the one hand Jesus is clearly identified in "kingly" terms: "the one who has been born king of the Jews" (2:2); the "Messiah" (2:4); the "leader who will shepherd my [= God's] people Israel" (2:6); and "my [= God's] Son" (2:15).[26] But on the other hand the single most prominent term used to designate Jesus throughout this narrative is the term "child" (*paidion*: 2:8, 9, 11, 13—twice, 14, 20—twice, 21), a term which implies weakness and dependence in contrast to political clout and personal power.

And if the narrator's explicit designation "child" implies the weakness and dependence of Jesus as a character in the narrative, this impression finds further support in the narrator's implicit characterization of Jesus through the events of the story. In seven instances Jesus is the subject of a verbal form. But in four of these instances the verbal form in question is not active but passive in voice. Matthew indicates that "Jesus [*is*] *born* [*gennēthentos*] in Bethlehem of Judea" (2:1, emphasis mine). The astrologers inquire about the location of "the one *who has been born* [*techtheis*] king of the Jews" (2:2, emphasis mine). Herod inquires of the Jewish authorities "where the Messiah [*is*] *to be born* [*gennatai*] (2:4, emphasis mine). And the apparent biblical citation in 2:23 states that "he *will be called* [*klēthēsetai*] a Nazarene" (emphasis mine). In one case the verb is merely a copulative: "the place where the child *was* [*ēn*]" (2:9, emphasis mine). Accordingly, only the prophecy cited by the Jewish authorities depicts Jesus as an actor in the narrative in his own right: "For out of Bethlehem *will come forth* [*exeleusetai*] a leader *who will shepherd* [*poimanei*] my [= God's] people Israel" (2:6, emphasis mine; cf. Mic 5:2).

By contrast there are sixteen instances in which Jesus is the effective object of the actions of other people. The astrologers "see his star" (2:2), "make a diligent search" for him (2:8), "find" him (2:8), "see" him (2:11), "worship" him (2:2, 11), and "present him with gifts" (2:11). Herod announces his intentions to "worship" Jesus (2:8), while in reality he intends

---

26. In 2:23 Jesus is likewise identified as the "Nazarene," a term not directly associated with his "kingly" identity.

Power and Powerlessness 33

to "seek" him (2:13; cf. 2:20) in order to "destroy" him (2:13). Joseph, for his part, "takes" Jesus first to Egypt (2:13, 14) and then back to Israel (2:20, 21) at the command of the angel of the Lord. And finally God "calls" Jesus (i.e., "my son") out of Egypt (2:15).

Accordingly, as the narrator portrays him on the lower level of the narrative, Jesus is a character who appears as powerless as Herod appears powerful. He has no voice of his own, nor does he initiate any actions. He is depicted rather as a helpless, dependent "child" who is acted upon, whether for good or evil, by all the other characters of the story. As a result there appears to be no question as to where "power" lies, and where it does not lie, in this narrative.

But appearances are deceiving. In reality the narrator has established the "facts" of a "powerful Herod" and a "powerless Jesus" only in order to undermine the reliability of these "facts" within the world of the narrative. As noted above[27] the narrator begins the process of undermining the "apparent facts" of his narrative already in 2:1–2, with the juxtaposition of "Herod the king" and "the one who has been born king of the Jews." The progress of this undermining process can then be traced through the respective character portrayals of Herod and Jesus from this beginning point all the way to the conclusion of the narrative.

The next clue which the narrator offers to the true character of Herod is the revelation that "King Herod" is "terrified" at the news of "one who has been born king of the Jews" (2:3 cf. 2:2). The revelation that the king is terrified of the child signals to the reader not only that Herod's position as "king over Judea" is being challenged but also that Herod's power is itself more appearance than reality.

This impression finds further support in Herod's discovery that he has been "tricked by the astrologers" (2:16 cf. 2:8). The irony is especially biting here, since it is Herod himself who has just been attempting to *trick the astrologers* with his "secret" activities (2:7) and his smooth doubletalk about "worship" (2:8). But now it becomes apparent that not only is Herod powerless to accomplish his own purposes through deceiving others; but in addition he is powerless to prevent himself from being "tricked" in turn by those same people.

Nor is this the end of the matter. What Herod does not know but what the narrator repeatedly makes clear to the reader is the reason for Herod's continuing failure to accomplish his primary goal. As the reader discovers, it is the prior initiatives of the angel of the Lord which consistently foil

---

27. See the discussion above of "Herod the king" and "the one who has been born king of the Jews."

Herod's best efforts to destroy the child.[28] Before Herod can get word of the whereabouts of the child (2:8), the angel of the Lord instructs the astrologers not to return to Herod with such information (2:12). Before Herod is able to send his henchmen out to find and destroy the child (2:13b), the angel of the Lord instructs Joseph to flee to Egypt together with his family (2:13a, 14). As long as Herod is alive and capable of pursuing the child (2:20b), Joseph keeps his family safe in Egypt as the angel of the Lord has commanded (2:13b). Only when Herod is no longer a threat to the child (2:19, 20b) does the angel of the Lord instruct Joseph to return to Israel (2:20a). And before Herod's son Archelaus has any opportunity to carry out what his father failed to do (2:22a), the angel of the Lord warns Joseph to settle his family in Galilee rather than Judea (2:22b-23).

Accordingly, the unfolding events of the narrative successively unmask Herod's apparent "power" as "king over Judea" as virtual powerlessness vis-à-vis the genuine power of divine initiative. The most prominent confirmation of this fact, however, lies in the threefold mention of the death of Herod (2:15, 19, 20). Here lies the ultimate irony of the narrative. In the end it is Herod "the king" (2:1, 3, 9; cf. 2:22), whose signal aim throughout the narrative has been to "destroy the child" (2:13; cf. 2:20), who himself lies dead; while his intended victim is alive and well in Nazareth of Galilee (2:22-23). Nor can there be any doubt that it is divine initiative which has once again foiled Herod's plans.[29]

And with this turn of events the true shape of reality is now clearly visible. All outward evidence to the contrary notwithstanding, Herod is not in fact the genuine "king over Judea" nor is his "power" genuine power. Instead true kingship belongs to Jesus "the one who has been born king of the Jews" (2:2); and true power belongs to Jesus "the child" (2:8, 9, 11, 13, 14, 20, 21), who says nothing, takes no actions, and is by contrast totally vulnerable to the initiatives of those around him. And with this fundamental redefinition of terms the narrator signals to the reader that from here on and throughout the narrative both "kingship" and "power" are realities to be understood in a paradoxical light and to be identified in the unlikeliest of forms and places.[30]

---

28. While there is no specific mention of the angel of the Lord in the dreams of 2:12 and 2:22, the parallels between these dreams and those of 1:20, 2:13, and 2:19 appear to establish the angel of the Lord as the speaker here as well.

29. As Patte observes (*Gospel*, 36), "For the readers of the Gospel, there is no doubt about who has the power of life and death over Herod: it is God."

30. Cf. Patte's observation (ibid., 37) that "true authority, divine authority, is not based on the use (or the threat of use) of power. Consequently, the recognition that Jesus has divine authority also demands abandoning one's commonly held views about authority: the views concerning political authority and also the views concerning religious authority."

Herod the tetrarch (14:1–12).

The second political figure to appear on the scene in Matthew's narrative is Herod the tetrarch (14:1–12), introduced into the story just as word about Jesus' ministry of "power" spreads throughout Galilee: "At that time Herod the tetrarch got word of Jesus. And he said to his servants, 'This is John the Baptist. He has been raised from the dead. And it is on this account that [these] powers are at work in him'" (14:1–2).

But while it is the ministry of Jesus which occasions the initial mention of Herod (14:1–2), it is the prior ministry of John the Baptist which figures in the events of the flashback recounted in the following verses (14:3–12). Accordingly, it is John the Baptist who serves as the primary counterpart to Herod the tetrarch within this narrative; and it is the character of John the Baptist against which Herod's character is highlighted.

Here, as with the character portrayal of Herod the king (2:1–23), Matthew's narrator paints a "lower-level" portrait of Herod the tetrarch as a man of significant power. To begin with, Herod's power becomes clear from the explicitly "powerful" titles attributed to him. While he is most frequently identified simply as "Herod" (14:3, 6—twice), he is initially introduced as "Herod *the tetrarch*" (14:1, emphasis mine) and later identified as "*the king*" (14:9, emphasis mine).

And beyond these explicit designations Herod's power becomes clear from a variety of implicit indicators. Herod has "servants" (14:2) who carry out the actions he "commands (14:9b; cf. 14:10–11). He exercises the authority to "seize" people, "bind" them, and "put [them] in prison" (14:3). And at the same time he likewise exercises the contrasting authority to "promise [others] . . . whatever [they] might request" (14:7). Most importantly, however, Herod the tetrarch, just as Herod the king before him, wields the ultimate power of life and death over his subjects (14:9b–11; cf. 14:5a).

Beyond these indications of power the narrator likewise attributes to Herod the tetrarch the same fundamental character traits previously visible in Herod the king. Herod the tetrarch is astute. He knows what actions are politically expedient at any given moment and responds accordingly (14:3a cf. 14:3b-4; 14:5a cf. 14:5b; 14:9b–11 cf. 14:9a). Nor is he any less brutal than Herod the king before him. It does not matter whom he has to destroy (14:5) nor how gruesome the actions he has to initiate (14:8, 11) as long as he accomplishes that which is politically expedient. The character of Herod the tetrarch, just as Herod the king before him, exhibits power put to work for evil purposes.

By contrast the narrator's "lower-level" portrait of John the Baptist shows John to be fundamentally powerless. Within the flashback itself

(14:3–12) John serves as the subject of only one active verb: "[B]ecause John *kept on saying* [*elegen*] to him, 'It is not proper for you to have her'" (14:4). Beyond this single action attributed to him, John does nothing. By contrast he functions 13 times as the effective object of the actions of others, actions sometimes good and sometimes evil.[31] The crowd "considers [John] to be a prophet" (14:5). Herod "seizes" John (14:3), "binds" him (14:3, "puts [him] in prison" (14:3), "wants to kill" him (14:5), "commands that [John's head] be given" (14:9), and finally "sends and has [John] beheaded" (14:10). At the prompting of her mother the daughter of Herodias demands that Herod "give" her the head of John the Baptist (14:8). And after John's head has been "brought" (14:11) and "given" to her (14:11), she then "brings" the head to her mother (14:11). Finally John's disciples "take" his corpse (14:12) and "bury" it (14:12). The contrast in power between Herod the tetrarch and John the Baptist could scarcely be more pronounced at the lower level of the narrative.

But once again appearances are deceiving. Here, as was also the case with Herod the king, the narrator creates a portrait of political power on the one hand only to subvert it on the other. This process of subversion begins in 14:1–2 with the introduction of Herod the tetrarch: "At that time Herod the tetrarch got word of Jesus. And he said to his servants, 'This is John the Baptist. He has been raised from the dead. And it is on this account that [these] powers are at work in him.'"

No sooner has the narrator introduced the reader to Herod, the powerful "tetrarch," who has "servants" to do his bidding, than he subverts his own portrait by showing Herod to be deeply superstitious and fearful. Here the reader learns what Herod does not know, namely that Herod is hearing reports about *Jesus, not John the Baptist*. To the reader, therefore, Herod's mistaken conclusion that this figure is "John the Baptist raised from the dead" signals, even in advance of the flashback itself, that Herod fears John and his "powers" as a man "raised from the dead" precisely because it is Herod himself who has put John to death.

The irony here is not to be overlooked. In spite of his apparently ultimate power over the life and death of his subjects, Herod's comments reveal the true state of affairs: Herod fears the man he himself has killed and in so doing implicitly acknowledges the futility of his own power. Herod has taken the ultimate action which he can take against John the Baptist; and his action has been in vain. As Herod sees it, his sentence of death has been

---

31. In some instances John functions as the object of an active verb and in other instances as the subject of a passive verb.

overturned by an act of God[32] and the one he has executed has now been invested with "powers" even greater than before.[33]

That this is not in fact the case merely heightens the irony of the situation. Not only does Herod himself implicitly acknowledge that he is powerless to achieve his own goals. But in addition the reader recognizes what Herod cannot see, namely that the object of Herod's fear ("John the Baptist . . . raised from the dead . . . in whom [extraordinary] powers are at work": 14:2) is no reality at all but rather a figment of his own imagination and the product of his own bad conscience.

This portrait of Herod as a man powerless to accomplish his own aims and frightened of his own imagination finds further support throughout the flashback account of 14:3–12. Here the narrator portrays Herod as a man who fears everyone with whom he comes in contact and a man whose actions are consistently motivated by those whom he fears: John the Baptist (14:3 cf. 14:4), the crowd (14:5a-b cf. 14:5c), his wife Herodias (14:9-11 cf. 14:3, 4, 8), the daughter of Herodias (14:9-11 cf. 14:6-8), the guests at the party (14:9c-11 cf. 14:9a-b).

As a result the reader encounters Herod the tetrarch as a man fundamentally powerless to carry out his own desires. When he wishes to kill John (14:5a), his fear of the crowds prevents him from doing so (14:5b-c). When he wishes to keep John alive (14:9a),[34] his fear of the guests at his party prevents him from sparing John's life (14:9b-10).[35] Even more ironic, however, is the fact that Herod's own apparent power is by the same token his most obvious weakness. It is precisely because Herod has promised the daughter of Herodias "whatever she might request" (14:7) that he finds himself compelled to act against his wishes and have John executed (14:9-10). Accordingly, in spite of his apparent power, Herod is effectively a puppet on a string, operated now by this outside force and now by that one. His fears render him incapable of taking independent initiatives and leave him the single option of reacting to the actions of others.

---

32. Herod's conclusion that John "has been raised from the dead" clearly points to the agency of God in the "resurrection" that Herod imagines to have taken place.

33. Herod's conclusion that there are "powers" at work in John the Baptist *because* [*dia touto*] *he has been raised from the dead* clearly implies that these "powers" were not at work in John's ministry prior to this time.

34. As the narrator portrays it, Herod's reticence to kill John reflects not a change of heart on his part but rather his ongoing fear of the crowds and their reaction to John's death. Cf. Patte, *Gospel*, 214.

35. As Patte notes (ibid., 208), "the social relationship of Herod with his guests when he does not want to retract his oath in front of them is valued more than John's life and more than his relationship with the people he governs."

By the same token John the Baptist, who at first glance appears powerless, in facts exhibits the real power which Herod lacks. To begin with, John has been carrying out among the people a ministry of such effectiveness that they have recognized him as a "prophet" (14:5). Further, John has exercised his prophetic role with a power of which Herod can only dream. In a face to face encounter with Herod John has thrown expediency to the winds and bluntly condemned Herod's marital relationship with Herodias, the wife of his brother Philip: "It is not proper for you to have her" (14:4b; cf. 14:3b).

The power of this act is manifest in its contrast to the actions of Herod. While Herod will shortly demonstrate his powerlessness to achieve his political aims or carry out his personal desires, John here exhibits the power to disregard the constraints of expediency and to act instead on personal conviction. The power of John's act is likewise manifest in its impact on the tetrarch. Herod fears John's condemnation to such an extent that he takes the penultimate initiative of seizing John, binding him, and putting him in prison in order to silence his voice (14:3a; cf. 14:4). Accordingly, John the Baptist is the "powerful" figure who makes things happen within this account; while Herod the tetrarch, for his part, is reduced to the "powerlessness" of a reactive role.

But the ultimate irony here lies in the outcome of this series of events. Herod, who thinks he has rid himself of his nemesis by executing John the Baptist (14:10), finds instead that he now faces a "John the Baptist raised from the dead" (14:2) who has even greater "powers" than the John he has executed. And since this outcome (14:1–2) is narrated prior to the events themselves (14:3–12), the reader knows all along what Herod finds out only when it is too late: Herod's actions, even when he take them, are futile in their impact; and Herod's power, even when he exerts it, is impotence *vis-à-vis* the power of God.

Pilate the governor (27:1–2, 11–38, 54, 62–66; 28:1–15).[36]

The final political figure to appear on the scene in Matthew's narrative is "Pilate the governor" (27:1–28:15), to whom Jesus is "handed over" by the Jewish authorities (27:1–2): "And when it was morning all the chief priests and elders of the people conferred against Jesus, in order to put him to death. And they bound him and led him away and handed him over to Pilate the governor."

---

36. I have intentionally limited the designated text to those segments of the broader narrative that make specific reference to Pilate and those acting at his behest.

Here, as was the case with Herod the king and Herod the tetrarch, the narrator paints a "lower-level" portrait of Pilate as a man of significant power. This power is visible on the one hand in the titles attributed to him. The narrator first introduces him to the reader as "Pilate *the governor*" (27:2, emphasis mine). And in the following accounts the narrator alternates between the designations "Pilate" (27:13, 17, 22, 24, 62, 65) and "*the governor*" (27:11—twice, 14, 15, 21; 28:14, emphasis mine). When the Jewish authorities themselves address Pilate, they do so with the respectful term "*Sir*" (*kyrie*, 27:63, emphasis mine).

Pilate's power as governor is likewise visible in implicit fashion in the words of those around him. Virtually all of the other characters who come on stage within this section of the narrative make pointed appeals to Pilate as the person with the real power to grant their requests. The chief priests and elders of the people first "bring charges" to Pilate against Jesus (27:12-13) and later urge him to "secure" the tomb where Jesus' body has been buried (27:62-64). Pilate's wife implores him to "have nothing to do with that righteous man" (27:19); while the crowds demand that Pilate carry out their wishes concerning Jesus (27:20, 22, 23) and Barabbas (27:20, 21). Even when Pilate is not on the scene, other characters attribute power to him in unmistakable fashion. The chief priests and Pharisees assure the Roman soldiers who have been delinquent in their task of guarding the tomb that "if this comes to the attention of the governor, we will . . . keep you out of trouble" (28:14).[37]

Nor is there any question as to the nature of Pilate's authority. As Roman governor he is, above all, the person who wields the power of life and death over his subjects, whether they be Jewish or Roman. When the chief priests and elders of the people want to "put [Jesus] to death" (27:1), they "hand him over to Pilate the governor" (27:2). Having done so, they then incite the crowds "to ask [Pilate] for Barabbas and to have Jesus destroyed" (27:20). The crowds, for their part, oblige the religious leaders by demanding that Pilate "release" Barabbas (27:21; cf. 27:15, 17) and "crucify" Jesus (27:22, 23). And in an only slightly veiled allusion to ultimate consequences the chief priests and Pharisees promise to "keep [the Roman guard] out of trouble" in the event that Pilate learns what has happened at the tomb.

Pilate himself confirms by his actions that power which others attribute to him. He questions Jesus, the prisoner handed over to him (27:11,

---

37. That the "guard" whom Pilate has sent to the tomb is comprised of Roman soldiers rather than an armed Jewish contingent (cf. 26:47) becomes evident from the very fact that they are accountable to Pilate for their actions (28:14a: "if this comes to the attention of the governor") and evidently fear for their lives as a result of their delinquency (28:14b: "we will . . . keep you out of trouble").

13–14); takes his seat on the *"bema"* in order to pass judgment (27:19); and finally "releases" Barabbas to the crowds (27:26) and "hands [Jesus] over to be crucified" (27:26). But Pilate's power is ultimately evident in the actions which others take at his command. At his word the soldiers of the governor take Jesus to Golgotha and crucify him along with several other criminals (27:31b-38). Pilate's power over the life and death of his subjects is not matter for debate.

By contrast the narrator's "lower-level" portrait of Jesus is a portrait of powerlessness. By way of titles the narrator offers the single designation "Jesus" (27:1, 11-twice, 20, 26, 27). Other characters within the narrative make use of titles which serve to evaluate Jesus but do not *per se* connote power ("that righteous man," 27:19 cf. 27:24; "that deceiver," 27:63). And even when Pilate and his soldiers designate Jesus with "powerful" titles ("Jesus who is called Messiah," 27:17, 22; "king of the Jews," 27:29; "Jesus the king of the Jews," 27:37), they do so precisely in contexts which highlight Jesus' powerlessness. "Jesus who is called Messiah" is a prisoner whom Pilate has authority to "release" (27:17) or "crucify" (27:22). The "king of the Jews" is a condemned man being tortured and mocked prior to his execution (27:27–31). "Jesus the king of the Jews" is an executed criminal hanging on a Roman cross (27:37).

Nor does the portrait of Jesus' powerlessness change when viewed from the perspective of actions taken or received. Three references are made to what Jesus has previously done or said: Pilate inquires "what evil [Jesus] has done" (27:23); and the religious authorities recount to Pilate what "that deceiver said [27:63] while he was still living [27:63]." Twice the narrator indicates that Jesus "does not reply" to words directed to him (27:12, 13). But only twice within this account does the narrator portray Jesus as an actor or speaker on stage in his own right: Jesus "stands" before the governor (27:11a) and "says" something in response to the governor's question (27:11b).

By contrast Jesus functions consistently throughout this account as the effective object of the actions of others. Jesus' opponents "confer against him" (27:1) in order to "put him to death" (27:1, "bind him" (27:2), "lead him away" (27:2, 31), "hand him over" (27:2, 18, 26), "ask him" questions (27:11), "say" things to him (27:13), "bring charges/witness against him" (27:12, 13), seek to "have him destroyed" (27:20), "scourge him" (27:26), "take him along" (27:27), "strip him" (27:28, 31), "put [clothing] around him" (27:28), "put [things] on/over his head" (27:29, 37) "put [something] into his right hand" (27:29), "kneel down before him" (27:29), "mock him" (27:29, 31) "spit on him" (27:30), "strike him on the head" (27:30), "dress him" (27:31), "crucify him" (27:35; cf. 27:22, 23, 26, 31), and "guard" him

(27:54). Pilate's wife, for her part, urges Pilate to "have nothing to do with" Jesus (27:19). There appears to be no question that Jesus is as powerless in this setting as Pilate is powerful.

But once again appearances are deceiving. Just as he did with Herod the king and Herod the tetrarch, the narrator subverts his own portrait of "Pilate the powerful governor" and unmasks him by stages as "Pilate the powerless puppet." This process of unmasking begins early in the narrative, continues to the end, and is one in which Pilate plays a decisive role through his own actions. The first signal of Pilate's powerlessness comes in the repeated indications that Pilate intentionally places himself at the mercy of the crowds and their wishes: "And at each feast the governor had a custom of releasing one prisoner to the crowd, *whomever they wished*" (27:15, emphasis mine); "So when they had gathered together, Pilate said to them, '*Whom do you want me to release to you?*'" (27:17, emphasis mine); "And the governor replied and said to them, '*Which of the two do you want me to release to you?*'" (27:21).

Pilate's vulnerability to the wishes of the crowds then progresses from the level of inquiry to the level of shouting match, a public debate in which Pilate and the crowds hurl questions and answers back and forth (27:17/20, 21a/21b, 22a/22b, 23a/23b) with ever increasing "vehemence" (27:23b) until a full-scale "riot" is underway (27:24). As the reader discovers, Pilate is manifestly powerless either to influence the views or to control the actions of the crowds.

Nor is this the end of the matter. Not only does the narrator reveal Pilate's powerlessness to the reader; but Pilate himself likewise acknowledges his own impotence *vis-à-vis* the crowds: "And when Pilate saw *that he was accomplishing nothing* . . . (27:24). And with this acknowledgment Pilate's powerlessness is open to full view, his humiliation is complete, and the narrator's irony has reached its peak. "Pilate the powerful governor" has been fully unmasked as "Pilate the powerless puppet."

From here on out the script has been written by the religious authorities. All that Pilate can do is to act against his own better wisdom and capitulate to the demands of the crowds. Pilate knows that the religious authorities have handed Jesus over to him out of "jealousy" (27:18). He has heard the counsel of his wife to "have nothing to do with that righteous man" (27:19). He knows in his own heart that Jesus "has done no evil thing" (cf. 27:23). Yet in spite of all this knowledge Pilate is powerless to act on his own convictions. Instead he "washes his hands" of the matter and, in an act of obvious expediency, grants the crowds their demand: "I am innocent of the blood of this man. See to it yourselves!" (27:24). And with this declaration he releases the "notorious prisoner" (27:16) whom the crowds want freed (27:26a) and hands over for crucifixion the "righteous man" (27:19) whom the crowds want dead (27:26b).

Pilate, the most powerful man in Palestine, is ultimately powerless to do the one thing he knows is the right thing to do. Rather the *governor* reveals himself as the puppet of those whom he purports to *govern*, namely the Jewish crowds and the religious authorities who stand behind them.[38] There has been no question all along that it is the religious authorities who have masterminded the death of Jesus and manipulated Pilate into executing their scheme (27:1–2, 12, 20; cf. 27:62–64). And in 28:12–14 the narrator offers one final confirmation of this fact: "And when [the chief priests] had gathered together with the elders and conferred, they gave a significant sum of money to the soldiers, saying, 'Say, His disciples came during the night and stole him while we were sleeping. *And if this comes to the attention of the governor, we will persuade him* and keep you out of trouble.'" Pilate, who has been manipulated once to bring about the death of Jesus, will be manipulated once again to ensure that Jesus forever "stays dead" in the public perception. "Pilate the powerful governor" is indeed "Pilate the powerless puppet."

But the ultimate irony here is one which reveals the powerlessness not only of Pilate but that of the crowds and the religious authorities as well. Jesus, the one whose execution has been masterminded by the religious authorities, demanded by the crowds, and carried out by Pilate, does not "stay dead." Instead, just as he has predicted (cf. 27:63) and the angel of the Lord has announced (28:5–7), Jesus "is raised from the dead" in an act of God which gives the lie to all human claims of ultimate power. Pilate the governor, just as Herod the king and Herod the tetrarch before him, does indeed have the power to take life away. But this power itself is revealed as impotence in the face of a God whose infinitely greater power "raises [people] from the dead." In the light of Jesus' resurrection human power is robbed of its potency and human powerlessness transformed by the power of God. And this, as Matthew sees it, is the ultimate irony of power.

---

38. Cf. the comments of Goldberg (*Jews and Christians*, 190): "Jesus' last hope would seem to be Pilate. Surely, if anyone has the power to save him, it ought to be the governor who is backed up by the might of imperial Rome. But up to now, other sources of human strength . . . have consistently failed to save . . . So too, the kind of dominion manifested by human government now proves equally powerless to rescue him from death. Pilate, though he has all of Rome behind him and though he knows Jesus to be guiltless, nevertheless, fears a riot brewing and thus, to keep the peace, determines that Jesus' life is expendable." Contra Patte's apparent conclusions (*Gospel*, 380), however, the narrator does not paint a portrait of Pilate's powerlessness in order to absolve him of guilt.

III. CONCLUDING OBSERVATIONS

In speaking about the function of irony as a literary strategy Duke offers the following observations:

> In using irony an author invites the reader to reject an ostensible structure of meaning. The meaning to be rejected is often far more than the literal meaning of a particular sentence or expression, but rather a whole structured "world" of meanings or values which the author spurns . . . On one level the reader's search is a literary one . . . If ultimate meaning or values are at stake in the irony, however, then when the literary search is over and the higher structure has been discovered, the excitement of that interpretive leap is easily transferred to the possibility of a more ultimate leap. Particularly when irony is artfully done, the choice to share the author's perspective on a narrative world may become a decisive step toward dwelling with that author in a deeper sense and embracing a new perspective on the real world.[39]

It is this "new perspective on the real world" to which Matthew invites his readers as he paints conventional portraits of political power on the one hand only to subvert them on the other. In specific Matthew invites his readers to join him on the high ground from which he and they together can view the impotence of all human power in the political arena *vis-à-vis* the genuine potency of divine initiative. In Matthew's view, it is this perspective on the real world which will empower the believers of the Matthean church for their inevitable encounters with the "Herod's" and "Pilate's" of their own day, the "governors and kings" before whom they will be called to bear witness to their faith (cf. 10:18). And it is this perspective on the real world which will enable the Matthean church to hear and to understand the words of Jesus: "Those who find their life will lose it; and those who lose their life for my sake will find it" (10:39).

---

39. Duke, *Irony*, 34, 37.

3

"Thus You Will Know Them by Their Fruits"[1]

The Roman Characters of the Gospel of Matthew

INTRODUCTION

IN THE INTRODUCTION TO *Matthew and Empire: Initial Explorations* Warren Carter points to a "simple observation" that he views as largely overlooked within Matthean scholarship, namely "that the Gospel [of Matthew] comes from and addresses a world dominated by the Roman Empire." And Carter concludes: "It seems difficult to imagine that this world left no mark on the Gospel as most interpretations seem to suggest by their sheer inattention to this context."[2] Carter's observations are surely correct. While Matthean scholars have always paid attention to the individual Roman characters or character groups of the Gospel of Matthew—and thus by implication to the Roman Empire which they represent and embody—Matthean scholarship has focused its attention primarily on the theological issues at stake between Matthew's church and the wider Jewish community with whom it is in debate.

This narrative assessment of the Roman characters within Matthew's Gospel will focus explicit attention on what has until recently remained

---

1. Matt 7:20. All biblical citations are taken from the New Revised Standard Version unless otherwise designated.

2. Carter, *Matthew and Empire*, 1.

largely implicit and unexamined, namely the impact of the Roman Empire and, in specific, its human functionaries on Matthew's story of Jesus. And while it is in some respects literarily unwarranted to focus on such ethnic distinctions,[3] the parameters of this study are for reasons of clarity and simplicity drawn to include only those characters within Matthew's story who can clearly be viewed as Romans: the centurion (*hekatontarchos*) who comes to Jesus on behalf of his sick servant (8:5-13); the emperor (*kaisar*: 22:15-22); Pilate, the governor (*hēgemōn*: 27:1-66; 28:11-15); Pilate's wife (*hē gynē autou*: 27:19); the soldiers (*stratiōtai*) of the governor, a cohort (*speira*) of troops (27:27-54);[4] the centurion (*hekatontarchos*) at Jesus' cross (27:51-54); and the guard (*koustōdia*) at Jesus' tomb (27:62-66; 28:11-15).[5]

This study will proceed in three stages. The first step will be to identify Matthean evidence pointing to the normal activities and roles of each of the Roman characters or character groups and to paint a "lower level"[6] portrait of Roman imperial power as it creates the socio-political backdrop to Mat-

---

3. That Matthew does not delineate his characters predominantly along the lines of "Roman" and "Jewish" becomes clear from several significant clues in his narrative. To begin with, the single most prominent face of the Roman occupation of Palestine is, for Matthew's Gospel, without question the ubiquitous "tax collectors" *(telōnai*: 5:46; 9:9, 10, 11, 12, 13; 10:3; 11:19; 18:17; 21:31, 32; cf. 17:25-26; 22:15-22), Jewish functionaries who work at the behest of their Roman overlords to collect the taxes assessed by Rome on their Jewish compatriots. Further, the Matthean Jesus refers in the same breath (10:18) to "governors and kings," a categorization which includes both Roman governors such as Pilate (27:1-66; 28:11-15) and local, part-Jewish client rulers such as "Herod the king" (2:1-23) and "Herod the tetrarch" (14:1-12). Most importantly, however, Matthew shapes his accounts of these three figures in such a way as to highlight the commonalities between them as political leaders, regardless of ethnic distinctions. On Matthew's parallel portrayals of these characters, see Weaver, "Power and Powerlessness," 179-96.

4. And while they are identified only obliquely, I likewise include the soldiers of Herod the Great (2:16, 20) and Herod the Tetrarch (14:3, 10) within Matthew's "lower level" portrayal of Roman soldiers.

5. The verb *echete* (27:65) is grammatically ambiguous and could be construed either as imperative "Take a [Roman] guard" or as indicative "You have a [Jewish] guard." But the fact that the Jewish authorities appeal to Pilate to "command that the tomb be secured" (27:64) suggests that the guard (*koustōdia*) authorized to "secure" the tomb (27:65) will be Roman and not Jewish. This conclusion is further supported by the concern of the Jewish authorities that word of the empty tomb and the failure of the guard (28:13) will "be heard by the governor" and thereby get the guard itself into trouble (28:14). Cf. M'Neile, *Gospel*, 428-29; Gundry, *Literary and Theological Art*, 584; Morris, *Gospel*, 731-32.

6. Thus Muecke in his book *The Compass of Irony*, where he describes irony (19-20) in terms of a "double-layered or two-storey phenomenon" in which "the lower level is the situation either as it appears to the victims of irony . . . or as it is deceptively presented by the ironist" and "the upper level is the situation as it appears to the observer or the ironist."

thew's narrative. But while Roman imperial power is the ultimate socio-political reality against which Matthew's narrative unfolds, this power stands necessarily and consistently in an ironic tension with the central reality of Matthew's story, namely, the "kingdom of heaven." And this "kingdom" has "come near" (4:17) in the person of Jesus of Nazareth through his life, death, and resurrection. Accordingly, the second step of this study will be to assess Matthew's treatment of each Roman character or character group within the ongoing plot of the narrative and to paint Matthew's own "upper level" portrait of Roman imperial power as viewed through the lens of the "kingdom of heaven" and ultimately as unmasked by that greater power.[7] The third step of this study will be to reflect on Matthew's overall portrait of the Roman characters within his Gospel and on the implications of this portrait for Matthean theology.

I. MATTHEW'S LOWER LEVEL PORTRAIT: THE EVERYDAY FACE OF ROMAN IMPERIAL POWER

Soldiers (*Stratiōtai*).

Beyond the ever-present Jewish "tax collectors" of Matthew's Gospel,[8] the most visible face of Roman imperial power for the characters of Matthew's narrative is surely that of the Roman "soldiers" (*stratiōtai*) stationed in their land as the military force of the Roman occupation. These soldiers—organized into "centuria" of 100,[9] "cohorts" (*speirai*: 27:27) of 600,[10] and "legions" (*legiōnes*: 26:53) of 6,000[11]—form the broad base of a powerful and extensive military hierarchy reaching all the way from the foot soldiers at the bottom (8:9; 22:7; 27:27-66; 28:11-15; cf. 2:16; 14:10) to the officers (8:5-13; 27:54), the client king (2:1-23; 14:1-12) or the governor (27:1-66;

---

7. See Weaver, *Power and Powerlessness*, 185-87, 188-91, 193-96. Cf. Carter's conclusion (*Matthew and Empire*, 1) that "the Gospel resists Rome with a *social challenge* in offering a vastly different vision and experience of human community, and with a *theological challenge* in asserting that the world belongs to God not Rome, and that God's purposes run through Israel and Jesus, not Rome."

8 See n3 above.

9. Thus Luz, *Matthew 8-20*, 10. While there is no specific mention of such "centuria" in Matthew's narrative, the repeated references to the title "centurion" (*hekatontarchos*: 8:5, 8, 13; 27:54) clearly imply their existence within the world of the story.

10. Thus Brown, *Death*, 248; Luz, *Matthew 8-20*.

11. Thus Brown, *Death*. While Matthew makes no mention of Roman legions within his narrative, Jesus' reference to "twelve legions of angels" (26:53) clearly evokes the parallel image of these massive Roman forces.

28:11–15), and ultimately the emperor himself at the top (22:15–22; cf. 17:25–26; 20:25).

As the persons of lowest rank within this military hierarchy the soldiers are subject to the commands of their superiors all the way up the line. They "go" and "come" at the command of their centurions (9:9). They perform the tasks that the client kings "send" them to do (2:16; 14:10; cf. 14:3). They carry out the decisions of the Roman governor (27:26, 31–38; cf. 27:62–66). And they ultimately serve as the "troops" (*strateumata*) "sent" by the emperor himself to do his bidding (22:7).[12]

But while the Roman soldiers of Matthew's Gospel have no authority over others within the Roman military establishment itself, they nevertheless wield genuine and fearsome power over the occupied populace. They have the authority to "find" civilians (27:32) at will and compel them into "forced" labor for stated tasks (27:32: carrying a cross for a condemned prisoner) and stated distances (5:41: one mile). They are the functionaries who carry out the official punishments decreed by the client king or the governor: arrest (14:3), binding (14:3), imprisonment (14:3), flogging (20:19; 27:26), beheading (14:10), and crucifixion (27:27–38, 51–54). Following executions they "keep watch" over the executed criminal (27:36, 54), "cast lots" for his clothing (27:35), and serve as a "guard" at the tomb (27:65, 66; 28:11; cf. 28:4). In addition the soldiers likewise carry out special military operations against the occupied populace (2:16: "killing all the [young] children" of Bethlehem; 22:7: "destroying . . . murderers" and "burning their city").

In addition to the everyday violence demanded by their designated tasks as the troops of an occupying army, the soldiers of Matthew's narrative exhibit a brutality well beyond the call of duty. When Jesus, already subjected to a pre-execution flogging (27:26a), has been handed over to the

---

12. The "king" in Jesus' parable of the wedding banquet (22:1–10) is a complex figure. Within Matthew's narrative Jesus tells the parable as an allegorical depiction of the course of salvation history and the bitter consequences for the Jewish people as a result of their role in that history. Central to the interpretation of Jesus' allegory is the identification of the "king" with God and of "his son" with Jesus himself. Accordingly, the death and destruction unleashed by the "enraged king" are an ominous prophecy concerning the judgment of God about to fall on the Jewish people. From the vantage point of Matthew's church, however, the parable of Jesus has taken on a new layer of meaning. In their post–70 CE world, the language of the "enraged king" who "sends his troops" to "destroy those murderers" and to "burn their city" is a vivid allusion to the Roman "king," namely, the emperor, and the "troops" he sent to lay waste to Jerusalem (23:37–38; 24:1–2). Accordingly, the "king" of Jesus' allegory is a complex and conflated image of God, whose judgment is falling on the Jewish people, and the Roman emperor, whose "troops" are the agent of that judgment. Cf. the conclusion of M'Neile (*Gospel*, 315): "These verses refer to . . . the sack of Jerusalem by the Roman armies, who, as God's instrument of punishment, are 'His armies.'"

soldiers for crucifixion (27:26b), they inflict their own crude mockery and physical abuse on him before carrying out the official sentence. Jesus has been tried and condemned as "King of the Jews" (27:11, 37; cf. 27:17, 22). Accordingly, the soldiers surround him and set up a mock-royal court at his expense. Their tactics are evident from their actions. They seek to intimidate Jesus by their overwhelming numbers (27:27: "the whole cohort") and to humiliate him with the public undressing (27:28, 31) and dressing (27:28, 31) to which they subject him. They ridicule him with mock-royal attire: a crimson robe (27:28), a "crown" of thorns (27:29), and a reed "scepter" (27:29). They "mock" him (27:29, 31; cf. 20:19) with their genuflections and their cries of "Hail, King of the Jews!" (27:29). And they abuse him physically as they "spit" on him and "strike" him with the reed (27:30).

For the Jewish characters of Matthew's narrative the Roman soldiers occupying their land are clearly a powerful and brutal force, widely recognized as those who are "evil" (5:39). The everyday face of Roman occupation is one of compulsory labor, unrequited humiliations, cruel torture, and bloody executions.

Centurions (*Hekatontarchoi*).

The centurions of Matthew's narrative are clearly people in the middle. As the leaders over centuria, detachments of 100 soldiers, they have considerable power. Not only are they men of rank, "having soldiers under [them]" (8:9; cf. 27:54); but they are also men of authority, issuing commands to soldiers and slaves alike and knowing that these commands will be carried out immediately. As one centurion explains (8:9), ". . . I say to one [soldier], 'Go,' and he goes, and to another, 'Come,' and he comes, and to my slave, 'Do this,' and the slave does it."

At the same time, however, Roman centurions are likewise "under authority" (8:9), receiving their own orders from higher up the military chain. The tasks that fall to them and their centuria are the routine tasks of military occupation: the crucifixion of condemned criminals (27:54 cf. 27:26-38), the posting of charges against those executed (27:37), and the subsequent vigil at the crucifixion site (27:36, 51-54).

Accordingly, centurions would appear to be people who inspire the same fear and hatred as their soldiers. As military leaders who issue commands to soldiers and civilians alike and expect immediate and unthinking obedience, centurions are clearly men whose word is to be feared. And as the captains of the Roman governor's torture and execution squads they are likewise conspicuous symbols of the oppressive Roman occupation.

The Governor (*Hēgemōn*).

Of all the Roman characters "onstage" within Matthew's story[13] Pilate, the Roman governor (27:2–66; 28:11–15), is farthest up the military chain of command and accordingly, from a "lower level" perspective, the most powerful figure within the narrative. The predominant power of the Roman governor within the world of the story is clearly evident throughout Matthew's narrative rhetoric.[14]

Matthew introduces the Roman ruler explicitly as "Pilate *the governor*" (27:2) and then intersperses references to "Pilate" (27:13, 17, 22, 24, 58—twice, 62, 65) with parallel references to "the governor" (27:11—twice, 14, 15, 21, 27; 28:14),[15] "thereby emphasizing his military and political power."[16] The Jewish authorities address Pilate accordingly with the respectful title "Sir" (27:63: *kyrie*), a title that carries with it the connotation of power and authority.

The power of the Roman governor also becomes visible in implicit fashion within Matthew's narrative, as the actions of the story flow toward him and appeals are addressed to him. The Roman governor is the one "before whom" prisoners are "dragged" (10:18), "to whom" they are "handed over" (27:2, 18; cf. 20:19), "before whom" they "stand" on trial (27:11), and "before whom" community leaders "gather" (27:62). He is likewise the one to whom people of position and power—family members (27:19), wealthy individuals (27:57–58), and Jewish authorities (27:62–66)—appeal for action on their behalf. And he is the one who inspires fear not only among the occupied populace but also among the soldiers under his command (28:14). As a "tyrant" over his subjects (20:25b) and one who can "lord it over" them (20:25a), the Roman governor has the ultimate power of "command," a power both acknowledged by his supplicants (27:64) and confirmed by his own actions (27:58).

But it is in the depiction of his official duties that the power of the Roman governor is most clearly visible. While on duty in Jerusalem during the Passover, the governor has military command over a cohort (27:27b), a force of 600 men who together comprise "the soldiers of the governor"

---

13. "Caesar," the Roman emperor (22:15–22; cf. 10:18; 17:25; 20:25), plays an unseen role in Matthew's narrative, as an "offstage" character to whom the actors in the story make reference.

14. Thus Weaver, *Power and Powerlessness*, 191–192; Carter, *Matthew and Empire*, 163–164.

15. Cf. Jesus' own references to "governors and kings" (10:18), "the rulers of the Gentiles" (20:25), and "their great ones" (20:25).

16. Matera, *Passion Narratives*, 104.

(27:27a) and who assist him in the task of "maintaining order"[17] among the crowds. And in this role the governor wields the awesome power of life and death over the occupied populace. Accordingly, he has the duty to hold prisoners (27:15–16), put them on trial (27:11a), interrogate them (27:11b, 13–14), listen to the charges brought against them (27:12, 13), and sit on the "judgment seat" to determine their fate (27:19). Depending on the outcome of the trial the governor then has the authority either to "release" prisoners (27:15, 17, 21, 26; cf. 27: 20) or to have them "flogged" (27:26a)[18] and "hand them over" (27:26b) to be "crucified" (27:22, 23, 26, 31, 35, 38, 44; 28:6; cf. 27:20).

For the inhabitants of the land the governor is hardly the most visible face of the Roman occupation on a day-to-day basis. But within the occupied territory he is without question the most powerful human symbol of Roman empire and domination.

The Emperor (*Kaisar*).

At the pinnacle of the Roman military hierarchy stands the emperor, the ultimate symbol (22:19–21) and the ultimate military power (22:7)[19] of the Roman imperial system. And while the emperor plays no "onstage" role within the plot of Matthew's narrative, he is nevertheless a powerful "offstage" character, whose impact is felt on the most mundane levels of existence as well as in the most profound human catastrophes. And it is no doubt the emperor above all others who inspires Jesus' words to his disciples about the "rulers of the Gentiles" who "lord it over" their subjects and "their great ones" who are "tyrants" over them (20:25).

The most obvious and widespread impact that the emperor has on the lives of his Jewish subjects within Matthew's narrative is the "taxes" (*kēnsos*: 17:25; 22:17, 19) and the "toll" (*telē*: 17:25) that he levies on them through the agency of ubiquitous and universally despised Jewish "tax collectors" (5:46; 9:9–13; 10:2–3; 11:19; 18:17; 21:31–32)[20] sitting at their "tax

---

17. Morris, *Gospel*, 692.

18. While the text of 27:26 associates the governor himself with the act of "flogging," this act of torture is without question delegated by the governor to soldiers who carry out the sentence.

19. See n12 above.

20. Within Matthew's narrative the term "tax collectors" is coupled variously with the terms "sinners" (5:46; 9:10, 11; 11:19), "prostitutes" (21:31, 32), and "Gentiles" (18:17). Tax collectors are associated derisively with the "Son of Man," whose reputation is that of "a glutton and a drunkard" (11:19). And Jesus identifies the tax collectors themselves as "the sick" (9:12) and "sinners" (9:13).

booths"(9:9). This taxation of the Jewish people by their own compatriots, in obvious collaboration with the Roman occupiers, is the more galling (22:21a) and controversial (22:15–18) because the taxes are collected in the form of a Roman coin (22:19: *dēnarion*) which bears both the "head" (22:20: *eikōn*) and the "title" (22:20: *epigraphē*) of the emperor himself.

But if taxes are the everyday face of the Roman emperor, violence, death, and destruction are the catastrophic face of the Roman imperial system and its powerful "king" (22:7).[21] In Jesus' allegorical parable of the wedding banquet the outlines of a Roman emperor and his military campaign against Jerusalem (already history from the perspective of Matthew's church) are clearly visible in the image of the "king" who "sends his troops" to "destroy those murderers" and to "burn their city." Shortly thereafter Jesus announces to "Jerusalem" (23:38), "See, your house is left to you desolate," an unmistakable allusion to the impending destruction of the Jewish temple. And as Jesus and his disciples then leave the temple, Jesus warns them (24:2) that "not one stone will be left here upon another; all will be thrown down." The devastation wrought by the military campaigns of the Roman emperors is clearly massive and overwhelming, both to human life and to the physical infrastructure that sustains human community.

Accordingly, while the emperor himself is not an "onstage" actor within Matthew's narrative, it is evident that his impact on the lives of the occupied populace extends both to the most mundane aspects of daily life and to the most terrifying of human catastrophes. Here is clearly the most powerful Roman of them all.

Pilate's Wife (*Hē Gynē Autou*).

The final Roman character present within the world of Matthew's narrative is the wife of Pilate, the Roman governor. Her portrait differs significantly from that of the other Roman characters in that she is neither male nor military. Accordingly, within her first-century Hellenistic context she clearly has less power than they. Matthew's narrative offers no clues to the normal role of Pilate's wife. But the narrative nevertheless implies that as the wife of the Roman governor she is a woman of considerable authority. Her appeal to her husband *"while he [is] sitting on the judgment seat"* (27:19a, emphasis mine), an action which interrupts him in the very course of his official duties, is one that could presumably be taken only by a person of such authority.

---

21. See n12 above.

II. MATTHEW'S UPPER LEVEL PORTRAIT: ROMAN IMPERIAL POWER UNMASKED

With the exception of Pilate's wife, Matthew's "lower level" portrait of the Roman characters within his narrative is a monolithic portrayal of brutal and oppressive military might exercised by an occupying power against a subject people. But first appearances are notoriously deceptive within Matthew's narrative. Even as the Roman military hierarchy exercises overwhelming power against the occupied populace, Matthew paints an "upper level" portrait of these Roman characters which effectively unmasks their powerful façade and reveals the true state of affairs.

Unlike the "lower level" portrait, however, this "upper level" portrayal is far from monolithic. While Matthew uniformly unmasks Roman imperial power wherever he finds it, he does not, however, offer a uniformly "damning" portrayal of the Roman characters within his story. Instead Matthew paints an astonishingly variegated portrait of these characters, mocking some of them with his narrative rhetoric and offering highest commendation to others.

The Centurion with the Sick Servant (8:5–13).

The first Roman character to walk "on stage" within Matthew's narrative is a figure who astonishes Jesus himself (8:10: *ethaumasen*). Matthew introduces this character with the powerful title, "centurion" (8:5). And the centurion himself acknowledges this power with his references to the "soldiers under [him]" (8:9a) and his authority to command them (8:9b). But ultimately Matthew's narrative rhetoric portrays this centurion revealing through his actions and confessing through his words his own effective powerlessness in the face of Jesus' genuine power.

The first indication of the true state of affairs lies in the reference to the centurion's servant (*pais*: 8:6, 8, 13; cf. 12:18; 14:2)[22] who is seriously ill. The urgency of the servant's condition is reflected in the corresponding urgency of the centurion's act in "appealing" to Jesus (8:5: *parakalōn*)[23] and in his vivid description of the servant himself, who is "lying at home paralyzed, in terrible distress" (8:6). In spite of his authority over soldiers and civilians, the centurion is clearly overpowered by the illness of his servant. And in this respect he stands in the same position as all other supplicants who come, are

---

22. While *pais* could also refer to a "child" (thus 2:16; 17:18; 21:15), the Lukan parallel to this story identifies the *pais* (7:7) unambiguously as a "slave" (*doulos*: 7:3, 10).

23. Cf. the urgency reflected in 8:31, 34; 14:36; 18:29, 32; 26:53.

brought, or appeal to Jesus for healing. The very fact that he appeals to Jesus itself indicates both that he himself has no power over human illness and, more importantly, that Jesus does have such power.

But not only is the centurion powerless vis-à-vis the illness of his servant, in pointed contrast to Jesus. He is also, in his own words, "unworthy" (*ouk . . . hikanos*) of the very presence of Jesus "under [his] roof" (8:8a). And this self-acknowledged "unworthiness" corresponds, in turn, to the centurion's reverential attitude towards Jesus himself. He addresses Jesus as "Lord" (*Kyrie*: 8:6, 8), an honorific title normally accorded to those higher up in the Roman imperial hierarchy, namely the governor (27:63) or the emperor (cf. 20:25), but now used by the centurion to express his subordination to Jesus.[24] He likewise acknowledges the "authoritative" position of Jesus,[25] a position parallel (8:9a) but clearly superior to his own, from which Jesus can "heal" others (8:8c) simply by "speaking the word" (8:8b cf. 8:9b). And Jesus, conversely, acknowledges the "faith" of the centurion (8:10: *pistin*; 8:13: *hōs episteusas*).

The overall impact of this narrative rhetoric is as "amazing" for Matthew's readers as the centurion himself is to Jesus. Here Matthew portrays a demonstrably powerful Roman centurion who, with his own words and actions, reveals to the contrary his true powerlessness over the circumstances of his life and acknowledges his subordination to Jesus as one with "authority" far beyond his own. And it is clear from Jesus' response to the centurion that Matthew in fact affirms this extraordinary self-assessment of Roman imperial power. Jesus offers the Roman (and thus Gentile) centurion the highest possible commendation ("Truly I tell you, in no one in Israel have I found such faith" [8:10]); and he offers him a space at the table "with Abraham and Isaac and Jacob in the kingdom of heaven" (8:11) at the expense of the Jewish "heirs of the kingdom" (8:12). Then he responds to the centurion's request, "speaks the word" (8:13a cf. 8:8b), and the "servant is healed" (8:13 cf. 8:8c).

Pilate the Governor (27:1-2, 11-54, 57-66; 28:11-15).

The next Roman character to appear in Matthew's narrative, Pilate the governor, does not fare as well, rhetorically speaking. While Matthew commends the centurion through his narrative rhetoric for recognizing Jesus'

---

24. Cf. 8:2; 9:28; 14:28, 30; 15:22, 25, 27; 17:15; 20:30, 31, 33.

25. According to the centurion Jesus is, like himself, a "man under authority" (8:9: *hypo exousian*), a phrase that clearly implies that Jesus' "authority" (cf. 7:29; 9:6; 10:1) has come from a source beyond himself (cf. 9:8; 21:23, 24, 27; 28:18).

superior "authority" (8:9) and placing his "faith" in Jesus (8:10, 13), there is no such commendation for Pilate. To the contrary Matthew portrays Pilate as a tragic figure, whose demonstrated powerlessness is compounded and made culpable by his failure to act on that which he knows to be true and to do that which he knows to be right.

Throughout the trial scene and even beyond, Matthew persistently unmasks the true powerlessness of this most powerful of all characters "onstage" in his narrative.[26] Ultimately Pilate's powerlessness is visible vis-à-vis every other character or character group present on the scene: Jesus; the Jewish crowd; the Jewish leaders; Pilate's wife; Pilate's soldiers; and Pilate himself.

Early in the trial scene Pilate is unable to get his prisoner to speak in his own defense (27:12–14).[27] In spite of the governor's best efforts (27:13), Jesus instead asserts the one freedom left to a "bound" prisoner (27:2) and maintains a complete silence vis-à-vis the charges brought against him by the Jewish leaders (27:12, 14). And in the end Pilate is capable only of "great amazement" (cf. 27:14).

As the trial scene progresses, Pilate's powerlessness is further highlighted as he intentionally places himself at the mercy of the crowd. He already has a dangerously flawed judicial policy in place for the Passover festival, namely, "to release a prisoner for the crowd, *anyone whom they wanted*" (27:15, emphasis mine). And in the midst of the trial Pilate invokes this policy and repeatedly abdicates his authority to the wishes of the crowd (27:17, 21), thus leaving himself powerless to adjudicate the trial according to his own best judgment and the dictates of justice (cf. 27:18, 19, 23). Instead he is forced into indecorous public debate with the crowd (27:17, 21–23), an escalating shouting match that Pilate eventually loses when it turns into a full scale "riot" (27:24b). And in the end Pilate is forced by his own self-imposed policy to grant the crowd their wishes rather than to enact the justice incumbent upon him.

Pilate is equally ineffective in his dealings with the Jewish leaders, the power bloc behind the crowd (27:20). These leaders, headed up by the high priest Caiaphas (26:3, 51, 57, 58, 62, 63, 65) and widely identified as "the chief priests and the elders [of the people]" (26:3, 47; 27:1, 3, 20; 28:11/12)[28] have already been prominently involved in the events that lead up to Jesus'

---

26. Cf. Weaver, *Power and Powerlessness*, 191–95.

27. Cf. Carter's observation (*Matthew and Empire*, 164) that "[Pilate] has not been able to intimidate Jesus into lying, begging, or recanting in order to save his life."

28. But see also the variant references in 26:14, 57, 59; 27:6, 41, 62.

trial before Pilate.[29] And throughout the trial itself it is these Jewish leaders, rather than Pilate, who succeed in setting the agenda (27:11–14, 17, 22 cf. 26:63, 65–68),[30] organizing public opinion (*against* the apparent views of Pilate: 27:20; cf. 27:15–18, 19, 21–23),[31] and manipulating the judicial system itself in order to accomplish their predetermined strategy for destroying Jesus (27:24–26 cf. 26:3–4, 59, 65–66; 27:1, 20).

After Jesus' death these Jewish leaders continue to orchestrate events by insisting that Pilate give them a "guard" for the tomb of Jesus (27:62–66). And two days later, faced with the double challenge of an empty tomb (28:11) and the dangerous implications of their own cover-up conspiracy (28:12–13), the Jewish leaders promise Pilate's soldiers that they will manipulate Pilate himself on the soldiers' behalf (28:14): "If this comes to the governor's ears, we will satisfy him and keep you out of trouble." As Matthew's narrative demonstrates, Pilate the powerful governor shows himself to be effectively and ironically powerless not only vis-à-vis the Jewish leaders, but also vis-à-vis his soldiers themselves.

But it is in contrast to the moral courage shown by his wife that Pilate's powerlessness comes into focus most prominently. Right in the midst of Pilate's futile shouting match with the crowd (27:19 cf. 27:17–18, 20–24a) Pilate's wife takes the clearly unusual step of interrupting her husband in the course of his official duties to give him an urgent warning (27:19, DJW): "Have nothing to do with that righteous man, for I have suffered many things today in a dream because of him." The urgency of her warning and its moral clarity stand in stark contrast to the feeble actions of Pilate vis-à-vis

29. They have "conspired to arrest Jesus by stealth and kill him" (26:4) and paid money to an informant who will "hand him over" (26:15, 16, DJW). They have come to Gethsemane "with swords and clubs" (26:47), "laid hands" on Jesus (26:50), and "arrested" him (26:48, 50, 57). They have put him on trial at the home of Caiaphas (26:57–64) and condemned him to death on the charge of "blasphemy" (26:65–66; cf. 27:1). Finally they have mocked and physically abused him (26:67–68) before "binding" him," "leading him away," and "handing him over" to Pilate (27:2).

30. Pilate's question about Jesus' identity as "King of the Jews" (27:11), his questions about "Jesus who is called Messiah" (27:17, 22), and the charge he posts above the cross (27:37: "This is Jesus, the King of the Jews") correspond directly to the "messianic" charges ("Messiah": 26:63, 68; "Son of God": 26:63) on which Jesus is condemned in his trial before Caiaphas the high priest.

31. That Pilate, contra Carter (*Matthew and Empire*, 165–167), does not view Jesus' identity itself as cause for execution is evident from the fact that it is only *after* the crowd repeatedly calls for Jesus' crucifixion (27:22, 23; cf. 27:20) that Pilate concludes that he is *ineffective* in his efforts (27:24), evidently to arrive at a *different* course of action than that demanded by the crowd. This conclusion is further confirmed by the prominent evidence to which Pilate has access that points to Jesus' innocence rather than his guilt. He is a "righteous man" (27:19, DJW) who has "done no evil" (cf. 27:23). And he has been framed by his enemies "out of jealousy" (27:18).

the crowd. Not only does Pilate have a policy already in place for abdicating his responsibility as the arbiter of justice (27:15). But by the time he receives the message from his wife, he has likewise committed himself to that expedient course of action (27:17). Accordingly, the outcome of Pilate's public debate with the crowd is never in doubt. Even as his wife exhibits the extraordinary courage to speak truth to power (27:19 cf. 14:3–4), Pilate is in the very process of abdicating that power to the wishes of the crowd and neglecting all corresponding questions of truth and justice.

And it is Pilate himself who makes the ultimate acknowledgement of his own powerlessness. Faced with the outbreak of an angry "riot" (27:24b) Pilate finally recognizes what Matthew's readers have been able to observe throughout the entire scene, namely that he *"[can] do nothing"* (27:24a: *ouden ōphelei*, emphasis mine[32]). And in the end Pilate is trapped by his own policies (27:15) and his own fears (27:24b) into disregarding everything that he knows to be true: the ulterior motives of those who accuse Jesus "out of jealousy"(27:18); the urgent, dream-inspired warning of his wife that Jesus is a "righteous man" (*dikaios*: 27:19, DJW); and his own internal conviction that Jesus has "done no evil" (cf. 27:23). And he is accordingly obliged to take the expedient and face-saving action of "wash[ing] his hands" in front of the crowd (27:24c) and proclaiming his own "innocence" (27:24d) in an obvious but futile attempt to rid himself of guilt for the manifest injustice that he is about to perpetrate.[33]

But if Pilate is ultimately shown to be powerless, he is not by the same token rendered "innocent," his own protestations notwithstanding. Pilate appears to believe that he has absolved his guilt by "washing his hands" (27:24c), proclaiming his own "innocence" (27:24d), and deflecting the responsibility for Jesus' death onto the crowd (27:24d). And for their part "the people as a whole" (27:25a: *pas ho laos*) willingly accept the responsibility

---

32. Or "was achieving [or benefiting] nothing." Cf. Carter, *Matthew and Empire*, 166. But, contra Carter, the implications of either translation are the same: Pilate is incapable of doing what he hopes to do.

33. Contra Carter (ibid., 165), who argues that, from Pilate's perspective, because Jesus "does not contest the title 'King of the Jews'" he is "not 'innocent' [*dikaios*]" but rather "guilty of rebellion and sedition." In fact the entire trial scene is structured rhetorically to highlight the moral dilemma of Pilate who is fully aware that he is faced with the condemnation of a "righteous man" (27:19, DJW) who has "done no evil" (cf. 27:23) but has been framed by his enemies "out of jealousy" (27:18). The evident innocence of this "righteous man" is rhetorically confirmed by the fact that his counterpart in the trial scene is depicted as a "notorious prisoner" (27:16). If Matthew intended to portray Pilate as believing his prisoner to be "guilty," there would be no need for the elaborate and self-serving scene in which Pilate seeks to establish his own "innocence" (27:24) vis-à-vis the (apparently culpable) act that he is about to carry out (27:26).

that Pilate has handed over to them: "His blood be on us and on our children!" (27:25b).

But the narrative rhetoric of Matthew's story does not absolve Pilate of his guilt. Instead Pilate's own words and actions portray him unmistakably as the character ultimately responsible for the death of Jesus. It is Pilate who "hands [Jesus] over to be crucified" (27:26b), the last link in a significant chain of characters who participate, each in their turn, in "handing Jesus over" to death.[34] It is Pilate who establishes the "charge" against Jesus that is subsequently posted over his head on the cross: "This is Jesus, the King of the Jews" (27:38 cf. 27:11). It is Pilate at whose "command" (27:58) the body of Jesus is given to a disciple for burial (27:57–59) and at whose further "command" (27:64–65) the stone is then "sealed" (27:66) and the tomb thereby "secured" against theft (27:64, 65, 66). And, in the ultimate and ongoing irony of Matthew's narrative rhetoric, it is Pilate who must, in a future out beyond the end of the story, be "satisfied" (28:14: *peisomen*) in the matter of the empty tomb.

In the rhetoric of Matthew's narrative there is in the end no commendation for Pilate. To be sure Matthew portrays Pilate as one who recognizes both truth (27:18, 19) and justice (27:23). But this awareness serves only to confirm Pilate's guilt. Ultimately Matthew's narrative rhetoric portrays Pilate as culpable for neglecting his own better judgment, abdicating his authority to the wishes of the crowd, intentionally perpetrating injustice, and failing in his attempt to absolve himself of the guilt for his actions.

Pilate's Wife (27:19).

Of all the Roman characters in Matthew's narrative Pilate's wife stands in a category by herself. She is the single non-military figure among the Roman characters. And she is likewise, *and apparently by the same token*, the sole Roman character whose power is not ironically unmasked before she receives commendation through the rhetoric of Matthew's narrative. The actions and the words of this woman mark her only for highest approbation.

That Pilate's wife takes the extraordinary step of interrupting her husband in the course of his official duties points implicitly to the urgency of her cause and the corresponding courage required for this act of advocacy. But her words themselves are an explicit pointer to the significance and the truth of her cause.

---

34. Thus Judas (10:4; 17:22; 20:18; 26:2, 15, 16, 21, 23, 24, 25, 45, 46, 48; 27:3, 4); the chief priests and scribes/elders of the people (20:19 cf. 20:18; 27:2 cf. 27:1); the crowd (27:18 cf. 27:15); and finally Pilate himself (27:26).

On the one hand Pilate's wife indicates that she has had a "dream." And in the world of Matthew's narrative "dreams" are important messages from "the angel of the Lord" (1:20, 24; 2:13, 19; cf. 2:12, 22). These messages call people to courageous action in the face of adverse public opinion (1:20), civil disobedience in the face of the powers that be (2:12) and timely response in the face of impending danger or its resolution (2:13, 19–20, 22). Accordingly the "dream" of Pilate's wife is likewise to be trusted as a divine message and one that calls her to courageous action.[35]

Pilate's wife does not reveal the specifics of her dream concerning Jesus. But she indicates that in this dream she has "suffered many things . . . because of him" (*polla . . . epathon . . . di' auton*). And while she does not explain this cryptic statement, Matthew's readers can hear in her words the overtones of Jesus' words to his disciples that they will be hated "because of my name" (10:22; 24:9: *dia to onoma mou*) and persecuted "on my account" (5:11: *heneken emou*).[36] Pilate's wife, while not formally identified as one of Jesus' "disciples," nevertheless "suffers," just as they will, "because of him."

Most significantly, however, Pilate's wife has become convinced—whether before, during, or after her dream—that Jesus is a "righteous man" (*tō dikaiō*) and accordingly not deserving of the death penalty which her husband is even at that moment "sitting on the judgment seat" to deliver. And in this confession Matthew's readers recognize a true word spoken about Jesus, who begins his ministry with an act carried out "to fulfill all righteousness" (3:15) and who proclaims "righteousness" as the hallmark of the kingdom of heaven (5:20; 6:33).[37]

But Pilate's wife is commended by Matthew not simply for her divinely inspired confession that Jesus is a "righteous man" and her corresponding "suffering" on his behalf. Ultimately she is commended for the action that she takes in response to her dream. Like Joseph the "righteous man" (1:19) and the "wise men from the East" (2:1), who took action "as the angel of the Lord commanded" (1:24; cf. 2:12, 14, 21, 22), Pilate's wife also responds immediately and faithfully to the dream that she has had.[38] And this prompt and faithful response sets the actions of Pilate's wife in sharp and positive contrast to those of her husband, who neglects the divine warning and takes action instead to save himself rather than his "righteous" prisoner.[39]

---

35. Cf. Heil, *Death and Resurrection*, 74.
36. Cf. 5:10.
37. Cf. Senior, *Passion of Jesus*, 114.
38. Cf. Matera, *Passion Narratives*, 108.
39. Cf. ibid.

In the end Matthew has only highest commendation for this extraordinary Roman woman.

The Centurion and "Those with Him" (27:54 cf. 27:27–53).

When Pilate, who does not heed the warning of his wife (27:19), finally succumbs to the expedient and "hands [Jesus] over to be crucified" (27:26), it is "the centurion and those with him" (27:54), namely "the soldiers of the governor" (27:27), who enter the narrative and take over the action. And it is these soldiers and their centurion, of all the Roman characters in Matthew's narrative, who exhibit the most radical shift in their actions and their perspectives from the beginning of the scene to the end.

As those who "flog" Jesus (27:26), "mock" him (27:31 cf. 27:27–29), physically abuse him (27:30), and finally "crucify" him (27:31, 35), these characters exhibit all the power and brutality expected of an occupying army, who can do what it will to the occupied populace. But this arrogance and apparent omnipotence are brought to a sudden and dramatic halt by the cosmic disruptions which accompany the death of Jesus: the "tearing" of the temple curtain "from top to bottom" (27:51); the "shaking" of the earth (27:51); the "splitting" of the rocks (27:51); the "opening" of the tombs (27:52); and the "raising" of the bodies of many "saints" (27:52).

In the face of this massive display of divine power (27:54: "the earthquake and what took place") the centurion and his soldiers recognize instantaneously that they are witnessing events far beyond their control and encountering power far greater than their own. And in this same instant their arrogance is transformed into abject "terror" (27:54: *ephobēthēsan sphodra*, "they were terrified") and their "mockery" (27:31) into confession of the highest order (27:54): "Truly this man was God's Son!"

The profound significance and the corresponding irony of this transformation are immediately evident to Matthew's readers. The "terror" of these Roman soldiers not only serves negatively to subvert their status as powerful occupiers; but it also serves positively to identify these soldiers with the followers of Jesus who are likewise "terrified" (17:6, DJW: *ephobēthēsan sphodra*; cf. 14:27, 30; 17:7; 28:5, 8, 10) at the visible evidence of God's power. And with their confession of Jesus as "God's Son" this Roman centurion and his soldiers give human voice, along with Jesus' disciples (14:33), Peter (16:16), and Jesus himself (26:63–64 cf. 27:43; cf. 21:37, 38; 22:2), to the central truth of Matthew's narrative, confirmed by none other than the voice of God (3:17//17:5; cf. 2:15): "This is my Son, the Beloved, with whom I am well pleased."[40]

In a profoundly ironic move Matthew's narrative rhetoric offers highest commendation to these Roman characters, *whose place in the narrative exists simply because they mock, torture, and crucify Jesus.* At the climactic moment of the narrative it is these Roman soldiers with their officer who proclaim the true identity of Jesus for all to hear. And in so doing they join a growing chorus of Gentile witnesses within Matthew's narrative who recognize Jesus' true identity (2:2; 8:6, 8; 15:22, 25, 27), place their "faith" in him (8:10, 13; 15:28), and "worship" him (2:2, 11), even as many of Jesus' Jewish compatriots fail to do so[41] and accordingly forfeit their position of privilege within the kingdom of heaven.[42]

The Guard at the Tomb (27:62–66; 28:2–4, 11–15).

The final Roman characters to show up "on stage" in Matthew's narrative are the soldiers of the "guard" (27:65, 66; 28:11: *koustōdia*; cf.28:4: *hoi tērountes*), requested by the chief priests and Pharisees (27:62–64) and authorized by "command" of Pilate (27:65 cf. 27:64). These Roman soldiers, whose commission and whose actions are integrally linked to the strategic concerns of the Jewish authorities (27:63–64; 28:12–13), receive no commendation from Matthew's narrative rhetoric. To the contrary, they are the victims of intense mockery within Matthew's narrative, as they demonstrate their inability to carry out their assigned task and face the ongoing consequences, both humiliating and dangerous, of this failure.

The first clue to Matthew's ironic treatment of the guard is that Pilate places these soldiers under the oversight of the Jewish leaders themselves, thus in effect subordinating the authority of the army of occupation to those whose land they occupy. Not only are the Jewish authorities, for their part, instructed to "take" (27:65: *echete*)[43] the guard and employ them to "secure" (27:65: *asphalisasthe*; cf. 27:64, 66) the tomb. But the soldiers of the guard themselves implicitly acknowledge their subordination to the Jewish authorities by going to them rather than to Pilate with their story of "everything that had happened" at the tomb (28:11).

But with this turn of events Matthew's unmasking of the power of the guard has only begun. The task of this guard is to "secure" a tomb (27:64,

---

40. Cf. Heil, *Death and Resurrection*, 87–88. See also 4:3, 6; 8:29; 27:40, 43.
41. Thus, for example, 21:32, 37–39; 22:2–3; 23:37; 27:20–23, 24–25.
42. Thus, for example, 8:11–12; 21:31, 43. Cf. Heil, *Death and Resurrection*, 87.
43. See n5 above.

65, 66) whose door has been closed with a "great stone" (27:60) and then "sealed" (27:66). The goals are to prevent the theft of a dead body from the tomb (27:64 cf. 28:13); and to forestall the spread of a rumor ("the last deception") that the one buried "has been raised from the dead" (27:64). But the "great earthshaking event" (28:2a, DJW: *seismos . . . megas*) instigated by the "angel of the Lord, descending from heaven" (28:2b) demonstrates that the soldiers on guard are powerless to carry out their task.

The guard is first outmaneuvered by the angel of the Lord, who "rolls back the stone" (28:2b: *apekylisen ton lithon*) which has been "rolled to" (27:60: *proskylisas*) the entrance of the tomb and "sits" on it (28:2b), thus effectively undoing the "seal" (27:66) and dismantling all "security" measures (cf. 27:64, 65, 66). The guard is then overwhelmed by the sight of this divine messenger, whose "appearance" is "like lightning" and whose "clothing" is "white as snow" (28:3).[44] And in a note of biting irony Matthew delivers the coup de grace (28:4): "For fear of him the guards shook [*eseisthēsan*] and became like dead men (*hōs nekroi*)."

Matthew's unmasking of the power of the Roman guard has now reached its climax, if not its conclusion. The military detail commissioned to "secure" a tomb instead witnesses all their "security" measures dismantled by a divine power that dwarfs their own human efforts. The soldiers employed to guard a dead man are instead "shaken" by the "earth-shaking" power of God and temporarily transformed by their own "fear" into "dead men" themselves. And the guards charged to prevent a corpse from being "stolen" will shortly discover[45] that in spite of their best efforts the body has disappeared undeniably from the tomb (cf. 28:11-15).

But this is not yet the end of their humiliation. Following the announcement by the angel (28:5-7) and the women's departure (28:8-10), "some of the guard" set off for Jerusalem to inform the chief priests about "everything that had happened" at the tomb (28:11). That they are not in fact aware of "everything that had happened" and have only an incomplete story to relate to the Jewish authorities is merely the first of their problems.

Once the chief priests have "assembled with the elders" and "devised a plan" (28:12a), the situation of the soldiers becomes both more humiliating and more dangerous. To begin with, the soldiers are bought off by the chief priests and elders with a "large sum of money" (28:12 cf. 28:15), a bribe intended to suppress the story about the angel and any possible rumors about

---

44. Cf. Matthew's similar depiction of the "transfigured" Jesus (17:2), whose face "shone like the sun" and whose clothes "became dazzling white."

45. The dead faint (28:4: *hōs nekroi*) into which the guards have fallen would appear to prevent them from overhearing the words of the angel (28:5-7). Note the pointed indication that the angel speaks "to the women" (28:5a).

Jesus' resurrection (28:13 cf. 27:63–64). The tenuous situation into which this secret alliance places the soldiers is heightened still further by the false story that they are obliged to repeat, a fabrication not only humiliating but also dangerously incriminating (28:13): "His disciples came by night and stole him away while we were asleep." That the Jewish authorities recognize the grave danger that this cover-up conspiracy poses to this Roman guard, ultimately answerable to Pilate himself, is evident from the contingency plans with which they reassure the soldiers (28:14): "If this comes to the governor's ears, we will satisfy him *and keep you out of trouble*" (emphasis mine).

Accordingly, the soldiers of this Roman guard have, by their own deliberate actions, put themselves under the power and at the mercy of the Jewish authorities for all time to come. The bribe that they have accepted from the chief priests and elders ensures that they will be obliged to keep on repeating the humiliating story of their own failure and the corresponding "success" of Jesus' disciples. And the real danger to which this story exposes them vis-à-vis the governor ensures that these Roman soldiers are at the ongoing mercy of the Jewish leaders for their own physical safety.

Faced with this dangerous dilemma the Roman soldiers guarding the tomb take the expedient step of "do[ing] as they are directed" (28:15a), thereby becoming the mindless and powerless puppets of the Jewish religious establishment. And Matthew notes the ironic success of their expedient response in terms of its ongoing afterlife within the Jewish community (28:15b): "And this story is still told among the Jews to this day."

Clearly Matthew's narrative rhetoric offers no commendation for this Roman guard, whose story is intimately intertwined with that of the Jewish authorities. Instead there is only unrelenting mockery of these powerful Roman occupiers who have chained themselves forever to the will and the word of their Jewish subjects.

The Emperor (4:1–11; 20:20–28; 22:15–22; 28:16–20).

The Roman emperor, the single most powerful human figure on the "lower level" of Matthew's narrative, does not play an "onstage" role. But his policies and actions nevertheless ensure his presence in the narrative as a powerful "offstage" character, whose name and reputation are invoked by the characters "on stage." But Matthew treats the emperor just as he does every other Roman military figure, subverting the power of the emperor through his narrative rhetoric and demonstrating the indisputable subordination of the emperor to the authority of God and God's Son, Jesus. Matthew's narrative offers three strategic indicators of the Roman emperor's true status in the cosmic scheme of reality.

The third and climactic temptation to which the devil subjects Jesus in the wilderness is the offer of "all the kingdoms of the world" in exchange for Jesus' "worship" (4:8–9). Implicit in this offer lies the stunning revelation that "all the kingdoms of the world," *including the Roman imperial power* (8:5–13 et al), in fact belong to Satan and are therefore at his disposal. Accordingly, just as Jesus is about to claim his messianic ministry as Son of God (3:17; cf. 4:3, 6) on behalf of the "kingdom of heaven" (4:17 et al), Matthew's narrative rhetoric implicitly depicts the Roman Empire, *and by the same token its emperor*, as the ultimate and "satanic" opposition to Jesus' own mission.[46] But the subsequent indications that Jesus rejects Satan's ultimate temptation (4:10a: "Away with you, Satan!") and forces Satan himself off the scene (4:11a: "Then the devil left him") confirm that neither the devil nor his "satanic" empire *with its emperor* are a match for Jesus, Son of God.

Jesus later makes explicit to the Pharisees that which the temptation scene communicates implicitly, namely the emperor's definitive subordination to the authority of God. Presented with the legal tender used for paying Roman taxes, a coin bearing the "head" and the "title" of the emperor (22:19–21a), Jesus offers an enigmatic, debate-stopping response to the Pharisees' query about taxes (22:21b): "'Give therefore to the emperor the things that are the emperor's, and to God the things that are God's.'" As Warren Carter cogently observes (p. 63), "Whatever else this cryptic comment may mean, it cannot in the Gospel's point of view mean that God and Caesar are the same, or equal, or unrelated, or that God is subordinate to Caesar."

And ultimately the Risen Jesus subverts the hegemonic claims of Satan altogether, *and by the same token those of the Roman emperor on Satan's behalf,* when he announces (28:18b), "All authority in heaven *and on earth* has been given to me" (emphasis mine), and sends his disciples out to carry on the mission of the kingdom of heaven in his authority and with his presence (28:19–20). As Carter concludes (*Matthew and Empire*, 63–64), "The center of the divine purposes is not Rome but the community that acknowledges God's reign. This community and its claims exist within the very heart of the Roman Empire in an ambivalent relationship to it. The emperor cannot be ignored, but he does not define ultimate reality. Caesar has power but God is sovereign."

---

46. Cf. Carter, *Matthew and Empire*, 62–63.

III. CONCLUSIONS: MATTHEW'S OVERALL PORTRAYAL OF ROMAN CHARACTERS

The world of Matthew's narrative is a deeply polarized world, with sharp divisions between the "good" and the "evil" (5:45a; 7:17-18; 12:35), the "righteous" and the "unrighteous" (5:45b), the "blessed" and the "accursed" (5:1-12 cf. 23:13-36; 25:31-46), the "faithful" (9:2, 22, 29; 15:28) and the "unbelieving" (21:25, 32; 27:42). But while other major characters or character groups consistently reflect either good [47] or evil traits,[48] Matthew paints an astonishingly complex portrait of the Roman characters within his narrative.

On the one hand they are powerful people. These Roman characters, with the single exception of Pilate's wife, comprise the military hierarchy that is the face of Roman imperial power for the people of occupied Palestine. And collectively they have powers ranging from the massive to the mundane. They can undertake military campaigns against rebellious cities (22:7); tax the occupied population (22:15-22); imprison, try, torture, and execute criminals (27:1-2, 11-54); perform guard duty following executions (27:62-66; 28:11-15); and compel civilians at will into forced labor on their behalf (5:41).

But even as Matthew invests these characters with power on the "lower level" of the narrative, he consistently subverts that same power through his own "upper level" narrative rhetoric. These demonstrably powerful Roman occupiers, from the foot soldiers all the way up to the emperor himself, are in the end portrayed as powerless vis-à-vis an entire range of challenges, natural and supernatural: physical illness (8:6), political riots (27:24), cosmic disruptions (27:51-54), and divine appearances (28:2-4). From the least of these Romans to the greatest Matthew unmasks their military might and demonstrates their subordination to the far greater power of God (22:21b) and the authority that God has granted to Jesus, his "Beloved Son" (28:18b; cf. 3:17b; 17:5b).

But while Matthew consistently subverts the military might of the Roman imperial power, he does not offer a monolithic condemnation of the Roman characters themselves. Instead Matthew evaluates these characters individually, according to their varied responses to Jesus. For those Romans who fail to do what they know to be right (27:24-26; cf. 27:18, 19, 23) or

---

47. Thus the supplicants who appeal to Jesus for healing. Cf. 8:1-4; 9:2-8, 27-31; 14:34-36; 15:21-28, 29-31; 17:14-20; 21:14.

48. Thus the Jewish authorities, who consistently challenge Jesus' actions. Cf. 9:2-8, 9-13, 32-34; 12:9-14, 22-32, 38-42; 15:1-9; 16:1-4; 21:23-27; 22:15-22, 23-33, 34-40.

to say what they know to be true (28:11–15; cf. 28:2–4), Matthew has nothing but unrelenting mockery. But for those Romans who acknowledge the power of Jesus (8:8–9); place their faith in him (8:10, 13); and confess his true identity as "Lord" (8:6, 8), "righteous man" (27:19), and "Son of God" (27:54), Matthew has only highest commendation. These Romans are ultimately counted among the "many" who "will come from east and west and will eat with Abraham and Isaac and Jacob in the kingdom of heaven" (8:11).

In the end Matthew's overall portrait of the Roman characters within his narrative is "round" and realistic rather than "flat" and ideologically driven. In this respect it closely resembles the group portrait of Jesus' disciples themselves. The Romans of Matthew's narrative are complex characters, capable, just as Jesus' own disciples, of extraordinary faith, tragic moral failure, and profound experiences of conversion. They are portrayed, in short, as real human beings, for whom Jesus' maxim holds true (7:20), "Thus you will know them by their fruits."

4

"What Is That to Us? See to It Yourself"

Making Atonement and the Matthean Portrait of the Jewish Chief Priests[1]

INTRODUCTION

TO READ THE GOSPEL of Matthew within its first-century religious context is to read an intensely Jewish narrative. This narrative opens with a Jewish genealogy (1:1, 2–16, 17), beginning with Abraham, the "father" of the Jewish people (1:1, 2, 17; cf. 3:9; DJW), and coming to its climax in the birth of Jesus the Jewish Messiah (1:1, 16, 17; cf. 1:18). And the narrative which follows—an account of the birth, childhood, ministry, death, and resurrection of Jesus Messiah—takes place against the backdrop of the Jewish religious world of first-century Palestine.[2] This is a world prominently peopled with

---

1. All biblical citations reflect the New Revised Standard Version unless otherwise designated. All chapter/verse references are likewise Matthean unless otherwise designated.

2. That is, the pre-70 CE world of Jesus' day. Matthew's narrative depicts the world prior to the destruction of the Jerusalem temple by the Romans in 70 CE. Matthew's narrative itself is written most likely in the mid-80's CE, a vantage point from which it looks back at the destruction of the temple through the words of Jesus, who foretells this event (22:7; 23:38; 24:1–2).

Jewish leaders (Pharisees[3], Sadducees[4], scribes[5], priests/chief priests[6], and elders[7]), closely associated with Jewish meeting places (synagogue[8], temple/house of God[9]) and Jewish feasts (Passover/Unleavened Bread[10], feast[11]), and regularly focused on Jewish scripture[12], the commandments[13], and what is lawful.[14]

This is likewise a world pervaded by the memory of the Jewish prophets of ancient days[15] and a history shaped by their prophetic pronouncements.[16] And the conflict which drives the plot of Matthew's narrative is a quintessentially Jewish conflict, the ongoing and ultimately deadly confrontation between Jesus Messiah and the Jewish leadership, who repeatedly contest his messianic status and "authority"[17] and who persistently seek to "destroy" him,[18] "kill" him,[19] or "put him to death."[20] Matthew's narrative retains its Jewish character and context up to its conclusion (28:20) and on into the

---

3. Thus *Pharisaioi*: 3:7; 5:20; 9:11, 14, 34; 12:2, 14, 24, 38; 15:1, 12; 16:1, 6, 11, 12; 19:3; 21:45; 22:15, 34, 41; 23:2, 13, 14, 15, 23, 25, 26, 27, 29; 27:62.

4. Thus *Saddoukaioi*: 3:7; 16:1, 6, 11, 12; 22:23, 34.

5. Thus *grammateis*: 2:4; 6:20; 7:29; 8:19; 9:3; 12:38; 15:1; 16:21; 17:10; 20:18; 21:15; 23:2, 13, 14, 15, 23, 25, 27, 29, 34; 26:3, 57; 27:41; cf. 13:52.

6. Thus *hiereis*: 8:4; 12:4, 5; *archiereis*: 2:4; 16:21; 20:18; 21:15, 23, 45; 26:3, 14, 47, 51, 57, 58, 59, 62, 63, 65; 27:1, 3, 6, 12, 20, 41, 62; 28:11.

7. Thus *presbyteroi*: 15:2; 16:21; 21:23; 26:3, 47, 57, 59; 27:1, 3, 12, 20, 41; 28:12.

8. Thus *synagōgē*: 4:23; 6:2, 5; 9:35; 10:17; 12:9; 13:54; 23:6, 34.

9. Thus *hieron*: 4:5; 12:5, 6; 21:12, 14, 15, 23; 24:1; 26:55; *naos*: 23:16, 17, 21, 35; 26:61; 27:5, 40, 51; *oikos/oikos tou theou*:12:4; 21:13. Cf. 23:38, where Jesus associates the temple about to be destroyed as "your house" (= the "house" of "Jerusalem, the city that kills the prophets and stones those who are sent to it!")

10. Thus *pascha*: 26:2, 17, 18, 19; *azymos*: 26:17.

11. Thus *heortē*: 26:5; 27:15.

12. Thus *nomos* (law): 5:18; 12:5; 22:36; 23:23; *nomos kai prophētai* (law and prophets): 5:17; 7:12; 22:40; cf. 11:13.

13. Thus *entolē/entolai*: 5:19; 15:3, 6; 19:17; 22:36, 38, 40.

14. Thus *exestin*: 12:2, 4, 10, 12; 14:4; 19:3; 20:15; 22:17; 27:6.

15. Thus 5:12; 12:39; 13:17; 16:4, 14; 23:29, 30, 31, 37. See also the references to John the Baptist (11:9, 13; 14:5; 21:26), Jesus (13:57; 21:11, 46; 23:37), and Jesus' disciples (10:41; 23:34) as "prophets."

16. Thus the "fulfillment citations" of Matthew's Gospel: 1:22: 2:5, 15, 17, 23; 3:3; 4:14; 8:17; 12:17; 13: 35; 21:4; 24:15; 26:56; 27:9, 35.

17. Thus *exousia*: 7:29; 9:2-8; 21:23-27; cf. 9:10-13; 12:1-8, 9-14; 15:1-9.

18. Thus *apollymi*: 12:14; 27:20.

19. Thus *apokteinō*: 16:21; 17:23; 21:38, 39; 26:4; cf. 23:37.

20. Thus *thanatoō*: 26:59; 27:1; cf. 20:18; 26:66.

world of Matthew's first readers with a reference by the narrator to a story which "is still told among the Jews to this day" (28:15b).

Central to the first-century Palestinian world of Jewish religious life depicted within Matthew's narrative are the Jerusalem temple, its primary administrators, the chief priests, and the sacrificial system which they are charged by Jewish law to officiate,[21] a system in which gifts are "offered" on the altar (5:23–24; 8:1–4; cf. 12:3–5), blood is "poured out" to make atonement (26:28),[22] and the "sins" of the people are "forgiven" (26:28b). The task of this essay is to assess the Matthean portrait of the Jewish chief priests of Jesus' day[23] against the scriptural (largely Levitical) backdrop which lays out their primary role within Jewish religious life, namely "making atonement" before God for the "sins" of the people.[24] In section one I will sketch out the Matthean portrait of the scripturally assigned role of the priestly class within Jewish religious life, connecting this portrait to its biblical antecedents. In section two I will then assess the overall performance of the

---

21. The primary scriptural locus of the Jewish laws governing the sacrificial system is Leviticus. For summary discussions of the sacrificial system depicted within Leviticus, see Hayes, "Atonement," 5–15; Ber, "Social Dimension," 110–24; Anderson and Culbertson, "Inadequacy," 303–28; Judisch, "Propitiation," 221–43. In a similar vein see also Weaver, "On Imitating God," 151–69.

22. Note the clarifying comments of Hayes (ibid., 6), who links atonement to the pollution of the sanctuary: "Basic to [rituals of atonement] in Leviticus is the view that human impurity and wrongdoing pollute the sanctuary. This concept is not made explicit in Leviticus, but is alluded to sufficiently to establish its importance." Hayes then points to Lev 15:31 (cf. Lev 20:3; Num 19:13, 20) as evidence of this underlying concept: "You shall set apart the Israelites from their impurity lest they die in their impurity by their polluting [rendering impure] my Tabernacle which is in their midst." Accordingly, the sacrifices offered in the sanctuary serve to cleanse the sanctuary itself of its pollution, a pollution brought about by human wrongdoing.

23. From a narrative critical standpoint the portrait of the Matthean chief priests has frequently been collapsed into the larger character group of "Jewish leaders," a category which includes Pharisees, Sadducees, scribes, Herodians, and elders/elders of the people. As Jack Dean Kingsbury notes ("Developing Conflict," 58), "Because the rhetorical effect of the way in which these several groups are presented is such as to make of them a monolithic front opposed to Jesus, they can, narrative-critically, be treated as a single character." And from his assessment of the evidence at hand Kingsbury then concludes (ibid., 60), "The notion that 'evilness' is the root trait, or fundamental quality, characterizing the Jewish leaders is in full accord with the tenor of Matthew's story." This observation, however, true as it may be within Matthew's narrative, allows Kingsbury and those who follow his lead to overlook the narrative critical necessity to hold the Jewish chief priests accountable to their scriptural calling vis-à-vis the people of Israel. This essay seeks to redress that oversight.

24. See, for example, Leviticus 16:34, describing the annual Day of Atonement: "This shall be an everlasting statute for you, *to make atonement for the people of Israel once in the year for all their sins*" (emphasis mine). See also Lev 4:20, 26, 31, 35; 5:6, 10, 13, 16, 18; 6:7; 16:16, 30, 34; 19:22; Num 15:25, 28.

Matthean chief priests against the backdrop of their assigned role, highlighting their prominent characteristics as Matthew portrays them.[25] In section three I will address the question of atonement. A crucial text here will be 27:3–10, the account of Judas Iscariot, who returns his 30 silver coins to the chief priests and announces to them (27:4a; emphasis mine), "*I have sinned*, because I have handed over innocent blood." Here I will highlight Matthew's ironic *modus operandi* as he portrays the chief priests' non-priestly response to an Israelite who comes to them confessing his sin.[26] And I will then contrast Matthew's portrait of the Jewish chief priests with a brief portrait of Jesus' own priestly ministry within the Jewish community, a ministry which fulfills the priestly role effectively abandoned by the chief priests,[27] namely mediating atonement vis-à-vis the "sins" of God's people (1:21; 26:27–28). I will conclude my essay in section four with brief reflections on the rhetorical impact of Matthew's portrait of the Jewish chief priests within his overall narrative.

I. "GO, SHOW YOURSELF TO THE PRIEST" (8:4B):

The Assigned Role of the Jewish Priestly Class within Matthew's Narrative

While Matthew nowhere sets forth a detailed description of the scripturally assigned role of the priestly class within the Jewish community of first-century Palestine, a close reading of Matthew's narrative yields significant bits and pieces of such a description. Fundamental to the task of the chief priests is their scriptural calling to maintain the Jerusalem temple—that is, the "house of God" (12:4), "my [= God's] house" (21:13//Isa 56:7), or the place where God "dwells" (23:21)—as a "house of prayer" for the people of Israel (21:13//Isa 56:7). It is the worship of God which lies at the root of the priestly calling. And it is this priestly calling to give oversight to the worship life of the Jewish community which Jesus proclaims to the chief priests as he enters the temple during his Passover visit to Jerusalem and physically

---

25. Cf. in this connection my essay on Matthew's portrait of Roman and Jewish political leaders and their use of political power: Weaver, "'They Did to Him.'"

26. Cf. 27:24, where Pilate, the Roman governor, responds with the same words ("See to it yourselves") to the Jewish crowds clamoring, at the instigation of the chief priests and the elders, for the crucifixion of Jesus (27:20–23).

27. Cf. 2:6b, where Matthew cites Micah 5:2 in identifying Jesus as one who will "shepherd my [= God's] people Israel," even as these same people are later depicted by Jesus himself (9:36; 15:24) as "the lost sheep of the house of Israel," *people thus apparently "unshepherded" by their designated religious leaders.*

overturns the commercial enterprise which he finds there (21:12–13). Here Jesus draws on the words of the Prophet Isaiah to remind the chief priests of their sacred charge vis-à-vis the wider Jewish community: "It is written, 'My house shall be called a house of prayer'" (21:13a//Isa 56:7).[28]

The *modus operandi* of Jewish priests for carrying out their priestly calling to the worship life of the Jewish community is, in turn, sacrificial in character. The Jewish "house of prayer" is in fact a house of sacrifice, where gifts are "offered" on the altar (5:23–24; 8:1–4; cf. 12:3–5), blood is "poured out" to make atonement (cf. 26:28a), and the "sins" of the people are "forgiven" (cf. 26:28b). And it is the priests who administer this sacrificial system, officiate at these sacrifices, and serve in this way as human agents of divine forgiveness. The everyday tasks of Jewish priests, as reflected within Matthew's narrative, point, detail by detail, to the requirements laid out in the Torah for the Jewish sacrificial system.

Day by day the priests sacrifice the "gifts" (*dōron*) brought by worshippers to the "altar" (*thysiastērion*) in the temple (5:23–24; 23:18–20; cf. 8:1–4). Following an elaborate ritual outlined in Leviticus 14:1–32, they examine those whose leprosy has made them ritually unclean, validate their cleansing, and sacrifice the required offering brought by those who have been cleansed: "[G]o, show yourself to the priest and offer the gift [*dōron*] that Moses commanded" (8:4).[29] And they deposit financial gifts in the temple treasury (*eis ton korbanan*: 27:6; cf. 15:5 *dōron*//Mark 7:11 *korban, ho estin dōron*).

Sabbath by Sabbath they "[eat] the bread of the Presence" (*tous artous tēs protheseōs*: 12:4; cf. Lev 24:5–9; Exod 40:23; 2 Macc 10:3), twelve loaves baked from "choice flour" (Lev 24:5), "set . . . in order before the LORD regularly as a commitment of the people of Israel" (Lev 24:8), and designated specifically "for Aaron and his descendants, who shall eat them in a holy place" (Lev 24:9). Sabbath by Sabbath they likewise carry out their

---

28. While Jesus' words initially appear to address the "money changers" and "those who [sell] doves," those whose commercial enterprise he overturns (2:13 cf. 2:12), it is in fact the chief priests and the scribes who not only "see" and "hear" what is going on (21:15) but likewise respond verbally to Jesus (21:16a). From Matthew's perspective, accordingly, it is these chief priests and scribes whom Jesus ultimately addresses with his words.

29. While Jesus and the leper are in the Galilee, near to Capernaum (cf. 8:5) and far from the Jerusalem temple, Jesus' command is nevertheless conceivable within Matthew's literary context. Keener (*Gospel of Matthew*, 263) notes that "[p]riests lived throughout Palestine and came to Jerusalem only during their course . . .; some Jewish traditions thus expect a leper to submit to local priests' inspection . . . before offering the sacrifice in the temple (Lev 14:2–3)."

regular priestly duties in spite of Sabbath work prohibitions (12:5; cf. Num 28:9–10).

And day by day and year by year the Jewish priests "make atonement" (*exilaskomai*) on behalf of the people,[30] so that their "sins" (*hai hamartiai*) might be "forgiven" (*aphiēmi*).[31] This happens both individually, on a case by case basis,[32] and collectively, in an elaborate, annual ritual on the Day of Atonement.[33] This annual ritual is enacted by the high priest inside "the curtain of the temple" (*katapetasma tou naou*: Matt 27:51: cf. Lev 16:2, 12, 15), that curtain which sets apart "the most holy place" (Exod 26:31—34), that is, the place in which God "dwells" (cf. Matt 23:21).[34] And this ritual, clearly the single most important of all Jewish rituals, is enjoined on the priests in due solemnity by the word of the Lord to Moses (Lev 16:34): "This shall be an everlasting statute for you, to make atonement for the people of Israel once in the year for all their sins."

Finally, in addition to their sacrificial work in "making atonement" for the people, the priests likewise play a crucial deliberative role in ensuring that the Jewish community is "absolved of bloodguilt" (Deut 21:8; cf. Matt 27:6 with its reference to "blood money") in those cases where "innocent blood" has been shed by an unknown perpetrator (Deut 21:1–9; cf. Matt 27:4). In the midst of an elaborate ritual of absolution carried out by the elders of the town nearest the dead body (Deut 21:1–4, 6–8), the priests are called into action as a deliberative group (Deut 21:5; emphasis mine): "Then

---

30. See n24 above.

31. Thus Lev 4:20, 26, 31, 35; 5:6, 10, 13, 16, 18; 6:7; 16:16, 30, 34; 19:22; Num 15:25, 28. While Matthew's narrative makes no mention of "atonement" (*hilaskomai/exilaskomai*), there is strategic reference to "forgiveness of sins" (*aphesis + hai hamartiai*) within a covenantal and sacrificial context: "This is my [= Jesus'] blood of the covenant which has been poured out for many for the forgiveness of sins" (26:28; cf. 1:21).

32. Thus the Levitical case laws governing the sacrifices to be brought and the atonement to be made for a wide range of sins and/or trespasses: Lev 4:13–21, 22–26, 27–31, 32–35; 5:1–6, 7–10, 11–13, 14–16, 17–19; 6:1–7, 24–30; 7:7–10. See by contrast Matt 27:4, where such a ritual of atonement should clearly take place but does not.

33. Thus Lev 16:2–34. Cf. Matt 26:28, which alludes to just such an annual atonement ritual.

34. There is sturdy scholarly discussion concerning which of two temple curtains, the "outer" curtain (cf. Exod 26:36) or the "inner" curtain (cf. Exod 26:31–33), is in focus within Matthew 27:51 (thus Carter, *Matthew and the Margins*, 536; Luz, *Matthew 21–28*, 565–66; Witherington III, *Matthew*, 521; Keener, *Gospel of Matthew*, 686–87). There is broad consensus, however, that Matthew's concept certainly *includes* the "inner" curtain, that which separates the "holy place" from the "most holy place" (Exod 26:33), even if it might not *exclude* the "outer" curtain. As Luz puts it (ibid., 565), "The narrator speaks of 'the curtain.' It does not appear to bother him that there is more than one." But see Carter's minority viewpoint (ibid., 536), which excludes the "inner" curtain from Matthew's consideration.

the priests, the sons of Levi, shall come forward, for the LORD your God has chosen them to minister to him and to pronounce blessings in the name of the LORD, *and by their decisions all cases of dispute and assault shall be settled.*" The urgency of their deliberative work in this ritual of absolution is apparent in the motive clause which concludes this piece of case law (Deut 21:9; emphasis mine): "So you shall purge the guilt of innocent blood from your midst, because you must do what is right [LXX: good and pleasing (*kalos kai arestos*)] in the sight of the LORD." The deliberative role of the Jewish priests in "purg[ing] the guilt of innocent blood" from the Jewish community is, accordingly, crucial to the broad covenantal commitment of the Jewish people spelled out in Deuteronomy 6:1–25, a commitment summarized in the call of Deuteronomy 6:18: "Do what is right and good [LXX: pleasing and good, *to areston kai to kalon*] in the sight of the LORD."

II. "AND THEY CONSPIRED" (26:4A):

The Narrative Portrayal of the Matthean Chief Priests vis-à-vis Their Priestly Calling

As Matthew portrays it, the scripturally assigned vocation of the Jewish chief priests is both liturgical and deliberative in its focus. Their calling, broadly framed, is to maintain the Jerusalem temple ("my [= God's] house"), as the "house of prayer" (21:13//Isa 56:7) for the Jewish people. Within that broad calling their primary tasks are to administer the sacrificial system carried out at the "altar" (5:23–24; 23:18–20, 35), to make atonement on behalf of those who have "sinned" (26:28; cf. 1:21), and to take deliberative action to remove the guilt of "innocent blood" from the midst of the community (cf. 27:4, 6).

But the chief priests who appear "on stage" within Matthew's narrative do not for the most part visibly carry out the activities which Matthew has outlined for them. While the narrative clearly *implies* that the chief priests are regularly engaged in a full range of liturgical tasks,[35] it does not for the most part *portray* them in the act of carrying out these tasks. Matthew offers his readers no real-time images of the chief priests serving at the altar in

---

35. Thus, for example, the references to "altar" (*thysiastērion*: 5:23, 24; 23:18, 19, 20), "gift" (*dōron*: 5:23, 24; 8:4; 15:5; 23:18, 19), and "Passover" (*pascha*: 26:2, 17, 18, 19), a celebration for which the priests must slaughter the lambs brought to the temple by the celebrants (cf. John 1:29, 36; 19:31). See also the reference in 21:12–13 to the market operated on the temple grounds for exchanging money into temple currency (cf. Exod 30:13) and for buying and selling sacrificial animals, in this case doves (cf. Lev 5:7; 12:8).

the temple,[36] offering the gifts brought by the worshippers, or mediating the forgiveness of God to those who have sinned. Nor do Matthew's readers witness the chief priests eating the bread of the presence or otherwise fulfilling their Sabbath duties. And where Matthew does portray the chief priests engaged in liturgical tasks, he does so only in ironic fashion.[37] Accordingly, Matthew's narrative portrayal of the chief priests within their real-world context bears little overt resemblance to the Matthean portrait of their scriptural calling.

The chief priests, as Matthew portrays them, belong to the highest echelon of Jewish society in first-century Palestine; and they have, accordingly, the greatest religious and political power within the Jewish community. One of their prime assets is their wealth in physical resources of all kinds. The Matthean chief priests appear to have significant money at their collective disposal (cf. 26:15b; 27:3; 28:12), evidently associated with the commercial enterprise which they have established at the Jerusalem temple, an enterprise based on the essential and thus legitimate sale of sacrificial animals (21:12: "those who sold doves" [*tas peristeras*; cf. Lev 5:7; 12:8]), the accompanying and necessary exchange of money for the requisite temple currency (21:12: "the moneychangers" [*tōn kollybistōn*; cf. Exod 30:13]),[38] and the collection of the "temple tax" (*to didrachma*: 17:24-27).

In addition to their disposable wealth the chief priests likewise oversee the maintenance of a massive and magnificent piece of real estate, the Jerusalem temple. This facility is unimaginably "great" in popular conception

---

36. But see Jesus' reference (23:35) to "Zechariah, son of Barachiah," a figure from Jewish history who was apparently on duty in the temple when he was "murdered between the sanctuary and the altar." For a discussion of the historical difficulties surrounding the interpretation of this Matthean reference, see Luz (*Matthew 21-28*, 154-55).

37. One such liturgical task which the chief priests perform "on stage" within Matthew's narrative, albeit in clearly ironic fashion, is to deal with the disposal of money brought to the temple (27:3-5), ostensibly for deposit in the temple treasury (27:6). Elsewhere Matthew portrays the chief priests frequently involved in the deliberative task of "taking counsel" (*symbouleuō*; *symboulion lambanō*: 26:4; 27:1, 7; 28:12). But these deliberations, in similar fashion, provide a bitterly ironic counterpart to the chief priests' calling to ensure that "innocent blood" be removed from the Jewish community.

38. As Long (*Matthew*, 236) notes, "The popular notion that the temple had become commercialized and Jesus was 'cleansing' it, restoring it to its previous sacred purpose, is false. The sacred role of the temple *was* the offering of sacrifices and the making of offerings under the direction of the priests. If these functions were to be fulfilled, then someone had to provide the animals to be sacrificed, and someone had to change the Greek and Roman coins the pilgrims brought with them into Jewish coins suitable for offerings." Instead, as Long concludes (ibid.), Jesus' temple action is not "reform" of the temple cultus but rather "revolution": "[Jesus] is not improving the temple; he is attacking the temple, and it is doomed."

(*megas/mega*; cf. 12:6; 23:17), a complex of "buildings" (*tas oikodomas tou hierou*: 24:1) that calls for special notice by travelers to Jerusalem. The temple is constructed "stone upon stone" (*lithos epi lithon*: 24:2) with huge Herodian ashlars, adorned with "gold" (*chrysos*: 23:16–17), and topped with an impressive landmark, "the pinnacle of the temple" (*to pterygion tou hierou*: 4:5), dangerously high above the ground far below (cf. 4:5–6). Central to this temple and crucial to the worship which takes place there are its "altar" of acacia wood (*thysiastērion*: 5:23, 24; 23:18, 19, 20, 35; cf. Exod 27:1–8) and a beautifully woven cloth, "the curtain of the temple" (*to katapetasma tou naou*: 27:51; cf. Exod 26:31), which sets apart "the most holy place" (Exod 26:31–34), namely the place in which God "dwells" (cf. Matt 23:21). This entire complex, then, serves as "the house" (*ho oikos*: 23:38) of the Jewish chief priests, their primary locus of engagement, and, by the same token, the quintessential gathering place of the entire Jewish people in the heart of their "holy city" (*tēn hagian polin*: 27:53).[39] This is the temple and this is the altar by which Jewish people "swear" when they make their solemn oaths to God (23:16–22). And this is the temple whose "destruction" is virtually unthinkable (cf. 26:61; 27:40) and whose predicted demise thus portends "desolation" for the entire Jewish people (cf. 23:38).

And if the chief priests have significant disposable wealth and a massive and strategic piece of Jerusalem real estate, they likewise have significant human resources. When they need to make arrests on behalf of the temple, they do so with the assistance of a temple guard, a "large crowd with swords and clubs *from the chief priests and the elders of the people*" (26:47; cf. 26:55; emphasis mine),[40] a guard which includes the personal slave of the high priest himself (*ton doulon tou archiereōs*: 26:51). And for his part the high priest Caiaphas (26:3, 57) has his own "palace" (*aulē*: 26:3, 58, 69), a residence large enough to house the gatherings of the entire Jewish "council" or Sanhedrin (*synedrion*: 26:59; cf. 26:3, 57; 27:1) and staffed both by personal "slaves" (cf. *ton doulon tou archiereōs*: 26:51) and by "guards" who oversee the court proceedings of the council (*tōn hypēretōn*: 26:58; cf. 5:25).

Along with their wealth in physical and human resources the Matthean chief priests likewise have significant social, religious, and political capital,

39. As Matthew depicts it, the Jerusalem temple is the gathering place for the entire Jewish community, from the greatest to the least: chief priests (21:15, 23, 45), scribes (21:15), elders of the people (21:23), Pharisees (21:45; 22:15, 34, 41), Sadducees (22:23, 34), Herodians (22:16), those who are buying and selling sacrificial animals (21:12), moneychangers (21:12), those who are sitting and teaching (26:55), Jewish visitors to Jerusalem (24:1), the blind and the lame (21:14), and children (21:15).

40. Cf. the comments of Keener (*Gospel of Matthew*, 640), who cites Luke 22:4, 52 among other sources and concludes: "The guards Judas led to Jesus probably belonged to the Levite temple guard . . . and the armed auxiliary police who worked for them."

both within the Jewish community and beyond. They associate regularly and strategically with other highly placed groups from the Jewish community: Pharisees (21:45; 27:62), scribes/scribes of the people (2:4; 16:21; 20:18; 21:15; 26:57; 27:41), and elders/elders of the people (16:21; 21:23; 26:3, 47, 57; 27:1, 3, 12, 20, 41).[41] They and their religious associates constitute, collectively, the *literati* of the Jewish community, those who "read" the Jewish scriptures[42] and parse out their meaning for the everyday lives of the Jewish people.[43] And the chief priests collaborate prominently with their religious associates on the Sanhedrin or "council" (26:59; cf. 26:3, 57; 27:1), a powerful Jewish deliberative body which meets in the high priest's palace (26:3; cf. 26:57), is moderated by the high priest (26:57, 62, 63, 65), and issues verdicts extending all the way to death sentences (26:65–66).

The social, religious, and political power of the Matthean chief priests within the Jewish community likewise positions them strategically as the prominent and crucial liaison with Rome, the ultimate political power of their day and their world. The chief priests of Matthew's narrative maintain regular and strategic collaboration with the Roman forces who occupy first-century Palestine. From the moment of Jesus' birth (2:1–6) to the moment of his death and even beyond (27:62–66; 28:11–15) the Matthean chief priests enjoy easy access to the local representatives of empire and mutually beneficial relationships with the Roman overlords of Palestine and/or their client rulers: Herod, the Jewish client king (2:3–6), "the Gentiles" (20:18), and Pilate, the Roman governor (27:1–2, 62–66; 28:11–15; cf. 27:12–13). And when they have need for human resources beyond their own, the chief priests have ready access to a Roman "guard" (*koustōdia*: 27:65; 28:11) comprised of Roman "soldiers" (*stratiōtai*: 28:12).

As Matthew portrays them, the Jewish chief priests are indisputably people of wealth and power. But from Matthew's perspective theirs is wealth and power gone corrupt on all fronts. In fact the chief priests of Matthew's

---

41. Note also Matthew's references to the Sadducees (3:7; 16:1, 6, 11, 12; 22:23, 34), a historically prominent Jewish group in first-century Palestine prior to the Jewish Revolt of 66–70 CE. The Sadducees are likewise (but for Matthew, only apparently) a constituent group of the Jewish Sanhedrin. While Matthew does not associate the Sadducees directly with the chief priests, Carter notes (*Matthew and the Margins*, 96; emphasis mine) that "Josephus attests the membership of both Pharisees and Sadducees among the wealthy . . . and politically powerful . . ., *including the chief priests*."

42. Matthew strategically associates each of these elite Jewish groups with the ability to "read": Pharisees (12:3, 5; 19:4), scribes (21:16; cf. 2:5–6), elders (21:42), and chief priests (21:16, 42; cf. 2:5–6), as well as Sadducees (22:31; see n41 above).

43. Thus, for example, questions concerning Sabbath observance (12:2; 10), divorce (19:3), payment of taxes (22:17), levirate marriage (22:23–28), the greatest commandment (22:34–36), oaths (23:16, 18), and tithing (23:23–24).

narrative direct all of their wealth and power to one central and overriding goal, namely, the destruction of their political rival, Jesus, whose "authority" they question (21:23–27), whose claim to "messiahship" they label "blasphemy" (26:63–65; cf. 21:15–16), and for whose messianic "inheritance" they ultimately kill him (21:38–39). Matthew's portrayal of the real-world performance of the Jewish chief priests vis-à-vis their scriptural calling is bleak and bitterly ironic throughout.

The Matthean chief priests are politically and religiously strategic in their words and actions, as they seek first to counter and then to destroy their rival. In response to a politically weighted question that Jesus puts to them concerning John the Baptist (21:24–25a), they choose their words with exquisite care and obvious expedience in order to avoid Jesus' censure on the one hand and the wrath of the Jewish people on the other (21:25b–27a): "'If we say . . . But if we say . . .' So they answered Jesus, 'We do not know.'"). They choose their actions with equal care and expedience, as they plot to arrest Jesus and kill him. Theirs will be a "stealth" operation (*dolō*: 26:4) and "not during the festival, or there may be a riot [*thorybos*] among the people" (26:5).[44] When they are faced with tainted "blood money" resulting from their police action against Jesus (*timē haimatos*: 27:6; cf. 27:3–4a), they weigh their options and take the religiously expedient decision (27:6–7).

And if the Matthean chief priests are strategic in their words and actions, they are likewise conspiratorial in their efforts against Jesus. Within Matthew's rhetoric the confluence of references to "gathering together" (*synagō*: 2:4; 26:3, 57; 27:17, 62; 28:12) and "taking counsel" (*symbouleuō*: 26:4; *symboulion lambanō*: 27:1, 7; 28:12) serves collectively to depict the Matthean chief priests as persistent conspirators.[45] They are introduced to the world of conspiracy when Herod the king "call[s] together [*synagō*: 2:4] all the chief priests and scribes of the people" and inveigles them into his own paranoid scheme against "the child who has been born king of the Jews" (2:2; cf. 2:3–8). Years later they themselves "gather" (*synagō*: 26:3) and "conspire" (*symbouleuō*: 26:4) against Jesus. They then "gather" (*synagō*: 27:57) in the house of Caiaphas the high priest to conduct a kangaroo court, seeking from the outset to condemn Jesus on the "false testimony" (*pseudomartyrian*: 26:59) of "false witnesses" (*pseudomartyrōn*: 26:60). They "confer together" (*symboulion lambanō*: 27:1) against Jesus before turning him over to Pilate. They "gather" (*synagō*: 27:62) before Pilate to demand measures to secure the tomb of Jesus and prevent a resurrection fraud by

---

44. Cf. 21:45, where the chief priests do not take action to arrest Jesus due to their fear of the crowds.

45. Cf. 12:14 and 22:15, where the Pharisees also engage in conspiracy (*symboulion lambanō*) against Jesus.

Jesus' disciples. And in their final appearance within Matthew's narrative (28:11–15) they "assemble" (*synagō*: 28:12) with the elders and "devise a plan" (*symboulion lambanō*: 28:12), their own resurrection fraud, to account for the empty tomb.

And the Matthean chief priests are as corrupt in their dealings as they are conspiratorial in their actions. Thus even as they carry out what are in principle legitimate priestly tasks, they fail to act with integrity. While they have legitimate funds to use for the purposes of temple worship (cf. 17:24–27; 21:12–13),[46] they use this wealth instead as capital for bribes paid to hit men (26:14–16), real-estate transactions that have the character of money-laundering (27:7–10), and hush-money paid to co-conspirators for passing on a false story (28:11–15). For his part Jesus accuses them of transforming the house of God (21:13a) into a "den of robbers" (21:13b//Jer 7:11a), to which they retreat for security after carrying out lives of injustice.[47]

When they engage their deliberative responsibilities as a council (26:3–5; 27:57–59), a task which should focus on removing the guilt of "innocent blood" from the midst of the Jewish community (*haima anaition*: Deut 21:8; cf. 21:5), they first conspire to kill their rival (26:4) and then intentionally corrupt their own judicial processes by engaging the services of "false witnesses" (*pseudomartyrōn*: 26:60) to provide "false testimony" (*pseudomartyrian*: 26:59). And when they ultimately pronounce the death sentence on the defendant in their trial (26:65–66), they ironically make themselves guilty of blood which they will shortly and implicitly acknowledge to be "innocent" (*athōon*: 27:4; cf. 27:6). Thus rather than fulfilling their covenantal commitment (Deut 21:9//6:18) to "do what is right in the sight of the LORD," they instead incur the very blood guilt that they are charged to remove from the Jewish community (cf. Deut 21:5, 8).

While the chief priests have access to the highest levels of Roman power in Palestine, access which could be used for the purposes of "righteousness" (*dikaiosynē*: 3:15; cf. 14:3–4),[48] they use this access instead for nefarious and self-serving purposes. When Herod the Jewish client king needs strategic information to assist him in destroying a political rival, the

46. See n38 above.

47. Cf. Jeremiah 7:8–11a: "Here you are, trusting in deceptive words to no avail. Will you steal, murder, commit adultery, swear falsely, make offerings to Baal, and go after other gods that you have not known, and then come and stand before me in this house, which is called by my name, and say, 'We are safe!'—only to go on doing all these abominations? Has this house, which is called by my name, become a den of robbers in your sight?"

48. John the Baptist, for example, who has been called by Jesus to join him in the task of "fulfilling all righteousness" (3:15), uses his access to Herod the tetrarch in order to speak truth to power (14:3–4), an act that costs him his life (14:5–12).

chief priests and scribes provide him with the intelligence he seeks (2:1–6). When the chief priests wish to destroy their own political rival (cf. 21:38), they hand him over to "the Gentiles" (20:18), namely, to Pilate the Roman "governor" (cf. 27:2). When the chief priests later fear resurrection fraud, they seek and gain an immediate audience with Pilate to express their concerns and to appeal for a remedy (27:62–66). And when the chief priests and elders face the terrifying conundrum of an empty tomb, they plot their own resurrection fraud and promise to "secure" the Roman governor, if the truth ever reaches his ears (28:11–15).[49]

And if the Matthean chief priests are conspiratorial in their actions and corrupt in their dealings, they are likewise cruel and abusive on levels both physical and emotional. In predicting his upcoming passion Jesus warns his disciples (16:21) that he will "undergo great suffering [*polla pathein*] at the hands of the elders and chief priests and scribes" and (20:19) that these same people will ultimately "hand him over [*paradidōmi*] to the Gentiles to be mocked [*empaizō*] and flogged [*mastigoō*] and crucified [*stauroō*]."[50] And Jesus' words are borne out vividly by the events that transpire in Jerusalem. After the high priest and the Jewish Sanhedrin have condemned Jesus to death (26:65—66), they themselves attack Jesus physically (26:67), "spitting" in his face [*emptyō*], "striking" him [*kolaphizō*], and "slapping" him [*rhapizō*]. And their physical abuse is matched, in turn, by their verbal abuse. As they spit and strike and slap, they taunt Jesus verbally (26:68): "Prophesy to us, you Messiah! Who is it that struck you?" Then, just as Jesus has predicted, they "hand him over" (*paradidōmi*: 27:2; cf. 26:2) to the Romans, to be "flogged" (*phragelloō*: 27:26) and "mocked" (*empaizō*: 27:29, 31) and "crucified" (*stauroō*: 26:2; 27:22, 23, 26, 31, 35; cf. 27:38). And as Jesus hangs dying on a Roman cross, the chief priests, scribes, and elders "mock" him (*empaizō*: 27:41) still further with a vicious onslaught of charges (27:42–43): "He saved others; he cannot save himself. He is the King of Israel; let him come down from the cross now, and we will believe in him. He trusts in God; let God deliver him now, if he wants to; for he said, 'I am God's Son.'"[51] And such is the portrait of cruelty and abuse by the Matthean chief priests.

---

49. Matthew does not clarify whether this action to "secure" the Roman governor will be one of friendly persuasion, bribe, or deceit. But regardless of their intended methods, the goal of the chief priests is self-serving and nefarious.

50. Here the chief priests are depicted as not only inflicting their own suffering on Jesus but also handing him over to others *precisely so that* these others can inflict even greater suffering on him.

51. The biting irony of Matthew's narrative, however, is that the chief priests, scribes, and elders both acknowledge and proclaim the deep truth about Jesus' identity,

III. "WHAT IS THAT TO US? SEE TO IT YOURSELF." (27:4B):

The Matthean Chief Priests and Atonement for God's People

Matthew's portrait is vivid; and his message is unmistakable. The consistent *modus operandi* of the Jewish chief priests reflects conspiracy, corruption, and callous cruelty. Their ongoing activities, as Matthew portrays them, stand in sharp and ironic contrast to their priestly vocation. In fact Matthew never depicts the Jewish chief priests carrying out their central scriptural calling and their covenantal commitment to "make atonement" before God for the "sins" of the people (cf. Lev 16:34). Remarkably absent from Matthew's Jewish narrative, a narrative in which matters of "sin"[52] and "forgiveness" (*aphesis*)[53] figure significantly (1:21; 26:28), are any real-time images of the Jewish chief priests dealing in person with the "sins" of the Jewish people. Despite their massive and amazing "temple" complex (cf. 4:5; 12:6; 24:1-2), with its "altar" for sacrifice (5:23, 24; 23:18, 19, 20, 35) and its "curtain" that closes off the place where God "dwells" (27:51; cf. 23:21), the chief priests are never visibly engaged in the act of "making atonement."

Instead, when they are called to this very act, the central and primary task of their priestly vocation, in a moment of crucial importance, the chief priests completely and callously abandon their priestly calling (27:4b) vis-à-vis an Israelite who confesses his "sin" to them in an act of suicidal desperation (27:3-4a, 5). Judas Iscariot has recently conspired with these same chief priests (26:14-16) and accepted a bribe of 30 silver coins in exchange for "handing [Jesus] over" to them (*paradidōmi*: 26:15, 16; translation mine).[54] But when he learns of Jesus' "condemnation" and realizes the deadly implications of his own actions (27:3a), Judas now "repents" (*metamelomai*: 27:3b) of his participation in this conspiracy against Jesus.[55] And in urgent

---

even as they mock him and ridicule his claim to be "God's Son."

52. Thus *hamartia*: 1:21; 3:6; 9:2, 5, 6; 12:31; 26:18; *hamartanō*: 18:15, 21.

53. Thus *aphesis* 26:28; *aphiēmi*: 6:12, 14, 15; 9:2, 5, 6; 12:31, 32; 18:21, 27, 32, 35.

54. Judas' act of "handing Jesus over" (*paradidōmi*: 10:4; 17:22; 20:18; 26:2, 15, 16, 21, 23, 24, 25, 45, 46, 48; 27:3, 4) is fundamentally no different in kind than that of the chief priests, scribes, and elders of the people who "hand [Jesus] over" (*paradidōmi*: cf. 20:19; 27:2, 18) to "the Gentiles" (20:19), namely to "Pilate the governor" (27:2,18). Nor does Judas' act differ essentially from that of Pilate himself, who "hands [Jesus] over" (*paradidōmi*: 27:26) to his crucifixion.

55. While the language of "repentance" (*metamelomai*: 27:3b) diverges here from that found in the proclamations of John the Baptist and Jesus (*metanoeō*: 3:2; 4:17; 11:20, 21; 12:41), this language nevertheless connotes a serious and life-changing response. As Matthew tells the story, Jesus himself uses this same term to rebuke the chief

distress he comes to the chief priests in the posture of a penitent seeking atonement,[56] bearing both the 30 silver coins (27:3c) and a damning self-confession (27:4a): "I have sinned by betraying innocent blood." Judas clearly knows the Jewish scriptures. And he is clearly aware that a "curse" hangs over him for his actions (Deut 27:25): "Cursed be anyone who takes a bribe to shed innocent blood." The issue that Judas brings to the chief priests is, therefore, not merely a matter of "sin" to be atoned, but even more crucially a matter of life and death (cf. Deut 19:11–13).

The chief priests know the scriptures well (cf. 2:4–6). And they likewise know what is at stake for Judas. But rather than carrying out their covenantal commitment and initiating a life-giving process to "make atonement" on behalf of Judas' sin,[57] the chief priests cynically abdicate all priestly responsibility as they throw Judas' sin back into his face with the words, "What is that to us? See to it yourself" (27:4b). The irony of Matthew's narrative rhetoric here is profound on not one but two levels. To begin with, the Jewish chief priests, who are bitter rivals of Jesus Messiah (1:1, 16, 17, 18) and who have conspired constantly and strategically to kill him and gain his messianic "inheritance" (21:38), have themselves instead, in one unguarded moment, given away any possible claim to their own religious and political leadership of the Jewish people. By abdicating their most fundamental task, namely "making atonement" on behalf of the "sins" of the Jewish people,[58] the Matthean chief priests have proven by their own words that they have no claim to be called the "shepherds" of Israel (9:36; cf. 2:6) and no claim on the "inheritance" of the Jewish "vineyard" (cf. 21: 33–46). In the words of David Garland, "[Judas] is turned away by the callous shepherds who have no regard for the sheep."[59]

---

priests and the elders of the people, because they have not "repented" (*metamelomai*: 21:32; cf. 21:29; DJW) at the preaching of John the Baptist (cf. 3:2, 7–10, where John's language of "repentance" *vis-a vis* the Pharisees and Sadducees is *metanoeō*). But see Hare (*Matthew*, 314) for the view that Judas' act of "repenting" (*metamelomai*) is not the "genuine repentance" reflected in the verb *metanoeō*.

56. Cf. Hare (ibid.), who does not credit the genuine character of Judas' "repentance" but notes nevertheless that Judas "lamely 'atones' for his sin by returning the tainted money."

57. As Witherington III notes (*Matthew*, 505), "[The chief priests] could have suggested various recourses, or even sacrifices for sin."

58. Cf. the comments of Carlson ("From Villain to Tragic Figure," 478): "Though given the role of absolving Israel of bloodguilt (Deut 21 1–9, 19 8–13), the religious leaders are no longer able to fulfill such a role because of their own bloodguilt (21 33–45, 23 29–36)."

59. Garland, *Reading Matthew*, 255.

But if the Matthean chief priests have abdicated their own calling and thereby given up any claim to the leadership of the Jewish people, theirs is an act of ironic necessity. As they acknowledge openly in conferring on the use of the 30 silver coins (27:6b), there is a clear reason why they cannot make atonement on behalf of Judas' sins. Since they themselves are the prime movers in the conspiracy against Jesus, the bribe they have paid to Judas is indeed "blood money" (27:6b).[60] Accordingly, they share both Judas' sin (27:4a) and Judas' "curse" (cf. Deut 27:25).[61] And they are in fact even more in need of atonement than Judas, since they have not "repented" of their actions (21:28; cf. 27:20, 41–43; 28:11–15). Ultimately, in the words of Garland, "Judas . . . [has made] a fatal mistake by returning to the temple to seek absolution through his co-conspirators when the temple is no longer the place of God's presence or the seat of forgiveness."[62]

Nor will ultimate outcomes be positive for the Matthean chief priests and their scripturally assigned role as "Atoners in Chief" of the Jewish people. When Jesus dies, the "curtain of the temple" will be "torn in two, from top to bottom" (27:51a) in a massive and symbolic display of divine power which will open the place where God "dwells" to the public view of Jews and Gentiles alike and will, by the same token, fundamentally reshape the geography of atonement. Ultimately Jerusalem, the "holy city" (4:5) of the Jewish people will itself be "burned" (22:7) and the entire temple complex, the central locus of the chief priests' current activities, will be "destroyed" so totally that "not one stone will be left . . . upon another," but "all will be thrown down" (24:2; cf. 26:61; 27:40). And in an act of profound and unintended irony the chief priests, even before the death of Jesus, have already pronounced the judgment of God on themselves and their leadership role within the Jewish community. In response to a story told by Jesus about conspiratorial and vicious vineyard tenants who kill the son of the vineyard owner and do not return the fruits of the vineyard, the chief priests (21:41) give voice to their own demise: "He [i.e., God, the divine vineyard owner] will put those wretches to a miserable death, and lease the vineyard to other tenants who will give him the produce at the harvest time." Within Matthew's narrative rhetoric there is thus no salvific future for the Jerusalem temple with its elaborate sacrificial system for "making atonement." Nor is

---

60. See n58 above.

61. Cf. Witherington III's comment (*Matthew*, 505), "But since [the chief priests] admit [the existence of 'blood money'], they also admit they are guilty of bribing someone to betray a Jew unto death. In other words, they are as guilty of Deuteronomy 27:25 in one sense as Judas is." In a similar vein, see Hare, *Matthew*, 313.

62. Garland, *Reading Matthew*, 255.

there a salvific future for the Jewish chief priests, who serve as the officiants of this sacrificial system.

Instead Matthew's narrative rhetoric pointedly replaces the priestly role of the Jewish chief priests with the priestly role of Jesus himself.[63] Jesus is the one whose name and whose life vocation, given to him before birth by divine agency, spell out the act of atonement for the "sins" of "his people" (1:21; emphasis mine): ". . . [A]nd you are to name him Jesus, for he will *save his people from their sins*." Jesus is the one who throughout his earthly ministry pronounces God's "forgiveness" to humans (*aphiēmi*: 9:2, 5) with divinely-given "authority on earth to forgive sins" (*aphienai hamartias*: 9:6). Jesus is the one who "saves" those who reach out or call out to him (*sōzō*: 8:25; 9:21, 22; 14:30). Jesus is the one who "shepherds [God's] people Israel" (*ton laon mou ton Israēl*: 2:6; cf. 9:36; 25:32; 26:31), is a "great light" to "the people who sit in darkness" (*o laos o kathēmenos en skotei*: 4:16//Isa 9:2), and ministers in their midst (*en tō laō*: 4:23; cf. 9:35). Jesus is the one who is "greater than the temple" (*tou hierou meizon*: 12:6) and whose ministry persistently reflects God's "desire" for "mercy and not sacrifice" (*eleos . . . kai ou thysian*: 9:13; 12:7; Hos 6:6). And in his ultimate act of faithfulness to the will of God (26:39, 42; cf. 26:44) Jesus himself becomes the sacrificial blood offering which transforms God's covenant with God's people for all time to come (26:28; cf. 20:28): "[T]his is my blood of the covenant [*to haima mou tēs diathēkēs*] which is poured out for many for the forgiveness of sins [*eis aphesin hamartiōn*]." The salvific and durative impact of Jesus' blood offering becomes visible for all to see at the very moment of his death, when God reaches down from heaven and "tears" the curtain of the temple "in two, from top to bottom" (27:51a), thus destroying, definitively and beyond reversal, both the hidden locus of the Jewish chief priests' activity in making atonement and, by the same token, the entire sacrificial system over which they officiate in order to make such atonement.

Thus in the penultimate irony of Matthew's narrative rhetoric—i.e., aside from the Resurrection, God's last laugh (cf. Ps 2:4–6)—it is the Jewish chief priests themselves, those who seek to *gain* the Jewish messianic "inheritance" through killing Jesus (cf. 21:38), who achieve instead the *devastation* of their temple curtain (27:51), the *destruction* of their temple (24:1–2), and ultimately, by the same token, the *loss* of their own priestly function as temple officiators. Accordingly it is the Jewish chief priests themselves who, in Matthew's unrelenting narrative irony, forfeit their own role as "Atoners in Chief" for the Jewish people. Instead atonement is enacted for all time

---

63. For a study of Jesus as source of atonement within Matthew's Gospel, see Gibbs, "Son of God," 211–25.

(cf. 28:20b) through the death of Jesus, who fills the role that the Jewish chief priests have abdicated and "saves his people from their sins" (1:21) through his "blood of the covenant which is poured out for many for the forgiveness of sins" (26:28).

IV. "SEE, YOUR HOUSE IS LEFT TO YOU, DESOLATE" (23:38):

Matthew's Narrative Rhetoric and the Ironies of God

Within the late first-century real world behind Matthew's narrative, a mere 15 years or so following the epoch-changing destruction of the Jewish temple in Jerusalem by the forces of the Roman empire, the narrative rhetoric of Matthew's Gospel is unrelenting in its condemnation of the Jewish chief priests of Jesus' day. In a real world where Jerusalem lies "burned" (22:7), its people "destroyed" (22:7), its leadership "put . . . to a miserable death" (21:41), and "not one stone" of the temple is "left . . . upon another" (24:2), Matthew's narrative rhetoric sees the unmistakable judgment of God in the downfall of Jerusalem, the destruction of the temple, and the dissolution of the sacrificial system officiated by the Jewish chief priests. In Matthew's view this divine judgment is charged above all to the account of the chief priests themselves, due to their cynical abdication of their scripturally assigned role not only in making atonement for the sins of their people (cf. 27:4) but also in ensuring that the guilt of "innocent blood" is removed from their midst (cf. 27:6). And in this post-70 CE world of massive devastation and disorientation, where the wider Jewish community of Palestine and the emerging Jewish messianic community reflected by Matthew and his church are struggling to rediscover their respective self-identities beyond the Jerusalem temple and the Jewish holy city, Matthew's narrative rhetoric speaks a bold and unmistakable word.

For the wider Jewish community Matthew's word is a mirror which reflects their present catastrophic reality (23:38): "See, your house is left to you desolate." The geography of atonement has shifted tectonically and for all time. The Jerusalem temple is no longer and will never again be the locus of atonement for the people of God. But in this very word of desolation lie the seeds of the ultimate "good news" of Matthew's Gospel. God will not be thwarted. God's passion for the atonement of human sin will never be abated. And in the stunning and salvific irony of Matthew's narrative rhetoric it is precisely those who abdicate their own role in the atonement of God's people who are the unwitting agents through whom God initiates that tectonic shift in the geography of atonement. Those who recognize the guilt of "blood money" in their hands (27:6) have no way of knowing in that moment that the very blood which occasions their guilt will shortly be "poured out for many," *people such as them included*, "for the remission of sins" *including such as theirs* (26:28). Atonement is God's last word. Such is the irony of Matthew's narrative rhetoric. And such is the ultimate "good news" of Matthew's Jewish Gospel. Let the reader understand.

5

"They Did to Him Whatever They Pleased"

The Exercise of Political Power within Matthew's Narrative

INTRODUCTION

TO READ THE GOSPEL of Matthew within the global context is to read Matthew's narrative against the backdrop of the urgent issues and challenges that face the global community as a whole and individual nations each in turn. One such challenge concerns the exercise of political power within the public arena and the honesty and integrity with which such power is exercised. Frequently such honesty and integrity become casualties of political expedience and the overweening drive to gain and retain power at all costs. Stories of lavish life styles, corruption, election fraud, assassination of rival politicians, torture and abuse of those who represent a political threat, repression of political opponents, and oppression of the powerless fill our television screens, our airwaves, and our newspapers with dismal frequency. Such recent geopolitical flash points as Myanmar, Kenya, Pakistan, Zimbabwe, Gaza, and Georgia are merely current illustrations of an ongoing and global reality. And the ongoing American "war against terror"—which includes such dubious features as "extraordinary rendition" to foreign prisons, the US detention facilities at Guantanamo Bay, and "enhanced interrogation techniques" (read "waterboarding" for one prominent example)—brings the exercise of political power into our own national life daily as a moral issue facing all those of us who are citizens of the US.

The Gospel Writer Matthew lived in a world little different from our own in this regard. In the course of his story about Jesus of Nazareth Matthew also paints a vivid portrait of the political power brokers of Jesus' world and the unsavory, cynical, and often brutal methods that they use to achieve their goals. From beginning (2:1–23) to ending (28:11–15) Matthew's narrative offers pointed and graphic depictions of political power as it is wielded by those in authority and as it impacts the lives of those who live and die within its domain. Accordingly, to read Matthew's Gospel with a focus on the exercise of political power is to discover a world astonishingly similar to the twenty-first-century world that we inhabit.

The following study will examine Matthew's narrative portrait of the first-century political leaders, both Roman and Jewish, who exercise power in the public arena of Palestine and the wider Roman Empire. Part one of the paper will examine the Roman and Jewish leaders within Matthew's narrative and the methods they employ to gain, retain, and exercise their political power. Part two will assess the effectiveness and/or ineffectiveness of such uses of power, as Matthew portrays this through the rhetoric of his overall narrative. Part three will offer brief pointers toward Matthew's contrasting portrait of positive leadership patterns as reflected in the ministry of Jesus. A brief conclusion will assess Matthew's overall narrative rhetoric as a tool for fruitful reflection on the use of political power within our twenty-first-century global community.

I. RULERS, GREAT ONES, AND VINEYARD TENANTS: A MATTHEAN PORTRAIT OF POLITICAL POWER

On all counts Matthew's Gospel is a deeply political document. Not only is its central and prominent agenda the proclamation of the "kingdom of heaven"/"kingdom of God" (*hē basileia tōn ouranōn/tou theou*), a factor which in itself establishes the thoroughly political character of Matthew's message.[1] But in addition Matthew's narrative of the life, death, and resurrection of Jesus is intricately interwoven from beginning to end with the realities and the structures of political power, both Roman and Jewish, in

---

1. Thus the following *basileia* references throughout Matthew referring variously to the realm of God: 3:2; 4:17, 23; 5:3, 10, 19, 20; 6:10, 13, 33; 7:21; 8:11, 12; 9:35; 10:7; 11:11, 12; 12:28; 13:11, 19, 24, 31, 33, 38, 41, 43, 44, 45, 47, 52; 16:19, 28; 18:1, 3, 4, 23; 19:12, 14, 23, 24; 20:1, 21; 21:31, 43; 22:2; 23:13; 24:14; 25:1, 34; 26:29. Note also the Matthean references to earthly "kingdoms": 4:8; 12:25, 26; 24:7.

place within first-century Palestine. Matthew has barely begun his narrative before he recounts in vivid fashion (2:1-23) the interface between the birth of Jesus Messiah (1:1, 16, 17, 18) and the political power structures in Jerusalem (2:1-23).[2] Throughout Matthew's narrative the life of Jesus is profoundly shaped by ongoing interaction with the political powers of the day, whether Roman[3] or Jewish.[4] And the penultimate incident of Matthew's Gospel (28:11-15) is one that pointedly highlights the political response of the Jewish leadership to the resurrection of Jesus and the ongoing impact of that political response from the time of Jesus on into the world of Matthew's own church.[5]

The political currents that run through Matthew's narrative are, on the one hand, Jewish in character, corresponding both individually and collectively to the various Jewish parties and leaders identified throughout the Gospel: Pharisees,[6] Sadducees,[7] elders [of the people],[8] chief priests and high priest,[9] scribes [of the people],[10] and Herodians.[11] By all accounts within Matthew's Gospel these are people and groups vested with significant authority within the Jewish community. Jesus himself acknowledges this authority as he speaks to them and to others. In the imagery of one of Jesus' allegorical parables (21:33-46) the chief priests and Pharisees recognize themselves as the "tenants"[12] (i.e., leaders) to whom the "landowner"[13]/

---

2. For a fuller discussion of the political portrait painted within 2:1-23, see Weaver, "Power and Powerlessness," 182-87.

3. Thus, for example, 8:5-13; 14:1-12; 27:11-37.

4. Thus, for example, Jesus' constant interactions with the Jewish authorities throughout the Gospel. But note in specific such texts as the following: 12:9-14; 16:21-23; 20:17-19; 21:33-46; 23:1-39.

5. For a fuller discussion of the political portrait painted within 28:11-15, see Weaver, "'Thus You Will Know Them,'" 122-24.

6 Thus *hoi Pharisaioi*: 3:7; 5:20; 9:11, 14, 34; 12:2, 14, 24, 38; 15:1, 12; 16:1, 6, 11, 12; 19:3; 21:45; 22:15, 34, 41; 23:2, 13, 15, 23, 25, 26, 27, 29; 27:62.

7. Thus *hoi Saddoukaioi*: 3:7; 16:1, 6, 11, 12; 22:23, 34.

8. Thus *hoi presbyteroi [tou laou]*: 15:2; 16:21; 21:23; 26:3, 47, 57, 59; 27:1, 3, 12, 20, 41; 28:12.

9. Thus *ho archiereus/hoi archiereis* : 2:4; 16:21; 20:18; 21:15, 23, 45; 26:3, 14, 47, 51, 57, 58, 59, 62, 63, 65; 27:1, 3, 6, 12, 20, 41, 62; 28:11.

10. Thus *hoi grammateis [tou laou]*: 2:4; 5:20; 7:29; 8:19; 9:3; 12:38; 15:1; 16:21; 17:10; 20:18; 21:15; 23:2, 13, 15, 23, 25, 27, 29; 26:3, 57; 27:41.

11. Thus *Hērōdianoi*: 22:16.

12. Thus *hoi geōrgoi*: 21:33, 34, 35, 38, 40.

13. Thus *ho oikodespotēs*: 21:33.

"owner of the vineyard"[14] (i.e., God) has entrusted the "vineyard"[15] (i.e., the people of Israel).[16] Jesus likewise announces to his disciples and the Jerusalem crowds gathered in the temple (23:2–3a): "The scribes and the Pharisees sit on Moses' seat; therefore, do whatever they teach you and follow it."[17] And the authority of these leaders also reaches well beyond the Jewish community. They are the biblical scholars to whom Herod the king appeals successfully for information concerning the birth of the Messiah (2:4–6). They are likewise the Jewish community leaders who have the political standing not only to gain audience with Pilate, the Roman governor (27:62) but also, by the same token, to turn prisoners over to Pilate for trial within the Roman jurisdiction (27:1–2). And much of Matthew's narrative focuses on the interchange between Jesus and these political leaders of the Jewish community.

But there are other political currents running through Matthew's narrative as well. These currents are Roman in character; and they correspond to the levels and structures of the Roman Empire visible and active within the "occupied territory" of first-century Palestine.[18] The Roman authorities within Matthew's narrative create a vast hierarchy of power which rules in imperial fashion over the entire Mediterranean world, Palestine included. As Matthew tells the story, this hierarchy includes the Roman emperor,[19] client kings ruling Judea and Galilee on behalf of Rome,[20] the Roman governor of Palestine,[21] Roman military officers such as centurions,[22] and the rank and file of Roman soldiers,[23] organized into legions of 6,000,[24] cohorts of 600,[25] and centuria of 100.[26] In speaking to his disciples Jesus identifies this

---

14. Thus *ho kyrios tou ampelōnos*: 21:40.

15. Thus *ho ampelōn*: 21:33, 39, 40, 41.

16. The imagery of Israel as the "vineyard" of God is well known within the Jewish community, as reflected in the prophecy of Isaiah 5:1–7. Cf. also other Matthean parables of Jesus focused on the imagery of the "vineyard" (20:1, 2, 4. 7, 8; 21:28).

17. All translations reflect the New Revised Standard Version unless otherwise indicated.

18. For a detailed discussion of the Roman imperial system in place within the first-century Mediterranean world, see Carter, *Matthew and Empire*, 9–53.

19. Thus *ho kaisar*: 22:17, 21.

20. Thus *ho basileus*: 2:1, 3, 9; 14:9 cf. 10:18; 11:8; *ho tetrarches*: 14:1.

21. Thus *ho hēgemōn*: 27:2, 11, 14, 15, 21, 23, 27; 28:14; cf. 10:18.

22. Thus *ho hekatontarchos*: 8:5, 13; 27:54.

23. Thus *ho stratiōtēs*: 8:9; 27:27; 28:12; cf. 2:16; 14:10.

24. Thus *ho legiōn*: 26:53.

25. Thus *hē speira*: 27:27.

26. Cf. 8:5, 13; 27:54. For a fuller discussion of the Roman imperial powers visible

hierarchy of Roman imperial power as "the rulers of the Gentiles" (*hoi archontes tōn ethnōn*: 20:25b) and "their great ones" (*hoi megaloi*: 20:25c). And Jesus implicitly acknowledges the authority of the emperor as he challenges the Pharisees (22:21b), "Give therefore to the emperor the things that are the emperor's . . ."[27] And while much of Matthew's narrative situates Jesus in intramural interaction with the Jewish community, it is Jesus' extramural interaction with the Roman imperial powers that both sets the stage for Matthew's narrative (2:1-23) and drives it inexorably toward its conclusion (27:1-2, 11-37).

Clearly there are significant social differences between the Jewish community portrayed in Matthew's Gospel, with its religious parties and temple functionaries, and the Roman Empire, with its political/military hierarchy extending from the emperor down to the common foot soldier. And there is likewise a vast power differential between the Jewish and Roman communities of Matthew's Gospel, the inherent differential between the occupying power and the occupied people. Within Matthew's Gospel this power differential is reflected most prominently in the unhindered prerogative of the Roman imperial forces to engage in military "search and destroy" missions in the face of political threats (2:1-23), to employ capital punishment as a routine sanction against its subject peoples (20:18-19; 27:1-2, 11-37), and to quash political uprisings with massive military force (cf. 21:33-46; 22:1-7; 24:1-2).

But what is perhaps most striking about Matthew's portrayal of these two highly distinct communities are the commonalities that their leaders exhibit as they exercise political power within their respective domains. While not all political strategies are reflected equally in both communities according to Matthew's narrative, there are far greater commonalities than differences in their respective political initiatives.

Lavish Lifestyles.

Surely one of the most ubiquitous symbols of political power is the lavish lifestyle that frequently accompanies and displays the wealth of the powerful. And on this front the political leaders of Matthew's narrative, whether

---

and active within Matthew's narrative, see Weaver, "'Thus You Will Know Them,'" 107-14. Strikingly, however, the most visible face of the Roman Empire within the world of Matthew's Gospel is that of the Jewish "tax collectors" (5:46; 9:9, 10, 11, 12, 13; 10:3; 11:19; 18:17; 21:31, 32; cf. 17:25-26; 22:15-22), who collaborate with the Roman overlords as they collect Roman taxes from their Jewish compatriots.

27. Cf. 17:25, where Jesus asks Peter, "What do you think, Simon? From whom do kings of the earth take toll or tribute? From their children or from others?"

Roman or Jewish, do not disappoint. While Matthew's depictions are spare by comparison with his Markan sources,[28] the images are nevertheless pointed and vivid. One indicator of lavish life style is dress. As Matthew indicates, those who live in "royal palaces" (*hoi oikoi tōn basileōn*: 11:8) likewise dress themselves in "soft robes" (*ta malaka*: 11:8a/b) of rich colors[29] and wear "crowns" (*stephanos*: 27:29) denoting their royalty. And in order to join in the festivities of a royal wedding celebration it is necessary to wear an appropriately lavish "wedding robe" (*endyma gamou*: 22:11, 12). The Jewish leaders of Matthew's Gospel, while they do not wear royal attire, nevertheless distinguish themselves extravagantly in the pious dress of their own religious community as they "make their phylacteries broad and their fringes long" (23:5b).

But lavish lifestyle goes far beyond matters of dress. Royal banquets—whether for weddings (22:1–14) or for birthday celebrations (14:1–12)—are likewise lavish events, with formal invitations,[30] a roomful of guests reclining at table,[31] a menu of choice meats (thus "oxen" and "fat calves": 22:4),[32] and fine dancing to entertain the king and his guests (14:6). Such royal banquets can also be the occasion for extravagant and conspicuous gift-giving to honor and award those in favor with the king. For her "pleasing" dance in front of Herod the tetrarch and his guests (14:6), Herod rewards the daughter of Herodias, "promis[ing] her on oath"—in the presence of his guests (14:9)—"to grant her whatever she might ask" (14:7).[33] The Jewish leaders may not be on the invited guest list for royal birthday parties or royal wedding banquets. But within their own community they are not to be outdone when it comes to conspicuous celebration. In Jesus' words (23:6), "[The scribes and Pharisees] love to have the place of honor (*tēn prōtoklisian*) at

---

28. Cf., for example, Matt 14:1–12 with Mark 6:14–29.

29. Thus the "scarlet robe" of 27:28. Clearly, in this context, for the soldiers to dress Jesus in a "scarlet robe" is to dress him in the attire of a "king," a symbolic mockery made indisputable by the addition of the "crown of thorns" (27:29a), the "reed" scepter (27:29b), and the acclamation, "Hail, King of the Jews!" (27:29c). While kings in fact wear purple (thus Mark 15:17, 20), Matthew has exchanged the "purple cloak" of Mark for a "scarlet robe," the attire of a Roman foot soldier and thus a readily accessible garment. Cf. Hare, *Matthew*, 318. But see Rev 17:3, 4; 18:12, 16 for mention of "scarlet" as a color of wealth and luxury.

30. Thus *hoi keklēmenoi*: 22:3, 4.

31. Thus *anakeimenoi*: 22:10, 11; *synanakeimenoi*: 14:9.

32. Thus *hoi tauroi . . . kai ta sitista*: 22:4. For further mention of the "fatted calf" as the prime menu for a banquet, cf. *siteutos* (Luke15:23, 27, 30).

33. Cf. Mark's version of the same incident (6:23), where the extravagance of Herod's act is made explicit in his promise to give Herodias' daughter anything she might wish up to "half of [his] kingdom."

banquets." The motif of lavish living and conspicuous celebration clearly connects the political leaders of Matthew's Gospel, Roman and Jewish alike, within a common lifestyle of privilege.

"I Say to One, 'Go'": The Power of Command.

No doubt the most basic and symbolic aspect of political power is the prerogative of political leaders to accomplish their goals by commanding others to carry out their decrees. The iconic image of the king on the throne issuing commands for his subjects to fulfill has been the stuff of folk tales and mythology for thousands of years of human society. And such power of command, whether exercised by kings or by other political leaders, is in fact the stuff of lived experience for people in all kinds of societies and social structures. Matthew's narrative, as a portrayal of the social community of the eastern Mediterranean world in the first century, depicts the exercise of power of command in ways characteristic to that world and that historical moment in time.

Within Matthew's narrative it is the Roman leaders and their proxies who exercise power of command in straightforward and uncomplicated fashion. From the top to the bottom of the Roman hierarchy political leaders or their agents simply issue commands which must be obeyed. Herod the king (2:1–23) has authority to "call"[34] people of prominence into his presence — including the local intelligentsia (2:4a: "all the chief priests and scribes of the people") and foreign dignitaries (2:7a: the wise men) — and to interrogate them[35] in order to acquire crucial information (2:4b-6; 2:7b, 16c). By the same token Herod likewise has the authority to "send" [36] people out to do his bidding. The wise men "set out" for Bethlehem (2:9) when Herod "sends" them (2:8); and Herod's henchmen carry out the gruesome task which he "sends" them to do (2:16). In similar fashion Herod the tetrarch (14:1–12) has straightforward authority to "command" that the head of John the Baptist be given to Herodias' daughter (*keleuō*: 14:9c) and to "send" and have John beheaded in the prison" (*apostellō*: 14:10). And Pilate the Roman governor (27:1-2, 11–27) exercises similar power of command as he "releases Barabbas" (*apolyō*: 27:26a) and "hands [Jesus] over to be crucified" (*apodidōmi*: 27:26b).

Farther down the Roman hierarchy centurions (cf. 8:5–13) have similar, if lesser, authority to command. As one such Roman centurion explains

---

34. Thus *synagō*: 2:4; *kaleō*: 2:7.
35. Thus *pynthanomai*: 2:4; *akriboō*: 2:7.
36. Thus *pempō*: 2:8; *apostellō*: 2:16.

to Jesus, "I also am a man under authority, with soldiers under me; and I say to one, 'Go,' and he goes, and to another, 'Come,' and he comes, and to my slave, 'Do this,' and the slave does it" (8:9). And even common foot soldiers in the Roman army can "force" others to carry burdens for a mile, some as onerous as the wooden cross on which a condemned criminal is about to be crucified (*angareuo*: 5:41; 27:32). Clearly the Roman imperial forces active in Palestine have no hesitation and find no hindrance in exercising their power of command over those under their authority.

The Jewish political leaders of Matthew's narrative are not portrayed as exhibiting the same power of command. To the contrary they find it necessary to use alternative means to accomplish their goals. To accomplish the arrest of Jesus, they must make a financial deal with Judas Iscariot, offering him money for services rendered (26:14–16). In order to ensure a Roman verdict against Jesus, they must "persuade" (*peithō*: 27:20) the Jewish crowds in Jerusalem to demand Jesus' death. And to quash any potential story of Jesus' resurrection, they must bribe the Roman guards with "a large sum of money" (*argyria hikana*: 28:12b) to disseminate a fabricated account about the empty tomb (28:11–15). What the Roman leaders can accomplish by simple command requires strategy, persuasion, and money on the part of the Jewish leaders. And such is the power differential between the "occupiers" and the "occupied."

First-Century "Photo-Ops": Public Relations Initiatives.

The terminology of "photo-ops" and the underlying political strategy of taking highly visible actions designed to impress the public and enhance one's popularity as a political figure have become a ubiquitous constant of present-day politics. Unforgettable images abound, from the 1993 handshake of Yitzhak Rabin and Yasser Arafat on the White House lawn to the 2003 speech of George W. Bush on a US aircraft carrier in front of a huge sign reading "Mission Accomplished" and well beyond. But while the "photos" of "photo-op" have been around only for some 150 years, the "opportunistic" political strategy behind the "photo-op" is no doubt as ancient as politics itself. And within Matthew's narrative the Jewish leaders, who have little access to simple power of command, are depicted as masters of the art of acting for public viewing and approval.

One of Jesus' persistent charges against the scribes and Pharisees is that they do their deeds in order to be "seen"[37] and "praised"[38] by others.

---

37. Thus *phainō*: 6:5, 16; 23:27, 28; *theaomai*: 23:5; cf. 6:1.
38. Thus *doxazō*: 6:2.

They "sound trumpets... in the synagogues and in the streets" to announce their acts of almsgiving (6:2). They "stand and pray" conspicuously "in the synagogues and at the street corners" (6:5). They "disfigure their faces" to publicize their acts of fasting (6:16). They "make their phylacteries broad and their fringes long" to display their piety in highly visible fashion to all who see them (23:5). They delight in public honor of all types: the "place of honor" (*tēn prōtoklisian*) at banquets (23:6a), the "best seats" (*tas prōtokathedrias*) in the synagogues (23:6b), respectful "greetings" (*tous aspasmous*) in the marketplaces (23:7a), and the honorific title "rabbi" (23:7b). In the face of all this evidence Jesus concludes that the scribes and Pharisees resemble "whitewashed tombs" which "look beautiful (*phainontai hōraioi*)" externally but on the inside reflect a very different reality (23:27). And in non-parabolic language he charges that they "look righteous (*phainesthe... dikaioi*)" on the outside, while being "full of hypocrisy and lawlessness" on the inside (23:28).

On the Roman front the portrait is noticeably different. For the most part Matthew offers no similar "opportunistic" depictions of the Roman imperial powers within his narrative, most likely suggesting that Matthew does not generally view them as either needing or attempting to curry favor with the Jewish populace under their military control.[39] By comparison with their Jewish counterparts, the Romans are engaged in no "hearts and minds" operation. Instead, as will be detailed below, the Romans routinely employ violence and military force to enact the will of the empire. The prominent exception to this rule, however, is reflected in the annual crowd-pleasing gesture of Pilate, the Roman governor, at Passover, when his custom is "to release a prisoner *for the crowd, anyone whom they [want]*" (27:15; emphasis mine). Here Pilate knowingly suspends his own powers of Roman jurisdiction and submits himself intentionally to the will of the Jewish crowd gathered in Jerusalem for the Passover. Clearly Pilate welcomes the approval of the crowd when he can gain it in opportunistic ways. And the highly public context within which Pilates exercises this political gesture ("so after they had gathered": 27:17a) demonstrates without question Pilate's interest in the greatest possible political benefit. Clearly the twenty-first-century "photo-op" has a long and well-practiced history.

---

39. Here I distinguish between unforced political opportunism of the "photo-op" variety and political expediency, in which political leaders are forced by political circumstances beyond their control into political actions that they would not otherwise take. Matthew charges Roman and Jewish leaders alike with "political expediency." On this point, see below.

Political Expedience: Acquiescence to the Necessary.

Just one small step beyond the ubiquitous political art of self-initiated action for public appearance lie the "expedient" responses forced on the political leader by external political necessity. Such actions clearly demonstrate the character of the political leader(s) in question by revealing the lengths to which they will go to do what is politically necessary, even when such actions contravene their own original intentions. And such actions likewise demonstrate the fundamental weakness of political leaders who find themselves forced into actions they have not chosen. Within his narrative Matthew indicts both Roman and Jewish leaders alike on the charge of political expedience.

The Jewish leaders, for their part, take politically expedient actions largely due to "fear"[40] of "the crowds"/"the people."[41] When Jesus asks the chief priests and the elders a question about John the Baptist (21:24-25a), they rehearse the two possible responses which Jesus has offered them and the respective risks involved (21:25b-26: "If we say . . . But if we say . . ."). And while they consider the shame that they would encounter for failing to "believe" one who has come "from heaven" (21:25b), it is ultimately their "fear" of the "crowd," who "regard John as a prophet" (21:26), that forces them to save their political reputations by responding, "We do not know" (21:27). When Jesus tells an allegorical parable in which the chief priests and the Pharisees recognize their own role as the villains (21:33-44 cf. 21:45), their immediate desire is to "arrest" Jesus (21:46a). But here as before their "fear" of the "crowds" prevents them from taking action, because the crowds regard not only John the Baptist but Jesus himself as a "prophet" (21:46b). And even when the chief priests and the elders of the people gather at the palace of the high priest and conspire "to arrest Jesus by stealth and kill him" (26:4), their plans are constricted ("Not during the festival . . ." [26:5a]) by their fear of the "riot" that may ensue "among the people" (*hina mē thorybos genētai en tō laō*: 26:5b).

In 27:3-10 the political expedience of the Jewish leaders appears to emerge from their fear of losing their reputation as those who do what "is lawful."[42] Faced with the need to dispose of the coins that Judas throws down in the temple (27:5a), the chief priests and the elders conclude that "It is not lawful (*ouk exestin*) to put them into the treasury, since they are blood money" (27:6). Their concern, ironically, lies not with the self-acknowl-

---

40. Thus *phobeomai*: 21:26, 46.
41. Thus *ho ochlos/hoi ochloi*: 21:26, 46; cf. *ho laos*: 26:5.
42. Thus *exestin*: 27:6. Cf. 12:2, 4, 10, 12; 14:4; 19:3; 20:15; 22:17.

edged truth that they have paid out "blood money" in the first place, but merely with the technical "legality" of putting such money into the temple treasury.[43] As a result they spend this money for an alternative and apparently "lawful" project, a burial field for foreigners (27:7-8).

But just as the Jewish leaders find themselves forced into expedient actions by their fear of the crowds, so also do the Roman imperial powers. Matthew's portrayal of Herod the tetrarch (14:1-12) shows him to be little more than a puppet on a string vis-à-vis the other characters in the story.[44] Herod has arrested and imprisoned John the Baptist due to John's outspoken political bluntness concerning Herod's marital affairs (14:3-5a). But when he wants to kill John, Herod finds his hands politically tied, since he "fear[s] the crowd," who "regard [John the Baptist] as a prophet" (14:5b). Later Herod is "grieved" at the request of Herodias' daughter, on behalf of her mother, for the head of John the Baptist (14:9a). But because he has just made an extravagant and highly public oath in front of a roomful of guests (14:6-7), Herod is forced once again into expedient action, this time "out of regard for his oaths and for the guests" (14:9b). John the Baptist ultimately loses his head because Herod fears the entire cast of characters at the banquet — his consort Herodias (14:8a, 11b), Herodias' daughter (14:6-7, 8b, 11a), and the guests reclining at table with him (14:6, 9b). And Herod's wide-ranging fear gives rise to political expediency of the most obvious and unprincipled sort.

Matthew's portrait of Pilate, the Roman governor, shows Pilate to be equally fearful of the crowds and equally skilled at the art of the expedient.[45] Like Herod the tetrarch, Pilate has tied his own hands politically in advance by establishing a completely open-ended and unquestionably crowd-pleasing Passover precedent vis-à-vis his Jewish subjects, namely "to release a prisoner for the crowd, *anyone whom they wanted* (27:15b; emphasis mine). Accordingly, when the crowd calls for the release of Barabbas (27:20-21) and demands that Jesus be crucified (27:22-23), Pilate has no other politically feasible options to consider. He knows that the Jewish leaders have acted out of "jealousy" in handing Jesus over (27:18). He has learned of the dream that his wife has had concerning "that righteous man" (*tō dikaiō ekeinō*: 27:19b, DJW). And he knows that Jesus has "done no evil"

---

43. Cf. the remark of Hare (*Matthew*, 313) on the expedient action of the Jewish leaders: "While [the Jewish leaders] openly deny their guilt . . . , *they are compelled to concede* that they cannot receive the money as a temple offering, because it is 'blood money'" (emphasis mine).

44. For a fuller discussion of Herod the tetrarch, see Weaver, "Power and Powerlessness," 187-91.

45. For a fuller discussion of Pilate, see ibid., 191-95.

(cf. 27:23a). So Pilate argues briefly with the crowds (27:23). But when a "riot" ensues (27:24a), Pilate knows that the game is up. Having given away his own political authority well in advance and fully aware of the extreme political danger associated with "riots,"[46] Pilate now has no choice but to do the politically expedient by "releasing Barabbas" for the Jewish crowd and "handing [Jesus] over to be crucified" (27:26).[47] Doing the politically expedient is clearly a typical modus operandi for the political leaders of Matthew's narrative, Jewish and Roman alike.

"Campaign Rhetoric": Verbal Attack and the Art of Persuasion.

To read the Matthean accounts of the controversies between the Jewish leaders and Jesus is to enter a world that strongly resembles a twenty-first-century election campaign between rival politicians. Here the Jewish leaders are mounting what appears to be an energetic political campaign in front of the Jewish crowds to discredit and defeat their political opponent, Jesus, and to win over the hearts and minds of the Jewish people for themselves.

The strategies that they adopt in this campaign are the standard tools of all political campaigns: verbal attacks on the opponent and persuasion of the supporters. The Jewish leaders open their campaign with virtually inaudible muttering (9:3, 4); but their attacks escalate to direct verbal challenges[48] and public pronouncements against Jesus (9:32–34; 12:22–24). They work indirectly, challenging Jesus' disciples on the actions of their "teacher" (9:10–13); and they take Jesus to task conversely for the actions of his "disciples" (12:1–8; 15:1–9) and the words of the children in the temple (21:14–16). They question Jesus "maliciously" (*tēn ponērian*: 22:18; cf. *ponēra*: 9:4) in public settings ranging from Galilean synagogues to the Jerusalem temple, in order to "accuse" him (*katēgoreō*: 12:10), to "test" him (*peirazō*: 16:1; 19:3; 22:35), and to "entrap" him (*pagideuō*: 22:15). They demand that he show them "signs [from heaven]" (12:38–42; 16:1–4). They challenge him to his face (21:23–27) and denounce him before the Jewish crowds in public proclamations (9:32–34; 12:22–24).

---

46. Cf. the similar fear of the Jewish leaders concerning the outbreak of a "riot" in 26:5.

47. Contra Carter (*Matthew and Empire*, 165), Matthew's emphatic threefold indication of Jesus' innocence, depicted as in the mind (27:18), in the hearing (27:19b), and on the tongue (19:23a) of Pilate himself, invites the reader to conclude that Pilate acts in spite of his own better knowledge and instincts.

48. Thus 9:10–13; 12:1–8, 9–14, 38–42; 15:1–9; 16:1–4; 19:3–9; 21:14–16, 23–27; 22:15–22, 34–40.

The campaign rhetoric of the Jewish leaders sounds two prominent themes. On the one hand the Jewish leaders challenge Jesus persistently on the question of what is "lawful" or "not lawful" (*exestin/ouk exestin*): plucking grain on the sabbath (12:1-8); healing on the sabbath (12:9-14); divorcing one's wife "for any cause" (19:3-9); and paying taxes to the emperor (22:15-22). In a similar vein they accuse Jesus' disciples of "break[ing] the tradition of the elders" by failing to "wash their hands before they eat" (15:2); and they castigate Jesus himself for "eat[ing] with tax collectors and sinners" (9:11). And to underscore their concerns about the law they "test" Jesus concerning the "greatest commandment in the law" (22:35-36).

But just as crucial to their rhetorical strategy is the challenge that the Jewish leaders raise with regard to Jesus' "authority" (*exousia*: 9:8; 21:23, 24, 27). They charge Jesus with "blasphemy" for pronouncing forgiveness of sins, while the crowds "[glorify] God, who [has] given *such authority* to human beings" (9:8; emphasis mine). They denounce Jesus as one who casts out demons "by [Beelzebul], the ruler of the demons" (9:34; 12:24; cf. 10:25) and thus implicitly not by the "authority" of God. And after Jesus has turned the temple upside down and thoroughly disrupted their financial enterprise (21:12-13), the chief priests and elders of the people accost Jesus as he teaches in the temple and put the question to him directly: "By what authority are you doing these things, and who gave you this authority?" (21:23b).

Ultimately, however, the success or failure of the Jewish political campaign to discredit Jesus and bring about his demise rests on the ability of the Jewish leaders to rally their own supporters, convince them vis-à-vis the cause in question, and engage them in effective political action. Throughout the Galilean segment of Matthew's narrative there is no evidence of any such successful efforts by the Jewish leaders at public persuasion. But at the most critical moment for their strategic purposes, Jesus' trial before Pilate, the Jewish power brokers in Jerusalem, the chief priests and the elders, finally succeed in their political efforts as they "[persuade] (*peithō*) the crowds to ask for Barabbas and to have Jesus killed" (27:20).

Matthew offers no hints as to how the Jewish leaders carry out this political "persuasion." All the readers witness is the outcome of their "persuasive" efforts. And to judge from the evidence at hand, this "persuasion" is hardly built on a nuanced argument which can be debated on the merits. Rather, the crowd has clearly been offered a standard "party line" response which can be supported only by increasingly vociferous repetition. When Pilate seeks to engage the crowds in rational discussion of the logic of their decision against Jesus—"Why, what evil has he done?" (27:23a)—the crowds have no reasoned argumentation to offer. Instead they merely repeat the "party line" that they have apparently been given by the Jewish leaders:

"Let him be crucified!" (27:23b). And, far from judicial debate, it is the ensuing "riot" (*thorybos*: 27:24a) caused by screaming crowds shouting their verdict repetitiously (27:23)[49] that brings about the desired political results. Pilate, who attempts to debate the judicial merits of the case in front of him (27:23a), ultimately accedes to the will of a screaming mob (27:23b-24a) and carries out their wishes (27:24b-26). To this extent the efforts of the Jewish leaders at political persuasion are indeed successful. And just days later they announce with confidence that they can "persuade" (*peithō*: 28:14; DJW) the governor himself, if political circumstances demand such action. Clearly the power of persuasion is a critical skill for the Jewish leadership in their political enterprise as the community organizers of the Jewish people.

The portrait is characteristically different for the Romans. Just as the Roman imperial powers depicted within Matthew's narrative do not frequently engage in opportunistic actions designed to win the hearts and minds of their subject peoples, so they likewise do not engage in verbal campaigns defaming their opponents or attempt, conversely, to garner the support of the masses through the art of rhetorical persuasion. Those who have military means to enact the will of the empire by the power of brute force have less need perhaps to "persuade" their subject peoples through political argumentation. Instead, for the Roman imperial hierarchy, it is military power itself that does the work of political persuasion. Thus when Herod, the client king over Judea, is "disturbed" at the news he hears (*etarachthē*: 2:3a; TNIV), Matthew notes that Herod's unease is shared by "all Jerusalem with him" (2:3b). As the events of the unfolding narrative suggest (2:13–18), it is sheer, and no doubt well-experienced, political instinct that infects the people of Jerusalem with the moods of Herod himself. Thus they realize instinctively that when Herod is "disturbed" (2:3; TNIV)—let alone "infuriated" (*ethymōthē*: 2:16a)—danger is never far away (2:16b). The moods of Herod and what they portend, accordingly, are shown to be as politically "persuasive" as the verbal rhetoric of the Jewish leaders.

Misspeaking the Truth: Public Lies and Political Deception.

While the campaign rhetoric of the political leaders in Matthew's narrative may be strong and harsh, the clear implication of the text is that this rhetoric, for the most part, reflects the honest opinions of its speakers. The controversies between Jesus and the Jewish leaders, for example, are generally portrayed as genuine controversies, in which the Jewish leaders actually

---

49. The imperfect form of the verb *ekrazon* in 27:23b clearly implies the repetitious character of the shouting.

believe the charges that they bring against Jesus. Matthew calls the reader to believe, for example, that the Jewish leaders honestly debate the "lawfulness" of Jesus' actions and honestly challenge his "authority." But political rhetoric, in the heat of the political battle, often extends well beyond honest differences into the realm of what is euphemistically called "misspeaking the truth" or in other words, public lies and political deception. And on this front Matthew paints both the Roman imperial powers and the Jewish leadership with the same brush.

Herod, the client king ruling Judea for the Romans, sets the stage for this type of cynical political behavior at the very beginning of Matthew's narrative. When the wise men are called to appear before Herod (2:7), they apparently make the assumption that they are simply receiving a royal welcome to Jerusalem and a private (cf. 2:7: "secret"/*lathra*) audience with a king who is vitally interested in the search that has brought them there. Matthew gives us no reason to believe that they are concerned about potential danger. They offer Herod the information he is seeking (2:7) and unhesitatingly obey his command to go to Bethlehem (2:9). And it takes nothing short of a divine dream-warning to deter them from returning to Herod with the information that he seeks (2:12).

But Matthew's readers are not fooled. Matthew has already clued the readers in to Herod's malicious intentions with his notice that Herod is "disturbed" at the news of Jesus' birth. So when Herod charges the wise men to "bring me word so that I may also go and pay him homage" (2:8), Matthew's readers know that danger is afoot. Surely Herod's "homage" is more threat than promise. But they are forced to look on helplessly for three interminable verses (2:9–11), while the wise men cheerfully carry out Herod's commands in blissful ignorance of Herod's evil intentions. Finally the dream-warning sends the wise men home "by another road" (2:12), a clear signal to the wise men themselves that Herod has in fact deceived them And in the following verses Matthew confirms for his readers what they have suspected all along: Herod is intent on "seek[ing] the child's life" (2:20) and "destroy[ing]" him (2:13). And in order to do so, he brutally annihilates an entire population of young children in Bethlehem (2:16). Herod's words about "homage," while they do not fool Matthew's readers, are intentional, and initially successful, political deception of the most cynical order for those to whom they are spoken.

And if Matthew's narrative opens with an account of political deception by the Roman imperial powers, it concludes with a depiction of just such deception carried out by the Jewish chief priests and elders (28:11–15). Faced with a missing body (28:5–6) and an unsatisfactory explanation by the soldiers set to guard the tomb (28:11), the chief priests and elders fabricate a dangerously self-incriminating version of events for the soldiers to disseminate (28:13b): "His disciples came by night and stole him away while we were asleep." Then they bribe the soldiers lavishly to pass on this fabrication (28:12–13a). And the Jewish leaders who could not find "false testimony" against Jesus at his trial in spite of their most strenuous efforts (26:59–60) are now successful in disseminating their own "false testimony" (28:15a), a story which in Matthew's words is "still told among the Jews to this day" (28:15b). Public deception is clearly standard practice for the political leaders of Matthew's narrative, whether Roman or Jewish.

Conspiracy to Destroy Political Enemies.

One of the most notorious, most ubiquitous, and, sadly, most successful strategies across the globe for gaining and/or retaining political power lies in the age-old art of political conspiracy , i.e., "join[ing] in a secret agreement to do an unlawful or wrongful act or to use such means to accomplish a lawful end."[50] Most frequently such conspiracies focus on the goal of destroying political enemies. Some conspiracies rise to the level of confirmed fact. Mere mention of the word "Watergate" evokes memories of one of the most notorious political conspiracies within American history, a conspiracy confirmed as fact day after day in congressional hearings during the summer of 1973 by the riveting testimony of such actual co-conspirators as John Dean, Counsel to then President Richard M. Nixon. Other conspiracies exist as undying yet seemingly non-provable theories. Oliver Stone's provocative movie, *JFK*, raises just such indestructible conspiracy theories concerning the 1963 death of President John Fitzgerald Kennedy. But, whether proven or unproven, conspiracies remain a notorious constant in the realm of worldwide politics.

Matthew's first-century narrative is awash with actual conspiracies, whether narrated to us by Matthew's omniscient implied author or confirmed for us by the words of the conspirators in question. Matthew's vocabulary offers us the technical terminology to denote conspiracy: *symbouleuō* (26:4) and *symboulion lambanō* (12:14; 22:15; 27:1, 7; 28:12).[51] And even in places where such technical terminology does not show up, Matthew uses

---

50. *Webster's Seventh*, 178.

51. This correlated terminology is variously translated by the NRSV as "conspire" (12:14; 26:4), "plot" (22:15), "confer together" (27:1), and "devise a plan" (28:12) as it denotes conspiracies. But see 27:7, where the same vocabulary depicts the chief priests and the elders (27:3; cf. 27:6) "conferring together" in non-conspiratorial fashion over how to dispose of the coins that Judas has thrown onto the temple floor (27:5).

alternative vocabulary or adopts other means to depict the conspiratorial actions of the characters in question (2:1–23; 21:33–46, and 26:57–68).

The conspiracies of Matthew's narrative focus on the characters of John the Baptist and Jesus. In the case of John the Baptist it is Herodias who conspires together with her daughter to bring about John's death. For her part she "prompts" (*probibazō*) her daughter to ask for the head of John the Baptist delivered up on a platter (14:8). And her daughter in turn plays her part in the conspiracy by verbalizing the request (14:8), receiving the head of John the Baptist on the requested platter (14:11a), and handing the platter and head over to her mother (14:11b).

In the case of Jesus Matthew's narrative portrays conspiracies on the part of his opponents to defeat him in debate (22:15), to kill him outright,[52] and to deny his resurrection (28:12–14). These conspiracies span the entire length of the narrative. And two of these conspiracies, recounted in 2:1–23 and 28:11–15, create a framing device that forms a virtual but penultimate "inclusio" around the narrative of Jesus' life, death, and resurrection.[53] Accordingly, the entire story of Jesus, as Matthew tells it, has as its fundamental counterpoint the motif of conspiratorial opposition to Jesus by the political leaders of the region, both Roman and Jewish.

The story is framed on the opening end by the quasi-conspiracy of Herod the king upon hearing news of "the one who has been born king of the Jews" (2:1). Herod first engages the unwitting collaboration of the Jewish chief priests and scribes of the people (2:4–6) on the one hand and the Gentile "wise men" from the east (2:1–2, 7–8, 16) on the other in a secret and deadly scheme of his own design to "seek the child's life" (2:20) and "destroy" him (2:13). Matthew's narration underscores the conspiratorial character of Herod's scheme with its vivid and evocative vocabulary. Herod "calls together" the chief priests and scribes for a high-level consultation.[54] He arranges a "secret" meeting with the magi (*lathra*: 2:7). And he interrogates his Jewish and Gentile informants closely[55] regarding the exact place where (2:4–6) and the exact time when (2:7, 16) this "king of the Jews" was born. Ultimately, Herod's quasi-conspiracy turns into a genuine conspiracy, as he sends his military henchmen out, fully aware of their task, to "[kill] all

---

52. Thus 2:4, 7–8, 13, 16, 20; 12:14; 21:38; 26:4, 59; 27:1.

53. Conspiracy against Jesus, as central as it is to the plot of Matthew's story, is neither the first word (1:1–25) nor the last word of this story (28:16–20). And the threat to Jesus, Messiah (1:1, 16, 17, 18) and Son of God (28:19; cf. 3:17; 17:5), which is posed by such conspiracy, has accordingly only "penultimate" power.

54. Thus *synagō*: 2:4. Cf. 26:3–4, 57/59; 28:12, where *synagō* and the vocabulary of conspiracy coincide.

55. Thus *pynthanomai*: 2:4; *akriboō*: 2:7, 16; cf. *exetazō akribōs*: 2:8.

the children in and around Bethlehem who [are] two years old or under" (2:16b). Clearly the Roman imperial powers are masters of the art of political conspiracy.

But as the narrative progresses, it is Jesus' Jewish opponents who mount repeated conspiracies against him. When Jesus heals a man on the sabbath (12:9–14), they conspire to "destroy him" (12:14). When Jesus defeats them in public debate, they conspire to "entrap him in what he [says]" (22:15). Eventually they conspire to "arrest Jesus by stealth" (26:4), charge him with "false testimony" (27:59), and "kill him" (26:4, 59; 27:1). And to carry out their plot they hire an informant from among Jesus' own disciples to "hand him over" to them (26:14–16).

The impetus for these conspiracies by the Jewish leaders is their intense political "jealousy" of Jesus, as Pilate clearly recognizes (27:18). Jesus himself identifies the source of this jealousy in the allegorical parable of the wicked tenants to whom the landowner sends his son (21:38, emphasis mine): "This is the heir; come, let us kill him *and get his inheritance*." Accordingly, the jealousy of the Jewish authorities and their conspiracies against him in Matthew's narrative reflect a fundamental power struggle with Jesus over leadership of the Jewish people, framed here as the "inheritance" of the Jewish "vineyard" (i.e., Israel; cf. Isa 5:1–7). And initially the Jewish leaders appear to win this power struggle, when they succeed in bringing about the death of Jesus (cf. 27:1–2, 15–26).

But when the dead body of Jesus disappears mysteriously from the tomb several days later (28:1–11), the chief priests and elders are forced to engage in a final, desperate conspiracy to counter the message of Jesus' resurrection (28:12–15) and assure their continuing hold over the hearts and minds of the Jewish people. The Jewish leaders pay a handsome bribe (28:12b: "a large sum of money") to the Roman soldiers to pass on the dangerously self-incriminating story that Jesus' disciples "came by night and stole him away while we were asleep" (28:13b). And with their significant powers of "persuasion" (*peithō*: 28:14b; cf. 27:20) the Jewish leaders promise to keep the soldiers out of trouble, in case their open admission of dereliction of duty reaches Pilate, the Roman governor (28:14a/c). This conspiracy is highly effective and enormously durable in the Jewish community. As Matthew acknowledges, the story is still being told "among the Jews" in his own day (28:15). Along with their Roman counterparts the Jewish leaders of Matthew's narrative are clearly well skilled at the art of political conspiracy.

Subversion of Justice: Judicial Systems Run Amok.

There is likely no more iconic image of the misuse of political power than that of a show trial, where the jury is stacked against the defendant, the guilty verdict determined in advance, or the outcome of the trial dictated by the emotions of a lynch mob. Images of such cynical travesties of justice span the centuries and circle the globe with grim and distressing regularity, leaving few nations or judicial systems innocent and untouched. One such vivid image comes to us from Matthew's account of Jesus' arrest and trials before Jewish (26:3–5, 14–16, 47–66; 27:1–2) and Roman (27:11–26) courts. And while Matthew portrays the Jewish leaders and the Roman governor as conducting their judicial affairs in significantly different fashion, he nevertheless lays unmistakable blame on both Jewish and Roman leaders for the miscarriage of justice over which they each in turn preside.

The Jewish miscarriage of justice begins days before Jesus' trial with the conspiracy of the chief priests and the elders "to arrest Jesus by stealth and kill him" (26:4). Both the language of "stealth" and the stated intention to "kill" Jesus offer vivid evidence in advance that there will be no legitimate judicial proceedings when Jesus is arrested. Instead, the outcome of the trial has already been determined; and "stealth" is accordingly a necessary strategy to conceal the blatant illegitimacy of the proceedings that lie ahead. The picture grows still darker when Judas Iscariot presents himself to the chief priests and offers his services to "hand Jesus over" (DJW) to them for a fee (26:14–16). The conspiracy is now full-fledged. And the "hit man" has now been hired.

The arrest of Jesus takes place both with the intended "stealth" but likewise with the trappings of enormous physical force. Judas seeks out Jesus at nighttime in Gethsemane (26:36), so the arrest can take place in a dark and secluded garden, well away from the light of day and the crowded city streets of Jerusalem. But Judas Iscariot brings along with him "a large crowd with swords and clubs from the chief priests and the elders of the people" (26:47b). And Jesus himself challenges the arrest posse both on the location of the arrest (26:55b: "Day after day I sat in the temple teaching, and you did not arrest me") and on the excessive force employed (26:55a: "Have you come out with swords and clubs to arrest me as though I were a bandit?"). With this depiction of Jesus' arrest Matthew's narrative imagery clearly suggests the fundamental illegitimacy of the proceedings at hand.[56]

---

56. Within the scope of this chapter I work strictly with the narrative force of Matthew's story. I make no attempt here to resolve any of the urgent historical questions surrounding the actual trial(s) of Jesus.

Nor do things improve when Jesus is brought before Caiaphas, the Jewish high priest, and the assembled Jewish leaders (26:57). Here there is neither interest in nor attempt at a genuine legal proceeding with the goal of uncovering the truth of the matter. To the contrary the chief priests and the "whole council" are engaged in a massive and energetic search for "false testimony against Jesus" toward the express goal "that they might put him to death" (26:59). Their failure to obtain "false testimony" apparently reflects their inability to find corroborating stories among the "many false witnesses" (26:60) who take the stand against Jesus.[57]

When Jesus refuses to respond to the apparently true charge finally brought against him by two witnesses (26:60c-63a),[58] the high priest adopts an alternative strategy, putting Jesus under oath to declare whether he is "the Messiah, the Son of God" (26:63b). The obvious ploy here, as confirmed by the unfolding events of the narrative, is to establish the capital charge of "blasphemy" against Jesus.[59] And Jesus' tacit affirmation (26:64a: "You have said so.") and the accompanying prediction about the coming Son of Man (26:64b) clearly provide Caiaphas with the ammunition he needs to pronounce the charge of "blasphemy" against Jesus (26:65) and to call forth the formal verdict from the assembled council (26:66b): "He deserves death." Here Matthew's irony is biting. While the Jewish leaders are unable to convict Jesus *on the "false testimony" that they are intentionally seeking* (26:59-60), they ultimately achieve their goal by pronouncing *a false verdict of which they are completely unaware*. As Matthew's readers know well, Jesus is indeed "the Messiah, the Son of God" (3:17; 17:5). Thus the verdict of the Jewish council is false, not because "blasphemy" itself is not a capital crime but rather *because Jesus is indeed the Messiah and Son of God and thus his witness to this effect is not blasphemy*. As a result the Jewish leaders preside over a judicial travesty both knowingly and unknowingly. And Matthew holds them accountable on both fronts.

---

57. Cf. Deut 19:15, where the Jewish law stipulates that "Only on the evidence of two or three witnesses shall a charge be sustained."

58. In pointed distinction to his Markan source which identifies the "temple destruction" charge against Jesus as "false" (14:57-58), Matthew carefully distinguishes the "many false witnesses" (26:60b) and the "two who came forward" (26:60c) and maintains that the Jewish leaders do not in fact find the "false testimony" that they are seeking (26:59a/60a).

59. Thus Lev 24:16a/b: "One who blasphemes the name of the LORD shall be put to death; the whole congregation shall stone the blasphemer." The historical question of whether Jesus' declaration would in fact have constituted "blasphemy" according to Jewish law *if it were not true* is a moot point for Matthew's narrative, which simply offers the verdict of Caiaphas and the council as the legal status of the question.

Nor is this the end of their culpability. In the morning, after the late night trial, the Jewish leaders consummate their conspiracy by "[binding] Jesus, [leading] him away, and [handing] him over to Pilate the governor" (27:1-2). With this act the Jewish leaders join Judas in the culpability for "handing over" an "innocent" man to certain death (27:3-4a); and they also disregard in cavalier fashion Judas' subsequent witness to the "innocence" of Jesus: "What is that to us? See to it yourself" (27:4b). Their final act in this judicial travesty is to stack the jury of public opinion against Jesus and "persuade" (27:20) the crowds gathered before Pilate to call for the release of Barabbas, a "notorious prisoner" (27:16, 17a, 20a, 21), and demand the death of Jesus by crucifixion (27:20b, 22-23). Matthew's damning account of the judicial culpability of the Jewish leaders concludes with the assessment of Pilate that they have acted not out of genuine legal concerns but rather out of a politically-motivated "jealousy" (*phthonos*: 27:18).[60]

But in spite of his political astuteness Pilate fares no better than the Jewish leaders in Matthew's narrative depiction. While Matthew charges the Jewish leaders with politically-motivated "jealousy" and a blatant attempt to gain advantage over their opponent by "false" means, Matthew accuses Pilate of the equally damning charge of political expedience.[61] And here Pilate's knowledge and his astuteness serve only to heighten his culpability in Matthew's assessment. Pilate has all the information, the political instinct, and the inherent authority that he needs to conduct an honest and fair judicial proceeding. He knows the innocence of the defendant (27:19, 23). He understands the political motivation of the plaintiffs (27:18). And he clearly has the authority as Roman governor to "release" defendants when the circumstances warrant (27:15, 17, 21; cf. 27:26). But in spite of all these qualifications Pilate presides over a miscarriage of justice just as egregious and just as culpable as that of the Jewish leaders.

His first false move is to hand his own judicial authority over to the Passover crowds in line with his annual custom "to release a prisoner for the crowd, *anyone whom they [want]*" (27:15; emphasis mine). Pilate then compounds his first error by overriding his own native instinct about the truth of the matter (27:18), neglecting the exculpatory evidence brought to his attention (27:19), and responding instead in expedient fashion out of his political fear of the crowds and the "riot" that they instigate in front of him (27:24a). Pilate then brings his miscarriage of justice to a vivid and bitterly ironic conclusion as he "washes his hands before the crowd"

---

60. Cf. 21:38, where apparent jealousy of the "heir" (*ho klēronomos*) and "his inheritance" (*tēn klēronomian autou*) is the self-identified motivation for the murder of the landowner's son.

61. See the discussion above on political expedience.

(27:24a),[62] claims his own "innocence" instead of the "innocence" of his defendant (27:24b),[63] releases a "notorious prisoner" to a shouting mob (27:26a cf. 27:16), and "hands [Jesus] over to be crucified" (27:26c). Just as Judas (26:15, 16, 48) and the Jewish leaders (27:2) have each done in their turn, Pilate now assumes the final culpability for "handing Jesus over" to death. And Matthew leaves his readers with no doubt that the political leaders of Jesus' day, both Jewish and Roman, are masters at the art of subverting justice on the judicial level.

The Politics of Violence: Ultimate Political Sanctions.

The ultimate and most egregious use of political power within any given society is reflected in those acts of emotional and physical violence by which political leaders seek first to demoralize and then to destroy their political adversaries in order to secure their own political power. Images and stories of such politically-motivated violence by powerbrokers of our world fill our newspapers, our airwaves, and our television screens regularly. Arrest and imprisonment of political adversaries, mockery and torture of political prisoners, kidnappings, disappearances, extra-judicial killings, assassinations, and the legalized imposition of capital punishment are, with alarming frequency, the standard "modus operandi" of those who wield political power in our twenty-first-century world.

The situation is no different in the world of Matthew's narrative. The use of violence as an ultimate political sanction is clearly an unquestioned assumption for the political leaders of Matthew's narrative, both Roman and Jewish. And such violence begins at very least with the arrest of prisoners. Within Matthew's narrative prisoners are "arrested,"[64] "seized,"[65] "dragged" before authorities,[66] "led away,"[67] and "handed over"[68] to prison,[69] trial,

---

62. Cf. Deut 21:6–7; Pss. 26:6; 73:13.
63. Thus *athōos eimi*: 27:24; cf. *haima athōon*: 27:4.
64. Thus *syllambanō*: 26:55.
65. Thus *lambanō*: 21:35, 39; *krateō*: 14:3; 21:46; 22:6; 26:4, 48, 50, 55, 57.
66. Thus *agō*: 10:18.
67. Thus *apagō*: 26:57; 27:2, 31.
68. Thus *paradidōmi*: 4:12; 10:17, 19; 17:22; 20:18, 19; 24:9; 26:2, 15, 16, 21, 23, 24, 25, 45, 46, 48; 27:2, 4, 26.
69. Thus *desmōtērion*: 11:2; *phylakē*: 14:3, 10.

and execution. Those who arrest prisoners "lay hands on" them,[70] "bind" them,[71] and use "swords and clubs" to carry out their arrests.[72]

Once arrested, prisoners then encounter both the emotional violence of mockery and the physical violence of torture. Those who hold prisoners in their power "mock" them both verbally[73] and in elaborately staged rituals intended to ridicule their victims (27:27-31). The vivid and detailed account of Jesus' "royal" mockery by an entire cohort of Pilate's soldiers—with the scarlet robe, the crown of thorns, the reed scepter, the genuflection, and the acclamation, "Hail, King of the Jews!"—appears to reflect the common means by which Roman soldiers entertain themselves at their prisoners' expense in the course of their military service for the governor. And the verbal taunts hurled at Jesus by those in authority, whether Jewish (26:68; 27:42-43) or Roman (27:29c), clearly reflect a culture in which verbal abuse of prisoners by those in authority is viewed by those same authorities as standard and acceptable practice.

Beyond the level of verbal abuse a prisoner may suffer the public indignity of being "stripped" of his clothing (*ekdyō*: 27:28, 31), dressed up for mockery (27:28-29), and then re-clothed with his own garments (*endyō*: 27:31). And the physical abuse and "mistreatment"[74] that prisoners endure extend from acts of public ridicule to acts of brutal torture. Prisoners are "spit on" in what is no doubt universally understood to be an act of contempt and shaming.[75] They are "slapped"[76] and "struck"[77] with the hands or with a rod. They are "beaten" with a rod[78] or "flogged" with a whip,[79] whether in Jewish synagogues (10:17; 23:34) or in Roman courtyards (cf. 20:19). And, surely most brutal of all, they are "flogged" with the Roman flagellum,[80] an instrument of torture that contains bits of lead and bone intended specifically to increase the pain and the physical injuries of the victims.

But torture is merely the prelude to the final act of violence. Prisoners who have been formally condemned to death (20:18; 26:66) or otherwise

---

70. Thus *epiballō tas cheiras*: 26:50.
71. Thus *deō*: 14:3; 27:2.
72. Thus *machairōn kai xylōn*: 26:47, 55.
73. Thus *empaizō*: 20:19; 27:29, 31, 41.
74. Cf. *hybrizō*: 22:6.
75. Thus *emptyō*: 26:67; 27:30.
76. Thus *rhapizō*: 26:67.
77. Thus *kolaphizō*: 26:67; *paiō*: 26:68; *typtō*: 27:30.
78. Thus *derō*: 21:35.
79. Thus *mastigoō*: 10:17; 20:19; 23:34.
80. Thus *phragelloō*: 27:26.

destined to die are then "killed"[81] in a manner consistent with the respective practices of the political powers in question. The Jewish leaders, when they assume the authority to carry out their own death sentences, stone their victims to death,[82] a practice legislated in the Torah.[83] Herod the tetrarch, acting on the wishes of his consort, Herodias, decapitates John the Baptist.[84] And the Romans, for their part, crucify political insurgents and common criminals.[85]

And in cases where there are no apparent judicial proceedings at all, Matthew's narrative depicts politically-motivated assassinations or "search and destroy" missions. At the behest of Herod the king countless children are "killed" (*anaireō*) en masse in a slaughter constituting collective punishment for the very young of Bethlehem (2:16c): "And [Herod] sent and killed all the children in and around Bethlehem who were two years old or under." Jesus, for his part, speaks of a Jewish prophet from an earlier era ("Zechariah, son of Barachiah"), who is "murdered" (*phoneuō*) in the Jerusalem temple "between the sanctuary and the altar" (23:35; cf. 23:31), an apparent allusion to the politically-motivated stoning death of "Zechariah, son of the priest Jehoida" at the command of King Joash, but apparently without a formal judicial hearing, due to the king's displeasure at Zechariah's unpatriotic prophecy against the people of Judah and Jerusalem (2 Chr 24:20–22). Elsewhere Jesus tells an allegorical parable of a landowner's servants and son who are "stoned" to death (*lithoboleō*: 21:35) or "killed" (21:35, 38, 39) by the vineyard tenants to whom they are sent to collect the produce of the vineyard. And in a similar vein Jesus likewise depicts servants who are "killed" (*apokteinō*: 22:6) or "murdered" (cf. *tous phoneis*: 22:7) by those whom they are sent to invite to the wedding banquet for the king's son.

In general terms the politically powerful within Matthew's narrative "persecute" their political opponents,[86] while "the violent take the [kingdom of heaven] by force" (11:12).[87] For their part the victims of the politically

---

81. Thus *thanatoō*: 26:59; 27:1; *apollymi*: 27:2; *apokteinō*: 10:18; 14:5; 16:21; 17:23; 23:34, 37; 24:9; 26:4; cf. 21:35, 38, 39; 22:6.

82. Thus *lithoboleō*: 21:35; 23:37. Cf. John 8:5, the account of the woman taken in adultery, and Acts 7:58–59, the account of the stoning of Stephen by a Jewish crowd in Jerusalem.

83. Thus, for example, Lev 20:2; 24:14; Deut 13:10.

84. Thus *apokephalizō*: 14:10. Cf. the references to John's "head" (*kephalē*) in 14:8, 11.

85. Thus *stauroō*: 20:19; 23:34; 26:2; 27:22, 23, 26, 31, 35, 38; 28:5; *systauroō*: 27:44; *ho stauros*: 10:38; 16:24; 27:32, 40, 42.

86. Thus *diōkō*: 5:10, 11, 12; 10:23; 23:34.

87. Thus *kai biastai harpazousin autēn*.

powerful "suffer"/"suffer violence" at the hands of the power brokers.[88] And the "blood" of "prophets,"[89] "righteous" ones,[90] and "innocent" victims[91] is shed by those who have the political will and power to do so. In speaking of the politically-motivated execution of John the Baptist at the hands of Herod the tetrarch, Jesus concludes in blunt and uncompromising language: "I tell you that Elijah has already come, and they did not recognize him, but *they did to him whatever they pleased*" (17:12; emphasis mine). In Matthew's view, there are no identifiable limits to the violence and brutality that the political leaders of his narrative exercise in order to retain their political power.

Failed Leadership: A Matthean Assessment.

Throughout his narrative Matthew passes unambiguous judgment on the political leaders in question, charging both Roman and Jewish power brokers with reprehensible use of political power. The evidence is straightforward.

Jesus himself assesses the Roman use of political power in a few brief but pointed words (20:25): "You know that the rulers of the Gentiles lord it over them [*katakyrieuousin autōn*], and their great ones are tyrants over them [*katexousiazousin autōn*]." To further reinforce this negative judgment, Jesus adds, "It will not be so among you" (20:26a); and he then delineates a radically new approach to being "great" (20:26b-28).

But Jesus saves most of his harsh words for the political leaders of the Jewish community. On the one hand he depicts the Jewish leaders as the "tenants" to whom God the "landowner" has leased the "vineyard" of Israel (21:33); and he identifies the Jewish leaders as those who "sit on the seat of Moses" (23:2). But Jesus grants authority to the Jewish leaders with one hand only to take it back with the other. The "tenants," as the Jewish leaders are forced to acknowledge in their own words,[92] ultimately prove themselves to be "wretches" (*kakous*) who face a "miserable death" (*kakōs apolesei*) and in the process forfeit the "vineyard" to others (21:41). And those who "sit on the seat of Moses" (23:2) and speak words which are to

---

88. Thus *paschō*: 16:21; 17:12; *biazomai*: 11:12.
89. Thus *tō haimati tōn prophētōn*: 23:30.
90. Thus *pan haima dikaion, tou haimatos tou Abel*: 23:35.
91. Thus *haima athōon*: 27:4; cf. 27:6, 24, 25.
92. In a remarkable verbal maneuver the Matthean Jesus obliges the Jewish leaders to pronounce a verdict on themselves as he asks them about the ultimate fate of the "tenants" in the story he has just recounted to them. Cf. Mark 12:1-9, where Jesus poses the question rhetorically and answers it himself.

be heeded (23:3a: "So do whatever they teach you and follow it") nevertheless prove themselves to be "hypocrites"[93] who "do not practice what they teach" (23:3c) and whose lifestyle Jesus accordingly warns his disciples not to emulate (23:3b: "But do not do as they do").

Matthew, for his part, charges the Jewish leaders with lacking the "authority" (*exousia*) that characterizes Jesus' teaching ministry (7:29). And he portrays them as failing repeatedly to lead the people under their charge. Not only do the scribes and Pharisees fail the "mercy" test to which Jesus submits their legal judgments (*eleos*: 9:13; 12:7; 23:23). But the chief priests and elders likewise fail to exercise their fundamental intermediary role between the people and God when Judas comes to them confessing that he has "sinned" (27:3-4a). Instead of caring for Judas in their priestly capacity, they throw his "sin" back into his face with the caustic words, "What is that to us? See to it yourself" (27:3b). Similarly, while the "God-forsaken" Jesus hangs dying on a Roman cross (cf. 27:46), the chief priests, scribes, and elders make no intermediary effort to plead with God on Jesus' behalf.[94] Instead they exhibit a cavalier disregard for human suffering, taunting Jesus to "save himself" (27:42a; cf. 27:40a) and "come down from the cross" (27:42b; cf. 27:40a). And they likewise exhibit a cynical distrust of God himself, taunting God in similar fashion to "deliver" Jesus "if he wants to" (27:43b).

Clearly the Jewish leaders of Matthew's narrative are not fulfilling the leadership role to which they have been called as "shepherds of Israel" (cf. Ezek 34:1-10). And Jesus accordingly "[has] compassion" on the Jewish crowds (cf. Ezek 34:11-16), because he views them as "harassed and helpless, *like sheep without a shepherd*" (9:36; emphasis mine).

II. "WHEN HEROD DIED": MATTHEW'S ASSESSMENT OF THE EFFECTIVENESS OF POLITICAL POWER

As illustrated above, Matthew's Gospel is replete with vivid depictions of the exercise of political power as carried out by Jewish and Roman political leaders in the world of Matthew's narrative. Along with these depictions, as also noted above, comes Matthew's consistently negative assessment of the ethical character of such political initiatives through the multi-faceted

---

93. Thus *hoi hypokritai*: 6:2, 5, 16; 7:5; 15:7; 16:3; 22:18; 23:13, 14, 15, 23, 25, 27, 29.

94. See, for example, Exod 33:1-6/12-23, where Moses pleads successfully with the LORD not to abandon God's people, as God has threatened ("I will not go up among you": v. 3b), but instead to "go with [them]" (v. 16a) to the land to which they are going. Cf. also Num 14:10b-25; 16:41-50; 21:4-9, where Moses likewise intercedes successfully with God on behalf of the people.

rhetoric of his storytelling. But there is another crucial means by which to evaluate the exercise of political power within Matthew's narrative *on its own terms*, namely the simple question of effectiveness. The manifest purpose for exercising political power is to achieve corresponding political goals, whether stated or unstated. Accordingly a crucial signal of Matthew's perspectives on the exercise of political power lies in the narrative depiction of the effectiveness or ineffectiveness of political initiatives to achieve their intended goals.

On this front Matthew exhibits a strong penchant for the ironic, as he paints political caricatures of the Jewish and Roman leaders, portrays the ineffectiveness of their political initiatives, and depicts their frequent failures to achieve the political goals they set out to accomplish. While political power can without question effect crucial results ranging from public influence on or persuasion of the masses (2:3; 27:20) to blatant miscarriage of justice (26:59; 27:15–26) and the resulting execution of the "righteous" or "innocent" (23:35; 27:3–4, 19, 23; cf. 2:16), the narrative rhetoric of Matthew's Gospel clearly and persistently depicts the limits of political power to achieve the ultimate goals of the political operatives in question. A review of the evidence will serve to establish Matthew's ironic and negative perspectives on the exercise of political power by the Jewish and Roman leaders within his narrative.

Lavish Lifestyle.

For Herod the tetrarch (14:1–12) lavish lifestyle appears on the surface to be its own reward. The life of partying, with a group of reclining guests (14:9; cf. 14:6), fine entertainment (14:6), and an extravagant and highly public award ceremony (14:7), is clearly a luxury for the wealthy and powerful to enjoy. But it is this same luxurious lifestyle that reveals Herod as a fundamentally weak character, a man forced into expedient actions (14:9–11) due to fear of his consort Herodias (14:3, 4, 6, 8, 11), her daughter (14:6, 7, 8, 9, 11), and the very guests he has invited to his dinner. And ironically, it is precisely Herod's extravagant oath, the oath of a "powerful" man, which reveals instead his fundamental weakness.

Power of Command.

The story of Herod the king (2:1–23) reveals a comparable truth. Herod wields a power of command that brings people into his presence (2:4, 7), sends them out (2:8, 16), and spells out death and destruction for many innocent victims (2:16). But with all his power of command Herod cannot save himself from being outmaneuvered and overpowered by the "angel of the Lord," who, unbeknownst to Herod, persistently foils his every effort to "seek the child's life" (2:20) in order to "destroy" him (2:13). At every point where the child's life is threatened, the angel of the Lord intervenes through the medium of "dreams" to rescue the child from the threat at hand (2:12, 13, 22; cf. 2:19). And in the end Herod not only proves himself incapable of achieving his key political goal, i.e., to "destroy" the child (cf. 2:19–23); but in a deeply ironic turn of events Herod himself "dies" instead of the child he has been seeking to "destroy" (2:19, 20). Herod's power of command proves useless in furthering his political aims.

Public Relations Initiatives.

The Jewish leaders, who take all their actions in order to "show" others their piety (6:16a) and to be "seen" (6:5a) and "praised" (6:2a) for their "righteous deeds" (6:1: DJW), ultimately find their actions no more effective than those of Herod the king (2:1–23) and Herod the tetrarch (14:1–12). While they clearly receive the momentary public praise and approval that they are seeking ("Truly, I tell you, they have received their reward": 6:2b, 5b, 16b), they do not receive the ultimate approbation of the Jewish crowds. Instead the crowds recognize that Jesus has an "authority" (*exousia*) that the Jewish "scribes" do not have (7:29; 9:8); and they are "astounded" by Jesus' teaching (*ekplēssō*: 7:28; 22:33) and "amazed" by his healing ministry (*thaumazō*: 9:33; 15:31; cf. *phobeomai*: 9:8; *existēmi*: 12:23). Consequently large Jewish crowds "follow" Jesus around the Galilean countryside;[95] and they swarm around Jesus as he enters Jerusalem and heals and teaches in the temple.[96] They "glorify God" on Jesus' account (*doxazō*: 9:8). They acclaim Jesus' deeds as unique in Israel: "Never has anything like this been seen in Israel" (9:33). They hail Jesus as the "Son of David" and "the one who comes in the name of the Lord" (21:9). And they proclaim him as "the prophet Jesus from Nazareth in Galilee (21:11; cf. 21:46). Clearly, in spite of all their best efforts at public relations, the Jewish leadership is totally ineffective for much of Matthew's narrative at winning over the hearts and minds of the Jewish crowds, while their opponent Jesus, to the contrary, is highly popular among the people.

---

95. Thus *akoloutheo*: 4:25; 8:1; 12:15; 14:13; 19:2; 20:29. Cf. 5:1; 8:18; 9:36; 14:14, where Jesus "sees" the crowds who have gathered around him.

96. Thus 21:9, where crowds likewise "go ahead" of Jesus (*proagō*) and "follow" him (*akoloutheō*) on his entry into Jerusalem. See also 21:14–15, 46; 23:1.

Nor do Pilate's efforts at winning over Jewish hearts and minds prove any more effective. Instead the public relations initiative that Pilate instigates in order to win the approval of the Jewish crowds at Passover (27:15) leads only to a noisy debate with the crowds (27:20–23) and the outbreak of a politically dangerous "riot" (27:24). Thus, as both Jewish and Roman leaders discover to their dismay, first-century "photo-ops" prove largely ineffective vis-à-vis the crowds.

Political Expedience.

If the lavish lifestyle of the politically powerful highlights (on the surface at least) the apparent success of their political endeavors, political expedience by contrast points to the undeniable failure of their political efforts. The very concept of "political expedience" implies by definition that the political operatives in question are forced by political exigencies beyond their control to do that which they would otherwise not do. Herod the tetrarch is "grieved" at the request of Herodias' daughter (14:9a), but sees no political alternative to executing John the Baptist (14:9b). The chief priests and the elders of the people, for their part, are clearly seeking to trap Jesus when they accost him with their question about his "authority" (21:23). But instead they themselves are effectively trapped ("We do not know": 21:27) by Jesus' counter question, which they find too politically dangerous to answer in definitive terms one way (21:25) or the other (21:26). In similar fashion the chief priests and the Pharisees find themselves incapable of "arresting" Jesus when he tells a story against them, due to their political fear of the Jewish crowds (21:45–46). And Pilate, for his part, finds himself forced by the political danger of "rioting" crowds (27:24) to execute a prisoner whom he knows to be innocent (27:19a, 23a) and whom he knows has been brought to trial for spurious reasons (27:18).

Whether these political leaders are ultimately effective in staving off the "sudden political death" that they fear is a question that Matthew answers variously or not at all. Herod the tetrarch disappears from the narrative abruptly after 14:1–12, with no further indication of his political success or failure. The Jewish leaders in Jerusalem ultimately succeed in winning over the Jewish crowd to their viewpoint (27:20–23, 25). Pilate, for his part, staves off a political "riot" by a symbolic "handwashing" (27:24–25), only to discover that the "Jesus case" refuses to disappear from his docket (27:62–66). And Pilate, the Roman governor, may ultimately find himself manipulated by his Jewish subjects and "persuaded" (28:14, DJW: read "bribed") into excusing a serious failure on the job by a military guard under his control. As Matthew portrays it, political expedience is clear evidence of political failure both going and (frequently) coming.

Campaign Rhetoric.

As noted above, the Jewish leaders depicted throughout Matthew's narrative find that their public relations initiatives are not effective in winning the hearts and minds of the Jewish people. They likewise make the same discovery with regard to their relentless campaign rhetoric against Jesus. Throughout Matthew's narrative the Jewish leaders trail Jesus doggedly, raising countless questions and objections and denouncing Jesus publicly whenever possible.[97] But no matter how often they speak or how loudly they denounce Jesus, they fail consistently in their efforts to defeat Jesus in public debate. For every challenge or question that they bring forward and for every "trap" that they set, Jesus responds with words that they can neither answer nor refute.[98] And Jesus' word is invariably the last word spoken, with the exception of conspiratorial threats muttered by the Jewish leaders among themselves (cf. 9:14; 21:45-46). Not once does Matthew offer the Jewish leaders the opportunity to get the last word in debate with Jesus. And Jesus' last direct word to them, a scriptural conundrum (22:41-45), is a question that silences them completely (22:46): "No one was able to give him an answer, nor from that day did anyone dare to ask him any more questions." If the Jewish leaders are, as it appears, waging a political campaign against Jesus, this campaign is, until very late in the narrative (27:20), spectacularly ineffective in achieving positive results.

Public Lies and Political Deception.

As Matthew indicates, both Roman imperial powers (2:8 cf. 2:16) and Jewish leaders (28:12-15 cf. 28:11) engage in the dissemination of public lies. And their efforts are likewise depicted as partially or wholly successful. Herod the king succeeds, without apparent difficulty, in persuading the wise men to "set out for Bethlehem" (2:9) on his behest under what the reader surmises to be false premises, Herod's supposed interest in "paying [the child] homage" (2:8). And the Roman guard, in collaboration with the Jewish chief priests and elders, disseminate a false story about the empty tomb of Jesus

---

97. Thus 9:2-8, 10-13; 12:1-8, 9-14, 22-37, 38-45; 15:1-9; 16:1-4; 19:3-9; 21:14-16, 23-27; 22:15-22, 23-33, 34-40; cf. 22:41-46.

98. Cf. the texts listed above in n. 97 to identify the questions posed and the answers given. There is no room to spell out the specifics of this wide ranging debate.

(28:12-15a) which maintains currency within the Jewish community up until Matthew's own day (28:15b). Clearly one can deceive all of the people (i.e., the wise men) some of the time or some of the people (i.e., "the Jews") all of the time.

But even here Matthew points in ironic fashion to the ultimate ineffectiveness of political deception as a strategy for political success. Herod the king, who thinks that he has successfully deceived the wise men into aiding him in his nefarious scheme to "destroy" the child" (2:8 cf. 2:13), has no notion that the "angel of the Lord" is about to undo his secretive efforts and communicate the ugly truth (2:13; cf. 2:12). Herod's efforts at deception are ultimately ineffective due to divine intervention of which Herod knows nothing. In Matthew's perspective God wills the truth to become public; and Herod can do nothing to prevent that from happening.

Matthew works differently, however, with the false message concerning Jesus' empty tomb (28:11-15). Here it is the worldwide proclamation of Jesus' own disciples (28:19-20) that puts the deceptive "story told among the Jews" (28:15b) in cosmic perspective and undercuts the ultimate impact of this blatant attempt at public deception. While the Jewish leaders' fabrication concerning the body of Jesus is still being passed on as truth in Matthew's own day, this false story is reaching "the Jews" alone (28:15b). By contrast the true message of the Risen Jesus is making its way to "all the nations" including the Jews[99] and creating a worldwide fellowship of disciples of Jesus,[100] of whom Matthew's own church is merely one small expression. In the narrative rhetoric of Matthew's Gospel public lies and political deception have no ultimate recourse against the will and the power of God to make known the truth.

Conspiracy to Destroy Political Enemies.

Matthew's narrative leaves no room for doubt concerning the significant power of conspiracies aimed at destroying political enemies. As becomes apparent throughout Matthew's story, such conspiracies can foment enormous evil in the world. Herod, who is conspiring against the one child that he fears (2:13), carries out a brutal massacre in Bethlehem (2:16) that leaves countless mothers bereft of their young children (2:17-18). John the Baptist

---

99. The climactic location of this saying of the Risen Jesus within the Gospel, the cosmic authority of the Risen Jesus, and the inclusively phrased formulation *panta ta ethnē* point to Matthew's intention to make an all-inclusive statement here. Cf. 24:9, 14.

100. Cf. 24:14: "And this good news of the kingdom will be proclaimed throughout the world [*en holē tē oikoumenē*] to all the nations [*pasin tois ethnesin*]."

loses his head due to the successful conspiracy of Herodias, the consort of Herod the tetrarch (14:8). The "tenants" to whom Jesus' allegorical "landowner" has "leased" his "vineyard" succeed in executing the brutal murder (21:39) that they have conspired to carry out (21:38). And the Jewish leaders are likewise successful in procuring the death of Jesus (27:24-26) by means of an entire web of conspiracies (12:14; 21:46; 26:14-16; 27:1-2, 20).

But within Matthew's narrative the political strategy of conspiracy to destroy one's enemies ultimately proves itself no more effective than that of public lies and political deception. Matthew's narrative rhetoric more often than not mocks those who conspire to do evil and depicts the ultimate ineffectiveness of their efforts. Herod the king, who seeks to "destroy" the child (2:13; cf. 2:20) is incapable not only of achieving his own goal (2:21-23) but also of saving his own life (2:19). The Jewish leaders who conspire to "entrap" Jesus in his words (22:15) find themselves totally incapable of defeating Jesus in public debate (cf. 22:46).[101] The "tenants" of Jesus' parable, who conspire to "get the inheritance" of the vineyard by "killing the heir" (21:38-39), discover instead that they themselves are about to face a "miserable death" (21:41a) and lose their stake in the vineyard altogether (21:41b). The Jewish leaders in Jerusalem, for their part, clearly intend their conspiracy against Jesus to be cloaked in secrecy: "And they conspired to arrest Jesus *by stealth* and kill him" (26:4; emphasis mine). But in fact Jesus has long known and spoken of their evil intentions (16:21; 17:22-23; 20:18-19). And the "stealthy" plans that the Jewish leaders lay for arresting Jesus and killing him (26:3-5) are, unbeknownst to the Jewish leaders themselves, no secret at all, since Jesus has just announced them, for the fourth and last time, to his disciples (26:1-2). And the conspiracy of the Jewish leaders to cover up the news of Jesus' resurrection maintains currency "among the Jews" alone (28:15b), while Jesus' disciples carry word of the Risen Jesus to "all nations" (28:19). Conspiracy, in Matthew's estimation, is ultimately a political strategy of dubious effectiveness.

Subversion of Justice.

In Matthew's narrative both Jewish and Roman political leaders clearly engage in subversion of justice, whether by prior conspiracy (26:3-5) or due to political expedience (27:24-26). And there can be no doubt about the effectiveness of the Jewish and Roman powers in achieving such subversion of justice, whether or not this is their stated goal. The Jewish leaders "conspire" against Jesus in advance (26:3-5, 14-16; cf. 27:1-2), arrest him by "stealth"

---

101. See the discussion above concerning campaign rhetoric.

(26:4, 55), seek "false testimony" against him at trial (26:59), and condemn Jesus on a charge of "blasphemy" which they fail to recognize as false (26:65-66). Thus the Jewish leaders clearly succeed in subverting justice as they put Jesus on trial. Pilate, in turn, subverts justice by first handing over his judicial authority to the Jewish crowd (27:15-18) and then responding in politically expedient fashion when he is backed into a corner by the "riot" that breaks out (27:24-26 cf. 27:20-23). In Matthew's view both the Jewish leaders and Pilate are equally effective in subverting the respective judicial systems over which they preside.

At the same time, however, Jesus himself makes it clear in advance that both Jewish and Roman leaders are able to carry out their subversion of justice precisely because their actions, completely unbeknownst to them, fulfill a divine mandate for the life of Jesus in which he "must (dei') go to Jerusalem and undergo great suffering at the hands of the elders and chief priests and scribes, and be killed" (16:21; cf. 17:12, 22-23; 20:18-19; 26:2). Accordingly, when Peter challenges this divine mandate, Jesus charges Peter with failure to "set his mind on divine things" (*ta tou theou*: 16:23). And in Gethsemane Jesus once again confirms this divine mandate as he identifies the reason for his arrest (26:56): "But all this has taken place, so that the scriptures of the prophets may be fulfilled." Thus even when the Jewish and Roman leaders succeed in what they believe to be their own designs to subvert justice and achieve their political goals, Matthew portrays these leaders in ironic fashion as unknowing actors in God's own divinely-initiated plan to "save his people from their sins" (1:21) through the person of Jesus of Nazareth, who is in truth "the Messiah, the Son of God" (26:63; cf. 27:40, 43, 54).

The Politics of Violence.

The ultimate power that the political leaders of Matthew's narrative can wield is the power of violence, reflected in the arrest, mockery, torture, and death of their victims. This power is genuine and fearsome. Herod the king (2:1-23) carries out a brutal massacre of young children in Bethlehem (2:16), leaving the mothers of Bethlehem (and no doubt the fathers as well) in deep grief (2:17-18). Herod the tetrarch (14:1-12) arrests, incarcerates, and finally decapitates John the Baptist (14:1-11), leaving his disciples to bury the body and report the grim news to John's successor, Jesus (14:12). Jesus himself is arrested by his Jewish opponents (26:47-56), tried before Jewish and Roman judiciaries (26:57-66; 27:11-26a), mocked and tortured by Jewish and Roman captors alike (26:67-68; 27:26b-31), and executed by crucifixion on a Roman cross between two common criminals (27:32–38). And Jesus warns his disciples that they too will encounter violent treatment from their own opponents in future (5:10–11; 10:16–23; 23:34, 37; 24:9–14), just as the prophets and righteous people before them have likewise suffered (5:12; 17:9–13; 23:29–31, 35). There can be no question that the Jewish and Roman leaders of Matthew's narrative wield violent power of major proportions.

But the power of violence, as genuine and fearsome as it may be, has distinct limits. And Matthew's ironic caricatures of the Jewish and Roman powerbrokers of his narrative come to their climax as Matthew mocks the violent power that they wield and robs it ironically of its potency. Those who mock and torture Jesus in fact do nothing more than proclaim his true identity loudly through their words (26:67–68; 27:29, 41–43) and visibly through their actions (27:28–30). As they announce publicly in their own mocking words, Jesus is indeed "Messiah" (26:68), "King of the Jews/Israel" (27:29, 42), and "Son of God" (27:43).[102]

And those who employ the power of violence to kill their victims find their power of life and death to be ultimately ineffective. Herod the king, who seeks to "destroy" the child (2:13), loses his own life instead (2:19, 20), while the once-threatened child ends up alive and well in Nazareth (2:23). Herod the tetrarch succeeds in killing John the Baptist (14:3–12) only to discover, as he believes, that his nemesis has now "been raised from the dead" with accordingly mighty "powers . . . at work in him" (14:1–2; cf. 13:58). And for the Jewish leaders, who successfully accomplish their political goal to bring about the death of Jesus (26:3–5; 27:1–2) and who ensure this political victory by setting a "guard" and "sealing the stone" in front of Jesus' tomb (27:66), Matthew spares no irony. Not only does the "angel of the Lord" commandeer the stone guarding the tomb, "rolling it back" and "sitting on it" (28:2). But in a narrative move ironic to the core Matthew informs his readers that those who have been guarding the dead body of Jesus "shake" at the sight of the angel and themselves "become like dead men" (28:4). And the Jewish leaders who have the power to orchestrate Jesus' death are, at the same time, powerless to keep Jesus dead and buried (28:11–15). Those who exercise the deadly power of violence find themselves massively outmaneuvered by divine initiative (28:1–4) and totally impotent vis-à-vis the power and the will of God to bring the dead to life (28:1–10, 16–20).[103] Clearly,

---

102. Cf. 21:38, where the vineyard tenants in their own words proclaim the son of the vineyard owner as the "heir" (*ho klēronomos*) to the vineyard.

103. On the irony of Matthew's resurrection account see Weaver, "Matthew 28:1-10," 398–402.

from Matthew's perspective, the exercise of violence as a political strategy is profoundly limited in its effectiveness.

Failed Leadership.

As the evidence indicates, the deep-rooted irony of Matthew's portrayal of the political leadership exercised by the Jewish and Roman powerbrokers within his narrative lies in a twofold failure on their part. On the one hand these political leaders fail to act with integrity in the execution of their legitimately assigned leadership roles. Roman imperial leaders exercise their power by "lording it over others" and acting as "tyrants" (20:25). And they achieve their political goals more often than not by suppressing justice (27:18, 19, 23, 24-26) and employing deadly violence against innocent people (cf. 2:13-23; 14:1-12; 27:31b-38). Jewish leaders, for their part, show themselves to be "hypocrites," who "do not practice what they teach" (23:3) and who live pious lives not out of concern for "mercy" (9:13; 12:7; 23:23) but rather out of the self-aggrandizing desire for public recognition and praise (23: 5-7). They likewise fail to live out the intermediary role between God and the people to which they have been called as leaders (27:3-4, 41-46). Instead they effectively abandon their charge and leave the people "harassed and helpless, like sheep without a shepherd" (9:36).

But this is not the extent of their failure, as Matthew makes vividly clear through his narrative rhetoric. If the political leaders of Matthew's narrative fail in the execution of their legitimately assigned tasks, they likewise fail, demonstrably and ironically, in the execution of their own nefarious schemes and misguided political initiatives. While they do indeed have the power to effect real evil in the real world (2:16; 14:1-12), their power is ultimately far more limited than they ever imagine (see section two above). The evil that they instigate through their political initiatives is at most penultimate in its impact[104] and in the end completely impotent vis-à-vis the genuine and overwhelming power of God (28:11-15 cf. 28:1-10/16-20). In the end the political leaders of Matthew's narrative, both Jewish and Roman, demonstrate profound and ironic failure in their exercise of political power—both in their sins of *omission* and in their sins of *commission*—even as they exercise the considerable power of their respective offices. And through this ironic portrait of the exercise of political power within the world of his narrative Matthew issues a sharp and unmistakable challenge

---

104. Cf. 10:28, where Jesus challenges his disciples, "Do not fear those who kill the body (*to sōma*) but cannot kill the soul (*tēn psychēn*)."

to the powerbrokers of his own world, and by centuries of extension, to the powerbrokers of our world as well.

III. "IT WILL NOT BE SO AMONG YOU": TOWARD A MATTHEAN MODEL FOR POLITICAL LEADERSHIP

In the above discussion I have sketched out Matthew's wide-ranging critique of the political leadership exercised by the Jewish and Roman powerbrokers within his narrative. To sketch out Matthew's contrasting portrait of positive political leadership would require an equally wide-ranging study of the character of leadership exhibited by Jesus and the characters associated with him (the prophets, John the Baptist, Jesus' disciples). But such a task lies well beyond the scope of the current essay and begs for further attention in a follow-up study. Here I offer merely a few basic pointers toward the thematic of such a study.

1) A primary question for consideration concerns the underlying vision or calling that gives character to the political leadership exercised by Jesus within Matthew's narrative. This question focuses, accordingly, on the central characteristics of the "kingdom of heaven" and the associated character portrait of God, the ruler of this domain. This question also includes attention to the specific "calling" of Jesus as reflected in the Matthean accounts of his baptism, temptations, and transfiguration.

2) A second question for consideration concerns the demonstrated character of Jesus' political leadership patterns within Matthew's narrative. This question includes attention to Jesus' basic leadership strategy of appointing and training disciples, to the overall character of Jesus' healing ministry, and to such central motifs of Jesus' teaching ministry as "love of God and neighbor," "compassion"/ "mercy," "servant leadership," and Jesus' rejection of violence by himself or his followers as an acceptable "modus operandi" within the "kingdom of heaven."

3) A third question for consideration concerns the demonstrated effectiveness and/or impact of Jesus' political leadership patterns as narrated within Matthew's story. This question includes attention to the specific effectiveness/impact of Jesus' "disciple-making" strategy as well as to the ultimate effectiveness/impact of Jesus' overall mission within the Jewish/Gentile community depicted in Matthew's narrative.

"They Did to Him Whatever They Pleased" 121

CONCLUSION: "ALL THE KINGDOMS OF THE WORLD"

As becomes clear from a search of the evidence, the narrative rhetoric of Matthew's Gospel pronounces sharp and uncompromising judgment on the political powerbrokers within Matthew's narrative, both Jewish and Roman. In the face of this potent political critique, what then does it mean for us to read Matthew's Gospel in our own world? And how does Matthew's narrative rhetoric assist us in reflecting on the exercise of political power within our twenty-first-century global village? Here I have neither time nor space to offer more than a biblical handful (seven!) of very basic observations that point toward the discussion that must take place among all those who read Matthew's Gospel as Scripture.

1. Within the "kingdoms of the world" political power is regularly put to use for evil purposes. Matthew's narrative rhetoric confirms for us what we already know from our own twenty-first-century world of experiences.

2. The task of Jesus' followers in response to abuse of power is the urgent and dangerous political task of speaking truth to and about the powerbrokers of the world. What John the Baptist and Jesus show us, among other things, is the courageous witness of those who directly address the abuses of the leadership of their day (14:1-12; 23:1-39).

3. The followers of Jesus will suffer for daring to speak truth to power. People can get killed for such audacity. John the Baptist and Jesus are prime examples of such people (14:1-12; 26:1-27:54).

4. Jesus' followers are called to respond in nonviolent fashion as they encounter suffering. Jesus himself sets the example for them (26:47-56) and calls them in turn to "love [their] enemies" (5:44) and "not to resist" those who are "evil" (5:39).

5. Justice belongs to God. It is the task of God, and not that of the followers of Jesus, to redress the wrongs of history (21:33-46; 22:1-10; 28:1-20).

6. The "kingdoms of the world" have far less power than they (and we!) imagine that they do. Witness the ways identified above in which such powers fail at their own evil tasks.

7. God's resurrection power trumps all human powers. And God's resurrection power always has the last word. The story of Jesus' resurrection (28:1-20) is God's last laugh (Ps 2:4; cf. 2:1-3) at all the pretensions of human power.

I conclude my study with a personal journal reflection on the exercise of political power, a story recounted in the spring of 1996, as I was a Visiting Scholar at Tantur Ecumenical Institute, right up the hill from the Israeli military checkpoint leading to Bethlehem. This story speaks of words from John's Apocalypse. But this story could just as well speak of the words of Matthew's narrative:

> April 7, 1996, Tantur. Saturday evening was the Easter Vigil at St. Anne's Church, just inside the Lion's Gate. And it was well into Easter Sunday morning before we got home and got to bed! But there was not much "rest for the weary." Jennifer had planned an Easter sunrise service to be held on the roof, that amazing vantage point from which we can not only look over to the mountains of Moab in Jordan, just across the Jordan Valley, but also and much more closely, directly down into the Israeli checkpoint on Hebron Road, just below Tantur. This was the place our service needed to be. We needed to claim and proclaim the Resurrection right here on this border location, with the signs of the military occupation both visible and audible just down below. It was a lovely service, very simple and reflective, with scriptures and recorded music and time for reflection. And the sun came up beautifully and passed through a tiny "slit" between the earth and the cloudbank above it. But the most powerful moment of all came at the end of the service. As the last piece of music Jennifer had chosen the Hallelujah Chorus. And there it was, right up above the checkpoint, that most visible sign of present oppression and occupation and military might, *there it was*, this incredible, powerful declaration about "the Lord God Omnipotent who shall reign for ever and ever" and "the kingdom of this world which has [*already*!] become the kingdom of our Lord and of his Christ." I stood at the railing and looked down into the checkpoint and simply exulted in the wonder of it all. What an enormous gift and what a powerful word of courage.

III. Matthew and the Irony of Power

The View from the Bottom Up

6

Rewriting the Messianic Script

Matthew's Account of the Birth of Jesus

THERE CAN BE LITTLE debate about the fact that Matthew's Gospel is a messianic narrative. Not only does he open this narrative with the phrase "the book of the origins of Jesus *Messiah*, the son of David, the son of Abraham" (1:1);[1] but he also brings the genealogy of 1:2–17 to its close and its climax with parallel references to "*Jesus, the one who is called Messiah*" (1:16) and "*the Messiah*" (1:17).

But while Matthew has written a messianic narrative, he has likewise altered the traditional messianic portrait which in popular Jewish perception belongs to such a narrative. This reworking begins in 1:1—2:23 with the account of the birth of Jesus. Here Matthew introduces into his narrative traditional messianic expectations with respect to the personal identity, character, and vocation of the Messiah. As the narrative unfolds, however, it becomes clear that Matthew, in ironic fashion, has introduced these expectations into the narrative only to redefine the messianic terminology on which they are built and rewrite the messianic script to which they give rise.

This study examines Matthew 1:1—2:23 in order to identify the traditional messianic expectations to which Matthew responds and the new messianic script which Matthew writes. In a three-step process which corresponds to the storylines of the three major actors (Joseph, Herod, the magi) the study addresses the questions of messianic identity (1:1–25: the story

---

1. All New Testament citations within this chapter represent my own translations of the texts in question. All Old Testament citations are taken from the New Revised Standard Version.

of Joseph), messianic character (2:1–23: the story of Herod), and messianic vocation (2:1–12: the story of the magi). The study concludes with a brief search for the appearance of this programmatic messianic script throughout the remainder of Matthew's narrative.

Messianic identity: the story of Joseph (1:1–25).

When one searches the text of 1:1–25 for clues to traditional expectations concerning the identity of the Messiah, one thing stands out above all: The Messiah is expected to come from the royal line of David, who himself in turn is a descendant of Abraham, the "father" of the Jewish people.[2] This becomes visible first of all through the language of the text. In 1:1 the narrator identifies Jesus as "the son of David, the son of Abraham." And the genealogy which follows in 1:2–16 begins with Abraham (1:2: "Abraham was the father of . . .") and includes David (1:6: "And Jesse was the father of David the King; and David was the father of . . .") as it moves to its conclusion in "Jesus, the one who is called Messiah" (1:16). The genealogical summary of 1:17 then reiterates this expectation when it first divides Jewish history into three eras, begun by Abraham, David, and the Babylonian deportation respectively, and then brings this history to its climax in the arrival of "the Messiah." And, at a crucial juncture in the narrative which follows, the angel of the Lord pointedly designates Joseph as "son of David" (1:20: "Joseph, son of David, do not be afraid to take Mary as your wife").

A second and closely related clue to the Davidic lineage of the Messiah lies in the form of the genealogy. Over a span of 15 verses (1:2–16) the reader encounters the formula "and _____ was the father of _____" ("*kai _____ egennēsen _____*") 39 times in succession, interrupted only occasionally by additional words or phrases. There can be little question that the signal intent of this formula is to establish a genealogical linkage stretching from the beginning of the list to its conclusion. And thus in this context, because Jesus has already been identified in 1:1 as "the son of David, the son of Abraham," it is apparent that the intended force of the genealogical formula repeated 39 times throughout 1:2–16 is precisely that of demonstrating the genealogical linkage of Jesus to David, and through David back to Abraham.

Accordingly, within 1:1–25 the narrator bears witness, through both the language and the structure of the text, to the traditional expectation that the Messiah will come from the line of David. But no sooner has the narrator

---

2. Cf. 3:9, where John the Baptist makes explicit reference to Abraham's role as "father" of the Jewish people.

established this expectation as fundamental to his messianic portrait than he begins, in ironic fashion, to alter this portrait by rewriting the messianic script and undercutting the very expectations which he has just set up.

This ironic rewriting can be viewed from two angles: (1) what the reader anticipates within the narrative and (2) what the reader actually discovers there. On the one hand, following the announcement (1:1) that Jesus is "the son of David, the son of Abraham" and the 39-fold repetition (1:2–16a) of the phrase "and _____ was the father of _____," the reader anticipates that the genealogy will conclude with the indication "and Joseph was the father of (*egennēsen*) Jesus, the one who is called Messiah." Instead, the reader learns (1:16b) that Joseph is "*the husband of Mary, of whom was born (egennēthē) Jesus, the one who is called Messiah.*" In short, just at the crucial juncture where, after 39 previous connecting links, Jesus himself is finally to be connected to the line of David, the narrator abruptly breaks his formula and, by the same token, destroys Jesus' connection to the Davidic line.

Nor is this in any sense an oversight on the part of the narrator. To the contrary, throughout the remainder of chapter one the narrator pointedly drives home the message that Joseph *is not and, under the announced circumstances, cannot be* the father of Jesus. Mary conceives her child "when [she] was engaged to Joseph, *but before they lived together*" (1:18; emphasis mine). The narrator assures the reader and the angel of the Lord assures Joseph that "that which has been conceived in her *is of the Holy Spirit*" (1:20; cf. 1:18; emphasis mine). The narrator adduces a biblical citation with reference to the "*virgin* [who] will be with child" (1:23; cf. Isa 7:14, LXX; emphasis mine). And, as if to prohibit any possible misinterpretation of his meaning, the narrator adds the intriguing note that Joseph "took [Mary] as his wife, but *had no marital relations with her* until she had borne her son" (1:24b-25a; emphasis mine).

But even more striking than that which the reader *anticipates but does not find* within the narrative, namely the linkage between Jesus and David, is that which the reader *does find but has not anticipated*, namely the significance of women within Jesus' genealogy. Here the narrator not only breaks open an undeniably patrilineal genealogy *in order to insert references to four mothers* (Tamar, 1:3; Rahab, 1:5; Ruth, 1:5; the wife of Uriah, 1:6); but in addition he brings the genealogy to its conclusion and its climax *with reference not to Joseph's fatherhood of Jesus but rather to Mary's motherhood* (1:16: "Joseph, the husband of Mary, of whom was born [*egennēthē*] Jesus"; emphasis mine). It thus appears that it is *the women in general and Mary in specific, rather than the men*, who hold the key to the significance of this genealogy. If this is indeed a patrilineal genealogy, it is so *precisely as interpreted through the presence within it of five women, the last and most crucial of which is Mary, the mother of Jesus.*

What is more, each of these women, Mary prominent among them, has at least the hint of sexual scandal attached to her name or her story.[3] Mary, for her part and as the climax to the list of women, is "found to be with child" before she and Joseph "live together" (1:18).[4] That this circumstance represents a serious scandal in societal terms becomes evident from the narrator's portrayal of the ethical dilemma faced by Joseph, who decides to "divorce [Mary] secretly" because he cannot bring himself to "make an example of her" (1:19). The words which the angel of the Lord speaks to Joseph serve only to confirm the seriousness of this scandal from Joseph's point of view: "Joseph, son of David, *do not be afraid* to take Mary as your wife" (1:20; emphasis mine). Thus if it is indeed the presence of the women which provides the clue to the significance of the genealogy, then that significance surely carries with it the overtones of sexual scandal.

Ultimately, in his own time and fashion, the narrator clears up both of the apparent "difficulties" with respect to Jesus' genealogy. On the one hand, as noted above, the narrator assures the reader that Mary is a "virgin" (1:23), whose child has been conceived "by the Holy Spirit" (1:18, 20), and who "does not have marital relations" with her own husband until after the birth of the child (1:25). On the other hand, Joseph, "son of David," ultimately "names" the child born to Mary (1:25) and in this way "adopts" Jesus into the line of David.[5] But the "damage" has already been done and the messianic script has effectively been rewritten. Jesus Messiah is indeed the Son of David. But he is so not through ordinary and respectable channels, as the biological son of Joseph. Rather Jesus Messiah is born through the extraordinary agency of the Holy Spirit and, from the human perspective, under a cloud of sexual scandal; and he must accordingly be "adopted" by Joseph into the line of David. Such is the identity of "Jesus Messiah, the son of David, the son of Abraham."

---

3. Tamar plays the role of "temple prostitute" (Gen 38:13–15, 21–22) and is very nearly burned to death as a "whore" (Gen 38:24) in order to trick her father-in-law Judah into fulfilling his promise to provide her with a husband. Rahab is a "prostitute" (Josh 2:1; 6:17). Ruth acquires her husband by going to the threshing floor at night, "uncovering his feet," and "lying down" with him (Ruth 3:4, 7, 8), a gesture with apparent sexual overtones and an action that accordingly "must not be known" (Ruth 3:14). The wife of Uriah bears a child to David after he has forcibly impregnated her, sent her husband to his death in battle, then claimed her as his wife (2 Sam 11:1–27).

4. The narrator's indication that Mary has conceived "by the Holy Spirit" (1:18) serves as a message to the reader but not as information available to Joseph, as the subsequent events of the narrative make clear.

5. Thus Brown, *Birth*, 139.

Messianic character: the story of Herod (2:1–23).

If the story of Joseph (1:1–25) serves to redefine the traditional messianic portrait with regard to personal identity, the story of Herod (2:1–23) rewrites the messianic script with regard to character.[6] Through the consistently ironic juxtaposition of "Herod the King" (2:1) and "the one who has been born King of the Jews" (2:2) the narrator reassesses traditional views on the character of the Messiah and redefines the concepts of "power" and "powerlessness."

There can be little question that traditional expectations portray the Messiah as a "powerful" figure. According to the titles applied to him in 2:1–23 the Messiah is the "one who has been born King of the Jews" (2:2), the "leader who will shepherd [God's] people Israel" (2:6), and "[God's] son" (2:15). And within the structure of the narrative the Messiah, the "one who has been born *King of the Jews*" (2:2; emphasis mine), stands in juxtaposition to Herod "*the King*" (2:1, 3, 9; emphasis mine), himself a demonstrably "powerful" figure, as the unfolding of the narrative makes clear. Accordingly, the reader has every reason to anticipate that Jesus Messiah will exhibit characteristics of "power" as the narrative takes shape.

As the narrative proceeds, however, what the reader discovers on the surface of the text stands directly counter to traditional expectations. Beyond the initial references to Jesus' messianic identity[7] the most prominent term used throughout the text to designate Jesus is "the child" (2:8, 9, 11, 13 [twice], 14, 20 [twice], 21). What is more Jesus "the child," far from exhibiting characteristics of "power," in fact does nothing at all within the narrative. To the contrary he is portrayed either as the subject of *passive* verbs or as the effective object of the actions of others, whether positive or negative in nature. Jesus Messiah is "born" of Mary (2:1, 2, 4), announced by a "star" (2:2, 9, 10), "worshipped" (2:2, 11) and "presented with gifts" (2:11) by the magi, "sought" by Herod (2:13, 20), "taken to Egypt" (2:13, 14) and then "taken [back] to Israel" (2:20, 21) by Joseph.[8]

Herod, by contrast, not only carries the "powerful" title of "King" (2:1, 3, 9; cf. 2:22) but also exhibits the characteristics of "power." He orders people into his presence (2:4, 7), questions them as he wishes (2:4–6, 7), and

---

6. For a more exhaustive treatment of the Herod narrative see Weaver, "Power and Powerlessness," 179–96.

7. Thus 2:2: "the one who has been born King of the Jews"; 2:4: "the Messiah"; 2:6: "[the] leader who will shepherd [God's] people Israel."

8. The only "actions" attributed to Jesus Messiah within 2:1–23 lie in the prophecy of 2:6 concerning the "leader" who will "come forth" (*exeleusetai*) out of [Bethlehem]" and "shepherd (*poimanei*) God's people Israel."

sends them out to do his bidding (2:8-9, 16). His moods and his reputation strike fear into the hearts of others (2:3, 22). And, what is most to the point, he has the authority to "seek and destroy" his enemies (2:13, 20) and he ruthlessly wields the power of life and death over them (2:16).

Accordingly, the surface of the text yields a portrait of Jesus Messiah as a "powerless" refugee child, whose life is endangered virtually from the point of his birth and whose parents must flee to a foreign country to protect him from the ravages of his counterpart, the demonstrably "powerful" King Herod. But this surface portrait of "powerlessness" and "power" is not ultimately reliable. Rather, behind the surface structures of the narrative the narrator is working in clearly ironic fashion to subvert the force of the surface portrait which he himself has painted.

On the one hand, the narrator is at work throughout the narrative undermining his own portrait of Herod as a "powerful" figure. The first hint of the narrator's ironic subversion of his own text lies in the account of Herod's "terror" (2:3) when he learns of the birth of "the one who has been born King of the Jews": The "king" who is "terrified" of a "[child] who has [just] been born" can hardly be so "powerful" after all. A further reassessment of Herod's "power" can be seen in the fact that Herod is not only "tricked" by his human counterparts, the magi (2:16), but ultimately thwarted altogether in his purposes by a divine power far greater than himself, namely the angel of the Lord (2:12, 13-15, 19-22). The final word which the narrator delivers on Herod's "power" lies in the threefold mention of Herod's death (2:15, 19, 20). The "powerful" king, whose very moods can terrify others (2:3) and whose commands can utterly destroy them (2:16), is ultimately "powerless" to prevent his own demise.

By contrast, Jesus Messiah the "powerless child" is shown to have power far beyond that which Herod the "powerful king" can claim for himself. In fact the very clues which point to the real "powerlessness" of Herod the King point by the same token to the real power of Jesus the refugee child. Not only does "the one who has been born" (2:2) strike "terror" into the heart of Herod (2:3); but Jesus "the child" (2:8, 9, 11, 13, 14, 20, 21), who does nothing at all throughout the narrative, is nevertheless protected through the powerful agency of the angel of the Lord (2:12; 13-15, 19-22). And it is ultimately Jesus the "powerless child" who arrives in Nazareth alive and well at the end of the narrative (2:22-23), while his "powerful" nemesis Herod the King lies dead (2:15, 19, 20).

And with this redefinition of surface realities the narrator has likewise redefined the messianic script with regard to the character of the Messiah. Not only is apparent "powerlessness" demonstrated to be real power and demonstrable "power" demoted to real powerlessness. But the life of Jesus

Messiah is by the same token definitively shaped by this newly conceived reality, this power which exhibits itself not through violence but rather through vulnerability. And such is the character of Jesus Messiah, the "leader who will shepherd [God's] people Israel."

Messianic vocation: the story of the magi (2:1–12).

There is one final step in the narrator's rewriting of the traditional messianic script as found in 1:1–2:23. Through the storyline of the magi (2:1–12) the narrator refutes traditional understandings of the vocation of the Messiah and in so doing redefines the categories of "outsider" and "insider."

Clues to the traditional script with regard to messianic vocation are not only prominent throughout 1:1–2:23 but also unmistakable in their intent. Jesus Messiah is announced in 1:1 both as the "son" of David, the Jewish king *par excellence* (1:6), and as the "son" of Abraham, the "father" of the Jewish people (cf. 3:9). The genealogy of Jesus Messiah (1:2–17) coincides with the history of the Jewish people, a history which begins with Abraham (1:2, 17), moves past David the King (1:6, 17) and the Babylonian deportation (1:12, 17) on the way to its climax in the arrival of the Messiah (1:16, 17). The birth of Jesus Messiah represents, detail by detail, the fulfilment of Jewish scripture (1:22–23; 2:5–6, 15, 17–18, 23). Jesus Messiah is "the one who has been born King of the Jews" (2:2) and "[the] leader who will shepherd [God's] people Israel" (2:6). And Jesus Messiah receives his name because "he will save his people (*ton laon autou*) from their sins" (1:21). There can be no question that the vocation of Jesus Messiah is to bring "salvation" to "[God's] people Israel," i.e., to the Jews.

But no sooner has the narrator established this traditional viewpoint on messianic vocation than he sets about to rewrite the messianic script which he has just laid out. On the one hand he portrays the Jewish people as astonishingly unaware of the Messiah in their midst and singularly unreceptive to his presence when they learn of it. King Herod and "all Jerusalem with him" are evidently unaware of the birth of the Messiah until alerted to this fact by foreign astrologers newly arrived in town; and when they hear of this event, they are uniformly "terrified" by the news (2:3). For their part, the "chief priests and scribes of the people," those with direct access to the Scriptures which point to the Messiah, consult their sources and pass on their information only after the fact and as the result of an official investigation (2:4–6). And the collective response of the Jewish people to the arrival of their Messiah can, finally, be seen in the deadly character of the "worship" which Herod, the King of Judea, seeks to offer to "the one who has been born King of the Jews" (2:8 cf. 2:13, 16–18, 20).

By contrast it is the magi, "astrologers from the East" (2:1) and outsiders altogether to the faith and the scriptural prophecies of the Jewish people, who follow a star all the way from "the East" to Bethlehem (2:1, 9) and in so doing find the Jewish Messiah which neither the King of Judea nor the Jewish intelligentsia from Jerusalem have succeeded in locating. And, what is of most importance, it is these Gentile magi who offer true "worship" to the Jewish Messiah (2:2, 11), in striking contrast to the deadly threats (2:13, 20) and the bloody murders (2:16–18) with which the Jewish people "welcome" their Messiah.

The messianic portrait painted by this scene can hardly be mistaken. Jesus Messiah is indeed portrayed as the one who brings "salvation" to "[God's] people Israel." But the Jewish people do not receive the Messiah sent to them. Instead, they "seek [his] life" in order to "destroy him". And in their place it is Gentiles "from the East," outsiders in every way, who both recognize the Jewish Messiah and offer him true "worship." And with this it becomes clear that Jesus, the one who has come to "shepherd [God's] people Israel" and to "save [them] from their sins," in fact has a "saving" mission which reaches far beyond the Jewish nation and the borders of Judea. And such is the vocation of Jesus Messiah, "the one who has been born King of the Jews."

Concluding reflections.

As demonstrated above, Matthew's narrator has taken up traditional messianic terminology and applied it to Jesus Messiah. But in so doing he has, in ironic fashion, effectively rewritten the messianic script which gives shape to this terminology. Jesus, "the son of David, the son of Abraham" (1:1), is born under a cloud of sexual scandal and must be "adopted" into the line of David. Jesus, "[the] leader who will shepherd [God's] people Israel" (2:6), exhibits a power which is characterized not by violence but rather by vulnerability. Jesus, "the one who has been born King of the Jews" (2:2), has saving significance which reaches far beyond Judea and "God's people Israel" to distant countries and to Gentile peoples. The reader of Matthew's Gospel has every reason to anticipate further evidence of this fundamentally altered messianic portrait as the narrative proceeds.

And Matthew's reader will not be disappointed. With regard to Jesus' messianic identity, character, and vocation Matthew's ongoing narrative paints a vivid portrait of a "Messiah with a difference."

On the level of identity Jesus' messianic status is widely acknowledged. The "voice from heaven" announces Jesus twice as "my beloved Son" (3:17; 17:5), while Satan (4:3, 6) and demonic spirits (8:29) likewise acknowledge this identity. Many people pronounce Jesus "Son of David": individuals who call on him for healing (9:27; 15:22; 20:30–31); amazed and enthusiastic crowds (12:23; 21:9); uninhibited children (21:15). From his vantage point in Herod's prison John the Baptist hears of "the deeds of the Messiah" (11:2); and he sends his disciples to inquire whether Jesus is "the one to come" (11:3). In rare moments of divine insight Jesus' disciples proclaim "Truly you are the Son of God" (14:33) and Simon Peter acknowledges Jesus as "the Messiah, the Son of the Living God" (16:16). And as Jesus rides triumphantly into Jerusalem to the accolades of the crowds, Matthew reminds his readers that Jesus here fulfils that which was spoken through the prophet, "Look, your king is coming to you!" (21:5b). From Matthew's perspective Jesus' messianic identity is indisputable.

But Jesus' messiahship is hardly one which corresponds with normal human expectations. While Jesus himself appears to claim this messianic identity implicitly with the Jewish authorities (21:37, 38; 22:2, 42–45) and explicitly with his own disciples (23:8, 10; cf. 24:5, 23; 25:34, 40), he strictly forbids his disciples from publicizing this fact among the crowds (16:20). Instead he warns them repeatedly that this messianic identity will lead him to suffering and death (16:21; 17:22–23; 20:18–19; 26:2), a scenario which they seek desperately to refute (16:22–23). But just as he has predicted, Jesus' messianic identity finds clear confirmation and public disclosure only as Jesus himself stands trial for his life before Jewish and Roman courts (26:63; 27:11, 17, 22), encounters the taunts of brutal captors (26:68; 27:29), and hangs dying on a Roman cross (27:37, 40, 42, 43). Accordingly, it is the centurion who witnesses Jesus' death into whose mouth Matthew places the ultimate public confession, "Truly this man was the Son of God!" (27:54). As Matthew sees it, Jesus, the suffering Messiah, has an identity which neither his friends nor his enemies are prepared to recognize.

On the level of messianic character, Matthew's portrait of Jesus is no less striking. Throughout the narrative Jesus' ministry is depicted on all sides as a ministry of "powerful deeds" [*dynameis*], as the words of Matthew (11:20; 13:58), Jesus (11:21, 23), the people of Nazareth (13:54), and Herod the tetrarch (14:2) bear witness. In addition Jesus is the one who "has power" (*dynamai*) to cleanse lepers (8:2); to give sight to blind men (9:28); to "bind the strong man" [i.e., Satan], "enter his house," and "plunder his belongings" (12:29); and to appeal to God his Father for the military support of angelic legions (26:53).

But in the crucial hours before his death, just when Jesus seems to have most urgent need of all the "power" and all the "powers" which have characterized his ministry thus far (cf. 26:53), Matthew instead paints a portrait of a Jesus who appears virtually "powerless." While the others around him seize the initiative in every possible way, Jesus does little and says even less.[9] From the moment of his arrest (26:57) until the moment of his death (27:50) Matthew attributes only four actions to Jesus: he "stands before the governor" (27:11); he "tastes [the wine offered to him]" (27:34) but "will not drink it" (27:34); and he "gives up his spirit" (27:50). Other than this Jesus does nothing at all, while the actions of others bombard him in an unrelenting and escalating sequence of violence. On the verbal level Jesus responds once to Caiaphas the high priest (26:64) and once to Pilate the governor (27:11). But even in the face of intense questioning (26:63; 27:14) and false accusations (27:12) Jesus says nothing more. Only as he hangs dying on the cross does Jesus break his self-enforced silence and cry out to God in his agony (27:46, 50).

And it is this silent and inactive Jesus at whom the Jewish authorities hurl the cruelest barb of all: "He saved others; he does not have the power [*ou dynatai*] to save himself!" (27:42a; cf. 27:42b-43). Appearances may be on their side. But their conclusions are wrong. They do not know of the angelic legions which Jesus could summon (26:53). They do not know that their taunts are merely the last in a lengthy list of messianic temptations to which Jesus has been subjected since the outset of his ministry (4:3, 5-6, 8-9; 16:22; 26:51; 27:39-40). They do not know that this is a Messiah whose true power is visible in vulnerability rather than in violence (cf. 2:13-23). Above all they do not know that God is at this very moment poised to vindicate Jesus Messiah and his messianic mission of suffering and death through an act of divine power which robs human power of its "potency" (28:11-15) and transforms death itself into life (27:51-54; 28:1-10). "Jesus the nonviolent Messiah" is no more recognizable to those around him than is "Jesus the suffering Messiah."

But it is on the level of messianic vocation where Matthew takes the most radical step of all in transforming the script for Jesus Messiah. On the one hand Matthew takes great pains throughout his narrative to reinforce the vocation of Jesus as Jewish Messiah, the one whose mission is "to save *his people* [i.e., the *Jewish* people] from their sins" (1:21; emphasis mine)

---

9. For a more exhaustive treatment of this portrait of Jesus and the others around him, see Weaver, *Missionary Discourse*, 144–46. See also Weaver, "Power and Powerlessness," 192–93.

and "to shepherd [God's] people *Israel*" (2:6; emphasis mine). Jesus is persistently identified with Jewish messianic titles: "Son of David,"[10] "Christ,"[11] "the one to come" (11:3), "king of the Jews,"[12] "king of Israel" (27:42), and "Son of God."[13] And Jesus knows himself as one "sent only to the lost sheep of the house of Israel" (15:24; cf. 10:6). As Matthew portrays it, Jesus' ministry is above all the ministry of the Jewish Messiah to his Jewish people.

But even as Jesus himself claims this apparently exclusive ministry to the Jews for himself (15:24, 26) and for his disciples (10:5-6), Matthew alerts his readers to the wider significance of Jesus' messianic mission. As Matthew observes, Jesus relocates himself to "Galilee *of the Gentiles*" (4:15; cf. Isa 8:23, LXX; emphasis mine) precisely in order to begin a ministry in which he will "proclaim justice to *the Gentiles*" (12:18; cf. Isa 42:1, LXX, emphasis mine) and in which these same "*Gentiles*" will "hope in his name" (12:21; cf. Isa 42:4, LXX; emphasis mine). Accordingly, in spite of his own calling to "the lost sheep of the house of Israel" Jesus finds himself compelled to reach out in "compassion" (15:32) and "amazement" (8:10) to the Gentiles beyond the "house of Israel"[14] to commend them for their "faith" (8:10-13; 15:28), to heal their illnesses (8:13; 15:28, 30), and to feed the hungry among them (15:32-39). In the face of such Gentile faith Jesus predicts that "many will come from east and west and recline with Abraham, Isaac, and Jacob in the kingdom of heaven" (8:11). And Jesus points his disciples to a time down the road when they themselves will proclaim the good news of the Kingdom "as a witness to all the nations" (24:14; cf. 10:18) as their final act of ministry before the "end of the age" (24:3; cf. 24:14) and the "coming of the Son of Man" (cf. 24:3, 30). Ultimately it is the Risen Jesus himself who opens the doors of the kingdom of heaven to all comers, Jewish and Gentile alike, as he sends out the eleven to "make disciples of all the nations" (28:19).[15] Clearly the "salvation" which Jesus Messiah has come to

10. Thus 9:27; 12:23; 15:22; 20:30, 31; 21:9, 15; 22:42, 43, 45; cf. 12:3.
11. Thus 11:2; 16:16, 20; 22:42; 23:8, 10; 26:63, 68; 27:17, 22.
12. Thus 27:11, 29, 37; cf. 21:5.
13. Thus 4:3, 6; 8:29; 14:33; 26:63; 27:40, 54; cf. 3:17; 16:16; 17:5; 21:37, 38; 22:2.
14. Thus a Roman centurion (8:5-13), a Canaanite woman and her daughter (15:21-28) and an apparently Gentile crowd (15:29-31, 32-39). The people of 15:29-39 address their praises to "the God of Israel" (15:31), a phrase that appears to identify them as Gentile "outsiders" rather than members of the Jewish community itself.
15. On this point, see Weaver, *Missionary Discourse*, 220n8. That Matthew intends for *panta ta ethnē* ("all the nations") to be inclusive of Israel as well is confirmed not only by "the all-inclusive character of the commission" itself (ibid.), but likewise by Jesus' pronouncement to the Jewish religious authorities shortly before his death, a statement that points unambiguously to the future mission work of Jesus' disciples: "Look! I am sending you prophets and wise people and scribes. Some of them you will

bring "his people" (1:21) is intended for all humankind and not merely for "the children of the kingdom" (8:12).

And with this universally inclusive word of commissioning Matthew completes his messianic narrative, the story of Jesus Messiah (1:1), and, by the same token, his radical and relentless rewriting of the messianic script which lies behind it. Jesus Messiah, as Matthew portrays him, is one whose messianic identity, character, and vocation stand as a profound challenge to all traditional notions of kingship, power, and social status. Let the reader understand.

---

kill and crucify; and some of them you will flog in your synagogues and persecute from town to town" (23:34; cf.10:17, 21, 23, 38).

7

Transforming Nonresistance

From *Lex Talionis* to "Do Not Resist the Evil One"

INTRODUCTION

STREWN ACROSS THE LANDSCAPE of the New Testament Gospels are numerous sayings which have over time gained notoriety as "the hard sayings of Jesus." These are the sayings which not only create controversy for the exegetes but also provide embarrassment for the expositors. They are the words which—if truth be told—we might wish that Jesus had never spoken[1] or that the Gospel writers had never preserved.

A prime case in point is the saying found in Matthew 5:38–42.[2] There can be little question that, word for word and phrase for phrase, this text has stirred up as much controversy and embarrassment as any of the so-called "hard sayings of Jesus":

> 5:38 You have heard that it was said,
>
> > Eye in place of eye [*opthalmon anti opthalmou*]
> >
> > and tooth in place of tooth [*kai odonta anti odontos*].

---

1. Here I refer to the claims of the Gospel writers concerning what Jesus said. I make no claims of my own concerning the *ipsissima vox* of Jesus; nor will the following essay engage in the search for that *ipsissima vox*. Rather, this study will focus its attention on the canonical form of Matthew 5:38–42 and the significance of this canonical text within its Matthean context.

2. See Matt 5:38–48//Luke 6:27–36.

5:39 But I say to you,

    Do not resist [*mē antistēnai*] the one who is evil [*tō ponērō*].

        But if someone strikes you on the right cheek, turn to them the other cheek as well.

5:40   And if someone wishes to sue you and take your tunic, let them take your cloak as well.

5:41   And if someone compels you to go one mile, go with them for two.

5:42   Give to the one who asks of you; and do not reject the one who wishes to borrow from you.[3]

Matthew 5:39a alone presents a whole spectrum of difficulties to the exegetes. The questions raised by this text range from the most specific exegetical issues to the most fundamental hermeneutical concerns. And at virtually no point is there consensus on how to resolve the difficulties or answer the questions.

The difficulties begin with the translation of the text. The command of 5:39a, *mē antistēnai tō ponērō*, contains only two key words, *antistēnai* and *ponērō*. The contextual force of both of these words is disputed.

The command *mē antistēnai* has traditionally been understood as a general call "not to resist [evil]."[4] As J. C. Fenton puts it, "The Law allowed a person who had been wronged to take an equivalent from the person who had wronged him. Jesus will not allow retaliation of this kind: evil actions are not to be resisted."[5] A variation on this interpretation views *mē antistēnai* as the call not to engage in *stasis*, namely, "violent rebellion," "armed revolt," or "sharp dissension" (cf. Mark 15:7; Luke 23:19, 25; Acts 19:40).[6] An alternative assessment of Matthew 5:39a, however, views this command as the

---

3. All biblical citations are my own translations either from the LXX or from the Greek New Testament.

4. Cf. Banks, *Jesus and the Law*, 196. On this interpretation of *antistēnai*, see Friedlander, *Jewish Sources*, 66; Allen, *Gospel*, 54; Klostermann, *Matthäus-Evangelium*, 48; Lagrange, *Évangile*, 112; Schniewind, *Evangelium*, 67; Clavier, "Matthieu 5:39," 44; Filson, *Gospel*, 89; Stendahl, "Hate, Non-Retaliation, and Love," 355; Fenton, *Saint Matthew*, 92; Gaechter, *Matthäus Evangelium*, 189; Albright and Mann, *Matthew*, 68; Banks, *Jesus and the Law*, 197-98; Piper, "'Love Your Enemies,'" 53; Strecker, *Sermon*, 82; Luz, *Matthew 1–7*, 329.

5. Fenton, *Saint Matthew*, 92. In a similar vein, see Strecker, *Sermon*, 83.

6. Thus Wink, *Violence and Nonviolence*, 13.

specific charge "not to testify against an evildoer in a court of law."⁷ In Stuart Currie's words,

> Matthew wants it understood that Jesus quoted Deut 19:21: "You have heard it was said, 'An eye for an eye and a tooth for a tooth,'" and then went on to add, "But I tell you, 'Do not protest against the wrongdoer. Don't file a complaint; don't make a court case of it, don't seek damages.'"⁸

The substantive *tō ponērō* fares little better than the verbal form *mē antistēnai*. Here the translation hinges on interpretation of the grammatically ambiguous dative singular form of *tō ponērō*. If *mē antistēnai* is interpreted in juridical terms ("Do not testify against . . . in a court of law"), then *tō ponērō* is most naturally construed as a masculine form and thus in personal terms ("the one who is evil").⁹ But those who interpret *mē antistēnai* in the more general sense of "do not resist" diverge in their understandings of the "evil" not to be resisted. *Tō ponērō* is alternately construed as a masculine form with a human referent ("the one who is evil"),¹⁰ as a masculine form with reference to Satan ("the Evil One"),¹¹ as a neuter form ("that which is evil"),¹² and as a fundamentally ambiguous term carrying both personal and impersonal force.¹³

---

7. Currie ("Matthew 5:39a," 140–45) is a major proponent of this interpretation. See also Schlatter, *Evangelist Matthäus*, 186; Grundmann, *Evangelium*, 171; Hill, *Gospel*, 127; Schweizer, *Good News*, 129; Guelich, *Sermon*, 219–20; Gundry, *Literary and Theological Art*, 94; Horsley, "Ethics and Exegesis," 14; Davies and Allison, *Matthew I–VIII*, 543.

8. Currie, "Matthew 5:39a," 145.

9. Thus Hill, *Gospel*, 127; Guelich, *Sermon*, 219–20.

10. Thus Klostermann, *Matthäus-Evangelium*, 48; Schniewind, *Evangelium*, 67–68; Filson, *Gospel*, 82; Stendahl, "Hate, Non-Retaliation and Love," 355; Albright and Mann, *Matthew*, 68; Strecker, *Sermon*, 82.

11. Thus Banks (*Jesus and the Law*, 197–98), who determines that *"ponēros*, as in 5.37; 6.13; 13.19, 38, must refer to Satan." Cf. Friedlander (*Jewish Sources*, 66–67), who translates *ponēros* as "the Evil One, i.e., the world." But while this interpretation reaches back to Origen and Chrysostom (Davies and Allison, *Matthew I–VIII*, 543), it is widely disavowed in more recent scholarship. See the comments of Kostermann, ibid.; Lagrange, *Évangile*, 112; Schniewind, *Evangelium*, 68; Gaechter, *Matthäus Evangelium*, 189; Strecker, *Sermon*, 82–83.

12. Thus Lagrange, *Évangile*; Gaechter, *Matthäus Evangelium*; Luz, *Matthew 1–7*, 329.

13. Thus Allen, *Gospel*, 54: "We need not ask as to the gender of *tō ponērō*. Just as in v. 37 it meant the evil and sinful element in life regarded from the abstract point of view, so here it is the same element contemplated as in action through an individual." See also Clavier, "Matthieu 5:39," 50–52; Fenton, *Saint Matthew*, 91. Cf. Piper (*"Love Your Enemies,"* 52–53), who translates the phrase as "Do not resist evil" but cites Jas

A second question with regard to Matthew 5:39a and the related sayings concerns the social context of these words of Jesus and the subsequent social settings within which they were handed down in the early church. Gerd Theissen cites first-century Jewish precedents for the effective use of nonviolent tactics as a means of social protest against the Romans.[14] He concludes from this evidence that Jesus formulated his sayings on nonviolence and love of the enemy in a setting in which such concepts would not have been rejected out of hand by those to whom Jesus spoke.[15]

Richard A. Horsley, however, rejects that notion. As he views it, "the focus of 'love your enemies' and the related sayings . . . is not on the Romans or even on domestic political enemies."[16] Instead, these words "depict circumstances of severe economic hardship among those addressed,"[17] circumstances in which "people are at each other's throats, hating, cursing, and abusing."[18] As a result, "these sayings of Jesus . . . call people in local village communities to take economic responsibility for each other in their desperate circumstances."[19]

The differences are not resolved when one moves from the level of oral tradition (the words of Jesus) to the level of sayings source (Q). Theissen attributes the transmission of the sayings in question to "wandering charismatics," Christian prophets who were often driven from town to town by the persecution which they encountered and for whom Jesus' words about nonviolence and love of the enemy would have had immediate relevance.[20] Here as well Horsley objects, maintaining that for Q, "the context indicated by the content of the individual sayings is that of social-economic relations in a village or town."[21]

5:6 ("the righteous person does not resist [the rich person]") as "an essential parallel" to Matt 5:39a.

14. Theissen, "Gewaltverzicht und Feindesliebe," 192–94. The first of these incidents took place in 26/27 CE under Pontius Pilate, the second in 39 CE under Gaius Caligula.

15. Ibid., 192–96. Theissen makes clear, however, that this in no way establishes a direct causal link between specific events in first-century Palestine and the words of Jesus. Cf. the comments of Wink (*Violence and Nonviolence*, 14), who in similar fashion locates the words of Jesus within the context of Roman oppression of the Jews.

16. Horsley, "Ethics and Exegesis," 23. Horsley in fact denies the existence of any established group of "Zealots" prior to 67–68 CE, at the time of the Jewish Revolt (ibid., 10).

17. Ibid., 21–22.

18. Ibid., 22.

19. Ibid.

20. Theissen, "Gewaltverzicht und Feindesliebe," 178–80.

21. Horsley, "Ethics and Exegesis," 20.

Nor is there consensus on the social setting of the Matthean text. Theissen assesses the Matthean context as that of the Jewish Revolt and the succeeding post-war era, a time in which Jesus' words about love of enemy would have contrasted noticeably with prevailing Jewish sentiment concerning the Romans.[22] Here Horsley acknowledges that "Matthew evidently reinterpreted the thematic saying he found in Q, 'love your enemies,' to refer to persecutors of Jesus' followers."[23] But he once again concludes that "most of the other sayings . . . refer to the internal relations of the local community."[24]

A third question, integrally linked to that of social context, relates to the focus of the sayings in question. Here viewpoints span the spectrum. On the one end Martin Hengel, citing Luke 6:27–36//Matthew 5:38–48 as his evidence, finds there both "the conscious rejection of violence" and "the heart of the proclamation of Jesus."[25] Hengel's view concerning the focus of these texts attracts wide scholarly support.[26] On the other end of the spectrum, however, Horsley draws the opposite conclusion from his study of the same texts:

> Perhaps Jesus advocated non-violence. Yet there is little or no evidence that he ever directly or explicitly addressed this issue of violence vs. non-violence. Surely non-violence was not the primary focus or purpose of his praxis and preaching . . . Since the sayings grouped with "love your enemies" do not refer to foreign or political enemies and do not focus on the question of violence, the lesser components of the usual picture of Jesus as advocate of non-violence will not hold together.[27]

But beyond the questions concerning the translation, social context, and focus of Matthew 5:38–42 lies an even more difficult question, one which concerns the ethical force of the text and the scope of its applicability. It is this question above all others which haunts the exegetes, embarrasses

---

22. Theissen, "Gewaltverzicht und Feindesliebe," 178–80.

23. Horsley, "Ethics and Exegesis," 20. He does not, however, specify who these "persecutors" might be.

24. Ibid.

25. Hengel, *Revolutionist*, 26–27.

26. See, for example, Friedlander, *Jewish Sources*, 66; Clavier, "Matthieu 5:39," 44; Lührmann, "Liebet eure Feinde," 412–38; Schottroff, "Non-Violence," 9–39; Strobel, "Macht und Gewalt," 71–112; Theissen, "Gewaltverzicht und Feindesliebe," 160; Lienemann, *Gewalt und Gewaltlosigkeit*; Lohfink, "Ekklesiale Sitz," 236–53.

27. Horsley, "Ethics and Exegesis," 24. It must be noted, however, that Horsley is able to arrive at these conclusions only by excluding Matthew 5:38–39a ("Matthew's redactional framing") from consideration (ibid., 13–14).

the expositors, and classifies Matthew 5:38-42 among "the hard sayings of Jesus."

Viewpoints on this issue divide into two major camps. A large majority of scholars view the sayings of Matthew 5:38-42 as words of Jesus addressed to individual disciples. As such, these words are applicable strictly on the personal level, between individuals, a sphere either explicitly or implicitly distinguished from that of social structures and state institutions.[28] The comments of Davies and Allison exemplify this approach:

> While in the Pentateuch the *lex talionis* belongs to the judiciary process, this is not the sphere of application in Matthew. Jesus ... does not overthrow the principle of equivalent compensation on an institutional level — that question is just not addressed — but declares it illegitimate for his followers to apply it to their private disputes.[29]

Other scholars, by contrast, view the words of Jesus as addressed not solely, nor even most importantly, to individual disciples but rather to the church itself as the community of disciples.[30] And viewed in this light, the words of Jesus are seen to have "political" implications which move well beyond the "private sphere." As Schottroff puts it,

> Non-resistance must be applied concretely in the area of politics. In this way Matt. 5:39-41 par. would have been understood in two different ways, the one within the community and the other toward outsiders. Within the community it would mean refusing to plan an insurrection or to put up a show of violent resistance. Toward those outside it would mean assuring everyone of peaceable intentions, making a political apology: We Christians are not revolutionaries.[31]

---

28. Thus Friedlander, *Jewish Sources*, xxiii; Allen, *Gospel*, 54; Klostermann, *Matthäus-Evangelium*, 48; Lagrange, *Évangile*, 112; Cunliffe-Jones, *Deuteronomy*, 118-19; Schniewind, *Evangelium*, 67; Filson, *Gospel*, 90; Fenton, *Saint Matthew*, 92; Gaechter, *Matthäus Evangelium*, 190; Grundmann, *Evangelium*, 172; Albright and Mann, *Matthew*, 68-69; Hengel, *Revolutionist*, 27; Hill, *Gospel*, 127-28; Thompson, *Deuteronomy*, 218; Craigie, *Deuteronomy*, 270n21; Gundry, *Literary and Theological Art*, 94; Davies and Allison, *Matthew I-VIII*, 542.

29. Davies and Allison, *Matthew I-VIII*, 542.

30. Thus Schweizer, *Good News*, 204-9; Schottroff, "Non-Violence," 26-27; Strobel, "Macht und Gewalt," 98; Lohfink, " Ekklesiale Sitz," 248-250; Strecker, *Sermon*, 82-83; Luz, *Matthew 1-7*, 330-31.

31. Schottroff, "Non-Violence," 26. Cf. the distinctly less eirenic tone of Lienemann (*Gewalt und Gewaltlosigkeit*) who points out (62) "dass der hier geforderte 'Weg der Friedfertigkeit' eine implizite Absage an die politische Theologie der zelotischen Bewegung darstellt, aber unverkennbar ist auch, dass Jesu Tod wie seine Verkündigung

Without any question, however, the most fundamental controversy surrounding Matthew 5:38-42 concerns the relationship between these words of Jesus and the Jewish law to which they respond, the *lex talionis* (Exod 21:22-25; Lev 24:19-20; Deut 19:15-21). Here, as elsewhere, viewpoints span the spectrum.

Piper represents one end of the discussion. In his words,

> Jesus' command not to resist evil (Mt 5:39-42) demands the opposite of the Old Testament legal principles, 'an eye for an eye and a tooth for a tooth'. . . . If and when Jesus' word is binding, then the other is not . . . The antithesis between this Old Testament legal principle and Jesus' command is real. Taken absolutely they exclude each other; they are contradictory. Jesus was in some sense abolishing the *lex talionis*.[32]

On the other end of the discussion Horsley rejects this "antithetical" approach. In its place he proposes an approach based on the concept of "fulfillment":

> These sayings do not constitute new Law in the broad sense, certainly not to the point of abolishing the old, Mosaic Law . . . Like many other assumptions and conclusions about these sayings, this misconception is rooted in the acceptance of the Matthean framing of the material into "antitheses." Since the early redaction criticism on Matthew and the Sermon on the Mount, it has been clear that Matthew implies no abolition of the old Law in favor of the new. Jesus has come to fulfill the Law, to restore the proper functioning of the Law to the true righteousness originally intended by God in giving the Torah.[33]

'Analogien zur Botschaft der Zeloten' enthalten, denn der von Jesus gebotene Gewaltverzicht fördert nicht Quietismus, sondern eine Aktivität, deren Stärke gerade durch ihre Gewaltlosigkeit gesteigert und damit durchaus als bedrohlich wahrgenommen werden muss. Die verkündete Nähe des Reiches Gottes ist ihrer Gestalt nach gewaltlos; ihrer Wirkung nach ist sie politisch brisant."

32. Piper, *"Love Your Enemies,"* 89. See also Piper's further discussion, ibid., 89-91. Cf. Theissen, "Gewaltverzicht und Feindesliebe," 164-65; Guelich, *Sermon*, 224; Lienemann, *Gewalt und Gewaltlosigkeit*, 61; Luz, *Matthew 1-7*, 278-79, 330. But note the significant difference in the approach of Davies and Allison (*Matthew I-VIII*, 540): "What Jesus rejects is vengeance executed on a personal level. He still assumes that God, the only wise and capable judge, will, in the end, inflict fitting punishment on sinners . . . So the law of reciprocity is not utterly repudiated but only taken out of human hands to be placed in divine hands."

33. Horsley, "Ethics and Exegesis," 15. Cf. Hill, *Gospel*, 127-28.

As the evidence indicates, Matthew 5:38-42 has over time been the object of intense scrutiny. Study of this text has led to significant controversy and virtually no consensus. The passage has clearly earned its reputation as one of "the hard sayings of Jesus." Nor is that reputation likely to be dislodged in future. Yet it is precisely for this reason that Matthew 5:38-42 continues to lure scholars back for yet one more examination of an elusive text. Such is the nature of the task at hand.

I. MATTHEW 5:38-42 IN CANONICAL CONTEXT: THE *LEX TALIONIS*

If Matthew 5:38-42 has aroused controversy on almost all fronts, there are nevertheless two points on which scholarship is unanimous: (1) Matthew 5:38 presents a citation, in the words of Jesus,[34] of the *lex talionis*, the "law of retaliation," as found in the Jewish scriptures (Exod 21:22-25; Lev 24:19-20; Deut 19:15-21);[35] and (2) Matthew 5:39-42 presents Jesus' words in response to that "law of retaliation." It is these two points of consensus which create the point of departure for the following study and provide its basic structure. If Matthew 5:38-42 is a response to the Jewish *lex talionis*, then analysis of this "law of retaliation" is prerequisite to analysis of the Matthean text.

The first matter for consideration, then, is the Jewish *lex talionis*. This law was neither unique to the Jewish people nor original with them.[36] The origins of the *lex talionis* reach far back—to "extreme antiquity"[37]—within Ancient Near Eastern society, apparently to legal formulations governing the inter-tribal relationships of nomadic peoples.[38] Widespread literary evidence—from the Code of Hammurabi and the Middle Assyrian Laws to

---

34. Here I make reference to "the words of Jesus" as represented by the Matthean text. See n. 1 above.

35. Thus Friedlander, *Jewish Sources*, 65; Allen, *Gospel*, 54; Klostermann, *Matthäus-Evangelium*, 48; Lagrange, *Évangile*, 111; Schniewind, *Evangelium*, 68; Schlatter, *Evangelist Matthäus*, 185; Filson, *Gospel*, 89; Fenton, *Saint Matthew*, 92; Gaechter, *Matthäus Evangelium*, 189; Grundmann, *Evangelium*, 170; Albright and Mann, *Matthew*, 68; Hill, *Gospel*, 127; Banks, *Jesus and the Law*, 196; Schweizer, *Good News*, 129; Piper, "Love Your Enemies," 51; Guelich, *Sermon*, 219; Gundry, *Literary and Theological Art*, 94; Davies and Allison, *Matthew I-VIII*, 540; Strecker, *Sermon*, 82; Luz, *Matthew 1-7*, 323.

36. Cf. the discussion of Anthony Phillips (*Criminal Law*, 96-97), who notes that the law cannot be Jewish in origin since there is no evidence of the practice of physical mutilation within Jewish society.

37. Noth, *Exodus*, 182.

38. Thus Boecker, *Law*, 174. Cf. Mayes, *Deuteronomy*, 291.

Greek, Roman, and Jewish formulations, both scriptural and rabbinic[39]—points to the virtual universality of such a "law of retaliation" in the ancient world.

The force of this law in its original formulation was unambiguous: The person who has injured another shall receive back in punishment the same injury which he or she has inflicted upon the victim.[40] The *lex talionis*, however, was not license for personal acts of vengeance against the evildoer. Instead, this law was invoked and carried out by the court of law as an act of public justice.[41] Accordingly, the intent of the law was to prohibit personal acts of vengeance by relegating justice to the courts and strictly delimiting the punishment to be meted out.[42]

It was this ancient and universal law which found its way into the Jewish scriptures and stands as the backdrop for the words of Jesus in Matthew 5:38-42. But before comparisons can be drawn between the Jewish *lex talionis* and the Matthean text, there is a prior question to be resolved. Since there are three versions of the *lex talionis* within the Jewish scriptures (Exod 21:22-25; Lev 24:19-20; Deut 19:15-21), it will be essential to establish which one of these formulations lies most directly behind the Matthean text.

A comparison of Matthew 5:38-39a and the three LXX versions of the *lex talionis* indicates that Deuteronomy 19:15-21 has the strongest verbal and contextual links to Matthew 5:38-39a. All three LXX passages mirror the Matthean text word for word in the language of the talionic formula, "eye in place of eye, tooth in place of tooth" (*ophthalmon anti ophthalmou, odonta anti odontos*).[43] But only in the Deuteronomic text does the verbal linkage move beyond the talionic formula to the description of the situation calling forth such punishment. In Deuteronomy, as in Matthew, the

---

39. See, for example, Strack and Billerbeck, *Evangelium*, 337-41; Daube, *New Testament*, 255-56; Mayes, *Deuteronomy*, 291; Strecker, *Sermon*, 82.

40. Cf. Noth, *Exodus*, 182. The extent to which this law was practiced in literal fashion within Ancient Near East society remains open to question. See, for example, ibid.; Rad, *Deuteronomy*, 129; Phillips, *Deuteronomy*, 132-33; Craigie, *Deuteronomy*, 270; Patrick, *Law*, 76-77.

41. Thus Friedlander, *Jewish Sources*, 65-66; Boecker, *Law*, 175.

42. Cf. Kline, *Treaty*, 104; Gundry, *Literary and Theological Art*, 94; Payne, *Deuteronomy*, 116-17.

43. Here it is evident, syntactically speaking, that the entire phrase *ophthalmon anti ophthalmou kai odonta anti odontos*, as it appears in Lev 24:20, Deut 19:21, and Matt 5:38, has been extracted verbatim from the syntactical setting of Exod 21:23, where the nouns *opthalmon* and *odonta* serve as the direct objects of the preceding verb and thus stand in the accusative case. See Gundry, *Literary and Theological Art*, 94; Davies and Allison, *Matthew I-VIII*, 540.

text focuses on matters of "opposition"/"resistance" (*anthistēmi*) and "evil" (*ponēros*).[44] And in light of the fact that these two terms constitute the key vocabulary of Matthew 5:39a, this linkage is of major significance. Accordingly, both the verbal and the contextual evidence identify Deuteronomy 19:15-21 as the literary backdrop to Matthew 5:38-42.[45]

This linkage is crucial to the understanding of the Matthean text. If the Deuteronomic version of the *lex talionis* provides the literary backdrop to Matthew 5:38-42, then by the same token it provides the theological backdrop to the Matthean text as well. And this raises a second question: What is the significance of Deuteronomy 19:15-21? Or in other words, what meaning does the *lex talionis* derive from its specifically Deuteronomic context?[46]

The answer to this question begins with an examination of the overall literary-theological context in which the talionic formula is found, the legal corpus of Deuteronomy. This body of laws is effectively framed by parallel formulations in Deuteronomy 6:1-3 (the words of Moses) and Deuteronomy 27:9-10 (the words of Moses and the Levitical priests) which characterize their substance:

---

44. Thus Deut 19:18-20: "And the judges shall examine the matter carefully. And if the unjust witness has in fact brought unjust witness and has opposed (*antestē*) his brother, then you shall do to him in the same manner as he planned to do evil (*eponēreusato*) to his brother. And in this way you shall remove the evil one (*ton ponēron*) from your midst. And when the rest of the people hear this, they will be afraid. And they will no longer carry out such evil (*to rhēma to ponēron touto*) in your midst." Cf. Matt 5:39a: "Do not resist (*antistēnai*) the one who is evil (*tō ponērō*)."

45. Thus Guelich (*Sermon*, 220), who likewise identifies the immediate proximity of the fourth antithesis (Matt 5:33-37 on "truthtelling") to the fifth (Matt 5:38-42) as a significant point of linkage between the Matthean and the Deuteronomic texts: "Of the three Old Testament parallels, Deut 19:21, LXX, fits 5:38-39a as though tailormade. First, the setting of Deut 19:16 involved the hypothetical trial of a false witness, a most appropriate and hardly coincidental sequel to the previous Antithesis. Second, the false witness had accused (*antestē*) his brother in court (19:18). Third, the penalty was based on the *lex talionis* principle by assigning to the false accuser the same penalty that would have been incurred by the accused. And fourth, the reason given for such action was to remove the evil one (*ton ponēron*) from the community. All four elements found in Deut 19:16-21 constitute the premise and antithesis of 5:38, 39a." See also Currie, "Matthew 5:39a," 141. It is important to note in this context that since the verbal linkage between Matt 5:38-42 and Deut 19:15-21 lies in the respective Greek texts, the following discussion will base itself on an examination of the LXX version of Deuteronomy and not the Masoretic Text.

46. While this question is crucial to the understanding of Matt 5:38-42, it has not, to date, exerted influence on the discussion of the Matthean text. By contrast, commentary on Matt 5:38-42 has long paid significant attention to the basic concept of retaliation expressed by the *lex talionis* in its various Ancient Near Eastern versions. See, for example, Strack and Billerbeck, *Evangelium*, 337-41.

6:1   And these are the commandments
and the regulations
and the decrees
    which the Lord our God commanded me
    to teach you
    that you should do thus
    in the land which you are entering, to inherit it,
       in order that you fear
       the Lord your God
6:2   and keep
       all his regulations
       and his commandments
       which I am commanding you today—
          you
          and your children
          and your children's children—
             all the days of your life,
             in order that you have a long life.
6:3   And you shall hear, Israel,
and you shall be careful to do
    these commandments and regulations and decrees,
       in order that it be well with you
       and that you be greatly multiplied,
          just as the Lord, the God of your ancestors,
          promised to give you,
          a land flowing with milk and honey.

27:9   And Moses and the Levitical priests spoke to all Israel, saying,
    Be silent and hear, Israel:
    On this day you have become
    a people belonging to the Lord your God.

> 27:10 And you shall obey
> the voice of the Lord your God,
> and you shall do
> all his commandments
> and his regulations
> which I am commanding you today.

As this framework makes clear, the legal corpus of Deuteronomy is addressed to the people of Israel as a unified body ("all Israel": 27:9a; "Israel": 6:3; 27:9b)[47] whose corporate identity lies in the fact that they are "a people who belong to the Lord [their] God" (*eis laon kyriō tō theō sou*: 27:9). The Deuteronomic legal corpus itself consists of "the commandments, the regulations, and the decrees" (6:1; 27:10) which, as Moses indicates to the people, "The Lord our God has commanded me to teach you" (6:1).

Prominently bracketing this legal corpus is the charge to the Israelite community to "hear and do" all those "commandments, regulations, and decrees" which Moses has received from the Lord and now passes on to them.[48] The urgency of this imperative relates to the two factors which have primary impact on the life of the Israelite community, the "land which they are entering" (6:1) and the "God to whom they belong" (27:9).

The "land which they are entering," on the one hand, is no empty territory. Rather, it is filled with nations which are not only "great" (*mega*: 1:28; 4:38; 7:1; 9:1) and "many" (*poly*: 1:28; 7:1, 17), but also "stronger" (*ischyroteron*: 4:38; 7:1; 9:1) and "more powerful" (*dynamoteron*: 1:28) than the Israelites. These nations have their own gods (*theoi heteroi*: 6:14; 13:6 [LXX, 13:7]; *theoi tōn ethnōn*: 6:14; 13:7 [LXX 13:8]; 29:18 [LXX 29:17]; cf. 12:30), who lead them in turn into "abominable deeds" (*bdelygmata*: 18:9) and "impious acts" (*asebeian*: 9:4, 5). It is these nations, their gods, and their evil practices which will physically surround the Israelite community in "the land which they are entering" and thus exert a powerful influence upon them.

---

47. The corporate nature of the reference to Israel also becomes visible not only in the evident abandon with which the Deuteronomist switches between second plural (*hymeis/hymas*) and second singular forms (*sy/sou/soi*) in addressing the Israelites as a people but even more in his apparent preference for second singular forms over the second plural alternatives. Cf. the comments of Paul-Eugène Dion ("Tu feras disparaître," 349) concerning the use of the second person singular form of address throughout Deuteronomy and the comments of Patrick (*Law*, 102) concerning the text of Deut 24:7.

48. The centrality, for the Deuteronomist, of the language of "hearing" (*akouō*) and "doing" (*poieō*) in conjunction with the language of "commandments/regulations/decrees" and other similar terms is immediately evident in consulting a concordance.

Transforming Nonresistance 149

The other factor which enters the picture, however, is the character of the God to whom the Israelites belong. "The Lord [their] God" is described on the one hand as "a faithful God (*theos pistos*: 7:9) who "keeps covenant . . . with those who keep [my] commandments" (*ho phylassōn diathēkēn . . . tois phylassousin tas entolas autou*: 7:9) and "does mercy . . . to those who love me" (*poiōn eleos . . . tois agapōsin me*: 5:10). On the other hand, however, this God is described as "a jealous God" (*theos zēlōtēs*: 4:24; 5:9; 6:15) who "repays the sins . . . of those who hate me" (*apodidous hamartias . . . tois misousin me*: 5:9; cf. 7:10) and will "utterly destroy [the Israelites] from the face of the earth" (*exolethreuse se apo prosōpou tēs gēs*: 6:15; cf. 7:10) if they worship the gods of the nations round about them.[49]

And it is because the Israelites live in the midst of "the nations" and yet belong to a "faithful"/"jealous" God that Moses impresses upon them the urgency of "hearing" and "doing" the "commandments, regulations, and decrees" of the Lord. This, then, is the overall literary-theological context of the *lex talionis* of Deuteronomy.

The fundamental task at hand, however, is the analysis of the talionic formula within its immediate context, Deuteronomy 19:15-21:

> 19:15 No single witness shall prevail against a person
>> with respect to any wrongdoing
>> or any transgression
>> or any sin which he might commit.
>
>> Instead, every charge shall be established
>> by the mouth of two witnesses or three.
>
> 19:16 But if an unjust witness sets himself against a person
>> and accuses him of impious actions,
>
> 19:17 then the two people who have the dispute shall stand
>>> before the Lord,
>>> and before the priests,
>>> and before the judges,
>>>> whoever they may be in those days,
>
> 19:18 and the judges shall examine the matter carefully.
>
>> And if the unjust witness has in fact brought unjust witness

---

49. That these two divine characteristics correspond to each other as "the two sides of the coin" becomes clear from the juxtaposition of descriptions in Deut 5:9-10 (where God is identified as "a jealous God") and Deut 7:9-10 (where God is identified as "a faithful God").

and has opposed [*antestē*] his brother,

19:19   then you shall do to him in the same manner

as he planned to do evil [*eponēreusato*] to his brother.

And you shall remove

the evil one [*ton ponēron*] from your midst.

19:20   And when the rest of the people hear this,

they will be afraid.

And they will no longer carry out

such evil [*to rhēma to ponēron touto*] in your midst.

19:21   You eye shall not spare him:

life in place of life,

eye in place of eye [*ophthalmon anti ophthalmou*],

tooth in place of tooth [*odonta anti odontos*],

hand in place of hand,

foot in place of foot.

This law concerns the bearing of witness in court. It is an apodictic law ("You shall/shall not . . .) which leads into a casuistic ruling ("If . . ., then . . ."). The overall formulation identifies the parties involved, the crime committed, the legal procedure to be followed in dealing with the crime, the punishment to be meted out to the offender, and the purposes to be achieved by carrying out this punishment. Accordingly, the following analysis of Deuteronomy 19:15–21 will focus on these issues.

The court case described here is one which, in one way or another, implicates the entire Israelite community as involved parties. The perpetrator of the crime is described as "The single witness" (*martys heis*: 19:15), "the unjust witness" (*martys adikos*: 19:16, 18), and ultimately "the evil one" (*ton ponēron*: 19:19). The victim of the crime is alternately described simply as a "person" (*anthrōpou*: 19:15, 16) or more specifically as "his brother" (*tou adelphou autou*: 19:18, 19). Beyond these "two people who have the dispute" (*hoi dyo anthrōpoi, hois estin autois hē antilogia*: 19:17) are "the Lord" (*kyriou*: 19:17), "the priests" (*tōn hiereōn*: 19:17), and "the judges" (*tōn kritōn*: 19:17), before whom the disputants are to stand as they await a decision on their case. And beyond the legal framework of the court lies the entire Israelite community, designated by the corporate second person singular form "you shall remove" (*exareis*: 19:19),[50] the second person plu-

---

50. That this is a corporate reference becomes evident not merely from the Deuteronomist's frequent use of second person singular forms in addressing the Israelite

ral references to "from your midst" (*ex hymōn autōn*: 19:19) and "in your midst" (*en hymin*: 19:20), and the third person plural reference to "the rest of the people" (*hoi epiloipoi*: 19:20). Accordingly, there is no sector of the Israelite community which lies beyond the impact of this law.

The crime in question relates to the words and the actions of the "unjust witness." He is variously charged with "setting himself against a person" (*katastē . . . kata anthrōpou*: 19:16), "accusing him of impiety" (*katalegōn autou asebeian*: 19:16),"bringing unjust witness" (*emartyrēsen adika*: 19:18), "opposing his brother" (*antestē kata tou adelphou autou*: 19:18), and "planning to do evil to his brother" (*eponēreusato poiēsai kata tou adelphou autou*: 19:19). His crime is then summarized—as is his identity itself (*ton ponēron*: 19:19)—as "this evil deed" or simply "such evil" (*to rhēma to ponēron touto*: 19:20).

As a result, the actions of "setting oneself against," "accusing," "bringing unjust witness," and "opposing" not only correspond to each other but likewise give specific and communitarian definition to the "evil thing" which has been planned by the "evil one." Here "evil" is no abstract moral reality, to be defined in absolute terms detached from all reference to specific context. Rather, "evil" is defined as the concrete act of "opposing the brother," an act which both presupposes the context of the community and at the same time destroys the reality which it presupposes. The crime in question is above all else a crime against the entire community.

The description of the judicial process by which the "evil" is to be brought to light and the "evil one" brought to justice reinforces this communitarian concept. Here, however, the language points away from the disputants and towards the leadership of the community. The "two people who have the dispute" are instructed to stand "before the Lord" (*enanti kyriou*: 19:17), "before the priests" (*enanti tōn hiereōn*: 19:17), and "before the judges" (*enanti tōn kritōn*: 19:17) to present their case for adjudication.

Since "evil" is viewed as a crime against the community, it is the community itself, in the persons of its leadership, which is to take the initiative for responding to this crime. There is no question here of personal acts of vengeance carried out by the one who has been wronged. Both the authority and the responsibility for responding to "evil" belong to the community *as community*.

This is no insignificant task. The judges are pointedly instructed to "examine the matter carefully" (*exetasōsin . . . akribōs*: 19:18). Nor is the authority granted to the community a matter of insignificance. When the

---

community (see n. 47 above) but from the immediate context of the verb as well: the preceding second person plural formulation "and you shall do" (*kai poiēsete*) and the immediately following phrase "from your [pl.] midst" (*ex hymōn autōn*).

disputants bring their case for adjudication, they stand not merely before the priests and the judges but ultimately before the Lord. And, by the same token, when the judges decide the case, they are acting not finally on their own authority nor on that of the priests but rather on the authority of the Lord. Accordingly, justice within the community of Israel is seen to be not only public justice, as opposed to private revenge, but also divine justice initiated through human agents, the justice of God set in motion by the community in the persons of its leadership.

And if the judicial process involves the entire community in the persons of its leadership, the punishment for the crime involves the entire community in the persons of its membership. To begin with, the punishment itself is defined in communitarian terms: "And you shall do to him *in the same manner as he planned to do evil to his brother* (*hon tropon eponēreusato poiēsai kata tou adelphou autou*: 19:19, emphasis mine). It is precisely that "evil" which was intended to harm the brother *and thus, in effect, destroy the community* which now becomes the standard for the community's punishment of the evildoer.

Further, it is the community itself which is charged with the execution of this punishment: "*And you shall do to him* (*kai poiēsete autō*: 19:19a, emphasis mine).[51] The divine justice authorized by the Lord of the community, initiated by the judges of the community, and defined by that crime which has destroyed the community is to be enacted by the community as a corporate body.

And, significantly, it is precisely within this communitarian context that the talionic formula itself appears: "Your eye shall not spare him: life in place of life, eye in place of eye, tooth in place of tooth, hand in place of hand, foot in place of foot" (19:21b). This ancient formula, which in light of its history certainly predates its present connection to the legal ruling concerning the "unjust witness,"[52] has now been impressed into service by the Deuteronomist as the explanatory gloss giving specific substance not only to the intended actions of the offender but, by the same token, to the nature of his punishment.

Accordingly, *hon tropon*, i.e., the "same manner" by which the evildoer is to be punished, ranges from capital punishment ("life in place of life") to the exaction of member for member and limb for limb ("eye in place of eye, tooth in place of tooth, hand in place of hand, foot in place of foot"). And it is this *hon tropon*, now linked by the Deuteronomist to the ancient

---

51. See n. 50 above.

52. Thus implicitly Phillips (*Criminal Law*, 96) and Mayes (*Deuteronomy*, 289), who identify the talionic formula as a secondary addition to the ruling concerning the "unjust witness."

talionic formula and defined by that same formula, which constitutes the fundamental response of the community to "the evil one in [their] midst." The evil deed intended against the "brother," and thus in reality against the community itself, determines *point for point* the punishment to be meted out to the evildoer by the community.

This linkage between the *lex talionis* and the law concerning the "unjust witness" has major hermeneutical implications. While question has been raised about the extent to which the *lex talionis* was literally enacted in the ancient world in general,[53] and about the centrality of the talionic principle within Israelite law in specific,[54] there can be little question about the role of the *lex talionis* within its Deuteronomic setting. By attaching the talionic formula to a law whose enforcement, contrary to that of the *lex talionis* itself, can scarcely be called into question, the Deuteronomist establishes the force of the talionic formula as that of viable legislation. The addition of the warning clause, "your eye shall not spare him"[55] confirms this conclusion. For the Deuteronomist the *lex talionis* is an active and enforceable piece of legislation which defines in specific terms the punishment to be meted out to the "unjust witness."

This is confirmed by the presence of "motive clauses," statements which indicate the purposes to be achieved through enactment of a law and in this way motivate the listeners to obey the law in question.[56] There are two such "motive clauses" attached to the ruling concerning the "unjust witness." The first of these points backward to the crime which has already been committed with the community: "And you shall remove the evil one from your midst" (19:19b). The second one points forward, away from the crime, to the future life of the community: "And when the rest of the people hear this, they will be afraid. And they will no longer carry out such evil in your midst." (19:20). Both of these clauses, however, serve the common function of linking the law of the "unjust witness" to a broader pattern of laws within Deuteronomy.

Most important in this respect is the first of the "motive clauses": "And you shall remove the evil one from your midst" (19:19b: *kai exareis ton ponēron ex hymōn autōn*). This formula—either verbatim[57] or in a variant

---

53. See n. 40 above. Cf. Phillips' discussion (ibid., 97–99) concerning the *lex talionis* and the prohibition of murder.

54. Thus Boecker, *Law*, 171–72; Lind, *Law*, 21–24.

55. Cf. Deut 13:8b (LXX, 13:9b); 19:13a.

56. See the discussion of Carmichael (*Laws*, 37–40) on the "motive clauses" in Deuteronomy.

57. Thus 17:7; 19:19; 21:21; 22:21, 24; 24:7.

formulation[58]—is found throughout Deuteronomy in a prominent series of legal rulings,[59] each of which deals with a capital crime[60] and each of which legislates capital punishment as the means for dealing with the offender.[61]

Accordingly, the series as a whole concerns itself with capital punishment. And this means that the primary emphasis of the law concerning the "unjust witness" lies on the first directive of the *lex talionis*, the call to exact "life in place of life."[62] While the talionic formula goes on from there to speak about "eye," "tooth," "hand," and "foot" as well, it is precisely the initial call—i.e., to exact "life in place of life"—which establishes the link between this legal ruling and the remainder of the series.

---

58. "And you shall obliterate the evil one from your midst" (*kai aphanieis ton ponēron ex hymōn autōn*: 13:5 [LXX, 13:6]; "And you shall remove the evil one from Israel" (*kai exareis ton ponēron ex Israel*:17:12; 22:22); "And you shall wash away the innocent blood from Israel" (*kai katharieis to haima to anaition ex Israel*: 19:13); "And you shall remove the innocent blood from your midst" (*sy de exareis to haima to anaition ex hymōn autōn*: 21:9).

59. 13:1-5 (LXX, 13:2-6); 17:2-7; 17:8-13; 19:11-13; 19:15-21; 21:1-9; 21:18-21; 22:13-21; 22:22; 22:23-27; 24:7; cf. 13:6-11 (LXX, 13:7-12); 18:15-22. For a detailed study of this series of texts and the "removal formula" which creates the series, see Dion, "Tu feras disparaître," 321-49. See also Weinfeld, *Deuteronomy*, 355-56; Mayes, *Deuteronomy*, 233-34.

60. The crimes include false prophesying (13:1-5 [LXX, 13:2-6]; cf. 18:15-22, where the crime of the prophet is speaking in the name of other gods, but where the "removal formula" is absent); serving and worshipping other gods (17:2-7; cf. 13:6-11 [LXX, 13:7-12], where the crime is that of inciting others to the worship of other gods, but where the "removal formula" is absent); disobeying the legal rulings of the priest in a court case (17:8-13); murder (19:11-13; cf. 21:1-9, where the case involves an unresolved murder case); false witness in court (19:15-21); rebellion against parents (21:18-21); loss of virginity prior to marriage (22:13-21); adultery (22:22); rape of an engaged woman (22:23-27); kidnapping and enslavement or selling of an Israelite (24:7). That the crimes in question are in fact "capital crimes" becomes evident precisely from the "capital punishment" that is legislated as the punishment.

61. The punishment is variously designated: the offender shall be "stoned with stones" (*lithoboleō en lithois*: 17:6; 21:21; 22:21; 22:24; cf. 13:10 [LXX, 13:11]); you shall "kill" the offender (*thanatoō*: 17:7; *apokteinō*: 22:22; 22:25); the offender shall "die" (*apothnēskō*: 13:5 [LXX, 13:6]; 17:6; 17:12; 19:12; 21:21; 22:21; 24:7; cf. 13:10 [LXX, 13:11]; 18:20; *teleutaō*: 17:5); the offender shall give "life in place of life" (*psychē anti psychēs*: 19:21); the neck of the heifer shall be broken (*neurokoptō*: 21:4, 6). On the direct correlation between the "motive clause" and these legal rulings calling for capital punishment, see Dion, "Tu feras disparaître," 327; Phillips, *Deuteronomy*, 132. But note Driver (*Deuteronomy*, 152) and Mayes (*Deuteronomy*, 233), who cite 19:19 as an exception with reference to the question of capital punishment. As noted in n60 above, there are two additional laws in Deuteronomy (13:6-11 [LXX, 13:7-12]; 18:15-22) that demand the death of the offender but do not contain any form of the "removal formula."

62. Cf. Mayes, Mayes, *Deuteronomy*, 289.

The implications of this linkage are significant. What this means in the broadest terms is that for the Deuteronomist the fundamental hermeneutical key to interpretation of the *lex talionis* lies precisely in its association with the "removal formula," an unambiguous reference to the enforcement of capital punishment against an offender.

What this linkage means in more specific terms can be seen from closer examination of the "removal formula" of 19:19b. The grammatical form of the text (*ton ponēron* = accusative singular masculine[63]) determines that the object of the verb "remove" is personal rather than impersonal in its force and must therefore be translated as "the evil one."[64] Accordingly, the Israelites are charged to remove from their midst not simply evil in general but rather the evil person in specific.[65]

Nor is there ambiguity about what this "removal" implies. As the talionic formula itself ("life in place of life") indicates and the linkage of this text to its broader context (laws mandating capital punishment) confirms, there is for the Deuteronomist one fundamental means for "removing the evil one from your midst," namely, *the execution of the offender by the community*.[66] This action alone will suffice to deal with "the evil one" and to "remove from the midst" of the community the "evil" which he has carried out.

Here the Deuteronomist's communitarian understanding of "crime and punishment" becomes most visible. The reference to "the midst" confirms that for the Deuteronomist "the evil one" is guilty not merely of "opposing his brother" by the "evil" which he has done but in fact of threatening the very existence of the Israelite community.[67] And viewed within the Deuteronomic context it is apparent why the community is obligated to "remove the evil one *from [their] midst*" (19:19b, emphasis mine).[68] The

---

63. Thus 13:5 (LXX, 13:6); 17:7; 17:12; 19:19; 21:21; 22:21; 22:22; 24:7.

64. Cf. Dion, "Tu feras disparaître," 329–30. But note 22:21, where the accusative singular masculine form remains inflexible, even though it is spoken with reference to a woman!

65. Cf. ibid., 330n43. The human agony involved in this charge is clearly alluded to in the blunt warning of 19:21: "Your eye shall not spare him."

66. Here it is not specified what form that execution shall take. Elsewhere, however (see n61 above), the mode of execution is explicitly defined in terms of "stoning": thus 17:6; 21:21; 22:21; 22:24; cf. 13:10 (LXX, 13:11), where no "removal formula" appears.

67. Cf. the comments of Craigie (*Deuteronomy*, 251) concerning 17:2–7, another of the legal rulings containing the "removal formula": "The capital punishment of the offender removed that evil which had by the nature of the crime, endangered the continuation of the covenant community of God." See also ibid., 224, 284–85, 307.

68. That the primary concern lies with the community is evident from the fact that it is precisely the communitarian language of the "removal formula" that concludes the ruling concerning the "unjust witness." Attention thus focuses on the life of the

Israelites are "a people holy to the Lord [their] God" (*laos hagios . . . tō theō sou*: 7:6; 14:2, 21; 26:19; cf. 27:9; 28:9). And the God to whom they are "holy" is a "jealous God" (*theos zēlōtēs*: 4:24; 5:19; 6:15), a God prepared to "utterly destroy [them] from the face of the earth" (*exolethreuse se apo prosōpou tēs gēs*: 6:15; cf. 7:10), if they worship the gods of the nations round about them. Accordingly, as "a people holy . . . to a jealous God" the Israelites cannot, by very definition, allow either "the evil one" or the "evil" which he has done to remain within their community.[69] Rather, the "evil" which has taken place *in their midst*, and which has in this way threatened the life of the community, must be removed *from their midst* through the execution of "the evil one."

Further, this execution must be carried out *by the community itself*: "And *you shall remove* the evil one from your midst" (19:19b, emphasis mine.[70] If "evil" is by definition an offense *against the community*, then it must be *the community as community* which takes action to rid itself of this offense by removing the evil one from their midst.[71]

The first "motive clause" (19:19b), then, points backward, to the crime which has already been committed, and instructs the community how to "remove" the "evil" which threatens both its identity and its existence. The

---

community as a whole and not on the question of justice at the individual level.

69. Cf. the comments of Wright, *Deuteronomy*, 417-18; Phillips, *Deuteronomy*, 95; Craigie, *Deuteronomy*, 293; and Bellefontaine, "Deuteronomy 21:18-21," 24.

70. See n50 above. The collective involvement of the community in the execution of the offender is made explicit in 13:9 (LXX, 13:10) and 17:7, where the first hands to be raised against the offender are "your hands" (*hai cheires sou*) / "the hand of the witnesses" (*hē cheir tōn martyrōn*) and the last hands to be raised against the offender are those "of all the people" (*pantos tou laou*).

71. Cf. the comments of Patrick (*Law*, 102-3; emphasis Patrick's): "As in all biblical law, the addressee of Deuteronomic Law is the people of Israel, but D has *collectivized* a significant portion of its law. The 'you' addressed is the people as a corporate entity . . . The people are addressed directly in the attached motive clause ('so you shall purge the evil from the midst of you') which explains the collective orientation of the law: the community must assume collective responsibility for serious offenses that occur within it and execute the offender to remove the guilt attached to it. If it did not do so, the whole community would be subject to divine judgment." Significant light is shed on this Deuteronomic conception of "crime and punishment" by the comparative studies of Weinfeld (*Deuteronomy*) and Dion ("Tu feras disparaître"). Dion, who traces the "removal formula" from its Deuteronomic form to earlier formulations, both within and beyond Israel, observes (ibid., 349) that the "innovation" of the Deuteronomist lies precisely in the "democratization" of a formula which had formerly been applied to the king as the leader of the people. Weinfeld observes (ibid., 239, 242) that in Deuteronomy, by contrast with the Book of the Covenant and the Priestly Code, "the concept of sin and punishment has . . . been transferred from the divine to the human sphere . . . In the deuteronomic view sin does not act of its own accord, nor is the malefactor cut off from his people by the natural course of events: the people themselves must purge the evil from their midst."

second "motive clause" (19:20) looks forward, away from the crime, to the ongoing life of the community: "And when the rest of the people hear this, they will be afraid. And they will no longer carry out such evil in your midst" (*Kai hoi epiloipoi akousantes phobēthēsontai kai ou prosthēsousin eti poiēsai kata to rhēma to ponēron touto en hymin*). This "fear formula"[72] shows the ultimate concern of the Deuteronomist to be ethical in nature and not merely sacral.[73] While the "evil one" and the "evil" which he has committed must be removed from the midst of the community which is "holy to the Lord," that is not the end of the matter but rather only the beginning.

The ultimate concern here is the ethical impact of this act of "removal" upon the community which hears of it. The ruling concerning the "unjust witness" will achieve its intended purpose only if the Israelite community "hears" of the incident, "fears" God,[74] and "no longer carries out such evil in [its] midst." The "fear formula" serves, in the first instance, to deter the remainder of the Israelite community (*hoi epiloipoi*) from following in the footsteps of "the evil one" and continuing on in his "evil" practices.[75]

But within the Deuteronomic conception "deterrence" is only the first half of the ethical concern. If the Israelites are called to the task of "removing the evil one from their midst" so that they will "no longer carry out such evil in their midst," this negative task merely highlights by contrast the positive task which lies beyond, namely, "doing what is good and right" (*poieō + to kalon kai to areston*: 6:18; 12:25, 28; 13:18 [LXX, 13:19]; 21:9), a formulation directly parallel to "doing the commandments, etc." (*poieō +*

---

72. Cf. the similar formulations which occur either in conjunction with the "removal formula" (17:13: "And when the whole people hears this, it will be afraid and will no longer act impiously" [*kai pas ho laos akousas phobēthēsetai kai ouk asebēsei eti*]; 21:21c: "And when the rest of the people hear this, they will be afraid" [*kai hoi epiloipoi akousantes phobēthēsontai*]) or in conjunction with the command to execute the offender (13:11 [LXX, 13:12]: "And when all Israel hears this, it will be afraid; and they will no longer carry out such evil in your midst" [*pas Israel akousas phobēthēsetai kai ou prosthēsousin eti poiēsai kata to rhēma to ponēron touto en hymin*]).

73. Cf. the comments of Weinfeld (*Deuteronomy*, 243): "According to Deuteronomy, the death penalty does not serve a sacral need for the destruction of the malefactor who had defiled the holy state (cf. Lev 20:3), nor is it an object in itself, that is, the removal of impurity. It serves as a deterrent 'so that all may obey and fear' (13:12; 17:13; 19:20; 21:21)."

74. While no object is supplied for the verb "fear" (*phobēthēsontai*), it would appear from the phraseological evidence of Deuteronomy that the object implied by the text is not "the punishment you have just heard about" but rather "the Lord your God." Cf. the references to "fear of God" in Deut 4:10; 5:29; 6:2, 13, 24; 8:6; 10:12, 20; 13:4 (LXX, 13:5); 14:23; 17:19; 25:18; 31:12, 13; cf. 5:5; 9:19; 25:58.

75. Thus Driver, *Deuteronomy*, 152; Kline, *Treaty*, 85; Phillips, *Deuteronomy*, 119; Thompson, *Deuteronomy*, 174; Craigie, *Deuteronomy*, 252-53; Dion, "Tu feras disparaître," 330; Patrick, *Law*, 103; Payne, *Deuteronomy*, 116.

entolas, etc.: 1:14, 18; 4:1, 5, 6, 14; 5:1, 27, 31, 32; 6:1, 3, 24, 25 and throughout). It is this positive imperative which defines the ethical import of the central command of Deuteronomy, "to love the Lord your God with your whole heart and your whole soul and your whole strength" (6:5).[76] Thus it is this positive imperative which constitutes the ultimate ethical concern of the Deuteronomist.

Accordingly the positive concern for "doing what is right and good" gives rise to the negative concern expressed in the "fear formula": The community cannot "do what is right and good" until they "fear [the Lord their God] and refrain from doing what is evil." And as a result, the call to "hear, fear, and not do evil" is a *negative* command necessitated precisely by the *positive* ethical concern of the Deuteronomist.

Here lies, finally, the answer to the question concerning the role of the *lex talionis* within the larger context of Deuteronomy. What can be said about the "fear formula" can be said as well about the *lex talionis* as a whole. The command to exact "life for life" and in this way to "remove the evil one from your midst" is, for the Deuteronomist, the fundamental means of eradicating "evil" from the community *and in so doing* of empowering the community to "do what is good and right." And this is the ultimate force of the *lex talionis* as found in Deuteronomy 19:15–21.

II. MATTHEW 5:38–42 IN MATTHEAN CONTEXT: THE RESPONSE OF JESUS

The task which remains is to examine the text of Matthew 5:38–42 in the light of its canonical context, the *lex talionis* of Deuteronomy 19:15–21. In order to highlight comparisons and contrasts between these texts the analysis of the Matthean text will follow the same outline as that of the Deuteronomic text.

The initial question thus concerns the literary-theological context of this saying of Jesus within Matthew's Gospel. The immediate context of Matthew 5:38–42 is the first major discourse of Jesus within the framework of Matthew's narrative, the so-called Sermon on the Mount (5:1–7:29).[77] Directly prior to this discourse Jesus has initiated his public ministry in Galilee and announced its fundamental concern, the kingdom of heaven

---

76. This is evident from the fact that it is precisely this language of "doing what is good and right" (*poieō* + *to kalon /to areston*) which creates the verbal contrast to the warnings against "doing what is evil" (*poieō* + *to ponēron/ta ponēra*) which effectively bracket the text of Deuteronomy (cf. 4:25–26//31:28–29).

77. See also 9:35–11:1; 13:1–53; 18:1–19:1; 24:1–26:1; cf. 23:1–39.

(4:17, 23; cf. 9:35; 11:1). Now in the Sermon on the Mount, Jesus' "inaugural address" to his listeners, he exposits his announcement of the kingdom of heaven by describing the characteristics and setting forth the imperatives of life within that kingdom. And, significantly, Jesus frames this discussion in thoroughly Deuteronomic language and concepts. The passages which bracket this address (5:17–20; 7:24–27) are strongly reminiscent, in both vocabulary and tone, of the passages which frame the Deuteronomic legal corpus (Deut 6:1–3; 27:9–10):

5:17   Do not think that I have come to repeal the law
and the prophets.
I have not come to repeal them but to fulfill them.

5:18   For I say to you, until heaven and earth pass away,
neither the smallest letter
nor the least stroke of the pen
will pass away from the law until all things
come to pass.

5:19   So whoever relaxes one of the least of these commandments
and teaches people to do the same
will be called "least" in the kingdom of heaven.
But whoever keeps the commandments
and teaches people to do the same
will be called "great" in the kingdom of heaven.

5:20   For I tell you, unless you exhibit surpassing righteousness,
greater than that of the scribes and Pharisees,
you will by no means enter into the kingdom of heaven.

7:24   So each one who hears these sayings of mine
and does them
can be compared to a wise man . . .

7:26   And each one who hears these sayings of mine
and does not do them
can be compared to a foolish man . . .

The correspondences between the Matthean text and its Deuteronomic counterpart are evident. The Matthean framework passages, as do those of Deuteronomy, focus on "doing the commandments/words" (*poieō* + *tas entolas/tous logous*: 5:19a; 5:19b; 7:24; 7:26) and emphasize the language of "hearing and doing" (*akouō + poieō*: 7:24; 7:26).[78]

But the differences between the two texts are equally striking. While the Deuteronomic text concerns itself with "doing the commandments," the Matthean text heightens the language to that of "fulfilling the law and the prophets" (5:17) and "exhibiting surpassing righteousness, greater than that of the scribes and Pharisees (5:20). As a result more is at stake in the Matthean challenge to "do the commandments" than mere repetition of Deuteronomic language or the simple restatement of an ancient biblical command.

This conclusion is confirmed by the "antitheses" which follow in 5:21–48 and which create the immediate context of 5:38–42. Here Jesus illustrates the character of "surpassing righteousness" through a series of six pronouncements (5:21–26; 27–30; 31–32; 33–37; 38–42; 43–48), each of which is structured in similar fashion: (1) "You have heard that it was said" + citation of a Jewish law; (2) "But I say to you" + saying of Jesus. Both the structure and the substance of these "antitheses" confirm that within the Matthean context "fulfilling the law and the prophets" and "exhibiting surpassing righteousness" move beyond the Deuteronomic conception of "doing the commandments."

Matthew identifies the addressees of the Sermon on the Mount as the disciples of Jesus, in distinction to the Jewish crowds: "And when [Jesus] saw the crowds, he went up onto the mountain. And when he had sat down, his disciples (*hoi mathētai autou*) came to him. And he taught them (*autous*)." (5:1–2).[79] The contents of the teachings point toward the same audience: "You are the light of the world" (5:13; "You are the salt of the earth" (5:14); "Blessed are you when they revile you and persecute you and say every evil thing against you, telling lies about you on my account" (5:11). The Sermon on the Mount is thus directed to the community of those who have left everything behind to become disciples of Jesus (cf. 4:18–22; 9:9; 19:27), children of the "Father who is in heaven" (5:16, 45, 48; 6:1, 4, 6, 8, 9, 14, 15,

---

78. See the corresponding discussion of Deuteronomy above.

79. The immediate proximity of the crowds to the disciples, however, becomes evident at the end of Jesus' address, when it is they (*hoi ochloi*: 7:28) and not the disciples who respond to the words of Jesus: "And when Jesus had finished these words, the crowds (*hoi ochloi*) were astounded at his teaching; for he was teaching them (*autous*) as one who had authority and not as their scribes" (7:28–29). If the disciples are in fact the inner circle to whom Jesus addresses his words (5:1), the crowds are nevertheless the outer circle who listen in from the periphery.

18, 26, 32; 7:11, 21), and family to each other (5:22, 23, 24, 47; 7:3, 4, 5; cf. 12:46–50).[80]

As with the Israelite community, the disciples live in the midst of a wider community with whom they come into close and frequent contact. This community is, for the most part, Jewish in makeup: scribes (*hoi grammateis*: 5:20; 7:29); Pharisees (*hoi Pharisaioi*: 5:20); the council (*to synedrion*: 5:22); tax collectors (*hoi telōnai*: 5:46); and people in general (*hoi anthrōpoi*: 5:16, 19; 6:1, 2, 5, 14, 15, 16, 18; 7:12). But this community includes as well those who are not Jewish, namely the Gentiles (*ta ethnē*: 6:32; *hoi ethnikoi*: 5:47; 6:7).

With few exceptions, however, this community of Jews and Gentiles is described as hostile to the disciples of Jesus who live in their midst. They are depicted as engaging in a variety of activities which display this antagonism. They are the ones who "revile" (*oneidizō*: 5:11), "persecute" (*diōkō*: 5:11, 44), "say evil things" (*legō pan ponēron*: 5:11), and "tell lies" (*pseudomai*: 5:11) about the disciples. They are the "adversary" (*ho antidikos*: 5:25) who initiates court proceedings; the "council" (*to synedrion*: 5:22) before whom people are brought to trial; the "judge" (*ho kritēs*: 5:25) who pronounces sentence; the "court assistant" (*ho hypēretēs*: 5:25) who throws people into prison. In simple terms they are "the evil one" (*ho ponēros*: 5:39a) and "the enemies" (*hoi echthroi*: 5:44).

The God to whom Jesus' disciples belong as they live in the midst of a hostile community is "King" of the "kingdom of heaven" (*basileia tōn ouranōn*: 5:3, 10, 19, 20; 6:10, 33; 7:21), the one who has heaven as "throne" (*thronos . . . tou theou*: 5:34) and earth as "footstool" (*hypopodion . . . tōn*

---

80. That Jesus here addresses himself to a "community" and not simply to individual "disciples" is evident from the prominent use of plural forms of address throughout the Sermon on the Mount. A prime (and relevant) example of this usage is found in the formulaic language of the "antitheses" themselves: "You [pl.] have heard . . . (*ēkousate*); but I say to you [pl.] . . . (*egō de legō hymin*)": 5:21/22, 27/28, 31/32, 33/34, 38/39, 43/44. But see Theissen's discussion of the antitheses ("Gewaltverzicht und Feindesliebe," 176). He notes that the antitheses are divided into two groups of three antitheses, a division which becomes evident from the fact that the complete formula introduced in 5:21 ("You have heard that it was said to the people of ancient days": *ēkousate hoti errethē tois archaiois*) is repeated only once, in 5:33 ("Again you have heard that it was said to the people of ancient days": *palin ēkousate hoti errethē tois archaiois*). Theissen correctly observes that the first group of three antitheses are casuistic in their formulation: "Everyone who . . ." (*pas* + participle), while the second group of three antitheses are apodictic: "You shall/shall not . . ." (imperative or infinitival form). Theissen's conclusion, however, that the first three antitheses are consequently directed to everyone, while the second three are addressed only to a particular group of persons is unwarranted. The very form of Jesus' address in all six antitheses ("But I say to you [pl.]": *egō de legō hymin*) indicates that the addressees of all the antitheses are the same group of people, namely, the community of Jesus' disciples in its entirety.

podōn autou: 5:35). This "King" has ultimate power over the destiny of humans, granting "reward in heaven" (*ho misthos en tois ouranois*: 5:12; cf. 5:46; 6:1, 2, 5, 16) and "casting into Gehenna" (*ballō eis geennan*: 5:29; cf. 5:30).

At the same time, however, this God is not only "King" of the "kingdom of heaven" but also the "Father who is in heaven" (5:16, 45, 48; 6:1, 4, 6, 8, 9, 14, 15, 18, 26, 32; 7:11, 21). And this "Father" is the one who "comforts" (*parakaleomai*: 5:4), "grants inheritance" (cf. *klēronomeō*: 5:5), "satisfies" (*chortazō*:5:6), "shows mercy" (*eleeō*: 5:7), grants "sight" (cf. *horaō*: 5:8), "provides [food and clothing]" (*prostithēmi*: 6:33), and "names his children" (*kaleō* + *huioi theou*: 5:9). Above all this "Father in heaven" is one who is "perfect" (*teleios*: 5:48), one who "lets the sun shine on both the evil (*ponērous*) and the good (*agathous*) and sends rain on the just (*dikaious*) and the unjust (*adikous*)" (5:45).

This is the setting of the Sermon on the Mount. It is this community of disciples—"followers" of Jesus and "children" of their "Father in heaven," who at the same time live in the midst of hostile neighbors—to whom Jesus addresses the words of Matthew 5:38–42. As is now evident, these words both parallel Deuteronomy 19:15–21 and move beyond it.

Moses' address to the people of Israel lays down the "commandments, regulations, and decrees" which are to govern the life of the Israelite community "in the land which they are entering, to inherit it" (Deut 6:1). The urgency of these "commandments, regulations, and decrees" stems from the fact that the Israelites live in the midst of nations with "other gods," while they themselves are "a people holy ... to [a jealous] God" (cf. Deut 7:6; 14:2).

Jesus' address to his disciples describes the "surpassing righteousness" which "fulfills the law and the prophets" and thus governs the life of the kingdom of heaven, that "kingdom" which the disciples are "entering" (Matt 5:20; cf. 5:3, 10) to "inherit" it (Matt 25:34). The urgency of this "surpassing righteousness" emerges from the fact that they who live in the midst of "evil ones" and "enemies" are nevertheless "children" of a "perfect Father in heaven."

The saying of Matthew 5:38–42 itself, as each of the other antitheses, consists of two sections: (1) the formulaic statement "You have heard that it was said" (5:38a) followed by the substance of the law in question (5:38b); and (2) the formulaic statement "But I say to you" (5:39a) followed by Jesus' response to the law in question (5:39b-42). The substance of Jesus' response, in turn consists of the command (5:39a) followed by two double sayings (5:39b/40; 5:41/42) which illustrate this command.[81]

---

81. Both of these double sayings exhibit the same syntactical structure in their two

5:38 You have heard that it was said,
> Eye in place of eye
> (*ophthalmon anti ophthalmou*)
> and tooth in place of tooth.
> (*kai odonta anti odontos*)

5:39 But I say to you,
> (*Egō de legō hymin*)
> Do not resist the one who is evil.
> (*mē antistēnai tō ponērō*)
>> But if someone strikes you on the right cheek,
>> (*all' hostis se rhapizei eis tēn dexian siagona sou*)
>> turn to them the other cheek as well.
>> (*strepson autō kai tēn allēn*)

5:40 And if someone wishes to sue you and take your tunic,
> (*kai tō thelonti soi krithēnai kai ton chitōna sou labein*)
> let them take your cloak as well.
> (*aphes autō kai to himation*)

5:41 And if someone compels you to go one mile,
> (*kai hostis se angareusei milion hen*)
> go with them for two.
> (*hypage met autou dyo*)

5:42 Give to the one who asks of you;
> (*tō aitounti se dos*)
> and do not reject the one who wishes to borrow from you.
> (*kai ton thelonta apo sou danisasthai mē apostraphēs*)

Two primary parties are in focus in this text, a protagonist and an antagonist. The saying itself is addressed to a collective protagonist, a plural "you" (*ēkousate*: 5:38a; *hymin*: 5:39a) which must within this context be a reference to the disciples of Jesus (*hoi mathētai autou*: 5:1; *autous*: 5:2), the designated addressees of the discourse as a whole.[82] Accordingly, this text,

---

halves: (1) "Whoever . . .": *hostis* + finite verb; (2) "[And] to the one who . . .": articular participle + *thelō*. Cf. Lührmann, "Liebet eure Feinde," 418; Davies and Allison, *Matthew I-VIII*, 538; Clavier, "Matthieu 5:39," 49–50.

82. See the discussion of this question above.

like its Deuteronomic counterpart, is communitarian in its thrust. While the "community" in question has shifted its identity from Israel to the disciples of Jesus, there can be little question about the fact that this text is addressed to a community *as community*.[83]

At the same time the saying concerns itself with an individual antagonist, whom Jesus characterizes in 5:39 as "the one who is evil" (*tō ponērō*).[84] In distinction to the Deuteronomic text, however, the Matthean saying distinguishes the corporate "you" being addressed from the "evil one" in question. This suggests that the "evil one" is not a disciple but rather a member of the larger community of Jews and Gentiles which surrounds the disciple community and is hostile to them.[85] Accordingly, this word of Jesus instructs the community of disciples how to deal with the "evil one" whom they encounter in the larger community of Jews and Gentiles within which they live.[86]

---

83. The fact that the individual illustrations provided in 5:39b–42 are formulated in terms of a singular addressee (*sou, soi, se*) does not undermine the collective thrust of the unit as a whole. Rather, as the form of the saying makes clear, it is the collective references of 5:38–39a (*ēkousate, hymin*) which introduce and thus interpret the singular references (*sou, soi, se*) and not the other way around. The individuals addressed in 5:39b–42 are called to act, accordingly, not on their own behalf but precisely as members of the community to which they belong.

84. That the grammatically ambiguous form *tō ponērō* is here to be construed as a masculine (rather than neuter; cf. 5:11; 9:4; 12:35) form and thus as a personal reference ("the one who is evil") becomes clear both from the preceding statement (5:38b) as well as from the illustrations which follow (5:39b–42). On the one hand the reference to "eye in place of eye and tooth in place of tooth" makes sense only in terms of the interactions between two individuals; and on the other hand each of the illustrations adduced in 5:39b-42 is phrased in terms of response to "the one who . . . ." Cf. France, *Gospel*, 126. It is as well this same context which excludes the possibility that Jesus is here making reference to Satan, "the Evil One" (cf. 5:37; 6:13; 13:19, 38). Accordingly, while 5:39a remains grammatically ambiguous, it is most naturally construed in personal terms, as a masculine singular form whose closest parallels are the unambiguous masculine plural forms *ponērous/tous ponērous* of 5:45, 13:49, and 22:10. The verbal and contextual linkage between this Matthean text and a Deuteronomic text which makes unambiguous reference to "the one who is evil" (Deut 19:19) confirms this conclusion.

85. At the same time, however, the very breadth of the examples cited in 5:39b–42 leaves room for the conclusion that the "evil one" could as well on occasion be another disciple. Horsley pushes the issue too far when he suggests ("Ethics and Exegesis," 19–20) that all of the illustrations cited in 5:39b–42 relate to inner-community relationships. That it is not unthinkable, however, for Jesus to identify one from among the disciple group as an "evil one" becomes clear from the text of 7:11, where Jesus classifies the entire group of addressees as "evil": "So if you who are evil people (*ei oun hymeis ponēroi ontes*) know how to give good gifts to your children, how much more will your Father who is in heaven give good things to those who make requests of him!"

86. Cf. the comments of Schlatter (*Evangelist Matthäus*, 186), who observes that it is precisely because the disciples are not outwardly separated from the Jewish community

The substance of the saying appears to confirm this conclusion. In 5:39c-42 Jesus identifies the "one who is evil" by means of an illustrative list of offenses ranging, in descending order,[87] from physical assault (5:39c) to financial importunity (5:42a/b). "The one who is evil" is that one who "strikes you on the right cheek" (5:39c), "wishes to sue you and take your tunic" (5:40), "compels you to go one mile" (5:41), "asks of you" (5:42a), and "wishes to borrow from you" (5:42b).

At the top of the list (5:39c) and gravest of the offenses is that of "striking [another] on the right cheek." This action could take place in any Jewish setting where one person grows angry with another; and it might well take place in those settings where the disciples of Jesus and the message they bring are unwelcome.[88] It is undeniably a physical assault upon the one thus struck.[89] But within such a context the slap "on the right cheek"—by very definition a "back-handed" slap—represents not so much an act of physical brutality which injures the victim as it does the supreme form of insult to the one who receives the blow, a much more serious insult than a slap with the open palm.[90]

---

at large that the question of how to respond to "evil" comes into sharp focus for them: "Nur darum bekam die Frage nach dem Recht für die Jünger Wichtigkeit, weil ihre eigene Gemeinschaft sie nicht von der völkischen Gemeinschaft schied. Der Boshafte, der Ohrfeigen austeilt und einen rechtlichen Anspruch auf ihren Chiton erhebt und zum Frondienst zwingt, steht nicht im Jüngerkreis. Solches Unrecht widerfährt ihnen von ihren Volksgenossen. Weil ihr eigener Verband sie nicht von der Judenschaft trennen kann und darf und sie doch für die anderen zum Gegenstand des Hasses macht, bekam die Frage, wie das Unrecht abzuwehren sei, für sie Gewicht."

87. Thus Clavier, "Matthieu 5:39," 49-50; Lohfink, "Ekklesiale Sitz," 240.

88. Cf. 5:11-12, where Jesus warns the disciples that they can expect people to "revile" them (*oneidizō*), "persecute" them (*diōkō*), "say all kinds of evil" about them (*legō pan ponēron*), and "tell lies" about them (*pseudomai*) on his account.

89. That this is so can be seen from the verbal links between this text and the Servant Song of Isaiah 50:4-9, where the Servant of the Lord announces (50:6), "I offered my back to scourges and my cheeks to blows (*tas de siagonas mou eis rhapismata*)." Cf. Gundry, *Literary and Theological Art*, 95; France, *Gospel*, 126; Davies and Allison, *Matthew I-VIII*, 544; but note Luz's caution (*Matthew 1-7*, 325) that "slaps are so widespread that it is unnecessary to awaken special reminiscences of the servant of God of Isa 50:6, who was beaten." The character of physical assault in *rhapizō* can also be seen from the verbal links between Matt 5:39b and Matt 26:67, where Roman soldiers strike (*rhapizō*: cf. the noun form *rhapisma* in Mark.14:65; John 18:22; 19:3) Jesus himself. Cf. France, *Gospel*; Levison, "Responsible Initiative," 234; Davies and Allison, *Matthew I-VIII*, 546.

90. Thus Daube, *New Testament*, 256-57; Clavier, "Matthieu 5:39," 53; Hill, *Gospel*, 128; Guelich, *Sermon*, 221-22; Gundry, *Literary and Theological Art*, 95; Lohfink, "Ekklesiale Sitz," 241; Horsley, "Ethics and Exegesis," 18; Wink, *Violence and Nonviolence*, 15; Davies and Allison, *Matthew I-VIII*, 543-44; Luz, *Matthew 1-7*, 325. The measure of insult implied by such a "backhanded" slap can be seen in the fact that

Second on the list of offenses (5:40) is that of "wishing to sue [another] and take [his] tunic." Here there is a clear allusion to the apparently common Jewish practice of seizing a person's garment in pledge for an unpaid debt. What is striking about this offense, however, is the type of garment which is seized, namely the tunic (*chitōn*) or undergarment. Jewish law (Exod 22:25-27; Deut 24:10-13, 17: cf. Amos 2:7-8) specifically prohibits extended seizure of the cloak (*himation*) or outer garment, since that is the garment which serves its owner at night as a blanket. No such restriction, however, applies to the tunic (*chitōn*) or undergarment; and it is therefore this garment which is requisitioned by "the one who is evil."[91]

The third offense (5:41), contrary to the first two, moves beyond a strictly Jewish setting to identify a Gentile, in specific a Roman, as "the one who is evil." Jesus' reference to "the one who compels you to go one mile" points to the Roman military practice according to which soldiers may "compel" (*angareuō*) individual civilians to carry military gear or other burdens for the distance of 1000 paces or one "mile."[92]

The final offenses on the list (5:42a/42b) fall under the common rubric of financial importunity. Here "the one who is evil" is one who "asks [money] of you" (5:42a) on the one hand or "wishes to borrow [money] from you" (5:42b) on the other. While neither of these actions is in and of itself "evil," their presence in the illustrative list of offenses committed by "the one who is evil" clearly implies that "asking" for money and "wishing to borrow" money are both viewed as importunate requests on the part of the one who asks.[93]

---

the fine imposed by the Mishnah as penalty for such a slap is twice as great as the fine imposed for a slap with the open palm: "If a man slapped his fellow, he gives him 200 *zuz*; if with the back of his hand, 400 *zuz*" (*Mishnah Baba Qamma* 8.6 cited by Daube, "Old Testament," 21).

91. For a discussion of the garments in question and the legalities surrounding seizure of a garment, see Davies and Allison, *Matthew I-VIII*, 544-46. Thus also Hill, *Gospel*, 128; Guelich, *Sermon*, 122; Gundry, *Literary and Theological Art*, 95; Lohfink, "Ekklesiale Sitz," 241; Horsley, "Ethics and Exegesis," 18; Luz, *Matthew 1-7*, 325-26. But note Wink (*Violence and Nonviolence*, 16-19), who appears to confuse the nature of the law suit and the type of garment demanded.

92. Thus Hill, *ibid.*; Theissen, "Gewaltverzicht und Feindesliebe," 176-77; Guelich, *Sermon*, 222-23; Lohfink, "Ekklesiale Sitz," 240-41; Davies and Allison, *Matthew I-VIII*, 546-47; Luz, *Matthew 1-7*, 326. Cf. Matt 27:32 and Mark 15:21, where soldiers "compel" (*angareuō*) Simon of Cyrene to carry Jesus' cross. But note Horsley ("Ethics and Exegesis," 19), who concludes that "the surrounding sayings, and especially the formulaic antithesis of 5:38-39a, force us to assume that this saying [5:41] is subordinated to the editorial framing [and thus apparently refers to inner-community rather than Roman-Jewish relations]."

93. Cf. Lohfink, "Ekklesiale Sitz," 240. While many scholars view the couplet of

The illustrative list of offenses committed by "the one who is evil" thus ranges broadly over the spectrum of "evil" circumstances which the community of Jesus' disciples might face as they live in the midst of hostile neighbors both Jewish and Gentile. They are subject to physical abuse and verbal insult, law suits and corresponding loss of property, forced labor at the behest of occupying forces, and financial importunity. And while the offenses which Jesus cites are specific in character (a slap on the *right* cheek; a law suit over a *tunic*), the form of the saying ("the one who . . . and the one who . . . and the one who . . .) implies that this list of offenses is merely illustrative in nature and could go on indefinitely, limited only by the real life experiences and the imagination of the disciples.[94]

Accordingly, the "evil" and the "evil one" to which Jesus refers do not differ in essence from the "evil" and the "evil one" of Deuteronomy 19:15–21. But there is a striking difference in the procedure to be followed in response to such "evil." In distinction to Deuteronomy 19:15–21 the setting of the Matthean text is not that of a court case. Not only is there no mention of an appearance "before the Lord, the priests, and the judges" (Deut 19:17); but there is also, significantly, no mention of any "careful examination" by the judges (Deut 19:18) to establish the guilt of the antagonist. By contrast, the character of the antagonist as "the one who is evil" is portrayed as a self-evident "given" of the situation. Further, the form of the saying encourages the community itself to define the character of "the one who is evil" by making its own additions to the open-ended list started by Jesus.[95] Within this context "evil" is neither that which requires definition by means of legal process nor that which demands recourse by the courts on behalf of the community.

This conclusion is confirmed by the "antithetical" form of the saying, even apart from its substance. Jesus opens with "You have heard that it was said, 'Eye in place of eye and tooth in place of tooth,'" an unambiguous reference to the well-established legal procedure for dealing with cases of personal injury.[96] And he goes on to add, "But I say to you . . . ,'" indication

---

5:42a/42b as only tangentially related to the preceding illustrations of 5:39b, 5:40, and 5:41 (thus Guelich, *Sermon*, 223; Davies and Allison, *Matthew I–VIII*, 547; Luz, *Matthew 1–7*, 329), Horsley ("Ethics and Exegesis," 18) views these illustrations, conversely, as conclusive proof that the text as a whole does not concern itself with the topic of non-retaliation.

94. Cf. the comments of Tannehill (*Sword of His Mouth*, 42), who notes that "a repetitive pattern embracing a series of particulars can point us beyond the literal sense of the words by suggesting that a series is open ended, that the pattern extends to many situations which have not been named." See also Levison, "Responsible Initiative," 233.

95. See n. 94 above.

96. There is considerable question about the status of the *lex talionis* within Jewish

that he is about to challenge the legal procedure to which he has just made reference. While the community is enjoined to take action, as becomes evident from the imperative which follows "But I say to you," this action lies beyond established courtroom procedures.

And if procedures differ from those outlined in the Deuteronomic text, so does the response of the community to "the one who is evil." The ancient biblical principle of "punishment in kind" (*hon tropon*) and the corresponding command to exact "injury in place of injury" and "life in place of life"[97] give way to a startling new command: "But I say to you, *Do not resist the one who is evil*" (emphasis mine). The startle effect (or as Tannehill describes it, the "imaginative shock"[98]) of this command derives from the form of the saying as well as from its substance.

The formulation of the saying as a *negative* command ("*do not* resist the one who is evil," emphasis mine) indicates first of all that what Jesus is here challenging is a *normal* human response or a *conventional* practice of society, that which people, individually or collectively, are most likely to do under ordinary circumstances. Accordingly "resisting the one who is evil" is just such an action, not only the instinctive reflex of the individual who has been wronged but even more significantly the corporate response of the community in accordance with established legal codes. And it is just such a

---

society during the first century CE. Indications from the Talmud (*Mishnah Baba Qamma* 8.6) and Josephus (*Antiquities* 4.8.35 [280]) suggest that physical retaliation had been replaced, at least in part, by monetary compensation for the harm done. Other evidence (cited by Strack and Billerbeck, *Evangelium*, 341–43) indicates that at least in certain circles the *lex talionis* was still understood in terms of physical retaliation. For a detailed discussion of this question, see Daube, *New Testament*, 254–65. See also Friedlander, *Jewish Sources*, xxii–xxiii; Banks, *Jesus and the Law*, 198–99; Guelich, *Sermon*, 219.

97. On this point Daube (*New Testament*, 258) finds it "noteworthy that when Jesus quoted the old Biblical maxim, he omitted the first clause 'Life for life' and mentioned only 'Eye for eye, tooth for tooth'. This is highly significant. In the case of homicide, the Rabbis did not abolish retaliation, at least not in theory: a murderer was liable to capital punishment, and even he who killed a man unwittingly could save himself only by escaping into a city of refuge. Accordingly the clause 'Life for life' was not divested by the Rabbis of its literal meaning in the way the other clauses 'Eye for eye, tooth for tooth' and so on were. The natural result was that the two parts of the maxim drifted apart, in law and in the minds of the people: the clause 'Life for life' belonged to criminal law, was connected with the death penalty, the other clauses 'Eye for eye' and so on belonged to private law, were connected with monetary compensation." See also Daube, "Old Testament," 21–22. Such a historical development, however, does not correspond to the literary evidence at hand; since according to the Deuteronomic text the *lex talionis*, through its attachment to the "removal formula," has as its signal purpose the illustration of a law prescribing capital punishment in response to a capital crime.

98. Tannehill, *Sword of His Mouth*, 54.

deep-rooted human/societal response which Jesus counters with the command "Do not resist . . ."

The impact of this negative command can hardly be overestimated. With the words "Do not resist" Jesus disallows both the principle of *hon tropon*, punishment in kind, and the *lex talionis*, the law of retaliation which embodies that principle. And in so doing he invalidates the most ancient and fundamental standard which individuals and societies have for dealing with "the one who is evil."[99]

Nor is this the only difficulty with these words of Jesus. There is an even greater obstacle here which arises not merely from the negative formulation of the command but from the specific substance of the imperative as well: "Do not *resist* . . . the one who is *evil*" (emphasis mine). This command appears to be nothing less than a counsel of capitulation, the command to adopt a passive and powerless response in the face of aggressive and overpowering "evil."[100] Here Jesus instructs his disciples to concede *in advance* the superior power of "evil" and to submit themselves *without resistance* to all the brutalities and injustices perpetrated by "the one who is evil." This is not merely a "hard saying" of Jesus; this is nothing short of scandalous.[101]

But this is neither the end of the saying nor the end of the matter. This word of Jesus does not stop with the command "Do not resist the one who is evil." Rather, the primary command (5:39a) opens out immediately into a series of secondary imperatives (5:39b-42), each of them highly specific in nature:

---

99. Contra Daube, who asserts (*New Testament*, 258-259) that "this part of the sermon on the mount . . . is not concerned—not even secondarily—with a certain historical system of punishment."

100. Cf. the comments of Luz (*Matthew 1-7*, 329), who sees in Matt 5:39a "a certain shift in . . . accent toward a Christian passivity" and Schottroff ("Non-Violence," 26), who defines the "non-resistance" of which Jesus speaks as "total surrender to the enemy's unjust demands."

101. Cf. Tannehill's discussion (*Sword of His Mouth*, 54) of the "imaginative shock" created by many of the synoptic sayings: "[T]he tension in synoptic sayings is a reflection of the fact that they seek to challenge men [sic] who already live in a structured personal world. New structure can arise only by attacking the old. Everything important to us has its place within our personal world, and the structures of this world are the means by which we interpret experience. We unconsciously fit whatever we experience into these structures, so experience does not ordinarily challenge them. These interpretive structures have a ravenous appetite, seeking to digest all that we encounter. If speech is to induce 'imaginative shock,' effectively challenging the old structures and suggesting new visions, it must resist such digestion. It must stick in the throat. Forceful and imaginative language can do its work only if it does not fit into our ordinary interpretive structures. The result is tension, which often finds its formal reflection within a text."

5:39b But if someone strikes you on the right cheek,
> *turn to them the other cheek as well.*

5:40 And if someone wishes to sue you and take your tunic,
> *let them take your cloak as well.*

5:41 And if someone compels you to go one mile,
> *go with them for two.*

5:42 *Give* to the one who asks of you;
> and *do not reject* the one who wishes to borrow from you. (Emphasis mine)

Here the true force of Jesus' call "not to resist the one who is evil" finally comes to light. In the form and the substance of these secondary imperatives lies the key to the interpretation of the primary command. With one exception these imperatives are positive in their formulation: "turn," "let," "go," "give," and "do not reject."[102] And it is precisely these positive imperatives which exegete the negative command of 5:39a ("do not resist"). As a result the command "do not resist" is neither a call to passivity nor a counsel of capitulation.[103] Even while it constitutes in grammatical terms a negative command and in semantic terms a call to inaction, Jesus' command "not to resist the one who is evil" is, paradoxically, a positive command and a call to action.

The substance of the secondary imperatives confirms this conclusion. The most striking feature of these imperatives as a group is the radically, even absurdly, unanticipated character of the responses to which they challenge the listeners.[104] Those who have been insulted and physically abused by a back-handed slap are to turn the other cheek as well to the one who has assaulted them. Those who have been taken to court and sued over their *chitōn* or undergarment are to offer up their *himation* or outer garment as

---

102. While the imperative "do not reject" is, to be sure, a negative formulation, the parallelism of the two final imperatives ("give" and "do not reject") indicates that even this negative formulation is to be understood as a positive command.

103. Cf. the comments of Theissen ("Gewaltverzicht und Feindesliebe," 177: "Die negative Forderung, nicht Widerstand zu leisten, wird durch eine positive ergänzt und übertroffen. So ist auch bei Mt nicht einfach an ein passives Sichfügen gedacht.") and Lienemann (*Gewalt* und *Gewaltlosigkeit*, 62: "Noch wichtiger aber ist, dass die Weisung Jesu durchgehend nicht auf eine passive Hinnahme des Erlittenen zielt, sondern, ganz im Gegenteil, zu einem aktiven Tun auffordert: Halte hin! Gib! Geh' mit!"). Luz, however, turns this argument on its head, arguing in precisely reverse fashion (*Matthew 1–7*, 329) that "it signifies a new tone that [Matthew] summarizes the *positive* exhortation of vv. 39b–42 in the *negative* formulation, 'do not resist.'"

104. Cf. Wink, *Violence and Nonviolence*, 18–20.

well to the adversary. Those who have been coerced into service carrying baggage for the occupying forces are to extend their services without coercion and carry the load for two miles instead of one. Those who have been importuned financially are to give without hesitation to those who ask money of them. The single observable principle which governs these responses is that they run directly counter to all human instinct, individual or societal.[105] As a result, the command "not to resist," far from being a call to passivity or a counsel of capitulation, constitutes a challenge to the most radical of human responses.

Nor is there any question about the ethical character of these responses. By placing the imperatives of 5:39b-42 in deliberate juxtaposition to the *lex talionis* ("eye in place of eye and tooth in place of tooth"), a law which is not merely violent but ultimately death-dealing, Jesus repudiates the essential violence of the talionic principle and establishes the character of his own call to action, by contrast, as fundamentally life-affirming.

Nor is this the end of the matter. While the imperatives of 5:39b-42 are without question real-life commands calling for real-life responses,[106] these imperatives in no way exhaust the meaning of Jesus' command "not to resist the one who is evil." Nor do they function as so many "legal rules" to be observed. Rather, they serve above all an "illuminating" function with respect to the command of 5:39a.[107] On the one hand these imperatives create an illustrative list of potential interpretations of the command "not to resist the one who is evil." On the other hand this list, because of its extreme specificity and vividness, calls for its own extension to all those other specific circumstances not here enumerated in which the community of Jesus' disciples likewise encounters "the one who is evil." And in this way the illustrative imperatives which Jesus sets forth not only suggest specific ethical alternatives for the community of disciples but ultimately reshape the entire

---

105. Cf. the comments of Tannehill, who notes (*Sword of His Mouth*, 70, emphasis Tannehill's): "In each case an *action* is commanded, and this action is the precise opposite of our natural tendency in the situation . . . I would suggest that these almost absurd commands were conceived by the simple device of reversing man's [sic] natural tendency."

106. On this point, cf. Lienemann's reference (*Gewalt und Gewaltlosigkeit*, 61) to "konkrete Weltverhältnisse" and Lohfink's similar reference ("Ekklesiale Sitz," 242; emphasis Lohfink's) to "*reale* Verhaltensweisen" in contrast to those commentators who effectively disarm the imperatives of 5:39b-42 by relegating them to the realm of the metaphorical or spiritual and thus denying them the force of literal commands (thus Daube, "Old Testament" 20; Davies and Allison, *Matthew I-VIII*, 541).

107. On this point, see Tannehill's discussion (*Sword of His Mouth*, 25-27) of the distinction between "legal rule" and "text as illuminator."

ethical landscape. Such is the force of the paradoxically *positive* command "not to resist."

But there is an even greater paradox which comes to light here. Not only do the illustrative imperatives of 5:39b–42 show Jesus' call "not to resist the one who is evil" to be a *positive* command despite its *negative* formulation. They also demonstrate that this command is one which *empowers* the community of disciples, even while it appears to enjoin a stance of *powerlessness*. The fact that Jesus does not merely invalidate the principle of *hon tropon* and the corresponding *lex talionis* but also illustrates a new mode of response to "the one who is evil" means that for the first time ever *initiative has been placed in the hands of the community*.

As long as the *lex talionis* was in force, the only option open to the community for responding to the evildoer was to repay the evil deed, in essentially mechanistic fashion, with punishment in kind. As a result, all prerogative for *action* remained with the evildoer; while the community, bound by its own legal code, could do nothing more than *react*.

Now all this has changed. Precisely through the scandalous command "not to resist the one who is evil" (5:39a) and the absurdly unanticipated imperatives which give it substance (5:39b–42) Jesus paradoxically holds out to the community of disciples a power they have never before experienced, *the power to act in the face of evil*.[108] Initiative no longer belongs solely to "the one who is evil." Now through the word of Jesus the community of disciples finds itself empowered and impelled to respond to the evildoer with initiatives of its own which are as daring and unexpected as they are positive and life-affirming.

This is Jesus' answer to the (Deuteronomic) law of retaliation. And at this point the saying ends. There are no motive clauses and no further words of explanation.[109] Following his listing of illustrative imperatives (5:39b–42)

---

108. Cf. the comments of Wink, who describes the imperatives of 5:39b–42 (*Violence and Nonviolence*, 19) as "a practical strategic measure for empowering the oppressed," and observes with reference to the command of 5:41 (21) that "the question here, as in the two previous instances, is how the oppressed can recover their initiative, how they can assert their human dignity in a situation that cannot for the time being be changed. The rules are Caesar's, but not how one responds to the rules—that is God's, and Caesar has no power over that."

109. See the comments of Davies and Allison (*Matthew I–VIII*, 546) and Luz (*Matthew 1–7*, 326–27) to this effect and the related comments of Tannehill (*Sword of His Mouth*, 70–71). Other scholars, to the contrary, fill the apparent *lacuna* in this saying of Jesus with "motives" appropriate to the Matthean context: the example of the life of Jesus (Strobel, "Macht und Gewalt," 94–98; Levison, "Responsible Initiative," 233–34); the awareness that judgment belongs to God alone (Hill, *Gospel*, 127; Lienemann, *Gewalt und Gewaltlosigkeit*, 75); the desire to win over the adversary (Lohfink, "Ekklesiale Sitz," 241). Even Luz, who claims to find no "motive" as such for the imperatives of 5:39b–42

Jesus simply moves on to the sixth and final antithesis (5:43–48). But here in this final antithesis Jesus puts into words that which till now has remained unspoken. The motive clause which is missing from the command "not to resist the one who is evil" finds clear expression in the saying which follows:

> 5:43 You have heard that it was said,
>
>> You shall love your neighbor and hate your enemy.
>
> 5:44 But I say to you,
>
>> Love your enemies and pray for those who are persecuting you,
>>
>>> *in order that you might be the children of your Father who is in heaven.*
>>>
>>> *For he makes his sun to rise*
>>>
>>>> *on the evil and the good [epi ponērous kai agathous]*
>>>
>>> *and he sends rain*
>>>
>>>> *on the just and the unjust [epi dikaious kai adikous].*
>
> . . . .
>
> 5:48 *You shall therefore be perfect,*
>
>> *as your Father in heaven is perfect.* (Emphasis mine)

The command to "love your enemies and pray for those who are persecuting you" (5:44a) states the obverse of the preceding command "not to resist the one who is evil" (5:39a). Accordingly the motive clauses attached to the latter command apply as well to the former. As a result the command of 5:39a reads as follows in its "completed" form (5:39a, 44, 48): "Do not resist the one who is evil . . . in order that you may be the children of your Father who is in heaven; for he makes his sun to rise on the evil and the good and he sends rain on the just and the unjust . . . You shall therefore be perfect, as your Father in heaven is perfect."

And with this connection the picture is now complete and the comparison clear. It is because the Israelite community "belongs to a jealous God"—a God who "will utterly destroy [them] from the face of the earth" if they follow the gods of the nations around them—that they are commanded to "remove the evil one from [their] midst" by exacting "life in place of life" and "member in place of member." And it is, by the same token, because the

---

(*Matthew 1–7*, 326–27), nevertheless appears to offer just such a "motive" (337) when he describes the renunciation of force as "a 'contrasting sign' of the kingdom of God or a part of a new way of righteousness which has been opened up by Jesus."

community of disciples are the "children of a perfect Father"—who "makes his sun to rise on the evil and the good and sends rain on the just and the unjust"—that Jesus now commands them "not to resist the one who is evil."

For Matthew, as for Deuteronomy, the ethics of the community of faith emerge directly from the community's theology, or in other words, from the community's understanding of the character of God. It is this shared reality which confirms that Jesus *is indeed "fulfilling the law and the prophets" (5:17), even as he proclaims "But I say to you" (5:21–48)*. And it is, accordingly, in the light of this same reality that the Deuteronomic command to "remove the evil one from your midst" finds its ultimate "fulfillment" in the command of Jesus "not to resist the one who is evil."

8

The Hard Sayings of Jesus in Real-World Context

Reading Matthew 5:38–48 within the Occupied Palestinian Territories

THE WORDS OF JESUS in Matthew 5:38–48 surely qualify for the proverbial list of Jesus' hard sayings. The commands "Do not resist the one who is evil" (5:39a, DJW),[1] "Love your enemies" (5:44a), and "Pray for those who persecute you" (5:44b) are words we might wish that Jesus had never spoken or that the Gospel Writers had never preserved. Such commands appear illogical, counter-intuitive, and even scandalous.

But within Matthew's narrative these words are vital to Jesus' call to greater righteousness (cf. 5:20a) and the life of the kingdom of heaven (5:20b). Accordingly, those who follow Jesus as his disciples face these hard sayings as the ongoing call to an extraordinary life of faithfulness within a real world peopled with evil ones, enemies, and persecutors.

Such is surely the case for present-day Palestinian Christians living in the Occupied Palestinian Territories.[2] Their community has lived for

---

1. All biblical citations reflect the New Revised Standard Version unless otherwise designated.
2. This may also apply to Palestinian Muslims. Note the response of Mohammed (not his real name), a Palestinian Muslim, when asked (in a "Life of Jesus" course for tour guiding students) to identify the "important themes" in the Sermon on the Mount: "I can't do this assignment. Jesus is a very important prophet for us. And everything that he said is important." Mohammed eventually submitted a paper far more extensive than that of any of his colleagues.

more than sixty years with the after-effects of the 1948 Nakba (catastrophe), in which they lost more than half of their ancestral lands to the State of Israel. And since 1967 they have lived under occupation by the State of Israel and under military rule by the Israeli Defense Forces. Accordingly, when Palestinian Christians read Matthew 5:38–48, they encounter the radical call of Jesus in a context where others (whom they might view as evil ones, enemies, and persecutors) build walls around their cities, expropriate their lands, destroy their homes, bulldoze their olive groves, put roadblocks in front of their villages, impose curfews and closures on their towns, and erect military checkpoints that restrict their freedom of movement.

This paper offers a twofold contextual reading of Matthew 5:38–48. The first reading utilizes narrative criticism to analyze the text from my own scholarly context as a student of Matthew's Gospel. This reading assesses 5:38–48 within Matthew's overall narrative, attending to narrative location, internal structure, use of vocabulary, biblical and real-world allusions, and ultimately the narrative/theological message for Matthew's first-century community.

The second reading assesses the pragmatic significance of these hard sayings of Jesus for twenty-first-century Palestinian Christians. What do these first-century words of Jesus mean to present-day Palestinian Christians living under Israeli occupation? And where does the call of Jesus become visible within the real world of the Occupied Palestinian Territories? This reading emerges from personal conversations with Palestinian Christians from the West Bank and Jerusalem, most of them longterm acquaintances, persons whom I have learned to know throughout frequent sojourns in Israel/Palestine as traveler, tour leader, and sabbatical scholar.

The paper concludes with a brief comparison of these two contextual readings. How do these readings relate to each other? Where are their coherences and/or divergences? What happens to scholarly biblical interpretation as biblical text engages with the real world? How does the twenty-first-century Israeli/Palestinian context impact the interpretation of this first-century Matthean text?

I. MATTHEW 5:38–48: A NARRATIVE READING

To read a text within its narrative context is to encounter that text sequentially within the flow of the narrative. The text therefore "derives its significance not simply from its content as such but from its relationship to the other 'events' in the unfolding narrative."[3] Accordingly, a narrative reading

---

3. Weaver, *Missionary Discourse*, 28.

of Matthew 5:38-48 must attend first to the preceding text (1:1—5:37), secondly to the text itself (5:38-48), and finally to the subsequent text (6:1–28:20).

Matthew's Narrative Pre-Information (1:1—5:37).

As David B. Howell notes in his study of narrative rhetoric within Matthew's Gospel, "The initial information about the attitudes, characters, and narrative world which is projected [within a narrative text] plays a large part in the process of teaching readers the correct interpretive techniques for reading the text."[4] And the initial information provided by 1:1–5:37 offers multiple clues to the interpretation of 5:38-48.

One such clue is the Jewish/messianic character of Matthew's narrative. This narrative opens with a Jewish/messianic genealogy beginning with Abraham (1:1, 2, 17), the ancestor of the Jewish people (cf. 3:9), continuing through (King) David (1:1, 6, 17) and the deportation to Babylon (1:11, 12, 17), and rising to its climax with Jesus the Messiah (1:1, 16, 17). Accordingly, Matthew's accounts of the birth and infancy of Jesus (1:18–2:23) feature Joseph, son of David (1:20) and Jesus the Messiah (1:18; 2:4), who "has been born king of the Jews" (2:1), who "is to shepherd [God's] people Israel" (2:6) and whose messianic designation is that of "my [= God's] son" (2:15; cf. Ps 2:7).

John the Baptist (3:1–17) is an eschatological Jewish prophet, "the Elijah who is to come" (11:7–15; cf. 17:10–13; Mal 4:5). John's water baptism (3:5–10, 11a) foreshadows the arrival of a messianic figure who is "more powerful" (3:11b) and will "baptize . . . with the Holy Spirit and with fire" (3:11d). And John's prophetic pointers toward the Messiah find prompt fulfillment.

Jesus is baptized by John (3:13–16a), endowed with the Holy Spirit (3:16b), and affirmed by the voice of God for his messianic ministry (3:17; cf. Ps 2:7). He is then "led up by the Spirit into the wilderness to be tempted by the devil" (4:1) in a series of encounters that highlight his messianic calling (4:3, 6; cf. 4:9). Jesus resists these temptations (4:4, 7, 10), dispatches Satan (4:10–11a), and is served by angels of God (4:11b). He then relocates from Nazareth to Capernaum in messianic fulfillment of the scriptures (4:12–16; cf. Isa 9:1–2). And from here Jesus Messiah commences his mission, proclaiming the kingdom of heaven (4:17), calling disciples (4:18–22), and engaging in a peripatetic and charismatic ministry of teaching and healing that draws massive crowds from all directions (4:23–25).

---

4. Howell, *Inclusive Story*, 115.

Within this highly charged messianic context Jesus goes up the mountain (5:1a), recasting the image of Moses at Sinai in a messianic and eschatological mode, and inaugurates his messianic ministry by teaching his disciples about the kingdom of heaven in the hearing of the crowds (5:1–7:29). In Terence Donaldson's words,

> [T]he gathering to Jesus on the mountain in Galilee . . . should be seen in the context of the eschatological gathering of the people of God. The disciples are the foundation of the eschatological community called into being by the messianic activity of Jesus, and the crowds are being invited to join their fellowship. The Sermon, then, is the messianic interpretation of the Torah for this community—the authoritative declaration of the characteristics which this community is called to exhibit.[5]

Jesus opens his inaugural address with blessings on those who exhibit the characteristics of the kingdom of heaven (5:3–12; cf. 5:13–16). He then defines his coming in terms of messianic fulfillment: "Do not think that I have come to abolish the law or the prophets; I have come not to abolish but to fulfill (5:17)." Following this programmatic declaration Jesus then illustrates his messianic fulfillment of scripture with a six-fold litany: "You have heard that it was said . . . But I say to you . . ." (5:21–26, 27–30, 31–32, 33–37, 38–42, 43–48). The text of 5:38–48 creates the conclusion and climax of this litany.

The implications of Matthew's messianic motif for interpreting 5:38–48 are manifest. Jesus Messiah has come to carry out God's messianic agenda: to bring Jewish history to its climax (1:1, 2–16, 17); to "shepherd [God's] people Israel" (2:6) as "king of the Jews" (2:2); to "fulfill all righteousness" (3:15); to resist the temptations of Satan as the true and faithful Son of God (4:1–11; cf. 2:15; 3:17); to proclaim the arrival of God's realm (4:17); and to "fulfill . . . the law [and] the prophets" (5:17). Accordingly, Jesus' scriptural citations ("You have heard that it was said . . .") find messianic fulfillment in Jesus' exposition ("But I say to you . . ."). Conversely, Jesus' calls to action reflect messianic interpretation of Jewish scripture.

A further interpretive clue is the narrative juxtaposition of King Herod (2:1) and Jesus "who has been born king of the Jews" (2:2). As one who "seeks the life of the child" (2:13, 20) and slaughters the infants of Bethlehem to execute this scheme (2:16–18), Herod undeniably demonstrates evil character. The irony of the narrative, however, is that Herod, in spite of his worst intentions and his manifest power, cannot carry out his single goal, namely to destroy the child. Instead Matthew portrays Herod as utterly

---

5. Donaldson, *Jesus on the Mountain*, 115.

powerless vis-à-vis the angel of the Lord, who persistently dispatches people just in time to foil Herod's plots and save the life of the child (2:12, 13, 19-20, 22). In the end Herod lies dead (2:15, 19, 20), while the child is alive and well in Nazareth (2:21-23). The message is clear. Evil people can create horrific human devastation (2:16-18). But they have far less power than they or others imagine. And it is God, not the powers of evil, whose agenda ultimately wins the day.

A related interpretive clue emerges from the beatitudes of Jesus' inaugural address (5:3-12). Here Jesus pronounces kingdom blessings on the "poor in spirit" (5:3) those who "mourn" (5:4), the "meek" (5:5), those who "hunger and thirst for righteousness" (5:6), the "merciful" (5:7), the "pure in heart" (5:8), the "peacemakers" (5:9), and those "who are persecuted for righteousness' sake" (5:10; cf. 5:11-12). And with these extraordinary blessings Jesus puts his listeners on immediate notice that the kingdom of heaven stands fundamentally at variance with "the kingdoms of the world and their splendor" (4:8) and ultimately with all human notions of power and greatness (cf. 16:21-23; 18:1-4; 20:24-28).

Responding to Evil Ones and Enemies (5:38-48).

The text of 5:38-48 concludes Jesus' litany on the greater righteousness. This litany deals with murder (5:21-26), adultery (5:27-30), divorce (5:31-32), swearing of oaths (5:33-37), retaliation (5:38-42), and hatred of enemies (5:43-48). Each section opens with the words, "You have heard that it was said," followed by a Jewish scripture. And each section ends with the refrain, "But I say to you," in the authoritative voice of Jesus Messiah, followed by Jesus' messianic fulfillment of the scripture.

In each section Jesus' greater righteousness contrasts sharply with what his listeners have previously heard. The prohibition of murder (5:21; cf. Exod 20:13//Deut 5:17) now extends to mere anger (5:22-26); and adultery (5:27; cf. Exod 20:14//Deut 5:18) reaches beyond the physical acts of the body to the lustful thoughts of the heart (5:28-30). Jesus prohibits divorce (5:31; cf. Deut 24:1) "except on the ground of unchastity" (5:32). And he forbids the swearing of oaths (5:33; cf. Lev 19:12; Deut 23:21), calling his followers to a simple "yes" or "no" response (5:34-37). The final two sections of Jesus' litany (5:38-42, 43-48) fit this same pattern, even as they depict the vivid challenges of everyday life for Jesus' disciples in a world of violence and oppression.

This is a world of physical assault and insulting behavior: "If anyone strikes you on the right cheek . . ." (5:39b). Within the honor-shame culture of Matthew's first-century Middle Eastern narrative, such a back-handed slap is considered an insult. In Warren Carter's words, "[A back-handed slap] expresses the power differential of a superior who disdains an inferior: a master with a slave, a wealthy landowner with a poor farmer or artisan, a Roman with a provincial, a wise man with a fool or a child . . ., a government official with a difficult prophet (2 Kgs 22:24), the religious elite with a dangerous preacher (Matt 26:67)."[6] But such an insult is likewise a brutality. Accordingly, Jesus depicts a world where his followers regularly encounter both physical assault and public insult.

This is a world where law suits against impoverished debtors are common: "If anyone wishes to sue you and take your tunic . . ." (5:40a). Jewish law prohibits taking and keeping a person's outer garment or cloak, since this may well be their only blanket (Exod 22:25–27; Deut 24:10–13; cf. Amos 2:7–8). But there is no such law against taking the tunic, the undergarment worn next to the body. Accordingly, Jesus reveals a convenient legal loophole for taking an impoverished debtor to court and demanding the very shirt off his back.

This is a world where Jewish civilians live under Roman military occupation. And the Romans, even the least among them, have all the privileges associated with military conquest and occupation. Here a Roman foot soldier may compel any civilian to carry his pack for one mile (5:41a; cf. 27:32).[7] And the civilian is obliged to comply with this command, no matter how inconvenient or burdensome.

This is also a world where Jesus' disciples encounter indigents on the streets who beg money from the passersby (5:42a) and friends and neighbors who seek to borrow from them (5:42b). In this world, profoundly impacted by "poverty and exploitative practices of tax and debt,"[8] desperate economic realities can create evil ones even out of poverty-stricken compatriots.

Finally, this is a world where Jesus' disciples encounter enemies and persecutors (5:43–44). Here one's very life is at stake. As Matthew's reader already knows, these people do such things as seek the lives of innocent children and carry out brutal massacres to destroy them (2:1–23). And throughout his public ministry, from Galilee (5:10–12) to Jerusalem (23:34–36), Jesus persistently identifies the persecution of God's faithful ones—presumably by their enemies—as the distinguishing mark of their faithfulness.

---

6. Carter, *Matthew and the Margins*, 151–52.

7. As Carter notes (ibid., 152–53), "The verb **forces** (. . . *angareusei*) refers to requisitioning labor, transport (animals, ships), and lodging from subject people (called *angaria*)."

8. Ibid., 153.

The prophets have already met this fate (5:12; cf. 21:33–36; 23:29–31), as will John the Baptist shortly (4:12a; 14:1–12; 17:9–13). Jesus will likewise die at the hands of others (16:21; 17:22–23; 20:17–19; 21:33–46; 26:1–2). And he promises his disciples the same persecution (5:10–12; 23:34–36).

Here in this brutal world Jesus' disciples have heard the scriptural calls to "eye for eye and tooth for tooth" (5:38; cf. Deut 19:15–21) and hatred of enemies (5:43b; cf. Lev 19:18[9]). "Eye for eye and tooth for tooth," the ancient *lex talionis*, calls for a measured but mandated response by the Israelite community to the evil in their midst. Deuteronomy 19:15–21, the closest biblical antecedent to Jesus' citation,[10] spells out a detailed legal process that establishes but strictly delimits the liability of the offender. The community must punish the offender with the identical violence that he/she has inflicted on the victim, no more and no less.[11]

But just as before (5:21–37), Jesus responds to these scriptural appeals ("You have heard . . .") with his own authoritative messianic interpretation ("But I say to you . . ."). And Jesus' responses surely scandalize his listeners.[12] Jesus' command "Do not resist" (5:39a) is an apparent affront to those who regularly suffer violence and oppression. And it resounds like a call to total capitulation to evil people and total passivity vis-à-vis evil powers.

But appearances are deceiving. Jesus immediately follows up this call to nonresistance (5:39a) with an illustrative list of nonresistant actions (5:39b, 40, 41, 42a, 42b). And each of these imperatives is an active verb: turn (5:39b); let . . . have (5:40); go (5:41); give (5:42a); do not refuse (5:42b). Even the single negative command (5:42b) clearly implies a positive action. Accordingly, Jesus' call to nonresistance is in fact a call to active response.

But Jesus' commands are not merely active. They are also unexpected. The very fact that Jesus identifies these actions as nonresistant implies that they do not fit expected norms. There is nothing natural or instinctive about these responses. Instead they need to be thought out instantaneously, in the thick of real-world challenges. They require mental agility, creativity, and spontaneity. Accordingly, these responses cannot be anticipated in advance.

---

9. Note, however, that Lev 19:18 refers only to "loving your neighbor" and does not mention "hating your enemy." For such language, see Ps 139:21–22.

10. Of the three (Septuagintal) versions of the *lex talionis* found within the Jewish scriptures (Exod 21:22–25; Lev 24:19–20; Deut 19:15–21), only Deuteronomy 19:15–21 includes the specific vocabulary of Matthew 5:39, namely *resist* (*anthistēmi*: Deut 19:16) and *evil one* (*ho ponēros*: Deut 19:19).

11. For a detailed discussion of Deuteronomy 19:15–21 vis-à-vis its messianic fulfillment in Matthew 5:38–48, see Weaver, "Transforming Nonresistance," 32–71.

12. Cf. 11:6, where Jesus pronounces a blessing on the one "who is not scandalized" (*mē skandalisthē*, DJW) by him or his messianic ministry (11:2–5).

Instead they take the evil one by surprise and disrupt all instinctive patterns of action and reaction.

These responses likewise bring the evil itself into clear focus and confront the evil one with the implications of their actions. The one who demeans another with a back-handed slap on the right cheek must treat the other as an equal, if they now issue a front-handed slap on the left cheek. The one who sues another for his tunic and receives the cloak as well now faces public shame when the defendant leaves the courtroom stark naked. And the soldier who compels a civilian to carry his pack one mile now faces dangerous legal consequences when the civilian carries his pack two miles instead.

Further, the casuistic (if . . . then) form of Jesus' commands clearly suggests that Jesus has not offered an exhaustive list of rules. Instead Jesus' repeated formula suggests that these illustrations serve merely as the first items in a list that extends indefinitely,[13] as far as changing circumstances demand and creative imagination enables. These imperatives are thus not rules to be rigidly applied. Rather they point toward a moving, growing, ever-transforming pattern for nonviolent living in a violent world.

Here Jesus shatters the ancient and seemingly indestructible linkage between action and reaction reflected in the *lex talionis*. In place of obligatory retaliation Jesus now frees his disciples to act rather than react in the face of evil and to take creative and nonviolent initiatives vis-à-vis their antagonists. The implications are revolutionary. As Warren Carter notes, "The servile refuse to be humiliated; the subjugated take initiative by acting with dignity and humanity in the midst of and against injustice and oppression which seem permanent."[14]

Now Jesus sets forth his final commands: "You have heard that it was said, 'You shall love your neighbor and you shall hate your enemy.' But I say to you, 'Love (and keep on loving) your enemies. Pray (and keep on praying) for those who persecute you'" (5:43–44, DJW). The shock effect of these words is manifest. Jesus' call transforms instinctive hatred into unimaginable love. Enemies and persecutors, those who arrest, torture, and kill Jesus' disciples (10:16–39; 22:1–10; 23:34–36; 24:9–13), are the very people whom they must love and for whom they must pray. And these responses are not once and done. The present tense imperatives "love" (*agapate*) and "pray for" (*proseuchesthe*) imply repetitive actions. Thus loving enemies and praying for persecutors are the ongoing agenda of everyday life. The challenge of Jesus' words is immense.

---

13. Thus Tannehill, *Sword of His Mouth*, 42, 69.
14. Carter, *Matthew and the Margins*, 154.

But Jesus' logic is also clear. Jesus offers a motive clause (5:45-48) grounding the actions of his disciples in their identity as children of their Father in heaven (5:45a) and, by the same token, in the character of the Father whose children they are (5:45b). Within the Hebrew thought world, to be children of another means above all to resemble that one in character and actions (cf. John 8:39, 42). Thus because God "makes his sun to rise on the evil and the good and sends rain upon the righteous and the unrighteous" (5:45b/c) and because God is their "Father in heaven" (5:45a, 48), Jesus' disciples are called to love their enemies. Since God bestows blessings with scandalous impartiality, the children of God will likewise reflect God's love for all people, even evil ones, enemies, and persecutors. In so doing they will fulfill the greater righteousness to which Jesus has called them (5:20; cf. 5:46-47). And they will also, through God's empowering grace,[15] exhibit God's perfection (5:48b) within their human existence (5:48a).

Matthew's Narrative Post-Information (6:1—28:20).

Jesus has issued an extraordinary challenge. But a question persists. How are these words of Jesus reflected in the actual lives of God's faithful ones, Jesus included? Matthew's answer to this question emerges in the story-lines of the prophets, John the Baptist, Jesus, and Jesus' disciples. These story-lines have begun prior to 5:38-48. And the collective portrait is unmistakable. God's faithful ones consistently suffer at the hands of evil ones. And they do so without retaliating in kind. The prophets were persecuted long ago (5:12b). John the Baptist has been arrested prior to Jesus' public ministry (4:12; cf. 4:17). Jesus' own life was threatened at birth (2:1-23); and he now faces renewed persecution (cf. 5:11). And Jesus assures his disciples that they too will one day "be persecuted . . . on [his] account" (5:11; cf. 5:10). Now these story-lines play themselves out. And Matthew's endings are consistent with his beginnings.

The story-line of the prophets (5:12; 23:29, 30, 31) reflects simple, nonviolent commitment to the mission to which they have been sent (21:34, 36). The parabolic slaves of the landowner go as they are sent and attempt their mission, namely "to collect his produce" (21:34). When their mission is rejected and they themselves are brutalized and killed, there is no mention of retaliation. Their calling is to "collect the produce" of the vineyard, not to

---

15. Cf. Jesus' promise to his disciples: "When they hand you over, do not worry about how you are to speak or what you are to say; for what you are to say will be given to you at that time; for it is not you who speak, but the Spirit of your Father speaking through you" (10:19-20).

take the lives of the tenants. And the suffering of the prophets (5:12; 23:29, 30, 31) is an ongoing reality, even as God persistently sends emissaries into a brutal world to carry out God's ongoing agenda (21:34/36a; cf. 23:34a).

The story-line of John the Baptist is similar. John, the one sent to prepare the way for Jesus (11:10; cf. 3:3), finds his mission ultimately rejected (14:3-4). Accordingly, John suffers the violence of the violent (11:12). And he forfeits his life in brutal fashion (14:8-11; 17:12) for the sake of righteousness (21:32a). But there is no hint that John engages in retaliatory violence vis-à-vis the violent powers of his world (11:12). John's calling as the "Elijah who is to come" (11:14b) is to "prepare the way of the Lord" (3:3) and proclaim the word of the Lord (3:2, 7-12; 14:4), not to enact the wrath of God (3:10, 12).

The story-line of Jesus highlights Jesus' profound commitment to a messianic mission that is nonviolent in character. Jesus teaches, proclaims, and heals (4:23//9:35; cf. 11:1) in a strongly life-affirming ministry where "the blind receive their sight, the lame walk, the lepers are cleansed, the deaf hear, the dead are raised, and the poor have good news brought to them" (11:5). Nevertheless Jesus knows that his ministry, like that of John, will ultimately be rejected (17:12).

But Jesus does not retaliate (cf. 26:53). Instead he heads deliberately toward Jerusalem, keenly aware of divine necessity (16:21-23; cf. 26:54). And he regularly predicts the brutal fate that awaits him there at the hands of his enemies (16:21-23; 17:22-23; 20:17-19; 26:1-2; cf. 21:33-46). Jesus' commitment to nonretaliation is firm and unshakable. When Peter challenges Jesus' prediction of suffering and death (16:21-22), Jesus rebukes him sharply (16:23). When Judas identifies Jesus for arrest (26:47-49), Jesus replies, "Friend, do what you are here to do" (26:50a). When a disciple wields a sword in Jesus' defense (26:51-52), Jesus issues a categorical rebuke: "Put your sword back into its place; for all who take the sword will perish by the sword" (26:52). And Jesus flatly rejects the option of divine retaliation: "Do you think that I cannot appeal to my Father, and he will at once send me more than twelve legions of angels?" (26:53). During his trial Jesus refuses to defend himself against the accusations of his opponents (27:11-14). And he suffers to the death (27:50b) rather than retaliating against his enemies (26:53) or responding to their taunts (27:40, 42-43).

The story-line of Jesus' disciples depicts them initially as impervious to Jesus' call to nonresistance (16:21-22; 26:51). But in the world beyond the end of the narrative the picture looks strikingly different. Here Jesus' disciples are sent by divine calling (9:38; 10:5, 16; 22:3, 4; 23:34, 37) to a mission that is life-affirming (10:7-8, 12-13), invitational (22:3a; cf. 22:2-4, 8-10), and gracious (10:8b). But this mission, like that of Jesus, will meet with rejection. In fact Jesus knowingly sends his disciples out "like sheep into the midst of wolves" (10:16). There they will be "maligned" (10:25b), "hated" (10:22a; 24:9b, 10), "mistreated" (22:6), "seized" (22:6), "flogged" (10:17b; 23:34b), "handed over" (10:17a, 19a, 21a; 24:9a, 10), "dragged before governors and kings" (10:18a), "persecuted" (10:23a), "stoned" (23:37), "crucified" (23:34b), "killed" (10:28a; 22:6; 23:34b), and "put to death" (10:21b; 24:9a).

But Jesus calls his disciples not to retaliation but rather to a surprising range of nonviolent responses. At times Jesus counsels prudence. The disciples must "leave" the houses where they are not welcome (10:14), "flee" from the towns where they are persecuted (10:23), "beware" of people (10:17a), and "be wise as serpents and innocent as doves" (10:16b). Elsewhere Jesus calls his disciples to throw caution to the winds: "Do not worry" (10:19a), "Do not fear" (10:26a, 28a, 31a, DJW), "Speak in the light" (10:27a, DJW), "Proclaim from the housetops" (10:27b), "Acknowledge me before others" (cf. 10:32a). Jesus even calls his disciples to vivid prophetic actions: "Let your peace return to you" (10:13b) and "Shake off the dust from your feet" (10:14b). But more than this is not theirs to do. Their calling is to carry out the peaceable mission to whom they have been sent and, like Jesus, to suffer without retaliation when others inflict violence.

But the story-lines of God's faithful ones do not end with suffering and death. Those who do not resist evil ones but instead love their enemies and pray for their persecutors ultimately "find" their life through "losing" it (10:39b) and are "saved" by "enduring to the end" (10:22b; 24:13). And Matthew's narrative ends with the same profound irony (2:1–23) and the same divine laughter (Ps 2:4) with which it began. In the Resurrection Narrative (27:62–28:20), as in the Birth Narrative (1:18–2:23), God gets the last laugh. Here Jesus' enemies discover that God has bested them at their own game, undone their death sentence, raised Jesus from the dead, and left the well-secured tomb empty. The message is clear. God alone has ultimate power. God alone has the prerogative to right the wrongs of history. And God alone will surely and powerfully vindicate God's faithful ones for their obedience in mission, their creative nonresistance to evil ones, their persistent love of enemies, their constant prayers for persecutors, and their faithfulness in suffering and death.

I. MATTHEW 5:38–48: A PALESTINIAN CHRISTIAN READING

To read Matthew 5:38–48 as a twenty-first-century Palestinian Christian is to encounter the radical call of Jesus day by day within the challenging context of the Occupied Palestinian Territories. This call comes to Christians across every spectrum. The sixteen people interviewed for this paper reflect a wide range of churches: Anglican, Armenian Orthodox, Baptist, Charismatic, Greek Orthodox, Latin Catholic, Lutheran, Melkite/Greek Catholic, and Quaker. They are women and men ranging in age from the twenties to the seventies. And they represent differing professions: health care, tourism, education, organizational administration, pastoring, writing, and public speaking. But in spite of the demographic differences, the responses reflect strong similarities.

The Challenge of Matthew 5:38–48.

Broad consensus emerges over the challenge of Jesus' words. From Samia's[16] perspective, "These are some of the very difficult passages that we [face] with the Occupation. It's not easy to be a Christian." Nora[17] notes the unique character of Jesus' words: "You don't find these verses in any of the other religions. For us the neighbor and the enemy are one." And like Samia Nora finds it challenging "to follow Jesus every single day under Occupation" and confesses her difficulty at times in completing the Lord's Prayer with its call to forgive. As Imad[18] explains, "When the enemy keeps on doing what [he/she] is doing, this is where the victim will not tolerate the oppressor. It is difficult for people oppressed on a daily basis to forgive the oppressor." Alex[19] notes that "because of our human nature . . . these teachings seem to belong to other creatures and not to us." Solomon[20] wonders, "How can Jesus tell us to do such a thing?" And Cedar[21] and Samia highlight the difficulty of

---

16. Samia Khoury, Board Member, Sabeel Ecumenical Liberation Theology Center.

17. Nora Carmi, Former Coordinator of Community-Building and Women's Programs, Sabeel Ecumenical Liberation Theology Center.

18. Imad Nassar, Program Manager, Wi'am Palestinian Conflict Resolution Center.

19. Rev. Alex Awad, Dean of Students, Bethlehem Bible College and Pastor, East Jerusalem Baptist Church.

20. Solomon J. Nour, Headmaster, Hope Secondary School (deceased August 5, 2011).

21. Cedar Duaybis, Board Member, Sabeel Ecumenical Liberation Theology Center.

explaining these words to children who witness daily the indignities and brutalities of the Occupation. Palestinian Christians clearly recognize the enormous challenge of Jesus' words.

Jesus the Palestinian under Roman Occupation.

But even as they struggle with Jesus' words, Palestinian Christians readily identify the single most crucial factor for them in interpreting these words, namely the identity of Jesus himself. In a 1996 conversation, Naim,[22] when questioned about the source of his courage to proclaim good news to his Palestinian congregation, replied simply, "We take courage from the fact that Jesus was a Palestinian who lived under Occupation." And this factor remains crucial for Palestinian Christians. In Rana's[23] words, "When people think about Jesus, they don't usually think of him as living under occupation." But she adds, "Jesus brilliantly understood power structures . . . and he really understood the context that [oppressed people] live in." As Fadi[24] observes, Jesus "was born under Roman occupation [and] knew that his disciples would face problems." And Alex refers to the "vicious military occupation" of Jesus' day, while Imad cites the massacre of the Innocents and the crucifixion of Jesus as vivid illustrations of the violence carried out by that regime. Without question it is their direct identification with Jesus, a first-century Palestinian Jew living under Roman occupation, which gives twenty-first-century Palestinian Christians the courage to engage these hard sayings of Jesus in their Israeli-occupied world.

Jesus and the Law.

Another crucial interpretive factor is Jesus' relationship to the Jewish law, the Torah. Issa[25] notes that Jesus "is abolishing the law, even though he said he was fulfilling it," while Solomon and Samia conclude that Jesus has "turned the tables upside down [from the Old Testament]." Solomon notes further that Jesus "was referring to the Sharia" and "wanted to change this concept." Mitri[26] draws a more detailed comparison between Jewish Torah

---

22. Rev. Dr. Naim Ateek, Anglican Priest and Founder/Director of Sabeel Ecumenical Liberation Theology Center.

23. Rana Khoury, Vice President for Development and Outreach, Diyar Consortium.

24. Fadi Al-Zoughbi, Minister, House of Bread Church.

25. Not his real name, Bethlehem tour guide.

26. Rev. Dr. Mitri Raheb, Pastor, Evangelical Lutheran Christmas Church, and

and Muslim Sharia. In his perspective both of these understandings of law lead to a "false" and "very exclusive" focus on purity laws. And out of his own twenty-first-century experience Mitri notes that "Torah and Sharia have a very very ugly face. As a Palestinian Christian I know what it means if religious groups try to impose religious laws on women, on other religious groups, and on the society at large, claiming God for such a behavior." By contrast Mitri observes that "The Gospel is in contradiction to Sharia . . . Jesus talks about an inclusive community, which thinks of the enemy as a potential neighbor. [So] Jesus wanted to say that [the] exclusion [reflected in the Torah] has nothing to do with God." And Mitri rephrases Jesus' concluding words (5:48) accordingly: "You need to be whole, because God is inclusive and not exclusive."[27] Issa, for his part, speaks of the "new scripture" that Jesus brings to his followers, a scripture summed up in the word *love*. Clearly Jesus' challenge to the Jewish scriptures is crucial to twenty-first-century Palestinian Christians.

Jesus' Call to Resist Evil, Not Evildoers.

Another interpretive clue relates to the definition of *nonresistance* and to the distinction between individuals and systems/structures. To begin with, Palestinian Christians are clear about what Jesus' call does not mean. In Rana's words, "No way is it about accepting injustice." Nora likewise affirms that "Jesus doesn't mean to accept being dehumanized." Nor does Jesus call his followers to be "passive" (Daoud[28]) or "apathetic" (Fadi), but instead to be "peace*makers*" (Fadi, emphasis Fadi's).

But Palestinian Christians are also clear about the need to distinguish between individuals and the systems/structures in which they participate. Mitri notes that "Jesus is not calling us to surrender to evil," but rather to "resist the system and love the people."[29] Zoughbi[30] distinguishes carefully between "public life" and "private life," observing that Jesus' call "not to resist" applies to individuals who do evil and not to the systemic/structural evil in which they engage: "Jesus was not against the person but against

Founder/President, Diyar Consortium.

27. As Mitri notes, however, there is a steep price to pay for such a radical challenge: "The cross was the consequence for daring to question the Torah."

28. Daoud Nassar, Founder/Director, Tent of Nations.

29. Cf. the words of Jean Zaru, Presiding Clerk of the Ramallah Friends Meeting ("We have to love the enemy, but we resist with nonviolence") and of Nora ("Jesus is saying, 'Do not resist the evil one *with evil*'" [emphasis Nora's].

30. Zoughbi Zoughbi, Founder/Director, Wi'am Palestinian Conflict Resolution Center.

the system . . . The enemy is a friend in waiting. The system is evil, not the person." Accordingly, Zoughbi recognizes "the potential of everyone to be transformed," citing Zacchaeus and Saul/Paul as biblical examples of such transformation.[31] But Zoughbi pointedly leaves the task of transformation in God's hands: "God will take care of those who are not transformed and give them time to be transformed." In the meantime Zoughbi sees "no limits to forgiveness on the personal level."

Accordingly, there is no room for personal vengeance, but only for the justice of God. In Zoughbi's words, "God judges. We don't." But he points to the "poetic justice" reflected in Jesus' warning that "all who take the sword will perish by the sword" (26:52). And Fadi appeals to the scriptural dictum placing vengeance in God's hands: "'Vengeance is mine, I will repay,' says the Lord" (Rom 12:19; cf. Deut 32:35).

But with vengeance out of the picture, the "hard question" remains for Alex: "How do we love the people we are resisting?" In Solomon's view, this challenge calls Palestinians "to differentiate between Israelis and their acts," namely to "hate the deeds and not the person." Salim[32] has an even more nuanced perspective, noting that Israelis who engage in oppressive acts are themselves "victims" of the system they support. Zoughbi likewise acknowledges this complex dynamic, referring to "the hyphenated character, the oppressed-oppressor." And both Salim and Zoughbi struggle with the challenge of defining *good* and *evil*. Zoughbi asks, "Who is righteous? Who is unrighteous?" And Salim ponders the situation of the Israeli security guard at the airport, whose aggressive actions appear evil to an innocent Palestinian traveler but who "thinks he is doing good." Accordingly, Salim concludes, "If we understand the context of the action of the oppressor, that helps us to forgive."

Ultimately, however, Palestinian Christians insist that evil systems/structures must be resisted. Salim affirms that "the whole political situation needs to change." The Kairos Document,[33] drawn up by Palestinian Christians in 2009 and signed by heads of churches, puts the issue as follows (4.2/4.2.1):

> Love is the commandment of Christ our Lord to us and it includes both friends and enemies. This must be clear when we find ourselves in circumstances where we must resist evil of

---

31. Cf. Solomon's comment: "These people can be changed . . . In every person there is something good and something bad."

32. Dr. Salim Munayer, Founder/Director, Musalaha, and Professor of Theology, Bethlehem Bible College.

33. "Kairos Document."

whatever kind. Love is seeing the face of God in every human being . . . However, seeing the face of God in everyone does not mean accepting evil or aggression on their part. Rather, this love seeks to correct the evil and stop the aggression. The aggression against the Palestinian people which is the Israeli occupation is an evil that must be resisted . . . Primary responsibility for this rests with the Palestinians themselves suffering occupation.

Alex ponders accordingly, "What if the evil is a government? . . . Is Jesus ruling out all forms of resistance? . . . When the authority . . . is evil, how do we know when resisting is legitimate and when it is not?" Zoughbi's response is that "Jesus didn't ask us to succumb, but to challenge the oppressor and to weaken the structure of violence." And as evidence of Jesus' own resistance to systemic/structural evil Zoughbi appeals to Jesus' exorcism of evil spirits ("Jesus calls us to get rid of evil.") and the cleansing of the temple ("Jesus didn't prevent us from resisting. He gave us an example when he turned over the tables."). Mitri, Rana, Jean, and Daoud likewise speak of "resistance" even as they associate this with "love" (Mitri) and "nonviolence" (Rana, Jean, Daoud). And Nora clearly implies "resistance" when she notes, "I think Jesus is saying, 'Do not resist the evil one *with evil*'" (emphasis Nora's).

Jesus' Strategy of Nonviolent Response.

To ask how Palestinian Christians interpret Jesus' strategy of nonviolent response is to engage a rich spectrum of reflections. Some people focus on the impact of nonviolent resistance on the evil person or system/structure. Zoughbi observes that to "turn the other cheek" is "humiliating" to the attacker: "Your hard strike didn't do anything. Try again!"[34] And he notes that to "give the cloak as well as the tunic" is to "[trivialize the evil person's actions] by showing that [he/she] is silly." Nora views "turning the other cheek" as "defying nonviolently," an action that serves to "[make] the [other] person ashamed of what they are trying to do." Rana speaks of "loving enemies" as "doing something beyond expectation," a response that will "stop them" in the course of their actions. In Solomon's words, "Loving the enemy is more harmful to the enemy than getting revenge. It makes the enemy think twice." And for Zoughbi, Jesus' strategy of nonviolent response serves ultimately to "expose the structure of the injustices" and, within the context of twenty-first-century Palestine, to "let the world see how the Israelis are acting."

34. Or, as Nora puts it, "I'm still here! I'm standing up!"

But Palestinian Christians see far more in Jesus' strategy of nonviolent response than humiliation, shame, and the exposure of injustices. Mitri depicts Jesus' strategy as one in which the "enemy" is "a potential neighbor," or in Zoughbi's words, "a friend in waiting." For his part Daoud notes that to adopt nonviolent resistance has the effect of "changing the other" in the process: "If you transform your enemy to be your friend, he will not shoot you." Imad affirms that "Jesus' strategy is to . . . employ love rather than hatred" and ultimately "to bring about tolerance." And Fadi asserts that "the teaching of Christ makes sense, because it encourages [Christians] to plant seeds of peace and justice rather than anger and revenge."[35]

Further, as Palestinian Christians recognize, Jesus' strategy of nonviolent response also has an impact on those who take such actions. In Mitri's perspective, "[Those who engage in retaliation] become victims in this spiral of violence. Jesus wants his disciples to be subjects, who act and do not just react." The issue is about "you becoming in control and not falling into the trap of reaction or revenge." In Rana's terminology, "Jesus is trying to empower [the] victim." Jesus' verbs call people "to act not react." And Jesus' words are thus "words of empowerment." As a result, Rana affirms, "You decide how you will be treated. So you will start thinking of yourself not as a victim but as empowered." Daoud notes that employing nonviolent resistance "needs strength from the inside" and requires "going deep." But such action clearly builds the same strength that it requires. When you "change the other" by "transforming your enemy to be a friend," Daoud asserts, "this is the strength that Jesus was talking about." And clearly this is strength gained through persistent practice. For her part Nora pushes this persistent practice out into a life-long perspective as she speaks of Jesus' call to perfection: "You retain the divine in you by reacting how you react . . . Our whole life leads us slowly and gradually to the divine. [And] every experience we have in loving the enemy leads us closer to that image."

Twenty-First-Century Implications: The Dynamics of Violence.

Palestinian Christians reflect solid agreement on the dynamics of violence and the explicit strategies of those who engage in it. As Mitri notes, "Jesus' words are definitely for the real world." And Palestinian Christian analysis of this real world is thoughtful and penetrating.

---

35. Conversely, Fadi notes that "revenge is not a way of life." And he invokes the words of Mahatma Ghandi that depict "the whole world as blind and toothless" if people continue to exact "eye for eye and tooth for tooth." Salim similarly notes that "at the end of the day resisting evil [violently] brings more evil than good."

There is strong consensus on the purpose of the violence carried out by the Israeli occupation. In Imad's words, "The enemy is trying to humiliate and intimidate you and lead you to use violent action," thus "driving you to the edge," while Amal[36] concurs that "they want to push us to violence." Daoud asserts in general terms that "resisting evil with evil is what the evil wants," while Rana makes the principle specific: "The Israelis want us to react in a certain way." Mitri notes that "the Occupation triggers things [that lead] you to react." And he illustrates this principle with the September 2000 incident on the Haram al Sharif/Temple Mount in Jerusalem that resulted in the major outbreak of hostilities now known as the Second Intifada: "[When] Sharon [came to the] Al Aqsa, he knew that he would trigger a reaction from the Muslim community." For Palestinian Christians it is clear that violence not only engenders violence but in fact requires counter-violence in order to thrive.

Ironically, however, Palestinian Christians likewise recognize that those who employ their power to oppress others also have deep fear of those whom they oppress. Amal recounts the story of a night when soldiers invaded the Tent of Nations and forced Amal and other family members out of the house into the cold. As they did so, Amal questioned them: "Why do you come now? Why not during the day? You are afraid of me?" And Daoud notes similarly that soldiers who "jumped out of the field" to detain him and his family and search their car late one evening were "very, very afraid."

A further point of clarity relates to the debilitating impact of violence on those who employ it. Nora has a question for the security guards at the airport, who put Palestinian travelers through intensive searches widely known as "the VIP treatment": "Do you enjoy doing what you are doing?" And she concludes, "They are dehumanizing themselves when they dehumanize us." Salim would like to see a study of the people who work in airport security, noting that "The guy that checks you [at the airport] is a victim [of the system he supports]." Imad describes an Israeli television documentary featuring a remorseful Israeli, trained as an assassin to kill wanted Palestinians, who eventually reached a "moment of truth" and realized that he himself had been turned into a "killing machine." And Samia recounts the story of a Jewish man who apologized to Palestinians for his role in evicting Palestinians from their homes in 1948, because, as he realized, "this was what the Nazis did to his family."

But Palestinian Christians are likewise clear about the crucial impact of their own responses to those who are violent. Rana notes that to counter

---

36. Amal Nassar, Physiotherapist, Caritas Baby Hospital, and Member, Tent of Nations.

violence with violence "will only play to the prejudices that some Israelis have of Palestinians." Imad asserts that "We should avoid violence, so that they don't have any excuse [to engage in further violence against us]." And Daoud comments, "When you act differently, this confuses the other, [because you are] resisting the evil with good." Rana concurs that to live out the words of Jesus not only "empowers [you]" but also "shatters what the Israelis may think." Salim ponders the missiological impact of his airport encounters: "How I respond to [security personnel] can force them to check their conscience. Maybe I will have an opportunity to tell them about Jesus." And Fadi cites Jesus' call (Matt 5:16) to "let your light shine before others, so that they may see your good works and give glory to your Father in heaven."

Twenty-First-Century Implications: Palestinian Christian Responses to Violence.

To inquire how Palestinian Christians respond in real life to the everyday violence that they encounter is to engage with poignant and courageous stories of faithfulness under duress and, at times, with stunning accounts of transformation at the least expected times and places. These stories reflect a wide range of circumstances and strategies.

Simple strategies are crucial for Nora and Salim. They take books with them to the airport and take care not to "lose control" (Nora) or to get "triangled emotionally" by security personnel (Salim). And Nora notes, "The Occupation has brought out the best in me. Not only has it taught me self control; but it has also helped me live the teachings of Jesus Christ." Amal and her family—whose farm has been threatened repeatedly by Israeli court cases, military incursions, and settler vandalism—"refuse to be enemies." Instead they choose to "act positively" and "stay on the land" rather than "emigrate, [resign themselves], or react violently." And they cite the story of Naboth's vineyard (1 Kgs 21:1–16) to explain why they will not "sell their heritage." Similarly Rana extends the strategic actions and attitudes of a moment or a day into a lifelong stance: "We internalize [our nonviolent resistance]. Immigration stops becoming an option. Immigration is what the oppressor wants. Nonviolent resistance means the conscious decision to stay in this land and thrive."

Fadi, Samia, Nora, and Cedar name prayer as a fundamental response to violence. When Fadi experiences "uneasiness and frustration" while waiting at checkpoints, he "[prays] for the situation, that the Lord will soften the hearts of the soldiers so that they do not yell . . . and that [they] will help the people." Samia speaks of a prayerful practice taught her by her father, who encouraged her to "evaluate the day" every evening before she goes to sleep and identify the places where reconciliation needs to happen. Nora tells of handing olive branches to Israeli soldiers at the Wall with the words, "We are praying for the inner walls to fall down." And Cedar recounts a poignant story about her "Arab Jewish" neighbor in Haifa, whose only son was conscripted into the Israeli Defense Forces during the Six Day War in 1967: "I used to stand with her and pray with her for her son to come home. I cried with her, I prayed with her, my neighbor, my enemy . . . You cannot *not* feel for your neighbor."

Forgiveness features significantly within Palestinian Christian responses to violence. Alex says of his mother, who lost her husband and her property in 1948: "She focused on forgiveness and moving forward rather than living in the past. For this reason she refused to go to a refugee camp [festering] with resentments and anger." Zoughbi, who recognizes "no limits" to personal forgiveness, comments that "if the Lord has mercy because we are sinners, then we need to reconcile with brothers and sisters [and clearly enemies as well]." Salim, who needs "a day or two to undo feelings of anger" after encountering airport security, nevertheless notes that "part of the ability to forgive is to understand the context of the action of the oppressor." And he adds, "It's not only important to forgive, which is a hard process in itself, but we also have to be engaged in a process of reconciliation with the other side in order to understand and to address their grievances." Cedar cites the "miracle story" about her son, who had at one time "lost his will to live" due to the violence in Nablus, but who later told his mother, "I don't want to hate. I forgave them." And Cedar herself, who has found great help in "reading spiritual books from other cultures about rising above pain," states simply, "I have faith in God and in human beings, even the ones who are torturing . . . I believe . . . that in everybody there is something of God . . . I can forgive. I don't have to try. I don't have enemies."[37]

Personal contact with people on all sides of the conflict is crucial for Daoud: "The issue is to listen and try to understand. When [the Israelis] come to know [you], it shows them that you are also a human being." And Daoud goes on, "Political moves [that is, high-level governmental negotiations] have no function. I cannot give you a gift I don't own. I cannot

---

37. But forgiveness does not necessarily come easily or automatically. Samia tells of an Israeli Arab man who requested a glass of water from her as he was working for the Israeli military in closing off the street in front of her house. Samia's initial response was "Go, let your masters give you a drink!" Samia's aunt then challenged her with the words "That's not how you were brought up!" This caused Samia to reconsider and to give the man a glass of water. "I hated myself for that," Samia reflects, "the way I reacted."

promise peace if I don't have it. It should start with [personal contact]." Amal comments, "You can't make peace without meeting people. If we don't talk, people appear to [us] like enemies. We have to be prepared to talk with people." And Daoud and Amal offer as illustration the story of a woman from a nearby settlement who was invited to a meeting one day at the Tent of Nations. As the meeting started, she sat with her arms crossed in a defiant gesture. But as Daoud described the difficulties of life on the farm without water or electricity—both forbidden by the Israeli authorities—the woman became very agitated. Daoud was certain that she was about to attack him verbally. Instead she interrupted him to say, "You have no drinking water. But we have swimming pools! I had no idea! I was brought from America. I was offered a house in the settlement. I have been living here for nine years. I never knew that I had neighbors. You are normal people." And the woman came back to the Tent of Nations with her husband at Rosh Hashanah to wish the family Happy New Year. "This is not peace," Daoud explains. "This is the foundation for peace."

Such stories of transformation emerge in widely varying contexts. Cedar recounts the story of a soldier who was once posted to a detail on the roof of her family's house. And as he went through her home one day and saw a Bible, he commented, "You are followers of Jesus!" "Yes," Cedar replied, "And you ought to be too!" This interchange led Cedar to open the Bible to Isaiah 7 and engage in serious Bible study with an Israeli soldier. Sometime later Cedar discovered a loaf of sliced bread in her kitchen (at a time when curfew had been on for a month and the pantry was bare). Cedar refused the loaf of bread, waiting for the soldier to "come back in civilian clothes." But, as she concludes, "We made a friendship."

For his part Alex tells of a letter disseminated by a "prominent Messianic Jewish brother" that "viciously attacked" Bethlehem Bible College following a BBC conference on "Christ at the Checkpoint." As conference organizer, Alex responded to this attack in a letter "that expressed a desire for healing and reconciliation," even as it acknowledged points of disagreement and causes of "offense." When the Messianic Jewish community read his appeal, Alex notes, "they were astonished by the letter and said, 'The Palestinians have taken the moral high ground.'" And Alex concludes, "Consequently, we met together, we ate a meal together (both Messianic Jews and Christians), and resumed fellowship and cooperation. Had I responded to [the] letter with the same spirit that was in [the] letter, the gap between us would not have been bridged."

For Daoud a moment of transformation began with a terrifying incident in which Israeli soldiers with faces painted "jumped out of a field" and stopped the vehicle in which he was traveling with his family late one evening. In spite of his plea that the children were sleeping, the soldiers demanded that the family leave the car, so that they could search it. So Daoud woke his children and said to them (in English that the soldiers could understand): "Don't worry. They are friendly soldiers." Half an hour later the soldiers finished their search. But before they left, one of the soldiers said to Daoud, "Please apologize to your family. We did something wrong." And Daoud concludes, "If you transform your enemy to be a friend, he will not shoot you."

But enemies do not always become friends. At times the only victory for the victim of violence is the shame of the aggressor and their own personal dignity. In his 1995 volume, *I Am A Palestinian Christian*,[38] Mitri recounts an incident from the First Intifada, at a time when the residents of Beit Sahour had instigated a tax boycott to protest the fact that they were receiving no services. The Israelis then retaliated against this boycott by confiscating the furnishings of the households involved. As Mitri tells the story (111), one day the tax collectors entered the home of an elderly Christian woman and her family and spent hours removing their furniture and household goods, while the family watched. As the tax collectors prepared to leave the empty living room, the woman said to them, "You forgot the curtains. Please do not forget to take them down too and remove them." And in Mitri's words (ibid.),

> An eerie silence descended on the room. Shamed and guilty, the soldiers left. They took everything but the curtains. At that moment the old woman had achieved dignity. At that moment the triumphant Israeli army had lost the battle. An old woman had defeated them. She gave her enemy, who wanted to sue her and take her dress, her coat also. That became reality. That was resistance.

At other times faithfulness to the call of Jesus must serve as its own and sole reward. In his 2004 volume, *Bethlehem Besieged: Stories of Hope in Times of Trouble*,[39] Mitri recounts the day when he was held hostage in his pastor's office while Israeli soldiers vandalized the building. Mitri's words to the soldiers, remarkably gracious though they were, elicited neither shame nor kindness in response (22):

> [A] soldier told me, while destroying a painting, "You have here a very beautiful facility." I said, "We love beauty. We worked so very hard to make this place beautiful. And we take daily care

---

38. Raheb, *Palestinian Christian*.
39. Raheb, *Bethlehem Besieged*.

to keep it like this." Another soldier started making fun of me: "You sound like a very wise person." I answered, "The real wise person is he who can transform his enemy into a neighbor, and not his neighbor into an enemy." The commander obviously did not like my answer at all. He shouted at me to shut up, and he ordered his soldiers not to talk to me anymore.

In the end, however, it is hope that energizes Palestinian responses to the violence of the Israeli occupation. For Amal (whose name means "hope") this hope is a palpable reality that not only energizes her but powerfully impacts both the friends and the enemies who encounter it. Amal credits her father with instilling in his children a resilient hope and a dream for a future built on reconciliation. "Don't give up hope," he told them. "If you give up hope, you can't stay [on the land] one day. You have to prepare people for peace. I want you to continue to fulfill my dream to bring about reconciliation." Such hope-filled action becomes, in Amal's words, "a power that you cannot resist" and a power that serves ultimately to "break the [cycle] of violence." So Amal and her extended family tend their farm tenaciously and creatively, host international work groups that volunteer on the land, organize children's camps, run computer classes in the nearby village, provide space for Israeli/Palestinian dialogue, and offer seminars about nonviolent defense of Palestinian lands. And for Amal even enormous setbacks can be transformed into victories. As she notes with manifest joy and clear emphasis, "[Israeli settlers] uprooted 350 trees, *but we replanted 700 trees!*" And she continues, "A Jewish group came and sponsored 100 olive trees and planted them *with their own hands!*" Such hope-filled actions draw the immediate attention of both enemies and friends alike. After the olive trees were replanted, Israeli settlers came back, asking angrily, "Why did your replant the olive trees?" But a Muslim woman asked Amal, "From where do you have this patience? I want to come and learn every day."

For Palestinian Christians the call of Jesus to nonviolence is ultimately a calling that involves all of life and creates the agenda for a lifetime. In Jean's words, "You can't preach love of the enemy in isolation. The inner and the outer go together." Rana notes, "It's everything. It's not segmented or compartmentalized. It's the whole life." And for Nora, "Our whole life leads us slowly and gradually to the divine. [And] every experience we have in loving the enemy leads us closer to that image."

CONCLUSION: FROM SCHOLAR'S DESK TO REAL WORLD.

To compare the narrative reading of Matthew 5:38–48 above and the Palestinian Christian reading of this text is above all to discover fundamental similarities at work. Common to both readings is a keen awareness of the harsh context of Roman occupation within which Jesus lived and in contrast to which he taught his followers about the kingdom of heaven. Common also to these readings is recognition of the extraordinary challenge of Jesus' call "not to resist the one who is evil" but instead to "love your enemies." In addition these readings both insist that Jesus' call to nonresistance is a call not to passivity but rather to nonviolent action. And ultimately both readings acknowledge in their own ways the divine irony that reveals that earthly powers of evil, regardless how powerful they may appear, are nevertheless powerless vis-à-vis the genuine power of God to transform death into life and enemies into friends.

But there are likewise divergences between these readings. On the one hand such scholarly emphases as the messianic cast of the Gospel of Matthew and the Matthean motif of fulfillment of the law and the prophets (cf. 5:17–20) contract in the real-world exegesis of Palestinian Christians into a strategic emphasis on the newness that Jesus has introduced. On the other hand real-world Palestinian Christian exegesis of Matthew 5:38–48 adds a wealth of biblical parallels and allusions (Naboth to Saul/Paul, Isaiah to Romans) that reach well beyond the scholarly confines of a narrative study based in the Gospel of Matthew. But perhaps most significantly, this real-world Palestinian Christian exegesis contributes a rich panoply of real-life perspectives and experiences to illustrate and confirm the truth of even the most challenging of Jesus' hard sayings. If Jesus' words are "definitely for the real world" (Mitri), then real-world exegesis is likewise crucial to the scholarly enterprise. Let the reader understand.

9

"As Sheep in the Midst of Wolves"

Mission and Peace in the Gospel of Matthew

TO EXPLORE THE INTERFACE between "mission" and "peace" within the Gospel of Matthew is to address an issue that at first glance appears insignificant. While Matthew is clearly concerned with the "mission" of the church,[1] he employs the vocabulary of "peace" only five times throughout his Gospel.[2] And even this evidence appears ambiguous. On the one hand Jesus instructs his disciples to "greet" (10:12) the houses which they enter with a word of "peace" (10:13); and he likewise pronounces blessing upon the "peacemakers" (5:9). But in the three remaining uses of this word group Jesus speaks about his own mission (10:34a/b) and that of his disciples (10:13b) in terms not of peace itself but rather of its absence. Accordingly, it appears at first glance hardly warranted to address the topic of "mission and peace" as a central focus of Matthew's Gospel.

But if one addresses this question to Matthew's narrative itself, the results are quite different. While Matthew does not give prominence to the vocabulary of "peace," he nevertheless paints a vivid portrait of "peace" through the events and the characters of his story. And this portrait of "peace" is integrally linked to the motif of "mission." It is precisely those who are "sent out" to carry out the work of the "kingdom of heaven"—the

---

1. Note the prominence of Matthew's "Missionary Discourse" (9:35—11:1), as it is "bracketed" within the portrayal of Jesus' own ministry (4:23-25; 9:35; 11:1); and the climactic focus on the "Great Commission" (28:16-20), with which Jesus not only reissues but also expands the commission of chapter 10.

2. The word "peace" appears twice in 10:13 and twice in 10:34; and the word "peacemakers" appears in 5:9.

prophets,[3] John the Baptist (11:10), Jesus,[4] Jesus' first disciples and all those to follow[5]—whose life or whose calling exhibits a profound commitment to the ways of peace. In order to pursue the linkage between "mission" and "peace" within Matthew's Gospel, therefore, it will be necessary to examine Matthew's narrative portrayal of those who are "sent out" and to observe the manner in which they carry out their respective vocations on behalf of the "kingdom of heaven."

I. "FOR IN THIS WAY THEY PERSECUTED THE PROPHETS WHO WERE BEFORE YOU"

Mission and Peace in the Portrayal of the Prophets

Within the world of Matthew's narrative the prophets of Jewish history play a crucial role in setting the stage for the events of Jesus' own ministry. And throughout the narrative a clear picture emerges with regard to their prophetic vocation. The prophets are "those who are sent out" (23:37; cf. 21:34, 36) by God[6] to the Jewish people. Their task is primarily verbal in character. They are the human channels through whom "the word of the Lord" (cf. 1:22; 2:15) is first "spoken"[7] to the people and then "written" (2:5) as "scriptures" (26:56) for their continuing instruction.[8] The prophets' vocation likewise moves beyond the "spoken" and the "written" word to the level of "sign" (12:39), that word which is enacted within the very life of the prophet.[9] And the prophetic vocation extends even to the inner "longings" of the prophets' hearts (13:17). Accordingly, the prophets are those whose entire existence—words, actions, and even inner longings—is shaped by their identity as people "sent out" by God.

---

3. Thus 23:37; cf. 21:34, 36.
4. Thus 10:40; 15:24; cf. 21:37.
5. Thus 10:5, 16; 20:2; 22:3, 4; 23:34.
6. It is God who "sends out" the "prophets," as indicated by the "theological passive" ("those who are sent") of 23:37.
7. Thus 1:22; 2:15, 17, 23; 3:3; 4:14; 8:17; 12:17; 13:35; 21:4; 24:15; 27:9. Cf. 11:13, where Jesus describes the task of the "prophets" in the language of "prophecy," and 12:38-42, where Jesus speaks of the "proclamation" (12:41) of the "prophet Jonah" (12:39; cf. 12:40, 41).
8. Cf. 5:17, 7:12, 11:13, and 22:40, where Jesus refers to "the law and the prophets" as a collection of written documents.
9. Thus Jesus' reference to "the sign of Jonah the prophet" (12:39), who was "in the belly of the sea monster for three days and three nights" (12:40).

But Matthew likewise paints a vivid portrait of the fate to which the prophets are destined. They are "without honor . . . in [their] own country and in [their] own house" (13:57).[10] They are "taken" (21:35), "persecuted" (5:12), "beaten" (21:35), "stoned" (21:35; 23:37), "killed" (21:35; 23:37), "murdered" (23:31; 23:35), and "entombed" (cf. 23:29) by others who thereby make themselves responsible for the "blood" (23:30) of these prophets. Nor is there any question about the cause of this brutal fate. The prophets encounter dishonor, persecution, and death precisely because they have faithfully discharged their duties as "those who are sent out." In the parable of the Wicked Tenants (21:33-46), the "slaves" who are "sent out" by the vineyard owner to "collect his fruits" (21:34; cf. 21:36) meet their fate at the hands of the wicked tenants precisely as they come to the vineyard to carry out their task. Similarly, Jesus' lament (23:37) that Jerusalem "kills the prophets and stones those who are sent out to it" implies that it is specifically in the course of their work, and because of it, that the prophets are struck down.

Most striking, however, about this portrait of the prophets is their peaceable response to the brutal reception which they encounter. In the story about the Wicked Tenants (21:33-46), the slaves who are sent out by the vineyard owner to "take his fruits" (21:34) instead allow themselves to be "taken," "beaten," "stoned," and "killed" (21:35; cf.21:36) by those to whom they have been sent. Their mission extends to the "taking" of "fruits" but not to the "taking" of human life.

Nor is the response of the slaves due merely to their impotence in the face of power greater than their own. Jesus' question to his listeners (21:40) and their perceptive response (21:41) make clear that the vineyard owner has power that will enable him to rain down "terrible destruction" (cf. 21:41) upon his tenants in his own time and manner. Accordingly, the vineyard owner could come to the immediate rescue of his beleaguered emissaries. Or he could authorize and empower the slaves themselves to retaliate against the brutalities to which they are repeatedly subjected. But instead, he persistently "sends out his slaves" (21:34, 36; cf. 21:37) to the "wicked tenants"[11] in his vineyard, armed only with the urgent knowledge that "the right time for the fruits has arrived" (21:34) and the certain knowledge that the vineyard owner has commissioned them to "take his fruits" (21:34).

Nor is this mere oversight on the part of the vineyard owner. Rather, it is with the clear awareness of what has happened to his first servants (21:35)

---

10. While Jesus is clearly referring to himself in this instance, he does so, as it appears, by appealing to "common knowledge" on the question of regard for prophets.

11. Thus 21:41; cf. 21:33, 34, 35, 38, 40.

and in direct response to their fate, that the vineyard owner then renews and even intensifies his efforts to retrieve the fruits of his vineyard (21:36a). And when this second and larger group of slaves meets with the same fate as the first (21:36b), it is with clear intention that the vineyard owner finally sends out the most important emissary of them all, his own son, in the hope that he will meet with the "respect" that his predecessors did not receive (21:37).[12]

It is clear that the vineyard owner will not let the persecution of his emissaries deter him from his ongoing "mission" (cf. 21:34, 36, 37) to retrieve the fruits of his vineyard. He will continue, in the face of all opposition, to "send out his slaves" to carry out the urgent task of "taking his fruits" (21:34). And if their mission is not received, then their calling is to suffer the brutalities which come to them (21:35, 36; cf. 21:38–39) without retaliating in kind. Such is the peaceable mission of the prophets of Jewish history.

But the prophets' mission and their suffering do not remain unvindicated. In both the parable of the Wicked Tenants (21:33–46) and Jesus' lament over Jerusalem (23:37–39), the threat of present, future, and eschatological judgment hangs over those who do not receive the "prophets" (23:37) and those "sent" to them (21:34, 36; 23:37; cf. 21:37). Already in the present, as Jesus assures Jerusalem, "your house is left to you deserted" (23:37), an apparent reference to the spiritual emptiness of the Jewish temple. And in a future both historical and eschatological the vineyard owner will rain down "terrible destruction" (cf. 21:41) on those who have rejected his servants; and he will "give away" (21:41) to others the vineyard presently under their control. This word, spoken by Jesus' listeners in unwitting judgment upon themselves, functions as a pointer not only to the coming destruction of Jerusalem (cf. 22:7; 24:1–2) but also to the eschatological judgment upon the Jewish leadership from whom "the kingdom of God will be taken away" (21:43). The prophets of Jewish history, called to face persecution and death peaceably and without retaliation as they carry out their "mission" to the Jewish people, are nevertheless assured of ultimate vindication by God, the one who has "sent them out" to their task.

---

12. But the vineyard owner's son meets the same end as do his slaves, that of death itself at the hands of the tenants (21:38–39). See the discussion of Jesus' ministry below.

II. "BUT THEY DID TO HIM WHATEVER THEY WANTED"

Mission and Peace in the Portrayal of John the Baptist

While the prophets of Jewish history are figures from a former era whose words and lives form the backdrop to Matthew's narrative,[13] John the Baptist strides onto the scene as a living, dynamic character in the present day world of Matthew's story. But there is much in the portrayal of John the Baptist which links him with the prophets of times past.

Just like his forbears, John has been "sent out" by God to carry out his task. John is "the one about whom it is written, 'Look! I send out my messenger before your face,'" a prophecy of Malachi spoken in the divine first person (11:10).[14] John likewise shares with his forbears their "prophetic" vocation. John appears in the wilderness of Judea "proclaiming" (3:1) the word of the Lord, which is at the same time the word of the coming reign of God (3:2): "Repent! For the kingdom of heaven has come near."

Accordingly, John is a prophetic figure, "the voice of one who is crying in the wilderness" (3:3; cf. Isa 40:3, LXX). And in John's call to "repentance" he fulfills the prophetic task of calling the people to "prepare [*hetoimasate*] the way of the Lord—here a reference to Jesus himself—[and to] straighten his paths" (3:3; cf. Isa 40:3, LXX). Jesus likewise identifies John with the prophetic "messenger" of Malachi, whose task—in words addressed in this context to Jesus himself—is to "prepare [*kataskeuasei*] your way before you" (11:10; cf. Mal 3:1, LXX).

For his part John "prepares the way before [Jesus]" (11:10) by proclaiming the message of "the one coming after me" (3:11; cf. 11:3) and by inaugurating a ministry of baptism[15] which he carries out at the Jordan river (3:6, 13; cf. 3:5) and for which he acquires the label of "the Baptist."[16] For their part the people "prepare the way of the Lord" (3:3) by coming to John to confess their sins (3:6; cf. 3:11), to receive his baptism,[17] and to hear his proclamation (3:7-12).

John's proclamation is unpolished, uncalculating, and uncompromising. He calls the crowds to "Repent!" (3:2). He denounces the religious leadership as a "brood of snakes" seeking to "flee from the coming wrath" (3:7),

---

13. Thus, for example, 11:13. See also 23:35, an apparent reference to the historical scope of the Jewish Scriptures.
14. Cf. Mal 3:1, LXX; Exod 23:20, LXX.
15. Thus 3:6, 7, 11, 13, 14, 16; 21:25.
16. Thus 3:1; 11:11, 12; 14:2, 8; 16:14; 17:13.
17. Thus 3:6, 7, 11; cf. 3:13, 14, 16.

accuses them of unwarranted reliance on their "Abrahamic parentage" (3:9), calls on them to "bear fruit worthy of repentance" (3:8), and warns them of impending and fiery judgment if they do not (3:10-12). And to Herod the tetrarch, who has married Herodias, the wife of his brother Philip (14:1, 3), John's word is blunt, and persistent:[18] "It is not lawful for you to have her" (14:4). John's proclamation has all the biting rhetorical character of the prophets of Jewish history.[19]

And because of his words, John acquires a "prophetic" reputation. Not only do the crowds consider John to be a "prophet" (14:5; 21:26; cf. 16:14); but Jesus himself also labels John "a prophet . . . and more than a prophet" (11:9). In fact, John fills no lesser role than that of the "Elijah who is to come,"[20] that final prophet who appears in advance of the "great and glorious day of the Lord" (Mal 3:22, LXX) in order to "restore all things" (17:11; cf. Mal 3:23, LXX). Not only does John wear the clothing of Elijah (3:4; cf. 2 Kings 1:8, LXX) and live a correspondingly "righteous" (21:32) and ascetic (9:14; 11:18) life. But Jesus also announces John's identity as "Elijah" both directly to the crowds (11:14) and indirectly to his disciples (17:10-13).

As a prophet, however, John encounters the same fate which has befallen his forbears. To be sure, John meets with a positive reception from the common people. The "crowd" reveres him as a "prophet" (14:5; 21:26). "Jerusalem and all Judea and all the surrounding areas of the Jordan" go out to receive his baptism (3:5-6); and even the "tax collectors and prostitutes" witness John's ministry and "believe him" (21:31-32). But from the leaders, both religious and political, John meets with a very different reception. For their part the religious leaders accept no single aspect of John's "prophetic" vocation—neither his ascetic lifestyle (11:18),[21] his verbal proclamation (21:31b-32; cf.21:28-31a), nor his baptism (21:25).[22] Instead, they fail to

---

18. The use of the iterative imperfect form *"elegen"* suggests that John spoke not once but repeatedly to Herod.

19. Cf., for example, the rhetoric of Nathan (2 Sam 12:7-12), Elijah (1 Kings 21:17-24), Amos (Amos 4:1-3), and Ezekiel (Ezek 34:1-10).

20. Thus 11:14; 17:10, 11, 12; cf. Mal 3:22, LXX.

21. Judging from the nature of the charges against John (11:18) and Jesus (11:19), it appears that Jesus is referring more nearly to the religious leadership than to the common people. Elsewhere it is the Pharisees who accuse Jesus of demon possession (9:34; 12:24) and castigate him for consorting with "tax collectors and sinners" (9:11); and it is the chief priests and elders of the people (21:23) who apparently view themselves over against "the tax collectors and the prostitutes" (21:31, 32).

22. While elsewhere (3:7, 11) the Pharisees and Sadducees do in fact come out to the Jordan and receive baptism from John, the harshness of John's rhetorical attack on them ("You brood of snakes," 3:7) clearly suggests that John does not trust the genuineness of their apparent "repentance" (3:8).

"recognize" the "Elijah" in their midst (17:12), accuse him of "demon possession" (11:18), and do not "believe him" (21:25, 31, 32) or respond to his ministry (21:30).

From the political powers John faces imprisonment and death. And just like the prophets of Jewish history, John meets this fate as the result of his prophetic vocation and in the course of his work. In true prophetic fashion John meddles in the affairs of Herod "the king" (14:9). And Herod responds to this affront by "seizing" John (14:3), "binding" him (14:3), "handing him over" (4:12), putting him "in prison" (*en tō desmōtēriō*, 11:2; *en [tē] phylakē*, 14:3, 10), and eventually "killing" him (14:5) by "decapitation" (14:10; cf. 14:8, 11) and leaving his "corpse" (14:12) to be buried by his disciples. Such is the fate of the one who comes "preparing [the Lord's] way" (11:10).

John meets this fate as one who is physically powerless and at the same time peaceable.[23] From the moment of his arrest John is portrayed above all not as an actor in his own right but rather as a victim of the actions of others. In the accounts of his imprisonment and death (4:12; 11:2-6; 14:1-12) there are only three active verbal forms which refer to John's own initiatives: John "hears" (11:2) about what "the Messiah" is doing, he "sends" (11:2) his disciples to Jesus, and he "says" (11:3) something to him.

By contrast John appears three times as the subject of passive verbs and nine times as the object of active verbs. John is "handed over" (4:12); and his head is "brought" (14:11) to the daughter of Herodias and "given" (14:11) to her. Others "seize" John (14:3), "bind" him (14:3), "put" him in prison (14:3) with the intent to "kill" him (14:5). They then "decapitate" him (14:10), "bring" his head to Herodias (14:11), "take" his corpse (14:12), and "bury" it (14:12). And Jesus' own comments concerning the death of John portray him in a similar light. To the crowds Jesus announces (11:12) that "from the days of John the Baptist until now the kingdom of heaven *[or John himself!]* has been subjected to violence and violent people *[or Herod the tetrarch!]* have taken it by force. And to his disciples Jesus offers this oblique epitaph for John: "And I say to you that Elijah has already come; and they did not recognize him, but did to him whatever they wished" (17:12).

This portrait of John's "passion" leads to several conclusions. Just as it was with the vineyard owner, God has "sent" John to his task (11:10). But God does not intervene in the tawdry and violent affairs of Herod in order to preserve John's life. Rather John, who has worked courageously at "preparing [the Lord's] way" (11:10), suffers and dies on account of his faithful

---

23. For a detailed treatment of Matthew's characterization of John the Baptist in 14:1-12, see Weaver, "Power and Powerlessness," 179-96.

service. And just like the vineyard owner's slaves, John does not retaliate against the violence which he encounters. Rather, the one who has called people to "do fruit worthy of repentance" (3:8) instead permits them to "do to him whatever they wish" (17:12). John's calling, like that of the prophets before him, is a calling to proclaim the word of God. And if that word is not received, John's calling, like theirs, is to suffer the violence of others without responding in kind.

But suffering and death are not the final word for John. Rather, just like his predecessors, John receives ultimate vindication by God for his faithful witness as the prophet of the Lord. Jesus acclaims John on the human level as "a prophet . . . and more than a prophet" (11:9) and claims that "among those born of women none has been raised up who is greater than John the Baptist" (11:11). And Jesus also makes it clear that John's prophetic ministry comes from "heaven" itself (21:25), or in other words, directly from God. As a result, it is "belief" or "nonbelief" in John's "heavenly" message of "righteousness" which will determine the eschatological status of John's hearers with respect to the kingdom of heaven (21:31–32; cf. 21:25). John, whose prophetic voice is overpowered by violence in the present day world of Herod the tetrarch, nevertheless speaks a prophetic word whose power extends into the eschatological future of the kingdom of heaven. Such is God's vindication of the faithful prophet.

III. "IN THIS WAY ALSO THE SON OF MAN WILL SUFFER AT THEIR HANDS"

Mission and Peace in the Portrayal of Jesus

If John the Baptist is the prophet whose task is to "prepare [the Lord's] way" (11:10), then Jesus is the "Lord" whose way John "prepares." Not only does Jesus appear on the scene immediately following John's announcement of "the one coming after me" (3:13 cf. 3:11–12) to request baptism from John (3:13–16a). But Jesus likewise receives a divine confirmation of his identity. The heavens open up (3:16b), the Spirit of God descends upon him in the form of a dove (3:16c), and a "voice from heaven," the voice of God, declares him to be "my beloved son, the one in whom I take pleasure" (3:17; cf. 17:5).

Accordingly, Jesus, the Son of God and the one empowered by the Spirit of God, knows himself to be "sent" by God to a ministry among the Jewish people (10:40 cf.10:6; 15:24; 21:37). Jesus likewise exhibits a clear sense of how he has "come" and what he has "come" to do. By accepting the accolades of the crowds, Jesus acknowledges that he is the one who comes "in the name of the Lord" (23:39 cf. 21:9). At the same time he acknowledges that he has come as an ordinary human, "eating and drinking" (11:19), in contrast to the ascetic practices of his predecessor John (11:18). Jesus likewise identifies the tasks to which he has been called. He has not come "to destroy the law or the prophets" (5:17), "to call the righteous people" (9:13), "to bring peace" (10: 34), or "to be served" (20:28). Rather, he has come "to fulfill the law and the prophets" (5:17), "to call the sinners" (9:13), "to bring the sword" which "divides" families (10:34–36),[24] "to serve" others (20:28), and "to give his life as a ransom for many" (20:28).[25]

Throughout Matthew's narrative Jesus works at the tasks for which he has "come" through a threefold ministry of "proclaiming," "teaching," and "healing" (4:23; 9:35; 11:1), a ministry which the people acknowledge as one of "wisdom"[26] and "powerful deeds".[27] This ministry of Jesus reaches well beyond that of John, his predecessor (cf. 14:1–2). Like John, Jesus announces the "nearness" of the kingdom of heaven and calls people to "repentance" in light of the approaching reign of God (4:17 cf. 3:2). But while Jesus can, like John, announce that "the kingdom of heaven has come near" (4:17 cf. 3:2), he can also, unlike John, cast out demons "by the Spirit of God," an act which proclaims that "the kingdom of God has [already] come upon you" (12:28).[28] In addition Jesus assumes what is widely recognized to be the divine prerogative to proclaim the "forgiveness of sins" (9:2, 5 cf. 9:3), an act which Jesus' opponents consider to be "blasphemy" (9:3) but which the crowds recognize that Jesus, precisely as a human being, has carried out through "God-given authority" (9:8).

Jesus also carries out a teaching ministry which is mobile, wide-ranging, and prominent throughout his public career. Jesus goes about "all Galilee" (4:23), through "all the towns and villages" (9:35; cf. 11:1), teaching sometimes "in their synagogues" (4:23; 9:35; 13:54) and at other times "on mountains" (5:1), "beside the sea" (13:1–2), "in the house" (13:36; 17: 25), or "on the way" (20:17). Jesus regularly engages in major teaching sessions, sometimes publically for his disciples and the crowds[29] and at other times

---

24. See Weaver, *Missionary Discourse*, 112–14.

25. Cf. 8:29, where demons cry out against Jesus and ask him whether he "has come to torment them before the time."

26. Thus 13:54; cf. 11:19; 12:42.

27. Thus 13:54; 11:20, 21, 23; 13:58; 14:2.

28. Cf. the comment of Herod the tetrarch, who attributes the "mighty deeds" of Jesus to a "John the Baptist [who] has been raised from the dead" and is "for this reason" capable of that which he could not previously do (14:1–2).

29. Thus 5:1—7:27; 13:1–35; 23:1–39.

privately for his disciples alone.[30] Jesus' teaching ministry likewise includes sharp and sometimes lengthy controversies with his opponents concerning the scriptures.[31]

Jesus' teaching ministry is characterized by its authority. He repeatedly offers his own word, "but I say to you" (5:22, 28, 32, 34, 39, 44), as the definitive response to that which his listeners have "heard" in the Jewish scriptures.[32] As a result the crowds express their "astonishment" (7:28) that Jesus is teaching them "as one who has authority and not as their scribes" (7:29). Even when Jesus' listeners are not willing to accept his teachings, they grudgingly acknowledge the "wisdom" of his words (13:54) and bear cynical witness to the "truthfulness" with which he "teaches the way of God" (22:16). Jesus' words evoke "astonishment" and "amazement" from all of his listeners alike—the crowds (7: 28; 13:54; 22:33), his disciples (19:25), and his opponents (22:22).

Jesus likewise carries out a ministry of "powerful deeds."[33] This ministry is all-inclusive in its geographical reach and encyclopedic in its medical scope. Jesus goes about through "all Galilee" (4:23), through "all the towns and villages" (9:35), and heals "all" those who are sick.[34] Jesus' healing ministry encompasses those who are "suffering"[35] with "disease"[36] and "illness"[37], the "sick" (14:14) and those with "infirmities" (8:17), those who are "tormented" (4:24; 8:6) and "demon-possessed,"[38] "epileptics" (4:24; 17:15), "paralytics,"[39] "lepers" (8:2; 11:5), those who are "burning with fever" (8:14), those who are "hemorrhaging" (9:20), the "blind,"[40] the "mute,"[41] the "lame,"[42] the "maimed" (15:30, 31), and those with "withered hands" (12:10). Jesus' healing powers extend even to the raising of the "dead" (11:5 cf. 9:18).

30. Thus 10:1–42; 13:36–52; 18:1–35; 24:1—25:46.
31. Thus 12:1–8; 9–14; 15:1–20; 19:3–9.
32. Thus 5:21, 27, 33, 38, 43, cf. 31.
33. Thus 11:20, 21, 23; 13:54, 58; 14:2.
34. Thus 4:24; 8:16; 12:15; cf. 14:14; 15:30; 19:2; 21:14.
35. Thus 4:24; 8:16; 14:35; 17:15.
36. Thus 4:23, 24; 8:17; 9:35.
37. Thus 4:23; 9:35.
38. Thus 4:24; 8:16, 28, 33; 9:32, 33, 34; 12:22, 24, 27, 28; 15:22; 17:18). See also Matthew's prominent references to Jesus' exorcistic ministry of "casting out" the "demons" or "spirits" (8:16, 31; 9:33, 34; 12:24, 26, 27, 28).
39. Thus 4:24; 8:6; 9:2, 6.
40. Thus 9:27, 28; 11:5; 12:22; 15:30, 31; 20:30; 21:14.
41. Thus 9:32, 33; 11:5; 12:22; 15:30, 31.
42. Thus 11:5; 15:30, 31; 21:14.

Jesus also carries out numerous other "powerful deeds," both acts of compassion and prophetic signs of judgment. Jesus calms a storm by "rebuking the winds and the sea" (8:26; cf. 14:32). He comes to his disciples "walking on the sea" (14:25) and empowers Peter, in similar fashion, to come to him "walking upon the waters" (14:29; cf. 14:28). And on two occasions he feeds a crowd of thousands with a few loaves and fish (14:13-21; 15:32-39). On his way into Jerusalem Jesus denounces a fig tree, which "withers immediately" (21:19). And at the temple he "throws out" all the sellers and the buyers, "overturns" the tables of the moneychangers and the seats of the dove-sellers, and accuses the merchants and moneychangers of making "the house of prayer" into a "den of robbers" (21:12-13).

And in all of these "powerful deeds" Jesus, Son of God, acts with divine authority. Not only do Jesus' deeds create "amazement" in the minds of those who witness them (8:27; 21:20) and cause people to inquire into the source from which they come (13:54). They also draw believers (8:9) and skeptics (21:23) alike to the conclusion that Jesus is acting with "authority" as he carries out his deeds of power.[43] And Jesus not only acknowledges that he is acting with "authority" (21:24, 27), but he also passes on this same "authority" to his disciples for their own healing ministry (10:1 cf. 10:8). Finally, as the Risen Jesus and his disciples stand together on the mountain in Galilee (28:16-17), he assures them that "all authority in heaven and on earth has been given to me" (28:18), a gift both cosmic in its extent and divine in its origin.[44]

Accordingly, Jesus' public ministry of proclaiming, teaching, and healing is both "authoritative" in its origins and "dynamic" in its outworkings. At the same time this ministry takes on contrasting characteristics depending on the persons or groups toward whom it is directed. Towards the crowds and those who come to him in faith, Jesus carries out a ministry of "mercy" and "compassion." Jesus "has compassion" on crowds who lack effective leadership (9:36), crowds who are hungry (15:32), crowds with sick persons in their midst (14:14), and individuals who come to him for healing (20:34). Jesus likewise teaches his disciples about forgiveness by telling them a kingdom parable about a lord who "has compassion" and "forgives the debt" of one of his slaves (18:27), a clear allusion to God's own compassionate "forgiveness" (cf. 6:12, 14, 15). Jesus repeatedly characterizes his own ministry in the words of the prophet Hosea, "I desire mercy and not sacrifice"

---

43. The chief priests and elders of the people do not dispute Jesus' "authority," but rather its source. Elsewhere the Pharisees attribute Jesus' power to "Beelzebul, the ruler of the demons" (12:24; cf. 9:34).

44. The use of the "theological passive," *edothē*, indicates that what "has been given" comes from God.

(9:13; 12:7). And Jesus grants the requests of all those who come to him begging for "mercy";[45] castigates the scribes and Pharisees for "neglecting the weightier matters of the law, justice and mercy and faithfulness" (23:23); and pronounces "beatitude" on the "merciful," who will themselves "receive mercy" from God (5:7; cf. 18:33).[46]

But it is prophetic "woes" which characterize Jesus' interactions with his opponents. Jesus pronounces "woes" upon Chorazin, Bethsaida, and Capernaum, cities which have not "repented" in spite of the "powerful deeds" which Jesus has done there (11:21; cf. 10:15). Similarly, he pronounces generic "woes" upon "the world"/"the one through whom offense comes" (18:7) and a specific "woe" upon "the one by whom the Son of Man is handed over" (26:24).[47] But it is the Jewish religious leadership for whom Jesus reserves his most scathing response, a sevenfold sequence of "woes" directed against the "scribes and Pharisees, hypocrites"[48] and the "blind leaders" (23:16) for actions which Jesus considers hypocritical abuse of their privileged position "on the seat of Moses."[49]

Jesus' mission to the Jewish people, accordingly, is a multifold ministry, which conveys "compassion" to some and "woe" to others. And this ministry likewise evokes sharply divergent responses from those who encounter Jesus. During most of his public career Jesus meets with an enthusiastic reception from the ordinary people. He is constantly surrounded by "crowds"[50] or "great crowds,"[51] who "come to" him (21:14), "gather around" him (13:2), "bring" their sick to him (4:24; 14:35), "go before" him (21:9), and "follow" him[52] wherever he goes. As people witness his ministry of

---

45. Thus 9:27; 15:22; 17:15; 20:30, 31.

46. See also 6:1, 2, 3, 4, in which Jesus assumes that his disciples will participate in the religious practice of doing "alms" (= "merciful deeds").

47. Note, in a somewhat different vein, the "woe" which Jesus pronounces on pregnant and nursing women at the time of eschatological tribulations (24:19). Here the focus lies not on the failure or the sinfulness of the women involved, but rather on the extreme severity of the tribulations which await Jesus' disciples.

48. Thus 23:13, 15, 23, 25, 27, 29.

49. Thus 23:2; cf. 6:2, 5, 16. See also 12:34, where Jesus refers to the Pharisees (12:24) as a "brood of snakes" whose "good" speech and "evil" character do not correspond with each other.

50. Thus 5:1; 7:28; 9:8, 33; 12:23; 14:13; 15:31; 21:11, 46; 22:33.

51. Thus 4:25; 12:15; 13:2; 14:14; 15:30; 19:2; 20:29; cf. 21:8.

52. Thus 4:25; 12:15; 14:13; 19:2; 20:29; 21:9.

word and deed, they are "amazed,"[53] "astonished,"[54] "astounded,"[55] "shaken up,"[56] and "awestruck."[57] They acknowledge his "wisdom" (13:54) and his "powerful deeds" (13:54; 14:2),[58] acclaim the uniqueness of his ministry within Israel (9:33), proclaim him "prophet" (16:14; 21:11, 46) and "Son of David" (21:9, 15; cf. 12:23), and "glorify God" on his account (9:8; 15:31). And as a result the "report" about Jesus[59] spreads throughout the countryside; and Jesus' popularity with the people grows to such an extent that his opponents fear a "riot" among the people, if they take action against him (26:5; cf. 21:46).

But Jesus likewise meets with sturdy and persistent opposition throughout his ministry. The source of this opposition is sometimes identified with the Jewish people in general: the proverbial "they" (11:19; 9:24); "this people" (13:15); "this [evil and adulterous] generation" (11:16; cf. 12:39; 16:4); "the cities in which [Jesus] has done most of his powerful deeds" (11:20); the people of Jesus' "hometown" (13:54);[60] the "crowd" at a Jewish wake (9:23, 25). More frequently, however, Jesus' opponents are identified as the religious leadership of the Jewish people: Pharisees, scribes, Sadducees, Herodians, chief priests, and elders of the people.[61]

Jesus' opponents challenge his words and his actions at every turn. They question him concerning table fellowship (9:10-11), fasting (9:14),[62] sabbath observance (12:2, 10), ritual washing (15:1-2), divorce (19:3), resurrection (22:24-28), and the "greatest commandment" (22:36). In addition they ask him for a "sign from heaven" (12:38; 16:1), question the source of his "wisdom" and "powerful deeds" (13:54-56), challenge his acceptance of the accolade "Son of David" (21:15-16), and demand to know on whose "authority" he acts (21:23). And most cynically of all, they seek to "test him" (22:35) or to "entrap him in words" (22:15).

---

53. Thus *thaumazō*: 8:27; 9:33; 15:31; 22:22.

54. Thus *ekplēsomai*: 7:28; 13:54; 19:25; 22:33.

55. Thus *existēmi*: 12:23.

56. Thus *seiō*: 21:10.

57. Thus *phobeomai*: 9:8.

58. As Matthew makes clear in 13:54, however, such acknowledgment does not necessarily lead to faith.

59. Thus *akoē*: 4:24; 14:1; *phēmē*: 9:26; cf. 9:31.

60. In a similar fashion note also the reference to "the whole city" (8:34) of the Gadarenes (8:28), which takes an opposing stance toward Jesus.

61. Consult a concordance for Matthew's extensive usage of these terms.

62. While "the disciples of John the Baptist" are not elsewhere portrayed as opponents of Jesus (cf. 11:2-7), their question in 9:14 sets them over against Jesus and his disciples with regard to ritual practices.

Nor do they stop with questions. Jesus' opponents accuse him of "casting out demons through Beelzebul, the ruler of the demons" (12:24; cf. 9:34). They castigate Jesus' disciples for "transgressing the traditions of the elders" (15:1–2). They label Jesus a "glutton," "drunkard," and "friend of tax collectors and sinners" (11:19) because of his non-ascetic lifestyle (11:19) and his scandalous social practices (9:10–11). And when Jesus assumes the prerogative to forgive sins (9:2; cf. 9:6), they charge him with "blasphemy" (9:3).

Accordingly, Jesus' opponents reject his ministry in its entirety, word and deed alike. Just as they previously failed to "believe" John's message of "righteousness" (21:32), so they now fail to "repent" in response to Jesus' "powerful deeds" (11:20). Jesus charges that they do not respond when they are "called" (11:16–19), that they have "closed their eyes" to the "mysteries of the kingdom of heaven" (13:15 cf. 13:11), and that they reject his efforts when he wishes, in the fashion of a mother hen, to "gather" them (23:37). Instead, they "laugh" at his words (9:24), "take offense" at his "wisdom" and his "powerful deeds" (13:57), and exhibit an attitude of "unbelief" (13:58).[63] Ultimately they "take counsel together" against him (12:14; 26:4; 27:1) in order to "seize" (26:4; cf. 21:46) and "destroy" him (12:14) by "killing" him (26:4; cf. 21:38) or "putting him to death" (27:1).

Jesus is keenly aware of this deadly opposition. Throughout his ministry he makes persistent references to the brutal fate which awaits him. And over the course of Jesus' public ministry these references create a detailed portrait of his upcoming "passion." As Jesus himself announces, he "has a cup to drink" (20:22; 26:39, 42) which is filled with "suffering" (16:21; 17:12). He knows that when he arrives at Jerusalem (16:21; 20:18), he will be "taken" (21:39), "seized" (26: 55), "arrested" (26:55), and "handed over"[64] to others. Jesus' opponents will then "condemn him to death" (20:18), "mock" him (20:19), "flog" him (20:19), and "kill" him[65] by "crucifying" him (20:19; 26: 2) on a "cross" (cf. 10:38; 16:24), after which he will be "buried" (26:12).[66] In parabolic language Jesus describes himself as the "vineyard owner's son" (21:37 cf. 21:33) who will be "thrown out of the vineyard and killed" (21:39) and the "shepherd" who will be "struck" (26:31). And in the metaphorical language of his ultimate prophetic sign Jesus identifies bread and wine as his

---

63. Cf. 8:34, where the Gadarenes "implore" Jesus to "leave their territory," after he has healed a demoniac and released the demons into a herd of pigs (8:28–34).

64. Thus 17:22; 20:18, 19; 26:2, 21, 23, 24, 45, 46.

65. Thus 16:21; 17:23; 21:38, 39.

66. Cf. also 26:38, where Jesus tells his disciples in the Garden of Gethsemane that his soul is "deeply grieved to the point of death."

"body" (26:26) and "blood" (26:28) which are "poured out for many for the forgiveness of sins" (26:28).

But Jesus is not merely aware of the suffering which lies ahead of him. Rather, as he proclaims to his disciples, he has "come" for this very purpose, namely "to give his life as a ransom for many" (20:28). Jesus' suffering, accordingly, is as integral a piece of his mission as his "sayings,"[67] and his "powerful deeds."[68] As a result Jesus sets out very deliberately to go up to Jerusalem (16: 21; 20:17; 21:1, 10). And when the moment comes, Jesus makes equally deliberate moves to accept the suffering that awaits him there.

To be sure, Jesus agonizes in the Garden of Gethsemane (26:38), prays repeatedly to his "Father" for release from the "cup" which is his to "drink" (26:39, 42; cf. 26:44), and confesses that "the flesh is weak" (26:41). But once he has submitted himself to the "will" of his "Father" (26:39, 42; cf. 26:44), there is no further hesitation. Jesus steps forward to meet Judas, the one who has "come near" in order to "hand him over" (26:46). As he does so, he grants Judas effective permission to carry out his intentions with the words, "Comrade, do what you came for" (26:50). And when "one of those with Jesus" responds by drawing his own sword (26:51), Jesus offers him an immediate and sharp rebuke (26:52). Then, in stunning fashion, Jesus reveals that he has already renounced the use of violent power far greater and more effective than that of the single sword just drawn on his behalf: "Or do you suppose that I do not have the power to appeal to my Father, who would immediately send me more than twelve legions of angels? (26:53).

And from this moment onward Jesus, whose ministry of authoritative word and powerful action has driven the narrative forward thus far, now becomes the silent and passive recipient of the harsh words and the brutal actions of others. From the moment of his arrest (26:46–56) until the moment of his death (27:50) Jesus does almost nothing and maintains an almost complete silence, while his religious and political opponents seize the initiative both verbally and physically.[69]

On the verbal level they "take counsel against" him (27:1), "say" things to him,[70] "adjure" him to proclaim his identity (26: 63), "ask" him questions (27:11), "bear [false] witness against" him,[71] "accuse" him (27:12), pronounce him "worthy of death" (26:66), "condemn" him (27:3), "mock"

---

67. Thus 7:28; 11:1; 19:1; 26:1; cf. 13:53.

68. Thus 11:20, 21, 23; 13:54, 58; 14:2.

69. Cf. Pilate's question to the crowds (27:22), "What then shall I do with Jesus, the one who is called Messiah?" For a detailed comparison of Matthew's characterizations of Pilate and Jesus in the trial scene, see Weaver, "Power and Powerlessness," 191–195.

70. Thus 26:62, 63, 68; 27:11, 13, 29, 40, 41.

71. Thus 26:62; 27:13; cf. 26:59, 60.

him (27:29, 31, 41), "blaspheme" him (27:39), and "revile" him (27:44). On the physical level they "approach" him (26:49, 50), "kiss" him in mock friendship (26:49; cf. 26:48), "lay hands on" him (26:50), "seize" him (26:48, 50, 57), "bind" him (27:2), "lead him away" (26:57; 27:2, 31), "take him along" (27:27), "gather" people to him (27:27) and "hand him over."[72]

Once he is bound and within their power, they "spit" on him (27:30) or in his face (26:67), "strike" him on the face (26:67) and on the head (27:30), "cuff" him (26:67), "slap" him (26:67), "hit" him (26:67), "take clothes off" him (27:28, 31), "put clothes on" him (27:31), "put [things] around" him (27:28), "put [things] on/over" his head (27:29, 37), and "bow down before" him in mock worship (27:29). Finally, they "scourge" him (27:26) and "crucify" him;[73] and in this way they "put him to death" (26:59; 27:1) or "destroy" him (27:20). Before he dies, however, they "give him something to drink,"[74] "divide" his clothes among them (27:35), and "keep watch" over him as he hangs on the cross (27:36).

In response to all this Jesus takes few actions and speaks even fewer words. On the active level he "stands before the governor" (27:11), "tastes [the wine offered to him]" (27:34) but "will not drink it" (27:34), and ultimately "gives up his spirit" (27:50). On the verbal level Jesus maintains a total silence in the face of "false witness" against him,[75] much to the amazement of both Caiaphas (26:62) and Pilate (27:13, 14b). Only when their questions correspond to the truth does Jesus respond (26:64; 27:11). And as he hangs dying on the cross, he cries out to God in his "forsakenness" (27:46).

Accordingly, just as his predecessors, the prophets and John the Baptist, Jesus accepts his sufferings peaceably and without retaliation. He completely renounces not only the puny and ineffective efforts of his disciples to take violent action on his behalf (26:51–52) but also the all-powerful violent option which lies within his reach as the "Son" of his "Father" (26:53–54). Jesus rejects all violent options as the means either for saving his own life or for retaliating against his enemies.

But just as with his predecessors, the story of Jesus' peaceable ministry and his rejection of violent options does not end when Jesus "gives up his spirit" (27:50). Rather, as Jesus himself has predicted,[76] his death at the hands of powerful enemies gives way to the infinitely more powerful act of God in "raising" him "from the dead." To his opponents Jesus speaks in the

72. Thus 26:48; 27:2, 3, 4, 18.
73. Thus 27:22, 23, 26, 31, 35; cf. 27:32, 38, 44.
74. Thus *edōkan piein*, 27:34; *epotizen*, 27:48.
75. Thus 26:60–61, 63a; 27:12, 14a.
76. Thus 16:21; 17:9, 23; 20:19.

metaphorical language of Psalm 118:22 about "the stone which the builders rejected, [which] has become the head of the corner," an act which "has taken place at the Lord's initiative" (21:42). In a similar vein he cites Psalm 110:1, which speaks about the "Messiah, Son of David" (22:42), whom "the Lord" calls to "Sit at my right hand until I place your enemies under your feet" (22:44). Thus it is none other than God who will vindicate the peaceable mission of the "beloved Son" (3:17; 17:5; cf. 21:37), reversing the sentence of death enacted on Jesus, raising his lifeless body to new life, and granting him authority of the highest order.

And, in Matthew's biting irony, this is exactly what comes to pass. In an indescribable act of divine power[77] God "raises Jesus from the dead"[78] and in so doing empties the tomb in which Jesus has been laid (28:6; cf. 27:59). Jesus' opponents, who have "secured the tomb, sealing the stone and setting [a] guard" (27:66; cf. 27:64), find themselves outwitted and overpowered by this divine initiative. Not only does "the angel of the Lord" descend in a "great earthshaking event" and co-opt their entire security system by "rolling back the stone and sitting on it" (28:2). But the angel likewise disarms "those who are keeping watch" over the tomb, instilling such "fear" into them that they themselves "shake" and "fall into a dead faint" (28:4). And when they recover, they have no explanation to offer for the empty tomb (cf. 28:13–14) which once held the body of Jesus. As a result they themselves ironically create and perpetuate the very "resurrection fraud" which they had intended to prevent by their elaborate security measures (28:11–15 cf. 27:62–66).[79]

Nor is this all. God, who has vindicated the peaceable ministry of the "beloved Son" by raising him from the dead, likewise accords to Jesus authority of the highest order. When the Risen Jesus encounters his disciples on the mountain in Galilee, he announces that "all authority in heaven and on earth has been given to me" (28:18). And he sends them out with a renewed and expanded mission to "make disciples" not only of "the lost sheep of the house of Israel" as before (10:6; cf. 15:24) but rather of "all the nations" (28:18). This same Risen Jesus, with "all authority in heaven and on earth" (28:18), will not only "be with" his disciples until "the consummation of the age" (28:20) but also, as the victorious Son of Man, "come"[80] to the inhabit-

---

77. Matthew makes no attempt to describe the resurrection of Jesus, contenting himself with pronouncements that Jesus "will be raised" (16:21; 17:23; 10:19; 26:32; cf. 27:63) and announcements that Jesus "has been raised" (28:6, 7; cf. 27:53, 64).

78. Thus 17:9; cf. 16:21; 17:23; 20:19.

79. For a detailed study of the irony within Matthew's resurrection narrative, see Weaver, "Matthew 28:1–10," 398–402.

80. Thus 10:23; 16:27, 28; 24: 30, 44; 25:31; cf. 23:39; 24:42, 43, 46; 25:10, 19, 27.

ants of the earth "on the clouds of heaven" (24:30), in "kingdom" (16:28), "power" (24:30) and "[great] glory" (16:27; 24:30; 25:31), along with "his angels" (16:27; 25:31), in order to "sit on his glorious throne" (19:28; 25:31) and serve as the judge of "all the nations" (25:32). As such he will separate the "sheep" from the "goats" (25:32), "confess" or "deny" humans before "[his] Father in heaven" (10:32–33), and "repay each person according to their deeds" (16:27; cf. 25:31–46).[81] Jesus, the one who has "come" to "give his life as a ransom for many" (20:28) and who has accepted suffering and death peaceably and without retaliation, is now accorded ultimate authority over the eternal destiny of humankind. Such is the vindication of God's "beloved Son," the one who rejects the way of violence.

IV. "AS SHEEP INTO THE MIDST OF WOLVES"

Mission and Peace in the Portrayal of the Disciples

As Matthew views it, Jesus' disciples stand at the end of a long and illustrious line of forebears. Just as "the prophets who were before them" (5:12), John the Baptist, and Jesus himself, these disciples have been "sent out" by God to a ministry of public proclamation and deeds of power and compassion. They have likewise been "sent out" to suffer, peaceably and without retaliation, the persecution brought on by this ministry. The direct correlation between the mission of Jesus' disciples and that of their forebears, most prominently Jesus himself, is difficult to overlook within Matthew's narrative.

Jesus' disciples know themselves to be "called" by Jesus (4:21) to "follow" (8:22; 9:9) or "come after" (4:19) him. And Jesus then "sends the disciples out"[82] to "go"[83] and carry forward his ministry (10:1 cf. 9:35), a "sending" which Jesus equates with the divine "sending" activities of the "lord of the harvest" (9:38) and the "king who gives a wedding banquet for his son" (22:3, 4). Jesus' disciples thus know themselves to be both "called" and "sent" by Jesus, Son of God, to the same divine vocation which he himself has claimed.

---

81. Cf. 11:20–24, where Jesus pronounces "woes" on Chorazin (11:21), Bethsaida (11:21), and Capernaum (11:23), the cities in which he has carried out most of his "mighty deeds" (11:20, 21, 23), because they have failed to "repent" (11:20, 21; cf. 11:23) in response to Jesus' ministry. Accordingly, Jesus warns that "on the day of judgment" it will be "more tolerable" for Tyre, Sidon, and Sodom than for these unrepentant cities (11:22, 24).

82. Thus 10:5, 16; 23:34, 37; cf. 10:2.

83. Thus 10:6; 28:19; cf. 22:9.

Initially this vocation "sends" the disciples to "the lost sheep of the house of Israel" (10:5a, 6), in direct correspondence with Jesus' own mission (15:24) and in clear distinction to any mission to Gentiles or Samaritans (10:5). During his own earthly ministry among the Jewish people Jesus commissions his disciples to join him in his task.[84] But following his resurrection the Risen Jesus expands the mission of his disciples into a cosmic focus on all the nations (28:19) and extends their mission temporally to the very "consummation of the age" (28:20). Thus the mission of Jesus' disciples begins with the call of the earthly Jesus to minister "here and now" to "the lost sheep of the house of Israel"; but the outward trajectory of this mission reaches beyond the Jewish people to "all the nations" and beyond the present time to the very "consummation of the age."

Jesus employs terminology both metaphorical and non-metaphorical to characterize the identity of his disciples as those "sent out" into mission. In the metaphorical language drawn from nature and material culture Jesus' disciples are the "salt of the earth" whose value lies in its "flavor" (5:13), the "light of the world" (5:14), the "city set on a hill" which "cannot be hidden" (5:14), and the "lamp on the lampstand" which "gives light to all in the house" (5:15). These metaphors focus on the positive influence which the disciples exert over the society around them. In metaphorical language drawn from human society they are "fishers for people" (4: 19), "workers in the harvest" (9:37, 38; cf 10:10), and "slaves" sent out to "call the invited wedding guests into the feast" (22:3, 4, 8, 10). These metaphors emphasize the "gathering" task central to the disciples' mission.

In non-metaphorical terms Jesus calls his disciples "prophets,"[85] "righteous persons" (10: 41), "wise persons" (23:34), "scribes" (23:34), and "little ones" (10:42). As such they have a multifold ministry. Jesus' disciples are called to a verbal ministry of "proclamation" (10:7, 27; 24:14; 26:13), "call" (22:3, 9), "witness" (10:18; 24:14), "speaking" (26:13), and "words" (10:14). This is a ministry in which the disciples "say" what they have been given to say.[86] And this ministry is largely invitational in character. The disciples are instructed to "greet" the houses they enter with a word of "peace" (10:12, 13); to "proclaim that "the kingdom of heaven has come near" (10:7; cf. 3:2; 4:17); and, as the slaves of the king, to "say": "See! My feast has been

---

84. There is no positive indication, however, in Matthew's narrative that the disciples actually carry out the mission of 10:5b–42 prior to their arrival on "the mountain in Galilee" to which the Risen Jesus has called them (28:16). On this point, see Weaver, *Missionary Discourse*, 126, 127–53.

85. Thus 5:12; 10:41; 23:34; cf. 23:37.

86. Thus *laleō*: 10:19, 20; *legō*: 10:27; 22:4.

prepared! My oxen and my fatted calves have been slaughtered and everything is now ready! Come to the wedding feast!" (22:4b cf. 22:2-4a).

Jesus' disciples are likewise called to a ministry of healing and other deeds of compassion. Jesus "authorizes" his disciples "to cast out evil spirits and to heal every disease and every sickness" (10:1), the very tasks which he himself has been carrying out among the people.[87] And he likewise empowers them to show "compassion" to the crowds (15:32; cf. 14:14) by "giving" them sufficient bread to feed thousands of hungry people (14:19-21; 15:36-38). Along with this authorization and empowerment Jesus calls his disciples into ministry: "Heal the sick, raise the dead, cleanse lepers, cast out demons, give [people] something to eat! You have received without cost; give without charge!" (10:8a; 14:16; 10:8b).

But this invitational ministry of "proclamation" and deeds of "compassion" will not assure the disciples of a positive reception by those to whom they go. Rather, just as the prophets, John the Baptist, and Jesus before them, the disciples will encounter significant opposition to their ministry. They will enter houses which are "not worthy" (10:13) and encounter persons who "do not receive [them] or listen to [their] words" (10:14). They will likewise encounter persecution (10:16-39), the same verbal and physical abuse which Jesus has already encountered and that which will lead to his death.

On the verbal level people will "revile" the disciples (5:11), "say all kinds of evil" about them (5:11), "lie" about them (5:11), and "call them Beelzebul" (10:25). On the emotional level the disciples will find their invitation "disregarded" (22:5) by others who "do not wish" to receive it (22:3). The disciples will likewise find themselves "separated" from their closest family members (10:35) and surrounded by "enemies," in their own households (10:36) and beyond (5:44), who will "hate" them (10:22; 24:9, 10) and "rise up against" them (10:21). On the physical level the disciples will be "slapped" on the cheek (5:39), "sued" by those who wish to "take [their] cloaks" (5:40), "forced" to carry burdens for Roman soldiers (5:41; cf. 27:32), and "mistreated" (22:6). They will likewise be "persecuted from town to town,"[88] "seized" (22:6), "handed over to councils" (10:17, 19), "whipped in synagogues" (10:17; 23:34), "dragged before governors and kings" (10:18), and "scattered" as "sheep" whose "shepherd" has been "struck" (26:31). Ultimately, they will "lose their lives" (10:39; 16:25) as they are "handed over

---

87. Thus 4:23; 9:35; cf. 8:1-4, 5-13, 14-15, 16-17, 28-34; 9:1-8, 18-19/23-26, 20-22, 27-31, 32-34.

88. Thus 23:34; cf. 10:23; 5:10, 11, 12, 44.

to tribulation/death" (24:9, 10; 10:21), "stoned" (23:37), "crucified" (23:34), "put to death" (10:21), and "killed."[89]

Nor can this brutal rejection be considered simply an unfortunate consequence of the disciples' ministry. Rather, this persecution is an integral element of their mission itself. Jesus commissions them with the words, "See, I am sending you out as sheep into the midst of wolves" (10:16). Accordingly, the very character of the disciples' mission is shaped by their identity as those whose lot it is to suffer at the hands of others. The reason for this circumstance is simple and obvious. Jesus' disciples are those who "follow" (4:20, 22; 8:22; 9:9; 10:38; 16:24) or "come after" (4:19; 16:24) him, which means that they must go where Jesus goes. Accordingly, as they "follow" Jesus, they have no choice but to "take up the cross"[90] which Jesus himself is about to carry (20:19; 26:2) and to "drink the cup" of suffering (20:22, 23) which Jesus himself is about to drink (26:39, 42, 44). And as they "lose their lives" (10: 39; 16:25), they do so "on account of [Jesus]" himself (10:39; 16: 25). As Jesus says, "The disciple is not above the teacher, nor the slave above his lord. It is sufficient to the disciple that he be like his teacher, and the slave like his lord. If they have called the master of the house "Beelzebul," how much more so the members of his household" (10:24–25).[91]

Accordingly, just as Jesus himself has "come" to "give his [own] life" (20:28), so he has also "come" to "bring the sword" which will "separate" his disciples from their closest family members (10:34–35), turn "members of the household" into "enemies" (10:36), and lead the closest of relatives to "rise up against" the disciples and "hand them over to death" (10:21). And just as the divine "vineyard owner" of Jesus' parable spares neither his "slaves" nor his "son" from the violence which is sure to be carried out against them (21:36–37 cf. 21:34–35), so Jesus himself does not promise to spare his own disciples from the fate which awaits them. Addressing the Jewish religious establishment in the temple shortly before his own death, Jesus announces to them (23:34): "See, I send out to you prophets and wise people and scribes! Some of them you will kill and crucify; and some of them you will whip in your synagogues and persecute from town to town." Just as the "vineyard owner" will not allow the inevitable persecution of his emissaries to deter him from his mission to "take the fruits" from his "vineyard" (21:33–37), so too will Jesus not allow the inevitable persecution of his disciples to halt his ongoing mission to the Jewish leadership (23:34) and

---

89. Thus 10:28; 22:6; 23:34, 37; 24:9.

90. Thus *lambanei*: 10:38 *aratō*: 16:24.

91. Cf. 9:34; 12:24, 27. On the "image"/"reflection" correspondence between the sufferings of Jesus and that of his disciples, see Weaver, *Missionary Discourse*, 146–47.

their people (10:6, 23). As Jesus himself suffers, so too will Jesus' disciples "follow" him into suffering.

And just as Jesus faces suffering peaceably and without retaliation, so he calls his disciples to do the same. With respect to the "evil persons" who harass and humiliate them day by day (5:39, 40, 41, 42), Jesus challenges his disciples to active "nonresistance" of the most radical and scandalous sort: "turning the other cheek" to the one who has "struck you" (5:39); "offering your cloak as well" to the one who has "sued you and taken your tunic" (5:40); "going two miles" with the Roman soldier who "compels you to go with him one mile" (5:41); "giving" to the one who "asks [money] of you" and "not turning away" from the one who "wishes to borrow from you" (5:42).[92] Vis-a-vis their "enemies" Jesus calls his disciples to a stance of "love" (5:44); vis-a-vis their "persecutors" Jesus exhorts them to "prayer" (5:44).

To those who reject their ministry, Jesus calls the disciples to a prophetic but nonviolent response. If the house which the disciples have entered is "not worthy," they are called to "let [their] peace return to [them]" (10:13). And if they and their words are "not received," the disciples are exhorted to "leave that house or town" and to "shake off the dust from [their] feet" as they do so (10:14). In this way the disciples will dissociate themselves both physically and symbolically from the unreceptive house or town and at the same time point prophetically to the divine judgment which will fall on that house or town. For those who reject Jesus' disciples and their mission the consequences will be severe.[93]

But all such consequences remain the sole prerogative of God and not of the disciples. The disciples are neither authorized, empowered, nor commissioned to retaliate against those who have rejected them and their ministry. To the contrary Jesus calls them to respond to persecution with a combination of caution, courage, and confidence. On the one hand Jesus cautions them to be "wise as serpents," (10:16), "innocent as doves" (10:16), and "wary of people" (10:17). When they meet resistance in one town, Jesus urges them to "flee to the next one" on a journey throughout Israel (and

---

92. For a detailed exegesis of Matthew 5:38–42, see Weaver, "Transforming Nonresistance," 32–71.

93. In the present time they will lose their opportunity to hear the disciples' proclamation (10:14). In an historical future (to which, however, Matthew and his congregation already look backward) those who have "murderered" Jesus' emissaries will themselves be "destroyed" (22:7), their city "burned" (22:7), the stones of their temple "thrown down" (24:2 cf. 24:1), and their house "left desolate" (23:38), vivid allusions to the destruction of Jerusalem. And in an eschatological future, on the "day of judgment," that "city" which "does not receive" the disciples will suffer a fate worse than that of "the land of Sodom and Gomorrah" (10:15).

ultimately, throughout the world) which will not reach its conclusion "before the Son of Man comes."[94]

But Jesus calls his disciples to continued and courageous proclamation in the face of rejection and persecution. They are instructed "not to worry" about how they are to speak or what they are to say when they are placed on trial (10:19); and they are assured that the words they need will be "given" to them as they have need (10:19) and "spoken" through them by "the Spirit of [their] Father" (10:20). They are repeatedly enjoined "not to fear" others who have the power to revile them and put them to death (10:26, 28, 31). Rather, they are to "say in the light" and "proclaim on the housetops" what Jesus has told them in private (10:27) and to "confess" Jesus openly "before people" (10:32). Even their rejection in one house or town and their flight to the next destination signal not the end but rather the continuation of a worldwide missionary journey which will occupy their energies until "the Son of Man comes" (10:23) at "the end of the age" (28:20; cf. 24:14).

In the end God will vindicate the disciples for their faithfulness. They will be "rewarded" for "what they have done" (16:27) and "saved" because of their "endurance" (10:22; 24:13). Those who "lose their life" on Jesus' account will "find it" (10:39; 16:25). Those who "acknowledge" Jesus before others in hostile settings (10:32; cf. 10:17-20) are assured that Jesus will likewise "acknowledge" them before his Father in heaven (10:32). Those who have "left" homes, family, and real estate on Jesus' account will "receive" a hundred times what they have lost and "inherit" eternal life (19:29). Those who are "vilified" and encounter "persecution" for Jesus' sake are "blessed" in the present world and will receive "great reward" in heaven (5:11-12).

Jesus' disciples will also play a crucial role in determining the eschatological status of those to whom they have been sent out. Those towns which "do not receive" Jesus' disciples nor "listen to [their] words" will find their situation less "tolerable" on the day of judgment than that of Sodom and Gomorrah (10:14); while individuals who "receive" Jesus' disciples as "prophets," "righteous ones," and "little ones" will be granted eschatological "rewards" (10:41-42).[95] And at the "renewal of all things" when the Son of Man will be "seated on his glorious throne," Jesus' disciples, who have "given up everything" and "followed" him, will likewise "sit on twelve thrones, judging the twelve tribes of Israel" (19:28; cf. 10:6, 23). Jesus' disciples, whose identity as missionaries is that of "sheep in the midst of wolves" (10:16) and whose life in mission will lead them to unavoidable persecution and death

---

94. Thus 10:23; cf. 24:14; 28:19-20.

95. The eschatological character of these "rewards" is apparent from their juxtaposition to the eschatological "judgment" of 10:14.

(10:17–19, 21–22; 23:34), will finally receive ultimate authority along with the Lord whose mission they have carried out and whose sufferings they have shared. Such is God's vindication of those sent out unarmed into a violent world to "make disciples of all the nations" (28:19).

10

"Suffering Violence" and the Kingdom of Heaven (Matt 11:12)

A Matthean Manual for Life in a Time of War

INTRODUCTION

THE TIME WAS NOVEMBER 2000. The place was Bethlehem. I was on assignment at the International Center of Bethlehem at Christmas Lutheran Church, teaching a course on the life of Jesus for Palestinian tour guiding students. But the circumstances were grim. The outbreak of violence now known as the Second Intifada had begun only weeks before, at the end of September. Fierce gun battles between Palestinian gunmen hiding behind olive trees in the Palestinian town of Beit Jala and Israeli soldiers stationed across the valley in the Israeli settlement of Gilo shattered the quiet of Bethlehem evenings on a regular basis. And the loud booms of exploding shells and the menacing drone of helicopter gunships with their terrifying bursts of machine gun fire called me frequently from my bed to the window for anxious nighttime vigils in which the only prayer I could muster was, "O God, no!"

And then one day in our staff meeting at the International Center, Rev. Mitri Raheb invited me to write an Advent meditation for the online newsletter of the ICB. I accepted his invitation. And as soon as I did, I knew exactly what I needed to write. There was no question and no hesitation. I was living in Bethlehem in a time of war. And I knew that the text for the moment was Matthew 2:1–23, Matthew's account of a similar time of military violence and unspeakable horror in Bethlehem. Within a few short hours "Bethlehem: An Advent Meditation"[1] virtually wrote itself. And the task of "Reading Matthew in a Time of War," far from being an academic exercise, became instead the urgent task of reaching out to Matthew's narrative for a profound word of hope in the midst of present chaos and violence.

Matthew the Gospel Writer has much to say about "suffering violence." As Jesus comments to his listeners in reflecting on the ministry of John the Baptist (11:12), "From the days of John the Baptist until now the kingdom of heaven has suffered violence (*biazetai*), and the violent (*biastai*) take it by force."[2] Jesus' words are surely true. But the truth they express extends well beyond the temporal framework delineated by "the days of John the Baptist" on the one hand and the "now" of Jesus' own ministry on the other. In fact the "violence" portrayed in Matthew's Gospel reaches all the way from "the blood of righteous Abel" (23:35) to the "great suffering" that precedes the end of the age and the coming of the Son of Man (24:21, 29). As Matthew sees it, "suffering violence" is a given fact of life for God's righteous ones throughout history: Abel (23:35); Zechariah, son of Barachiah (23:35), the prophets (5:12; 23:37), and those "sent" to Jerusalem (21:34–36; 23:37); Joseph with "the child and his mother" (2:13–15, 19–23); the mothers and infants of Bethlehem portrayed as "Rachel" and her "children" (2:16–18); John the Baptist;[3] Jesus;[4] and Jesus' disciples.[5]

Through the narrative rhetoric of his Gospel Matthew offers multi-layered perspectives to his readers on life lived in the face of ongoing violence. These perspectives reflect (1) the lived experiences of the righteous ones in Matthew's narrative as they encounter and respond to violence, (2) the words of Jesus depicting or predicting the sufferings of himself and others, (3) the words of Jesus calling people to faithful responses to the violence they encounter, and (4) Matthew's own narrative rhetoric offering theological reflection on the suffering of the righteous.

This study proposes to examine, in a threefold summary overview, the Matthean theme of "suffering violence": (1) The first section of the paper will focus on the nature and cause of the violence faced by the righteous ones within Matthew's narrative; (2) the second section of the paper will

1. This essay was later published as Weaver, "Massacre," 54.

2. All biblical citations in this chapter are taken from the New Revised Standard Version unless otherwise designated by bracketed retranslations marked "DJW."

3. Thus 4:12; 11:2–19; 14:1–12; 17:9–13.

4. Thus 12:14; 16:21–23; 17:22–23; 20:17–19, 22–23, 28; 26:1—28:20.

5. Thus 5:10–12, 38–42, 43–48; 10:16–39; 16:24–26; 20:20–28; 22:1–14; 23:29–39; 24:1–31.

focus both on Jesus' call to faithful responses to violence and on actual lived responses to violence as reflected within Matthew's narrative; (3) the final section of the paper will focus on the rhetorical strategy of Matthew's narrative vis-à-vis the question of violence and assess Matthew's theological reflections on the suffering of the righteous. The study will conclude with brief reflections on the present-day implications of Matthew's text for living "in a time of war."

I. THE NATURE AND CAUSE OF VIOLENCE FACED BY THE RIGHTEOUS

To read the Gospel of Matthew with the question of "suffering violence" in focus is to discover a broad stream flowing through the heart of the Matthean landscape, a stream that intersects prominently with the lives of the righteous within Matthew's narrative and shapes their experiences profoundly. As Matthew sees it, "suffering violence" is a fundamental characteristic of the life and calling of those who are righteous.[6] Accordingly, from the outset of his narrative to its conclusion Matthew paints a vivid and unrelenting portrait of the violence inflicted on and suffered by these righteous ones. This violence ranges from the personal attacks of one individual against another[7] to the official and unofficial punishments meted out by authorities of the religious community or of the empire[8] to the widespread devastation of wars carried out by powerful military forces (24:6, 7). And the vocabulary depicting this violence ranges from general and/or metaphorical to concrete and very specific.

Speaking in broad and general terms Jesus refers to the "persecution" (*diōkō, diōgmos*) that the prophets have encountered in the past (5:12) and that which the disciples will encounter in similar fashion in the future.[9]

---

6. Thus, for example, Jesus' words in commissioning his disciples for ministry (10:23a): "See, I am sending you out like sheep into the midst of wolves." The very character of the disciples' mission, as Jesus portrays it, is shaped from its inception by the violent response that the missioners will receive from those to whom they go. See Weaver, Missionary Discourse, 92. In this respect Jesus' disciples share the calling not only of the prophets who preceded them in suffering "persecution" (*ediōxan*) 5:12) but also of John the Baptist, who "suffered violence" *biazetai*: 11:12; cf. 17:12) on behalf of the kingdom of heaven, and of Jesus himself, whose very mission means that he "must ... undergo great suffering" (*dei . . . polla pathein*: 16:21; cf. 17:12, 22–23; 20:17–19; 26:1–2).

7. Thus 5:25, 38, 39; 10:21–22.

8. Thus 2:16; 5:12; 10:17–18; 14:10; 26:67; 27:27–31, 35.

9. Thus 5:10, 11, 44; 10:23; 13:21; 23:34.

Synonymously Jesus speaks of "trouble," "torture," or "suffering" (*thlipsis*) that awaits his disciples whether in the present era (13:21) or in the eschatological future (24:9, 21, 29). In metaphorical language Jesus tells of the bridegroom that will be "taken away" (*apairō*: 9:15), the cup that he must "drink" (*pinō*: 20:22, 23; 26:39, 42), the life that he will "give" (*didōmi*: 20:28), and his blood that will be "poured out" (*ekchynnō*: 26:28). And Jesus warns his disciples of their status as "sheep [in] the midst of wolves" (10:16; DJW) and of the "cup" that they too must "drink" (*pinō*: 20:22–23).

At the personal level, individual versus individual, violence of various sorts—emotional, verbal, legal, and physical—affects the righteous ones of Matthew's Gospel. In the realm of emotions Jesus speaks of "enemies"[10] and those who "hate"[11] the disciples. And he warns of the "sword" (*machaira*: 10:34) that will "divide" (*dichazō*: 10:35; DJW) family members from each other: "a man against his father, and a daughter against her mother, and a daughter-in-law against her mother-in-law" (10:35//Mic. 7:6). In the verbal realm people "revile" Jesus and his disciples,[12] "utter all kinds of evil" against them,[13] and "call [them] Beelzebul."[14] On the legal front Jesus speaks of the "evildoer" (*ponēros*) who wants to "sue" you (*krinō*) and "take" (*lambanō*) your outer garment (5:38, 40); and he warns (5:25) of the "accuser" (*antidikos*) who will take you "to court"[15] and "hand you over" (*paradidōmi*) to the "judge" (*kritēs*). In the realm of physical violence Jesus speaks (5:38–39) of the "evildoer" (*ponēros*) who "strikes you (*rhapizō*) on the right cheek"; and he refers to the *lex talionis*, the law of retaliation invoked when one individual attacks another and gouges out their "eye" or knocks out their "tooth" (5:38).[16] And well beyond the level of "eye" and "tooth" physical violence, even among the most intimate of relations, is often deadly. Jesus points back through Jewish history to the "blood of righteous Abel" (23:35), a man murdered by his brother (Gen 4:8–11); and he warns of a time to come when "brother will [hand over (*paradidōmi*)] brother to death, and a

---

10. *echthros*: 5:43, 44; 10:36//Mic 7:6.

11. *miseō*: 10:22; 24:9, 10; cf. 5:43.

12. *oneidizō*: 5:11; 27:44.

13. *legō pan ponēron*: 5:11; cf. 26:62; 27:13.

14. *Epikaleō . . . Beelzeboul*: 10:25; DJW.

15. The words "to court" are not found in the Greek original, but are clearly implied by the context.

16. The punishment for such an offense ("an eye for an eye and a tooth for a tooth": 5:38) is, however, not an act of personal revenge but rather a corporate punishment carried out officially by the wider community (thus Deut 19:15–21). On the communal character of this punishment see Weaver, "Transforming Nonresistance," 37–47.

father his child, and children will rise up (*epanistamai*) against parents and have them put to death (*thanatoō*)" (10:21; DJW).[17]

But while violence of all types at the personal level is clearly a fact of life for the righteous ones in Matthew's narrative, the predominant depiction of violence is of that which happens at the judicial level. Here official or unofficial punishment is meted out by the authorities of the religious community or of the empire in accordance (or not!) with legal statutes governing such actions. These acts of violence as portrayed in Matthew's narrative fall into a handful of broad categories: (1) conspiracy; (2) arrest and imprisonment; (3) court trials and verbal abuse; (4) physical abuse and torture; and (5) execution and/or murder.

Cynical and clearly extra-judicial acts of conspiracy lie behind much of the judicial violence depicted in Matthew's narrative. Herod, the Jewish client king ruling Judea at the time of Jesus' birth, engages in conspiratorial actions (2:7-8) designed to "destroy" (*apollymi*: 2:13) his rival, the "child who has been born king of the Jews" (2:2). The wicked tenants of Jesus' parable (21:33-46) take similar conspiratorial steps to "seize" (*lambanō*: 21:39) and "kill" (*apokteinō*: 21:38, 39) the son of the vineyard owner. The religious leaders—Pharisees, chief priests, and elders of the people—then fulfill the words of Jesus' parable by "conspiring" or "devising plans" against Jesus[18] to "arrest" him (*krateō*: 26:4), "kill" him (*apokteinō*: 26:4), and "destroy" him (*apollymi*: 12:14). Characteristics of these conspiracies are "secrecy" (*lathra*: 2:7) and "stealth" (*dolos*: 26:4), bribery (26:14-16) and "blood money" (*timē haimatos*: 27:6; cf. 27:3-4), "jealousy" (*phthonos*: 27:18), and the political clout necessary to "persuade" the masses (*peithō*: 27:20), cause public "riots" (*thorybos*: 27:24; cf. 27:23), and force the hand of the Roman governor (27:24).[19]

The correlated acts of arrest and imprisonment begin the formal process of judicial violence as Matthew portrays it. The predominant technical term for this process is that of "handing over" (*paradidōmi*), a term widely used to depict the arrests of John the Baptist (4:12), Jesus,[20] and Jesus' dis-

---

17. The family members of 10:21 are not depicted as murderers who kill with their own hands but rather as those who "hand over" their next of kin for execution by the powers that be.

18. *symboulion lambanō*: 12:14; 27:1; *symbouleuō*: 26:4.

19. Cf. 2 Chr 24:20-21, which depicts the people of Judah "conspiring" (*qāšar*) against Zechariah, an act that leads to his stoning death in the temple court. See also Matthew's depiction of the "resurrection conspiracies" devised by the Jewish leaders first to ensure that Jesus' body stays in the tomb (27:62-66) and then to explain away the story of Jesus' resurrection (27:11-15).

20. Thus 10:4; 17:22; 20:18, 19; 26:2, 15, 16, 21, 23, 25, 45, 48; 27:2, 3, 4, 18, 26.

ciples.[21] A roughly similar sequence of events is depicted for such arrests. Jesus warns his disciples (5:25) of the "accuser" (*antidikos*) who hands a person over to the "judge" (*kritēs*), who in turn hands them over to the "guard" (*hypēretēs*). Elsewhere the arrest is instigated by a ruler (presumably acting by proxy; 14:3) or by a crowd—on occasion armed with "swords and clubs"(*machairōn kai xylōn*: 26:47, 55) as one would do to arrest a bandit (26:55)—who "lay hands" on someone (*epiballō tas cheiras*: 26:50), "seize" them,[22] and "bind" them (*deō*: 14:3; 27:2). Then the "prisoner" (*desmios*: 27:15, 16) is "led away" (*apagō*: 26:57; 27:2, 31), "dragged" before the ruling authorities (*agō*: 10:18),[23] and "handed over" to them (*paradidōmi*: 27:2). Typically the prisoner is then "put" (*apotithēmi*: 14:3) or "thrown" (*ballō*: 5:25) into "prison."[24]

Beyond the violence of arrest and imprisonment the righteous ones of Matthew's narrative also encounter the judicial (and extra-judicial!) violence connected with court proceedings. And they experience verbal abuse both within and beyond the courtroom. At the house of Caiaphas the religious leaders seek "false testimony" (*pseudomartyria*: 26:59) against Jesus and call forward "false witnesses" (*pseudomartys*: 26:60) to tell lies about him. Before Pilate they "accuse" Jesus (*katēgoreō*: 27:12; cf. 12:10) and "make accusations against" him (*katamartyreō*: 27:13). For his part Caiaphas the high priest charges Jesus with "blasphemy" (*blasphēmia*: 26:65), while the passersby at Golgotha "blaspheme" Jesus themselves (*blasphēmeō*: 27:39; NRSV footnote) and call on him to "save himself" (27:40). Before Caiaphas the religious authorities ridicule Jesus' apparent powers as "Messiah" and demand that he "prophesy" to them (26:68), while the Roman soldiers at the governor's headquarters "mock" Jesus verbally (*empaizō*) as they kneel before him and acclaim him "King of the Jews" (27:29, 31; cf. 20:19). After the crucifixion the chief priests, scribes, and elders likewise "mock" Jesus verbally (*empaizō*: 27:41), deriding his apparent inability to "save himself," taunting him to "come down from the cross," and calling on God to "deliver him now, if he wants to" (27:42-43). Nor does the verbal abuse end when Jesus dies. Following Jesus' death these same religious authorities pronounce Jesus a "deceiver" (*planos*: 27:63). And they refer to the potential story of his resurrection as the "last deception" (*eschatē planē*) which would be "worse

---

21. Thus 5:25; 10:17, 19, 21; 24:10.

22. *krateō*: 14:3; 21:46; 22:6; 26:4, 48, 50, 55, 57; *lambanō*: 21:35, 39; cf. 21:36.

23. Here the disciples appear before unnamed "governors and kings." Jesus, for his part, appears first before Caiaphas the high priest and the scribes and elders gathered at his house (26:57) and then before Pilate the governor (27:2).

24. *phylakē*: 5:25; 14:3, 10; *desmōtērion*: 11:2.

than the first" (27:64), presumably that "deception" carried out by the life and ministry of Jesus "the deceiver."

The litany of physical abuses suffered by the righteous ones of Matthew's narrative at the hands of Jewish or Roman authorities is lengthy; and the punishments range from insult and humiliation to torture and brutality. Insult and humiliation are reflected in such actions as "spitting" in someone's face (*emptyō*: 26:67; 27:30), "shaking one's head" at another person (*kineō*: 27:39), "gathering" a large crowd around someone in order to mock them (*synagō*: 27:27), publicly stripping a person of their clothing (*ekdyō*: 27:28, 31), publicly dressing them in other clothing (*peritithēmi*: 27:28; *endyō*: 27:31), "putting" things on the head or in the hand of another (*epitithēmi*: 27:29), "kneeling" before them in mock homage (*gonypeteō*: 27:29), and "dividing" someone's clothing after their execution (*diamerizō*: 27:35) through the casual game of "casting lots" (*ballō klēron*: 27:35). And a well-known and no doubt especially galling method of humiliation within the occupied Palestine of Matthew's story was for a Roman soldier to "force" or "compel" a Jewish civilian to carry a burden—in some cases a heavy wooden cross—for the distance of one mile (*angareuō*: 5:41; 27:32).

But the physical abuse suffered by the righteous in Matthew's narrative moves far beyond humiliation and insult. Torture and brutality are reflected in such acts as the Jewish communal practice of exacting "an eye for an eye and a tooth for a tooth" from the one who has assaulted another (5:38; cf. Deut 19:15–21)[25] and the ugly Roman game of twisting thorns into a sharp and painful "crown" to "put" (*epitithēmi*: 27:29) onto the head of a prisoner. And the list of official brutalities goes on. The righteous ones are "mistreated" (*hybrizō*: 22:6), "struck" with the hand (*kolaphizō*: 26:67) or with a rod (*typtō*: 27:30), "slapped" (*rhapizō*: 27:67), "hit" (*paiō*: 26:68), "beaten" (*derō*: 21:35; cf. 21:36), and "flogged" in Jewish synagogues (*mastigoō*: 10:17; 23:34) and on Roman military bases (*mastigoō*: 20:19; *phragellō*: 27:26). Physical abuse and torture of all kinds are clearly considered acceptable as judicial or extra-judicial punishment by Jewish and Roman authorities alike within the world of Matthew's narrative.

And beyond physical abuse and torture lies the ultimate social sanction, the judicial execution or extra-judicial murder of the righteous ones. Matthew's narrative is replete with references to such judicial or extra-judicial killings; and the grim vocabulary of violent death ranges widely. Death at the hands of Jewish or Roman authorities is frequently depicted with the simple metonym "blood" (*haima*) or "blood that is shed/poured out" (*haima ekchynnomenon*): "the blood of the prophets" (23:30); "all

---

25. See n. 16.

the righteous blood shed on earth" (23:35); "the blood of righteous Abel (23:35); "the blood of Zechariah, son of Barachiah" (23:35); "my blood . . . which is poured out" (26:28); "this man's blood // his blood" (27:24, 25).²⁶ Death by official violence is likewise depicted as "seeking the life" of another (*zēteō tēn psychēn*: 2:20) or, from the opposite point of view, "losing one's life" (*apollymi tēn psychēn*: 10:39; 16:25) or "giving one's life" (*didōmi tēn psychēn*: 20:28). The powers that be, whether Jewish or Roman, plot to "destroy" (*apollymi*: 2:13; 12:14; 27:20) the righteous ones and go to great lengths to carry out their conspiracies to "kill" them (*anaireō*: 2:16). After they have arrested and tried the righteous ones, they pronounce them as "deserving death" (*enochos thanatou*: 26:66) and "condemn them to death" (*katakrinō thanatō*: 20:18; 27:3).

Framed in broad and general terms the authorities then "put [the righteous] to death" (*thanatoō*: 10:21; 26:59; 27:1),²⁷ "kill" them,²⁸ "murder" them (*phoneuō*: 23:31, 35; cf. 2 Chr 24:20–21), or "do whatever they please" to them (17:12), an unmistakable euphemism for an ugly and brutal execution (14:8–11). And for his part Herod the Jewish client king mounts a massive and vicious pre-emptive strike against the young children of Bethlehem in a desperate attempt to "kill" his rival (*anaireō*: 2:16). Depicted in specific terms the Jewish authorities are portrayed as "stoning" their victims (*lithoboleō*: 21:35; 23:37; cf. 21:36),²⁹ while Herod the tetrarch, in a gruesome act of political expediency, "beheads" his prisoner (*apokephalizō*: 14:10; cf. 14:8, 9, 11). The Roman authorities, for their part, "crucify"³⁰ their prisoners on wooden "crosses"³¹ that the condemned themselves or other conscripted civilians are forced to "take up" or "carry" (*lambanō*: 10:38; *airō*: 16:24; 27:32) to the place of execution.

Beyond judicial and extra-judicial killings the righteous ones of Matthew's narrative ultimately face the massive terror and disruption of international warfare. In depicting the events preceding the "end of the age" (24:3, 6, 13, 14) Jesus speaks of chaotic conflict—"wars and rumors of wars" (*polemos*: 24:6)—in which nations and kingdoms will "rise" against each other

---

26. Cf. 27:4, where Judas refers to the "innocent blood" (*haima athōon*) that he has "handed over (DJW)."

27. Cf. 15:4, where, according to Jewish law (Exod 21:17; Lev 20:9), the one who speaks evil of father or mother "must surely die" (*thanatō teleutaō*).

28. *anaireō*: 2:16; *apokteinō*: 10:28; 14:5; 16:21; 17:23; 21:35, 38, 39; 22:6; 23:34, 37; 24:9; 26:4 Cf. 21:36.

29. See also 2 Chr 24:21, where Zechariah (Matt 23:35) is likewise "stoned" to death (LXX: *lithoboleō*).

30. *stauroō*: 20:19; 23:34; 26:2; 27:22, 23, 26, 31, 35, 38; 28:5.

31. *stauros*: 10:38; 16:24; 27:32, 40, 42.

(*egeirō*: 24:7). This international conflict will be characterized by "famines" (*limos*: 24:7), natural disasters such as "earthquakes" (*seismos*: 24:7), the desecration of sacred spaces by foreign military incursions (24:15),[32] the urgent and difficult "flight" of refugees from war-torn heartlands to the safety of the mountains (*pheugō*: 24:16; cf. 24:17-20), and "suffering" of cosmic proportions (*thlipsis*: 24:21, 29; cf. 24:22). For the righteous ones of Matthew's narrative "suffering violence" has been a constant reality ever since the murder of "righteous Abel" (23:35; cf. Gen 4:8-11) at the beginning of time; and they will continue to live this reality throughout history all the way to the cosmic "suffering" that precedes the "end of the age" (24:4-29).

To ask about the causes of this unrelenting violence is to look in two directions simultaneously, both toward the actions of the righteous ones themselves and toward the corresponding responses of those who oppose them. For the righteous ones the picture is unambiguous. Suffering comes to them precisely as they go about the tasks of their vocation and precisely due to these vocational activities.[33] It is in the course of the duties that they are "sent"[34] to carry out that the righteous ones encounter persecution and death; and their "sending" itself is defined in terms of the unavoidable suffering faced by "sheep [in] the midst of wolves" (10:16; DJW). The vocation for which these righteous ones suffer includes verbal tasks: "proclaiming" the arrival of the kingdom of heaven (*euangelizomai*: 10:7 cf. 10:16), "inviting" people to the wedding banquet for the king's son (*kaleō*: 22:3-4 cf. 22:5-6), fulfilling the prophetic ministry of "Elijah" (17:9-12a cf. 17:12b), pronouncing prophetic judgment on the sins of the people of God (2 Chr 24:20 cf. Matt 23:35//2 Chr 24:21), and speaking fearless truth to the powers that be (14:4 cf. 14:2-3, 8-11; 26:63-64 cf. 26:65-66). The vocation for which the righteous ones suffer also includes deeds of power as well as everyday acts of faithfulness: "restoring" physical wholeness to broken bodies (*apokathistēmi*: 12:13; cf. 12:14), offering acceptable sacrifices to God (Gen 4:2-5 cf. Matt 23:35//Gen 4:8-11), living a life of "righteousness" (*dikaiosynē*: 5:10), in parabolic language "collecting the produce" of the landowner on his behalf (*lambanō tous karpous*: 21:34 cf. 21:35, 36),

---

32. From the perspective of Matthew's readers Jesus' reference to "the desolating sacrilege standing in the holy place" clearly points to the desecration of the Jewish temple by the Roman army, an historical event in 70 CE of which Matthew's readers were intensely aware. Similar proleptic depictions of the destruction of Jerusalem and its temple lie in Jesus' parable of the king who gives a wedding banquet for his son (22:7) and in Jesus' warning to Jerusalem that "your house is left to you desolate" (23:38).

33. See n6. For a wider discussion of the relationship between mission and suffering, see Weaver, "As Sheep," 123-43.

34. *apostellō*: 10:16; 21:34, 36, 37; 22:3, 4; 23:37.

"following" Jesus (*akoloutheō*: 16:24a cf. 16:24b), and living life on his "account" (*heneken emou*: 5:11; 10:18), in his "name" (*dia to onoma mou*: 10:22; 24:9), and as "those of his household" (*oikiakoi autou*: 10:25). As Matthew makes clear to his readers, God's righteous ones suffer at the hands of their opponents precisely because of their faithfulness and obedience to the call of God.

For those who oppose the righteous ones of Matthew's narrative the picture is one of diametrical opposites. Here the causes of violence reflect a gamut of negative human impulses and paint a portrait of human weakness and brokenness. Matthew spells out some of these causes explicitly through his omniscient narrator; and he depicts other causes implicitly through his narrative rhetoric.

Prominent among these causes is the primal emotion of fear. Herod the king is "frightened" (*tarassō*: 2:3) when he hears of "the child who has been born king of the Jews" (2:2). And it is this urgent fear of his political rival that fuels his initial conspiracy against the life of the child (2:4–8) and its vicious consummation in the massacre of the children of Bethlehem (2:13, 16). Herod the tetrarch, for his part, is depicted as a man consumed by the fear of everyone around him: John the Baptist (14:1–2, 3–4), the crowd (*phobeomai*: 14:5), Herodias and her daughter (14:6–11), the guests at the party (14:6–11). And this all-consuming fear leads Herod to carry out a gruesome act that he "grieves" (*lypeō*: 14:9) even as he "commands" it done (*keleuō*: 14:9). The authorities in Jerusalem, both Jewish and Roman, exhibit deep fear of the Jerusalem crowds and the "riots" (*thorybos*: 26:5; 27:24) of which they are capable. This fear (26:5) is a prime factor in the conspiracy of "stealth" (*dolos*: 26:4) that the chief priests and elders instigate against Jesus. And this same fear (27:24a) ultimately drives Pilate to take an expedient political act for which he vainly seeks to establish his "innocence" (*athōos eimi*: 27:24b) even as he "hands [Jesus] over" (*paradidōmi*: 27:26) to be crucified. Clearly fear is a hugely debilitating emotion, as Matthew portrays it, one that consumes the individuals caught in its grip and drives them into violent actions that defy their own better wisdom (27:18, 19, 23)[35] or even their own wishes (14:9).[36]

A second prominent cause of the violence against the righteous ones in Matthew's narrative is jealousy and the political rivalry associated with it.

---

35. Pilate is aware that the religious leaders are acting out of "jealousy" (27:18). He learns from his wife that Jesus is an "innocent" man (27:19). And he knows for himself that Jesus has done no "evil" (27:23).

36. Thus Herod's "grieving" (14:9) at the act he nevertheless carries out. For a wider discussion of the character of the three political leaders in Matthew's narrative, see Weaver, "Power and Powerlessness," 179–96.

Pilate knows that the Jewish authorities have handed Jesus over to him out of "jealousy" (*phthonos*: 27:18). Jesus paints this same portrait of the Jewish authorities as he depicts the conspiracy of the wicked tenants against the son of the landowner (21:38): "This is the heir [*klēronomos*]; come, let us kill him and get his inheritance [*klēronomia*]." And the chief priests and elders prove Pilate and Jesus right as they fret over the "riot" (*thorybos*: 26:5) that will ensue if they arrest Jesus, whom they implicitly acknowledge as highly popular, during the festival.

Anger is a third prominent causal factor in the violence against the righteous ones. The final precipitating cause in the massacre of the children of Bethlehem is Herod's "infuriation" (*thymoomai*: 2:16) at being "tricked" (*empaizō*: 2:16) by the magi in an act that thwarts his initial conspiracy against his child-rival (2:12; cf. 2:7–8). Jesus' uncanny ability to outwit the religious leaders at verbal sparring (12:9–12; 21:23–22:45)—in spite of their best efforts to "test" him (*peirazō*: 22:35) and "entrap" him in his words (*pagideuō*: 22:15)—leaves them "amazed" (*thaumazō*: 22:22), "silenced" (*phimoō*: 22:34) and incapable of "answering" (*apokrinomai*: 22:46a) or "asking" (*eperōtaō*: 22:46b) Jesus anything more. And it also leaves them angry *enough to wish for his* "arrest" (*krateō*: 22:46) and conspire to "destroy" him (*apollymi*: 12:13).[37]

Additional factors leading to acts of violence against the righteous of Matthew's narrative are the avaricious search for financial gain (26:14–16; 27:3–10) and the callous and even sadistic delight in entertainment at any cost (27:27–31). As Matthew depicts him, Judas is clearly motivated by the desire for money ("What will you give me [*didōmi*]": 26:15a) as he goes to the chief priests with his scheme for Jesus' arrest (*paradidōmi*: 26:15b). And he is similarly motivated by the thirty pieces of silver that they "pay" him (*histēmi*: 26:15c) as he carries out his part of the plot: "And from that moment he began to look for an opportunity to [hand him over: *paradidōmi*]" (26:16). The Roman soldiers, for their part, appear to be motivated by callous delight in mocking and torturing a helpless prisoner who is at their mercy (27:27–31). Their detailed efforts to create a mock-royal scenario, complete with clothing, crown, scepter, and homage (27:28–29), suggest the actions of soldiers who seek elaborate entertainment to alleviate their boredom at life in the barracks. And their physical abuse of Jesus (27:29–30) gives evidence of sadistic pleasure at the pain and humiliation of others.

The picture is grim for the righteous ones of Matthew's narrative. They have faced consistent suffering throughout history at the hands of their

---

37. Cf. 2 Chr 24:20–21, where anger at Zechariah's words of judgment against the people of Judah likewise appears to be the predominant factor leading to his stoning death.

opponents, both Jewish and Gentile. And Jesus tells them that this situation will continue all the way to the end of the age. Further, they face this suffering not because of their wrongdoing but precisely because of their work on behalf of the kingdom of heaven, the mission that they have been "sent" to carry out (10:16; 21:34, 36, 37; 22:3, 4; 23:34). It is in short their lives of faithful obedience to God that engender massive fear, jealousy, and anger on the part of their opponents and make the righteous ones victims of avarice and callous brutality.

But this is not the end of the matter, so far as Matthew is concerned. Violence is not the last word; and suffering is not the last reality for the righteous ones of Matthew's narrative. If Matthew paints a grim and ugly portrait of the violence suffered by the righteous ones, he paints an equally vivid and frequently surprising portrait of their responses to this violence. Through the words of Jesus and the lived experiences of the righteous ones Matthew depicts for his readers the widely divergent characteristics of faithful response to violence.

II. THE CHARACTERISTICS OF FAITHFUL RESPONSE TO VIOLENCE

As Matthew tells his story, faithful response to violence comprises an entire spectrum of discrete responses ranging from the highly intuitive to the profoundly counter-intuitive and from silence and apparent passivity to bold and fearless public action. This wide spectrum of discrete responses, taken together, then creates an overarching portrait that is multi-faceted, complex, and well beyond the ordinary. Matthew paints this complex and extraordinary portrait by way of illustrations both positive and negative.

At the pragmatic end of the spectrum Matthew depicts "flight" as an obvious, sensible, and divinely-sanctioned response to the threat or the reality of violence. In light of Herod's imminent attempt to "search for the child, to destroy (*apollymi*) him" (2:13b), it is none other than the angel of the Lord who instructs Joseph to "get up, take the child and his mother, and flee (*pheugō*) to Egypt, and remain there until I tell you" (2:13a).[38] As Jesus commissions his disciples for ministry, he instructs them, "When they persecute you (*diōkō*) in one town, flee (*pheugō*) to the next" (10:23a).[39]

---

38. The motif of "flight" is also implicit in 2:22, where Joseph is "afraid" (*phobeomai*) to return to Judea, is "warned" (*chrēmatizō*) in a dream, and "goes away (*anachōreō*) to the district of Galilee" instead.

39. The disciples' "flight" (10:23a), however, is linked not to their personal safety but rather to their ongoing mission to the Jewish towns and cities: "For truly I tell you,

Similarly, as Jesus tells his disciples of the chaos and turbulence that will precede the coming of the Son of Man, he warns them, "So when you see the desolating sacrilege standing in the holy place, . . . then those in Judea must flee (*pheugō*) to the mountains" (24:15–16). And he adds, "Pray that your flight (*phygē*) may not be in winter or on a Sabbath. For at that time there will be great suffering (*thlipsis*) such as has not been from the beginning of the world until now, no, and never will be" (24:20–21). For his part Jesus himself "departs" (*anachōreō*: 12:15) in similar fashion when he learns that the Pharisees have "conspired against him, how to destroy (*apollymi*) him" (12:14); and he once again "withdraws" (*anachōreō*: 14:13) upon news of the death of John the Baptist.[40] Clearly, as Matthew sees it, there are times when "flight" or "withdrawal" is both appropriate and necessary in the face of present or impending danger.[41]

When appropriate "flight" is not possible, however—or perhaps even when it is (cf. 24:20–22)—Jesus calls his followers to a life of sturdy "endurance." In the face of inevitable suffering and death Jesus promises his disciples that "the one who endures (*hypomenō*) to the end will be saved (*sōzō*)" (20:22; 24:13). Such "salvation" does not, to be sure, imply personal safety in the present moment. The settings that call forth this "endurance" are ones where "hatred" (*miseō*) of the righteous ones is endemic among Jews (10:22), Gentiles (24:9), and even former followers of Jesus (24:10) "because of [his] name" (*dia to onoma mou*: 10:22; 24:9). They are also settings where close family members or other opponents will "hand over" (*paradidōmi*: 10:21a; 24:9a) the righteous ones to be "tortured" (*eis thlipsin*: 24:9a) and "put to death" (*eis thanaton*: 10:21a; *thanatoō*: 10:21b; 24:9b). "Endurance" is, accordingly, a stance of sturdy faithfulness to the "name" and the mission of Jesus to the "end" (*telos*) of one's own life.[42]

A life of "endurance" brings with it, in turn, certain social obligations that serve as established personal or communal rituals linked to suffering

---

you will not have gone through all the towns of Israel before the Son of Man comes" (10:23b). See Weaver, *Missionary Discourse*, 99–100.

40. Jesus' "withdrawal" at the death of John the Baptist (14:13) might, however, best be interpreted not in terms of "flight" but rather as an act of "mourning" over John's death and preparatory to a time of "prayer" (14:23) See the discussion of "grief and lament" below.

41. But when "flight" implies the "desertion" of Jesus, it is for Matthew no longer appropriate but rather an act of cowardice and failure: "Then all the disciples deserted him (*aphiēmi*) and fled (*pheugō*)" (26:56).

42. The obvious counterpart to "endurance" is for Matthew the human tendency to "fall away" or "become deserters" (*skandalizomai*: 13:21; 26:31, 33), a failure to which not only Peter but "all the disciples" in the Garden of Gethsemane ultimately fall prey (26:33, 35 cf. 26:56).

and death. One of these rituals is burial. Looking toward his upcoming violent death Jesus commends the woman who has "poured" very costly ointment on his head (*katacheō*: 26:7) for "preparing my body for burial" (*pros to entaphisasai me*: 26:12). And following the gruesome execution of John the Baptist (14:10–11), John's disciples "bury" his body (*thaptō*) and "notify" Jesus (*apangellō*: DJW) of his death.

A ritual, both personal and communal, that is closely associated with burial is the outward expression of grief and lament. In his own editorial response to the horrific massacre of the children of Bethlehem, Matthew invokes the words of Jeremiah 31:15: "A voice was heard in Ramah, wailing (*klauthmos*) and loud lamentation (*odyrmos polys*), Rachel weeping (*klaiō*) for her children; she refused to be consoled (*parakaleō*), because they are no more" (2:18). Pointing metaphorically toward his violent demise, Jesus speaks of his disciples as those who will mark that event by "mourning" and "fasting": "The wedding guests cannot mourn (*pentheō*) as long as the bridegroom is with them, can they? The days will come when the bridegroom is taken away from them (*apairō*), and then they will fast (*nēsteuō*)" (9:15). In the Garden of Gethsemane Jesus laments his own death in audible and visible fashion: "grieving deeply . . . even to death" (*lypeō*: 26:37; *perilypos . . . thanatou*: 26:38), "being agitated" (*adēmoneō*: 26:37), and "throwing himself on the ground" (literally "falling on his face": *piptō epi prosōpon autou*: 26:39). And as he hangs dying on the cross Jesus "cries out with a loud voice" (*boaō . . . phōnē megalē*: 27:45; cf. 27:50) in the words of Psalm 22, a psalm of lament: "My God, my God, why have you forsaken me?" (Ps 22:1a).

For Matthew it is clear that the personal and communal rituals of burial and lament are crucial responses for those who suffer violence. Preparing the "soul" (*hē psychē*: 26:38; DJW) and the "body" (*to sōma*: 26:12) for death and "weeping" (2:18) and "mourning" (9:15) for those who have died are often the only options available to the righteous ones overtaken by the violence of the powerful. And Jesus' words to his disciples in the Garden of Gethsemane make it clear that "grieving" is in fact the calling of the entire community of righteous ones as they gather around the suffering individual: "I am deeply grieved, even to death; *remain here (menō) and stay awake (grēgoreō) with me*" (26:38; cf. 26:40, 41; emphasis mine).[43]

Flight, endurance, and lament represent pragmatic and/or instinctive responses to violence. These responses come instinctively to mind in the moment of crisis (flight) or may happen without any formal thought at all (lament). Or these responses make pragmatic sense to the righteous ones

---

43. This is, however, a calling that Jesus' disciples miss as they "sleep" (*katheudō*: 26:40, 43, 45) rather than "staying awake" (*grēgoreō*: 26:38, 40, 41).

(endurance) in a world where violence cannot be avoided. But on the other end of the spectrum Matthew points his readers toward responses to violence that are highly counter-intuitive in character. These responses by their very nature demand careful thought and represent acts of the will that run directly contrary to human instinct. At the same time these responses are grounded in the character and the enabling power of God.

One such counter-intuitive response is reflected in Jesus' extraordinary negative injunctions against "worry" (*merimnaō*: 10:19), "fear" (*phobeomai*: 10:26, 28a, 31), and "alarm" (*throeomai*: 24:6) and his equally extraordinary positive injunction to "rejoice" (*chairō*) and "be glad" (*agalliaō*) in the face of "persecution" and verbal abuse (5:11-12). Depicting threatening legal contexts where his disciples will one day be handed over to Jewish "councils" and dragged before "governors and kings" to stand trial and bear "testimony" (10:17-18), Jesus nevertheless calls his followers "not to worry" about their legal defense: "When they hand you over, do not worry about how you are to speak or what you are to say" (10:19). Envisioning confrontational settings in which others will "malign" the disciples (10:25) and life and death settings in which people will "kill" their "bodies" (10:28), Jesus challenges his followers to "have no fear" of their opponents (10:26, 28a, 31). Pointing toward the chaos and violence of international warfare before the end of time (24:6-8), Jesus encourages his disciples "not to be alarmed" (24:6). And in place of their worry, fear, and alarm, Jesus calls his disciples to "rejoice and be glad" as they face "persecution" (5:11-12).

In light of the confrontational, dangerous, and even deadly settings depicted, Jesus' injunctions—whether negative or positive—make no sense on the human level. But viewed from a divine vantage point, these injunctions take on a totally new character. Jesus' disciples can release their "worries" about legal defense because their words will come to them as divine gift: "For what you are to say will be given to you at that time; for it is not you who speak, but the Spirit of your Father speaking through you" (10:19b-20). They can release their "fears" of verbal abuse since none other than God is at work through their own proclamation (10:27) to "uncover" hidden truth and "make it known" (10:26).[44] They can release their "fears" of death in the confidence that God their "Father" has "counted the hairs of their head," accords his children infinite "value," and will be with them in their suffering, since nothing happens "apart from" him (10:29-31). They can release their "alarm" at the turbulent course of human events in the sure knowledge that the "end" of history will proceed on God's timetable (24:6-8; cf. 24:14). And they can "rejoice and be glad" at their sufferings, since it is God who will ulti-

---

44. See Weaver, *Missionary Discourse*, 107-8.

mately "reward" them "in heaven" for their faithfulness (5:12). Accordingly, it is the character of God and God's power at work within human history and beyond that give ultimate meaning to Jesus' extraordinary injunctions.

A second counter-intuitive response to violence, one that corresponds inversely to Jesus' negative injunctions against worry, fear, and alarm, is that of bold proclamation and the courage to speak truth to power. As Matthew depicts it, righteous ones who are no longer consumed by worry or paralyzed by fear of the violence to come can exhibit the courage of their own moral convictions and can proclaim the truth of God boldly, regardless of the personal consequences that they may face. John the Baptist exhibits just such courage of conviction as he issues persistent and blunt rebukes to Herod the tetrarch concerning Herod's liaison with Herodias, the wife of his brother Philip: "It is not lawful for you to have her" (14:4).[45] John's courage of conviction lies beyond dispute. To speak blunt truth to political leaders is a highly dangerous proposition in any world and surely in the world that John inhabits; and to do so repeatedly proves in fact to be an affront deemed worthy of imprisonment and death (14:3, 5).

Jesus exhibits the same courage of conviction in an equally dangerous setting. When Caiaphas puts Jesus "under oath before the living God" to reveal his identity as "the Messiah, the Son of God" (26:63), Jesus responds with a fearless and powerful affirmative proclamation[46] that brings down on his head the charge of "blasphemy" from the high priest (26:65), the sentence of "death" from the members of the Jewish council (26:66), and ugly verbal and physical abuse (26:67). Jesus clearly views his calling as that of speaking truth to power, regardless of the violent consequences.

Jesus' disciples, for their part, have the same vocation. As Jesus prepares his disciples for mission, he calls them to fearless and highly public proclamation precisely in those contexts where their lives are endangered by those who will "malign" them (10:25) and "kill their bodies" (10:28): "What I say to you in the dark, tell in the light (*eipate en tō phōti*: 10:27a); and what you hear whispered, proclaim from the housetops (*kēryxate epi tōn dōmatōn*: 10:27b)." In the next breath (10:32) Jesus affirms those who "acknowledge" him "before others" (*homologeō . . . emprosthen tōn anthrōpōn*), an implicit warning that such "acknowledgement" will not take place without significant personal cost.[47] And, as Jesus alerts his disciples, it

45. The imperfect verb *elegen* (14:4) implies that John has been repeating this rebuke over and over.

46. "You have said so. But I tell you, from now on you will see the Son of Man seated at the right hand of Power and coming on the clouds of heaven" (26:64).

47. This is, however, a cost that Peter is not willing to pay when he is confronted in the courtyard of the high priest (26:69-75). Instead of "acknowledging" Jesus

is precisely within the context of the horrific violence that precedes the end of the age (24:9–10) that "this good news of the kingdom will be proclaimed (*kēryssō*) throughout the world, as a testimony (*martyrion*) to all the nations" (24:14a). Then and only then will the end come (24:14b). Fearless proclamation in the face of deadly violence will be the calling and the challenge for Jesus' disciples throughout history to the very end.[48]

But beyond the call to fearless proclamation lies what is surely an even more radical call to response in the face of violence. In the Sermon on the Mount (5:39, 44) Jesus issues corresponding challenges to his disciples "not to resist" (*mē antistēnai*) the "evildoer" (*ponēros*) but rather to "love" (*agapaō*) your "enemies" (*echthros*) and "pray" (*proseuchomai*) for "those who persecute you" (*diōkō*). The juxtaposition of vocabulary in these corresponding commands is breathtaking in its audacity. These commands, each in their own way, are profoundly counter-intuitive, presenting themselves to Jesus' hearers and to Matthew's readers as nothing short of scandalous.[49]

The call "not to resist an evildoer" (5:39a) represents Jesus' repudiation of the long-established Jewish law of retaliation, the *lex talionis* setting forth the rules by which the community was to respond in kind to an act of "evil" done in its midst.[50] Jesus' radical reversal of this time-honored community response to violence appears at first glance to be total capitulation to the "evildoer." But the negative command ("Do not resist"), which at face value appears completely passive in character, gives way to an entire sequence of imperatives that are both genuinely active and shockingly unanticipated: "But if anyone strikes you on the right cheek, turn the other also; and if anyone wants to sue you and take your coat, give your cloak as well; and if anyone forces you to go one mile, go also the second" (5:39b–41).[51] Within the framework of Jesus' overall saying (5:38–42) it is these active imperatives (5:39b–41; cf. 5:42) that serve to interpret the negative command (5:39a) and give it meaning. Accordingly, Jesus' call "not to resist the evildoer" is

---

(*homologeō*: 10:32) before the bystanders in the courtyard, Peter "denies" Jesus (*arneomai*: 26:70, 72; cf. 26:74) just as Jesus has challenged the disciples not to do (*arneomai*: 10:33) and just as Jesus has warned Peter that he is about to do (*aparneomai*: 26:34).

48. Note, however, Jesus' "silence" (*siōpaō*: 26:63) in the face of false witnesses (26:59, 60) and his failure to "answer" (*apokrinomai*: 27:12, 14) the many accusations brought against him (26:12, 13). Clearly there are also appropriate times for silence.

49. Cf. Jesus' pointed appeal to the disciples of John the Baptist (11:6): "And blessed is [the one] who takes no offense at me (*skandalizō*)." Jesus' words in 5:39 are surely cause for "offense."

50. For a wider discussion of this saying of Jesus (5:38–42) vis-à-vis its Deuteronomic counterpart (Deut 19:15–21), see Weaver, "Transforming Nonresistance," 32–71.

51. The parallel commands of 5:42 complete Jesus' list of responses; but they do not represent responses to violent acts in the same way as the commands of 5:39b–41.

in fact a bold challenge to active response of a profoundly nonviolent but equally provocative character.[52] And these nonviolent responses, shocking as they may appear, in fact put initiative for the very first time into the hands of the righteous ones rather than those of the "evildoer." As long as the "law of retaliation" is in force, it is only the "evildoer" who has the power of initiative, since those who suffer violence can do nothing but respond in kind. But with Jesus' stunning repudiation of the *lex talionis*, the righteous ones now have the authority to take bold yet nonviolent initiatives in response to the violence that they encounter.[53]

Jesus' call to "love your enemies and pray for those who persecute you" (5:44) and his corresponding blessing on the "peacemakers" (*eirēnopoioi*: 5:9) reflect the obverse of the command "not to resist an evildoer" (5:39a). The negative formulation "not to resist" finds its ultimate meaning in the positive commands to "love," "pray," and "make peace."[54] And these astonishing commands, profoundly counter-intuitive as they are, have their basis in the very character of God and their ethical appeal in the call to "be children of God [your heavenly Father]" (5:9; cf. 5:45, 48: DJW). Because God "makes his sun rise on the evil and on the good and . . . sends rain on the righteous and the unrighteous" (5:45b), Jesus calls his disciples to "love" and "pray for" those they would rather hate (cf. 5:43). And because God's mission is to make peace,[55] Jesus calls down a "blessing" on those who are "peacemakers" (5:9). And where the character of God is in focus, there the empowerment of God is likewise present. When Jesus calls his disciples to "be children of God, your heavenly Father," Jesus' words do not imply "bootstrap" theology but rather divine empowerment. The same "Father" whose "Spirit" will be speaking through the disciples when they need words in crucial situations (10:19-20) will likewise empower his "children" to respond to violence with "love," "prayer," and "peacemaking."

---

52. The clear implication of these illustrative responses to violence is that they will not only break the vicious cycle of action and reaction, but that—in the honor/shame culture of first-century Palestine—they will also shame the perpetrators of violence into an awareness of the "evil" of their own actions.

53. The disciple who draws a sword in the Garden of Gethsemane and attacks the slave of the high priest (26:51) is clearly not yet courageous enough for Jesus' bold command "not to resist the evildoer." Accordingly Jesus instructs him to "put [his] sword back into its place" (26:52a), warning him that the only other alternative is in effect that of the *lex talionis*: "For all who take the sword will perish by the sword" (26:52b).

54. Cf. Jesus' similar appeal (5:25) to "come to terms (*eimi eunoōn*) with your accuser (*antidikos*)".

55. While it is not stated explicitly, this is the clear implication of the "blessing" on the peacemakers in 5:9.

But without question the most prominent of the counter-intuitive responses to violence reflected in Matthew's narrative is obedient commitment to the mission of God in a dangerous world and the correlative willingness to suffer violence because of that mission if necessary. Such commitment and willingness to suffer is reflected above all in Jesus' repeated words about the divine necessity of his own suffering. During his Galilean ministry Jesus announces to his disciples that he *"must (dei) go to Jerusalem* and undergo great suffering *(polla pathein)* . . . and be killed *(apokteinō)"* (16:21: emphasis mine).[56] Jesus rebukes the disciple who seeks to defend him violently in the Garden of Gethsemane with the words, "Do you think that I cannot appeal to my Father, and he will at once send me more than twelve legions of angels? *But how then would the scriptures be fulfilled (plēroō), which say it must happen in this way (houtōs dei genesthai)?"* (26:53-54; emphasis mine). And to the crowd who has come to arrest him he says, "Day after day I sat in the temple teaching, and you did not arrest me. But all this has taken place, *so that the scriptures of the prophets may be fulfilled (plēroō)"* (26:55-56; emphasis mine).

Clearly Jesus views his suffering as a necessary component of the overarching mission to which he has been "sent" by God *(apostellō:* 10:40; 15:24; 21:37), namely a mission to "fulfill the scriptures" (26:54, 56; cf. 5:17). And Jesus is obedient to this divine calling. When Peter tests this commitment and tempts Jesus to avoid suffering (16:22), Jesus rebukes Peter sharply and charges him with "setting your mind not on divine things but on human things" (16:23).[57] When the moment of crisis comes, Jesus responds obediently, accepting God's "will" over his own personal desires *(thelō//thelēma:* 26:39b, 42b; cf. 26:44) and committing himself to "drink the cup" that has been set before him *(potērion pinō:* 26:39a, 42a; cf. 20:22, 23; 26:44). And as he hangs dying on a Roman cross Jesus refuses the temptation posed by the religious leaders who taunt him to "save [himself]" *(sōzō:* 27: 40; cf. 27:42)[58] and "come down" from the cross *(katabainō:* 27:40, 42).

The same unswerving commitment to the mission of God in the face of certain and unavoidable suffering, is also reflected in the past lives of the prophets of Jewish history and projected into the future lives of Jesus'

---

56. Cf. 17:12, 22-23; 20:17-19, 22-23; 26:1-2.

57. Cf. the temptations that Jesus faces as he hangs on the cross, namely to "save" himself *(sōzō:* 27:40a, 42a) and to "come down from the cross *(katabainō:* 27:40b, 42b). Here Jesus does not rebuke the tempters but as with Peter he does not yield to their temptations.

58. Here Jesus puts to the test his own challenge to his disciples: "For those who want to save their life will lose it, and those who lose their life for my sake will find it" (16:25; cf. 10:22b//24:13).

own disciples.[59] In his parable about the landowner and the wicked tenants (21:33-46) Jesus depicts the prophets as the slaves who are "sent" (*apostellō*) by the landowner to "collect his produce" (*lambanō tous karpous*: 21:34; cf. 21:36). And even when it becomes clear that the first crew of slaves thus "sent" has suffered violence and death on account of their mission (21:35), the second crew of slaves nevertheless goes out obediently as "sent" by the landowner (21:36a) and meets with the same fate (21:36b). In similar fashion Jesus tells a story about a king who "sends" (*apostellō*) his slaves to "invite" (*kaleō*) people to the wedding of his son (22:1-14), a pointed reference to Jesus' own disciples and their mission on behalf of the kingdom of heaven (10:7). Here as well the slaves who are "sent" respond in obedience to their calling (22:3a, 4), even as it becomes apparent that their mission is rejected (22:3b) and their very lives endangered (22:5). And Jesus paints the same portrait of faithful obedience when he says to the Jerusalem leaders, "Therefore I send you (*apostellō*) prophets, sages, and scribes, some of whom you will kill and crucify, and some you will flog in your synagogues and [persecute] from town to town" (23:34; DJW; cf. 10:23). As Matthew sees it, unshakeable commitment to the dangerous mission of God and willingness to accept the suffering that this entails is a prime characteristic of faithful response to violence.

Finally, in light of the wide array of faithful responses to violence depicted in Matthew's narrative, actions ranging from flight out of harm's way (2:13-23; 24:15-22) to bold, nonviolent initiatives in the very face of "evil" (5:38-48), Matthew offers his readers two crucial clues to discerning the right response in any given moment. The first of these clues lies in the urgent call to be attentive to one's surrounding circumstances. As Jesus sends his disciples out "like sheep into the midst of wolves" (10:16a), he enjoins them to be at one and the same time "wise (*phronimoi*) as serpents" and "innocent (*akeraioi*) as doves" (10:16b). This seemingly paradoxical imperative is in fact a call to keep one's eyes and ears open to impending danger (2:22)[60] and to "beware" of people and the violence they will unleash (*prosechō*: 10:17a). It is also a call to resistance vis-à-vis false loyalties: the public pressure to "believe" (*pisteuō*: 24:23, 26b) propaganda concerning "false messiahs" and

---

59. In the present moment, however, Peter openly exhibits his unwillingness to face suffering as he rebukes Jesus for predicting his passion (16:22). And he once again proves his unwillingness to suffer as he "denies" Jesus in the courtyard of the high priest (26:69-75). The sons of Zebedee, for their part, appear overly optimistic as they glibly announce that they are "able" (20:22b) to "drink the cup" that Jesus is "about to drink" (20:22a; cf. 20:23). In fact they, along with the rest of the disciples, "desert" Jesus and "flee" when their own lives appear endangered (26:56).

60. Joseph's attentiveness to the danger posed by the rule of Archelaus (2:22a) is affirmed in effect by the divine "warning" that Joseph receives in a "dream" (2:22b).

"false prophets" (24:24a); the human propensity to be "misled" (*planaō*: 24:24c) by the public campaign of "great signs and wonders" carried out by these charlatans (24:24b); and the powerful urge to "go out (*exerchomai*: 24:26a) and join their entourage. It is just such "wise innocence" or "innocent wisdom" that will equip Jesus' disciples for responding appropriately in the moment of crisis when violence overtakes them.

But just as importantly Matthew's readers hear another urgent call as well, the call to be attentive to the voice and the will of God. The magi (2:12) and Joseph (2:13, 22) respond to impending violence as they hear and obey the "angel of the Lord" (2:13) who speaks the words of God to them in "dreams" (*kat' onar*: 2:12, 13, 22).[61] And Jesus, for his part, attends to the voice of God through urgent prayer before his crucifixion. In the Garden of Gethsemane Jesus pleads with his Father three times for the "cup" of suffering to be taken from him (27:39; cf. 27:42, 44). But each time and in the very next breath he commits himself, just as he has taught his disciples to do in their own prayers (6:10b), to his Father's "will." His first prayer concludes with the words "Yet not what I want (*thelō*) but what you want" (27:39) and the second with the petition "Your will (*thelēma*) be done" (27:42; cf. 27:44).

The crucial significance of this attentiveness to the will of God becomes clear in Jesus' words to Peter, one of his sleeping disciples: "So, could you not stay awake with me one hour? Stay awake and pray *that you may not come into the time of [temptation]; the spirit indeed is willing but the flesh is weak*" (26:40b-41; NRSV footnote, emphasis mine). Jesus' words are as true for himself as they are for his disciples. Jesus himself faces profound temptation. And while his own spirit is willing, he acknowledges that his own flesh is weak. But precisely because he has stayed awake and prayed, he is now empowered to respond faithfully to the violence that will shortly overtake him.[62] Clearly, as Matthew tells the story, attentiveness to the voice of God, whether in dream or in prayer, is for God's righteous ones the ultimate key to faithful response vis-à-vis the challenges of a violent world.

---

61. Cf. the actions of Pilate's wife, who seeks, in vain as it turns out, to forestall impending violence against Jesus in response to a "dream" that she has had concerning him (*kat' onar*: 27:19). See Weaver, "'Thus You Will Know Them,'" 119-21.

62. The disciples, to the contrary, have slept through their prayer time (26:40, 43, 45) and are completely unprepared to deal appropriately with the violence that overtakes Jesus and threatens their own lives. They respond by striking back with the sword (26:51), deserting Jesus and fleeing (26:56), and denying any acquaintance with Jesus (26:69-75).

III. SUFFERING VIOLENCE AND THE NARRATIVE RHETORIC OF MATTHEW'S GOSPEL

In his story about Jesus Matthew paints a vivid portrait of a world in which God's righteous ones "suffer violence" (11:12) at the hands of brutal and powerful opponents precisely as they go about their mission on behalf of the kingdom of heaven and precisely because they do so. The violence they suffer is in many cases deadly. As a result the righteous ones, who have in fact been "sent out" to their work like "sheep into the midst of wolves" (10:16),[63] encounter death in the commission of their appointed task. This narrative portrait is a bleak one, taken at face value and read at the "lower level" of Matthew's narrative.[64] And the surface implications of this portrait are that violence wins the day, God's righteous ones are defeated by the powers of evil, and the kingdom of heaven is diminished by its opponents.

But these "lower level" implications prove entirely unreliable within the thoroughgoing irony of Matthew's narrative. While Matthew paints a vivid and convincing "lower level" portrait of the power of the violent and the impact of their violence, he simultaneously subverts his own effort with an astonishing "upper level" portrait that gives the lie to apparent reality. Matthew's "upper level" portrait is one that turns conventional wisdom on its head and redefines the significance both of violence and of suffering.

In the world of Matthew's story military empire and its subsidiaries are the supreme powers of the day[65] and state-sanctioned violence is the standard tool for maintaining such empire (2:13-23; 14:1-12; 27:1-2, 11-54). The religious authorities of the Jewish world, for their part, also wield significant power and carry out violence in their own sphere. Against this backdrop Matthew paints a stunning portrait of the powers that be, both Roman and Jewish, unmasking the utter futility of their violence and ridiculing their very image as powerful leaders.[66]

Herod the king, for all of his political clout (2:3), his power of command (2:4-6, 7-9), and his military might (2:16), cannot achieve his single goal, the death of his new-born rival (2:7-8, 13, 20). Instead he is thwarted at

---

63. Cf. 21:34, 36, 37; 22:3, 4; 23:34, 37.

64. Muecke (*Compass of Irony*, 19-20) defines irony as a "double-layered or two-storey phenomenon" in which "the lower level is the situation either as it appears to the victims of irony . . . or as it is deceptively presented by the ironist" and "the upper level is the situation as it appears to the observer or the ironist."

65. For a wider discussion of the portrayal of empire within Matthew's Gospel, see Weaver, "'Thus You Will Know Them,'" 107-24.

66. For a wider discussion of this theme, see Weaver, "Power and Powerlessness," 179-96.

every step of the way by the "angel of the Lord" who warns others in advance about Herod's evil designs so that they can take evasive actions (2:12, 13–14; cf. 2:19–21, 22). And in the end it is Herod who lies dead rather than the "child" he has been seeking to kill (2:19–20). Herod the tetrach, ruler of the Galilee, shows up in Matthew's narrative as a paranoid weakling, pulled now this way and now that by his fear of all the other characters: John the Baptist (14:1–2, 3–4), the crowd (14:5), Herodias and her daughter (14:6–11), the guests at the party (14:9). And even after he has employed the ultimate violence at his disposal and executed his nemesis (14:9), he finds himself newly haunted by an even more powerful "John the Baptist" who has been "raised from the dead" (14:1–2). Pilate, governor of Palestine and the highest ranking Roman on Matthew's narrative stage, unleashes the full violence of empire against Jesus "the king of the Jews" and turns him over for crucifixion (27:26), only to discover (or perhaps not!) that the superpower of the world has been upstaged by a divine coup in which God has raised Jesus from the dead and emptied the tomb in which he was laid (28:14). For their part the Jewish religious leaders come up as "short-handed" as the powers of empire. For all their scheming and conspiracy (12:14; 21:45–46; 26:3–5, 14–16), their "false witnesses" (26:59–61), their accusations against Jesus (27:12–14), their public manipulation of the crowds (27:20–23), and their private manipulation of Pilate (27:62–66; 28:14), the Jewish leaders end up with an empty tomb for which they have no good explanation (28:11–15) and a "last deception" that is for them truly "worse than the first" (27:64). As Matthew paints the portrait, the violence of the powerful is singularly ineffective in achieving the goals of those who employ it. To the contrary the violence of the powerful serves only to reveal the limits of their power and to make a mockery of their trust in the use of violent force.

Matthew's portrait of the suffering of the righteous is as extraordinary and paradoxical as his portrait of the violence of the powerful. This portrait is filled with images of the vindication of the righteous in the very face of their sufferings and precisely because of them. Many of these images come from the words of Jesus. In his inaugural address to his disciples Jesus pronounces a "blessing" on those who are "persecuted for righteousness' sake" (5:10) and those whom people "revile," "persecute," and against whom they falsely speak "all kinds of evil" on account of Jesus himself (5:11).[67] Jesus promises these righteous ones the inheritance of the "kingdom of heaven" (5:9) and "great reward" in that realm (5:12). And he designates those who "love their enemies," "pray for their persecutors" and live as "peacemak-

---

67. In pronouncing a "blessing" on his disciples ("Blessed are you . . .": 5:11) Jesus also includes the "prophets who were before you" (5:12).

ers" as "children of God, their heavenly Father" (5:9 and 5:48; cf. 5:45). As John the Baptist languishes in Herod the tetrarch's prison (4:12), Jesus heaps commendation on his head, announcing that "[A]mong those born of women no one has arisen greater than John the Baptist" (11:11). And in almost the next breath he adds pointedly, "From the days of John the Baptist until now the kingdom of heaven has suffered violence, and the violent take it by force" (11:12). After John the Baptist's death Jesus once again commends John, identifying him as the eschatological Elijah: "[B]ut I tell you that Elijah has already come" (17:12a). And once again he associates his commendation of John with John's suffering: "[A]nd they did not recognize him, but they did to him whatever they pleased" (17:12b). As he prepares his disciples for their mission work on behalf of the kingdom of heaven, Jesus promises that when his followers are put on trial before the religious and civil powers of the world that "the Spirit of [their] Father" will speak through them and give them the words they need to say (10:19-20). He reminds them of their infinite value in the sight of a God who cares even about the death of sparrows (10:29-31); and he affirms by comparison that nothing will happen to them "apart from [their] Father" (10:29). In ultimate terms Jesus promises his disciples that if they "endure to the end" they will be "saved" (10:22//24:13).

And beyond the words of Jesus crucial events of Matthew's narrative confirm in powerful fashion the truth of which Jesus has spoken. In a pointed prolepsis at the beginning of Matthew's story God vindicates the life and the mission of the "child who has been born king of the Jews" (2:2) by protecting the child from harm in the face of imminent and deadly threat from Herod the king (2:7-8, 13, 20). And as that episode concludes, it is the "child" who is alive and well in Nazareth (2:23), while Herod himself lies dead (2:19). In parallel scenes interpreting first Jesus' earthly ministry (3:13-17) and then, significantly, Jesus' suffering and death (17:1-8) the voice of God enters the story to acknowledge Jesus as "my Son the Beloved" (3:17; 17:5), while the Spirit of God "descends" on Jesus (3:16) and the power of God "transfigures" Jesus with heavenly glory (17:2). At the moment of Jesus' death God unleashes the powers of the universe in a proleptic act of cosmic vindication, as he "tears" the curtain of the Jewish temple in two, "shakes" the earth, "splits" the rocks, "opens" the tombs of the departed faithful, and later "raises" their bodies to life (27:51-53). And on the "third day" (16:21; 17:23; 20:19; 27:63, 64) God takes final and definitive action to vindicate Jesus the "Beloved Son" for the faithful and nonviolent life he has lived and the obedient death he has died. In an act of unparalleled power God overturns the death sentence of the Jewish council (26:66), condemns the mob actions of the Jewish crowd (27:22, 23, 25), and reverses the state-sponsored crucifixion of Jesus (27:26, 35) as he raises Jesus from the dead

(27:64; 28:6, 7), empties the tomb in which he was laid (28:1–6), grants Jesus "all authority in heaven and on earth" (28:18), and restores him to his followers (28:7, 8–10, 16–20) as the Risen Lord who will be "with [them] always, to the end of the age" (28:20).

Here then is Matthew's ultimate word to his readers about the violence of the powerful and the suffering of the righteous. It is a paradoxical word that defies human reason and flies in the face of all human instinct. And, as the lived experiences of Jesus' own disciples within Matthew's narrative make clear, it is no easy word to receive. But for those prepared to receive it, Matthew makes clear that this word is nothing less than the transformative power of God at work in the human realm, obliterating the evident achievements of those who carry out violence and transforming the very real sufferings of the righteous into present "blessing" and future resurrection.

A FEW CONCLUDING REFLECTIONS

From beginning to end this project has taken shape against a vivid and ugly backdrop of brutal warfare and horrifying violence. Last spring as I submitted my proposal, my thoughts were on the Israeli-Palestinian conflict that has turned especially deadly within recent years and on the warfare and ghastly bloodletting now engulfing the people of Iraq. As I began work in July, my efforts were punctuated daily by heartbreaking accounts of death and destruction from the vicious little hot war between Israel and Hezbollah. And in the inscrutable providence of God it is September 11, 2006 as I conclude this study.

To read Matthew's story in this world is to experience the call to a discipleship breathtaking in its audacity and virtually inconceivable in its vulnerability. In this world of empire and military might, a world stockpiled with weapons of mass destruction, Jesus' disciples are called to renounce all use of violence and to "put [their] sword back into its place" (26:52). In this world, where patriotic emotions are aroused daily by the public vilification of terrorists and the hideous violence that they unleash, Jesus' disciples are called to lay aside hatred and revenge and to "love [their] enemies" in imitation of their "Father in heaven" (5:44). In this world where military violence is the "knee-jerk" response of nation states to political conflicts of all sorts, Jesus' disciples are called to the dangerous and potentially deadly vocation of "peacemaking" (5:9). In exchange for this inconceivable vulnerability Jesus' disciples are promised life lived through the resurrection power of God and in the ongoing presence of the Risen Jesus. It is the calling of a lifetime, fraught with challenge and pregnant with Good News.

11

"Wherever This Good News Is Proclaimed"[1]

Women and God in the Gospel of Matthew

TO SPEAK OF "WOMEN and God" within the Gospel of Matthew is to trace a significant yet seldom explored motif within Matthew's narrative.[2] A search of the canonical Gospels for a prominent focus on women leads readily to the detailed and colorful stories of women recounted uniquely by Luke[3] and John.[4] Matthew's narrative portrayal of women, by contrast, derives largely from stories found in his prominent literary sources, Mark and Q. And Matthew's unique additions are few in number and sparse overall in their depictions of women.[5]

---

1. Matt 26:13a. All biblical citations are from the New Revised Standard Version unless otherwise designated.

2. But see Levine, "Matthew," 252–62; Dowsett, "Matthew," 517–41; Levine with Blickenstaff, eds., *Feminist Companion*.

3. Thus Elizabeth and Mary (1:5–25, 26–38, 39–56, 57–60; 2:1–52), Anna (2:36–38), Martha and Mary (10:38–42), the crippled woman (13:10–17), the woman searching for her coin (15:8–10), the widow seeking justice (18:1–8), the widow with the two coins (21:1–4), and the "daughters of Jerusalem" (23:26–31).

4. Thus Jesus' mother at Cana (2:1–12) and at the cross (19:25–27), the Samaritan woman (4:1–42), Mary and Martha (11:1–45), and Mary Magdalene (20:1–18).

5. Thus the women of Matthew's genealogy (1:3, 5, 6, 16), Mary and the women of Bethlehem (1:18–25; 2:1–23), the "antithetical" saying on adultery (5:27–30); the prostitutes who enter the kingdom of God (21:28–32); Pilate's wife (27:19). The one extended story about women unique to Matthew's narrative is the parable of the wise

But while Matthew's narrative portrayal of women appears, at first glance, less prominent and vivid than those of his counterparts, a careful examination of Matthew's narrative reveals a striking portrait of those who in the patriarchal world of first-century Palestine are largely people of little power and low esteem. And Matthew's corresponding narrative depiction of "Women *and God*" offers significant food for theological reflection.

Matthew's portrayal of women, set against the backdrop of a thoroughgoing patriarchal context and reflecting Matthew's own patriarchal worldview,[6] lends an undeniable irony to the character of Matthew's story. This irony is a two-level phenomenon in which the evident realities of Matthew's narrative world (i.e., the "lower-level" portrait) are frequently subverted by Matthew's own narrative rhetoric, as he paints for the discerning reader a crucially different "upper-level" portrait.[7] Thus to ask about "Women and God" within Matthew's Gospel is to delineate both the lower-level portrait of women visible within the broad outlines of Matthew's narrative world and the upper-level portrait which emerges ironically from Matthew's surprising subversion of his own story. To bring God into the story of women is ultimately, for Matthew, to overturn conventional social and religious perspectives and to grant women extraordinary and unanticipated significance for the life and the faith of the people of God.

I. WOMEN IN THE WORLD OF MATTHEW'S NARRATIVE: THE LOWER-LEVEL PERSPECTIVE

To assess the women of Matthew's Gospel from a lower-level perspective is to look primarily at their socio-cultural status within the world that they inhabit. A primary socio-cultural indicator is family relationship. Matthew identifies women largely by means of their relationships or their marital status within family structures. These women are "virgins" who join in the wedding festivities of the village (25:1, 7, 11) and "virgins" engaged to be married (1:23 cf. 1:18). They are "daughters" (9:18; 10:35, 37; 14:6; 15:22, 28) and "sisters" (12:50; 13:56; 19:29), "mothers-in-law" (8:14; 10:35) and

---

and foolish virgins (25:1–13).

6. Cf. Anderson, "Matthew," 29.

7. Thus Muecke (*Compass of Irony*, 19–20), who depicts irony as a "double-layered or two-storey phenomenon" in which "the lower level is the situation either as it appears to the victims of the irony... or as it is deceptively presented by the ironist" and "the upper level is the situation as it appears to the observer or the ironist."

"daughters-in law" (10:35), "wives,"[8] "divorced" women (5:31, 32; 19:3, 7, 8, 9), and childless widows (22:23–28).

Their most prominent role, however, is to conceive and give birth to children. The women of Matthew's narrative are those who "come together" with their husbands in sexual union (1:18; cf. 19:5), those "in whom" children are "conceived" (1:20), those who are "pregnant" or "with child" (1:18; 24:19), those with children in their "womb" (19:12), those of whom children are "born" (1:3, 5, 6, 16; cf. 2:1; 11:11), those who "bear" children (1:21, 23, 25; cf. 2:2), and "those who nurse" their infants (24:19; cf. 21:16). Women are frequently associated with their "children,"[9] whether "daughters" (10:35, 37; 14:6; 15:22, 28) or "sons" (20:20, 21). These are the "mothers"[10] of Matthew's narrative, a designation occurring almost as frequently as the word "woman/wife."[11] Within the patriarchal worldview of first-century Palestine the dual roles of "wife" and "mother" are clearly the preeminent and socially sanctioned means by which women participate in the life of the local community and fulfill their destiny within society.

Matthew likewise portrays women who live out alternative social/sexual roles, namely as "prostitutes" (*pornē*: 21:31, 32)[12] and those guilty of "unchastity" (*porneia*: 5:32; 19:9). But the shame associated with such women is reflected in the colloquial association of "prostitutes" with "tax collectors" (21:31–32), Jewish collaborators with Rome, who have a notorious reputation in their own community (5:46, 47; 9:11; 11:19; 18:17; 21:31, 32). And John the Baptist is blunt and unyielding in his legal challenge to Herod, vis-à-vis Herodias, the wife of his brother Philip: "It is not lawful for you to have her" (14:4).

Matthew also identifies women in terms of ethnicity, social status, and daily activities. The ethnic profile of the women of Matthew's narrative is predominantly Jewish, but includes Canaanite (15:22; 1:5 cf. Josh 2:1),[13] Moabite (1:5; cf. Ruth 1:4), and Roman (27:19) elements as well.[14] And ac-

---

8. Thus 1:20, 24; 5:31, 32; 14:3; 18:25; 19:3, 5, 8, 9. 10, 29; 22:24, 25, 28; 27:19.

9. Thus 2:11, 13, 14, 18, 20, 21; 14:21; 15:38; cf. 18:25; 19:13, 29.

10. Thus 1:18; 2:11, 13, 14, 20, 21; 10:35, 37; 12:46, 47, 48, 49, 50; 13:55; 14:8, 11; 15:4, 5, 6; 19:5, 12, 19, 29; 20:20; 27:56.

11. Matthew uses the term "mother" twenty-seven times and the term "woman/wife" thirty times.

12. See also Matthew's references to women in Jesus' family line who are viewed as "prostitutes": Tamar (1:3; cf. Gen 38:1–30) and Rahab (1:5; cf. Josh 2:1–21; 6:22–25).

13. Tamar (1:3) is a woman whose identity in Gen 38:6 might be "Canaanite" along with that of her mother-in law Shua (Gen 38:2). But see Levine's note to the contrary ("Matthew," 253).

14. "The wife of Uriah [the Hittite]" (1:6 cf. 2 Sam 11:3; 12:10) is identified in 2

cording to biblical history the "queen of the South" (12:42) hails from Sheba deep in the Arabian Desert (1 Kings 10:1; 2 Chron. 9:1).

In terms of social status the women of Matthew's narrative range from persons of power and privilege—"the wife of Uriah" (1:6); "the queen of the South" (12:42); Herodias and her daughter (14:3-4, 6-8, 11); and the wife of Pilate (27:19)—to young servant girls in the household of Caiaphas (27:69, 71). Women of power and privilege lead lives reflecting their status. Royal consorts give birth to renowned offspring (1:6; cf. 12:42). Queens travel extraordinary distances to "listen to the wisdom" of other monarchs (12:42). Daughters of privilege "dance" before rulers and their guests to celebrate auspicious occasions (14:6). Powerful mothers instigate nefarious plots against political enemies and "prompt" their daughters to enact them (14:8, cf. 14:9-11). Wives of Roman governors "send word" to their husbands on behalf of political prisoners (27:19). And even ordinary women occasionally emerge as people with "very costly" items in their possession and at their disposal (26:7).

But the majority of women within Matthew's narrative are ordinary village women from Bethlehem (1:18-25; 2:1-23), Nazareth (13:54-58; cf. 2:23; 12:46-50), and the Galilee.[15] Accordingly, women's activities within Matthew's story are largely the typical duties of those who maintain village households: "grinding" at the mill (24:41); "mixing" yeast and flour to make bread dough (13:33); "buying" lamp oil from the merchants (25:9-10); "trimming" the lamp (25:7); "lighting" the lamp and "setting" it on the lampstand (5:15); "spinning" wool (6:28); "nursing" their children (24:19; cf. 21:16); and "serving" men (8:15; 27:55; cf. 6:25, 31). These women also participate actively in the celebrations and death rituals of village life, escorting bridegrooms to wedding festivities (25:1-13) and anointing the bodies of the dead for burial (cf. 26:6-13).

But beneath all the apparent normalcy and routine of this women's world lies a profound vulnerability pervading the lives of these women and shaping their life experiences in crucial, challenging, and sometimes brutal ways. Much of this vulnerability relates to women's status within a male-dominated society and patriarchal family structures. These women are the objects of "lust" by men who "look at" them with evil intentions (5:28) and the victims of harassment by men who "trouble" them in verbal interactions (26:10; cf. 26:8-9). They are subject to regular and sometimes prolonged ritual impurity due to their menstrual bleeding (9:20). Unmarried women

---

Sam 11:3 as the "daughter of Eliam," a man with a Hebrew name. Thus she is evidently Hebrew and not Hittite. Cf. Levine, ibid.

15. 8:14-15; 9:18-26; 14:21; 15:38; 20:20-21; 27:55-56, 61; 28:1-11a. Cf. 19:13, where it seems most likely that mothers have brought their children to Jesus.

run the fearsome risk of being "found . . . with child" and suspected of inappropriate sexual liaisons (1:18). And they face the shame and danger of being "exposed . . . to public disgrace" (1:19) due to such pregnancies.[16]

Married women are likewise vulnerable. On the one hand their husbands may save them from "public disgrace" (1:19), protect them from physical dangers (2:13–14, 19–21; cf. 2:22–23), and support them as childless widows through levirate marriage (22:24–28; 1:5 cf. Ruth 3:1–4:15). On the other hand their husbands may divorce them "for any cause" (19:3; cf. 1:19; 5:31; 19:7, 8). If tragedy strikes, their next of kin may simply abandon them to their fate as childless widows rather than providing them with new husbands (1:3; cf. Gen 38:1–26). And men of power can do as they wish with married women and their husbands (1:6; cf. 2 Sam 11:1–27).

Beyond the vulnerability of women's status within a patriarchal society lies the vulnerability associated with women's physical and political powerlessness vis-à-vis the forces of violence in the world that they inhabit. Women can be thrown into debtor's prison along with their husbands and children (18:23–25). They are vulnerable to vicious death threats on their children that transform entire families into political refugees (2:13–15; cf. 2:22). They experience the brutal massacre of their infants at the instigation of paranoid tyrants (2:16). They witness the grim horror of public executions, carried out by the occupying powers against their Jewish compatriots (27:55–56). And they face the bitter prospect of enduring chaos and suffering as "pregnant" women and "nursing" mothers (24:19; cf. 24:15–22). And in the face of all this violence these women can do nothing more than "weep" for their murdered infants (2:17–18), "look on from a distance" at public crucifixions (27:55), "see" the tombs of those who have been executed (28:1), and, when necessary, "flee to the mountains" to save their own lives (24:16; cf. 24:20).

Such is the real world for the women of Matthew's story. And such is their fundamental vulnerability. Matthew's narrative paints a compelling and realistic lower-level portrait of women and their secondary and often endangered status within the patriarchal society and the Roman-occupied world of first-century Palestine.

---

16. According to Jewish law such "public disgrace" calls for the execution of the woman along with her sexual partner (Lev 20:10; Deut 22:22–24); cf. John 8:5). But Matthew does not specify the "public disgrace" that Joseph seeks to avoid (1:19).

II. WOMEN AND GOD IN MATTHEW'S NARRATIVE: THE UPPER-LEVEL PERSPECTIVE

But for Matthew this lower-level portrait of women serves merely as the backdrop for a narrative in which everyday reality is frequently turned on its head and delicious ironies abound. Matthew's upper level portrait of "Women and God" is stunning in its impact and far-reaching in its implications. And this upper level portrait stretches from the opening lines of Matthew's narrative (1:1-25) all the way to its concluding scenes (28:1-20).

Women, God, and the Birth of Jesus (1:1—2:23).

Matthew's narrative opens with the genealogy of Jesus, a patrilineal family line that traces Jewish history from Abraham (1:1, 2, 17) to Jesus the Messiah (1:1, 16, 17). In standard patrilineal fashion this genealogy proceeds from "father" to "son" ("and _____ was the father of _____") through 42 generations neatly subdivided into three 14-generation eras of Jewish history: "from Abraham to David" (1:17a; cf. 1:2-6), "from David to the deportation to Babylon" (1:17b; cf. 1:6-11), and "from the deportation to Babylon to the Messiah" (1:17c; cf. 1:12-16). The sheer force of verbal repetition, the seemingly endless list of men's names, and the inexorable movement from Abraham, the "father" of the Jewish people (cf. 3:9, DJW), to his most prominent "son" (1:1), "Jesus . . . who is called the Messiah" (1:16), clearly suggest to the reader that it is men who give Jewish history its meaning and propel history towards its climax. Even more crucially, this genealogy stretching from Abraham (1: 2, 17) to "the Messiah" (1:1, 16, 17) points to the inevitable conclusion that God acts through men—specifically fathers and sons—to accomplish God's plans for God's people.

But into this undeniably patriarchal genealogy with its unmistakable patriarchal theology Matthew inserts the names of four women "by whom" sons are born to fathers—Tamar (1:3), Rahab (1:5), Ruth (1:5), and the "wife of Uriah" (1:6)—all of them women whose lives reflect sexual irregularities. Tamar (Gen 38:1-30) poses as a prostitute in order to trap her father-in-law Judah into doing his duty and raising up offspring for her dead husband. Rahab (Josh 2:1; 6:22, 25) is a prostitute by vocation. Ruth (Ruth 3:1-14) presents herself to Boaz at the threshing floor during the night in a manner that "must not be known" (Ruth 3:14) to the people of Bethlehem. And the "wife of Uriah" (2 Sam 11:1-27) is taken from her husband's house to be the consort of David, King of Israel.

And with these four female interlopers in his patrilineal genealogy Matthew alerts the reader to a crucial shift. No longer does the significance of the genealogy lie solely in the fact that "fathers" give rise to "sons" in unbroken lineage from Abraham onward to the Messiah. Instead the very fact that women's names break the clearly established pattern of the genealogy suggests that women—and specifically, women of vulnerable reputations—play a crucial role within this patrilineal genealogy. And now it becomes clear that God works not only through men but also through women, even women of vulnerable reputations, to accomplish God's plans for God's people.

But the ultimate significance of these women for Matthew's genealogy does not become fully visible until the end of the family line (1:16). Here, in a stunning rhetorical move that takes the reader by surprise, Matthew breaks the linkage between Joseph and Jesus just at the crucial moment. Having followed the line of "fathers" and "sons" from Abraham onward, the reader anticipates that the genealogy will conclude with the standard formula "and Joseph was the father of Jesus . . . who is called the Messiah." This is what the story demands, since Matthew has already identified Jesus in 1:1 as "the son of David, the son of Abraham." And the tightly formulaic structure of the genealogy clearly demands an equally formulaic conclusion. But instead the reader learns that Joseph is merely "the *husband of Mary, of whom Jesus was born*, who is called the Messiah" (1:16; emphasis mine). Thus Joseph is not the father of Jesus. Instead Jesus' linkage to the messianic family line depends on Joseph's relationship to Mary, the fifth and climactic woman in Matthew's genealogy. And the reader now knows that there is far more at stake in Matthew's genealogy than a simple progression of fathers and sons.

In 1:18–25 Matthew expands his oblique reference to "Mary, of whom Jesus was born" into a full-blown narrative. And here the strategic role of the previous women finally comes into clear focus. Tamar, Ruth, Rahab, and the wife of Uriah appear in the messianic family line as women of vulnerable reputations precisely to point the way toward Mary, who shares their sexual vulnerability and faces the "public disgrace" (1:19) that accompanies such a status. Here the reader learns that Mary, who is "engaged" to Joseph but has not yet "lived together" with him, is "found to be with child" (1:18b), an evident sign of her premarital unfaithfulness.

The danger could not be greater for Mary and the child in her womb. Joseph's response could mean not only "disgrace" for Mary, but also the ultimate failure of Abraham's family line to reach its God-intended climax in the birth of "the Messiah" (1:1, 16, 17, 18). But Joseph knows nothing of God's messianic plans for Jesus. Matthew's immediate clarification that

Mary's child is "from the Holy Spirit" (1:18c) is clearly information offered to the reader alone and not to Joseph. So Joseph responds as he must. While he ponders the unthinkable legal response of "public disgrace" for Mary (1:19b), he is a "righteous man" (1:19a) who opts instead for a private divorce (1:19c).

But just as Joseph is about to act (1:20a), an "angel of the Lord" appears to him (1:20b), telling him what Matthew's reader already knows (1:20c-21). This is a "God thing." Mary's child is not the child of her unfaithfulness but rather a child "conceived from the Holy Spirit" (1:20c). This child has a divinely-ordained vocation, to "save his people from their sins" (1:21c). This vocation corresponds to the name "Jesus," which Joseph himself must give to the child (1:21b). Accordingly, Joseph must "not be afraid" to marry Mary (1:20b). When Joseph wakes, he responds obediently to the command of the angel. He marries Mary, but does not consummate the marriage until her child is born (1:24-25a). And the messianic crisis introduced in 1:16, where Matthew breaks the genealogical link between Joseph and Jesus, now finds resolution as Joseph "names [the child] Jesus" (1:25b) and adopts him into the messianic family line.[17]

The ironies are multiple and manifest. Matthew sets up a tightly-structured patrilineal genealogy only to subvert its force and transform its significance through the strategic insertion of women's names. Even more crucially Matthew sets up a messianic genealogy intended to climax in the birth of "Jesus the Messiah" (1:1, 16, 18; cf. 1:17) only to break the genealogical linkage between Jesus and his male forbears just at the crucial moment (1:16). On the lower level of the story Joseph suspects Mary of sexual unfaithfulness, even as Matthew informs the reader in upper-level discourse that the child she carries is "from the Holy Spirit" (1:18, 20). And Joseph, whose first thought is to "dismiss [his unfaithful fiancée] quietly" (1:19), learns from a divine messenger that God is at work within Mary's womb, carrying out God's ultimate plan to "save" God's people (cf. 1:21).

Role reversals abound. In spite of his narrative prominence Joseph's role in this divine initiative is secondary and supportive as he "takes" Mary as his wife (1:20) and "names" her child (1:21). Mary is primarily the object of others' actions. But her single act, namely "bearing" the son (1:21, 25) conceived in her womb by the Holy Spirit (1:18), is the crucial "God event" in the story and consequently the single event around which all other actions revolve. And Matthew confirms the world-transforming significance of Mary's single act with an ironic upper-level message to the reader identifying Mary, the woman of Joseph's erstwhile suspicions, with the Isaianic

---

17. Thus Brown, *Birth*, 139.

"virgin" who will "bear a son" whose name will be "Emmanuel" and whose life will signify that "God is with us" (1:23; cf. Isa 7:14).

Similar rhetorical irony appears in 2:1–23. Here again Matthew depicts Mary as the object of others' actions (2:11, 13, 14, 20, 21), while men play leading roles: King Herod (2:1–22), the "wise men from the East" (2:1–12), and Joseph (2:13–23). But here again Mary lies at the center of the drama, since she is inseparable from her child. When the wise men "enter the house" (2:10–11a; cf. 2:1–2), they encounter "the child *with Mary his mother*" (2:11b, emphasis mine). When the wise men depart, the "angel of the Lord" appears to Joseph with an urgent message concerning "the child *and his mother*" (2:13, emphasis mine). And as the story unfolds (2:13–15, 19–23), the focus lies on Joseph's unhesitating obedience to the angel's repeated commands to "take the child *and his mother*" to places of refuge safely away from the murderous grasp of Herod and his son Archelaus (2:13/14–15a, 20/21; cf. 2:22a/22b). Thus once again Joseph plays a secondary and supportive role, this time to "the child *and his mother*," whose urgent need for safety serves as the catalyst for all of his activities. And Mary, a powerless "mother" with an endangered "child," is in the ironic rhetoric of Matthew's narrative one whose plight, in tandem with that of her child, stirs heaven and earth into urgent and extraordinary action.[18]

As Matthew reveals through his narrative rhetoric, God is at work in the lives of women in unanticipated and extraordinary ways. Women of vulnerable reputation assume crucial significance within the messianic genealogy. A woman suspected of marital unfaithfulness serves as the maternal agent through whom God comes to "be with" God's people and "save" them. And an "angel of the Lord" repeatedly summons an ordinary man into extraordinary service to protect a powerless woman and her endangered child. Thus from the outset Matthew's story of "Women and God" breaks patriarchal patterns, reverses patriarchal roles, and reframes the patriarchal history of God's salvific acts among humankind.[19]

---

18. Nor does Matthew overlook the women of Bethlehem (2:16–18) with his ironic rhetoric. These women have no power to prevent the unspeakable horror that overtakes them. When Herod instigates the massacre of their children (2:16), they can only raise their "voice" in "wailing," "loud lamentation," and "weeping" for their murdered infants (2:18). But Matthew ironically invests the grief of these powerless women with powerful significance, as they assume the role of their ancestral mother "Rachel" (2:18), fulfill the words of their ancestral prophet Jeremiah (2:17; cf. Jer 31:15), and re-enact the tragic history of their ancestors.

19. See Weaver, "Messianic Script," 376–85.

Women, God, and the Ministry of Jesus (3:1–25:46; 27:55–56).

Matthew's portrayal of women in the opening scenes of his narrative (1:1—2:23) finds a reflection in his portrayal of the women associated with Jesus' ministry. Since Jesus is, for Matthew, none other than "God with us" (cf. 1:23), to ask about "Women and God" is to look above all at the ministry of Jesus and his encounters with women. And Jesus' ministry is clearly an "equal opportunity" outreach involving women and even children along with men.

When Jesus engages in large-scale healing and feeding ministries (14:13–21; 15:32–39), Matthew pointedly amends his Markan source to highlight the presence of "women and children" in the crowds along with the "men" (14:21 cf. Mark 6:44; 15:38 cf. Mark 8:9).[20] Jesus heals women on his own initiative (8:14–15)[21] and at the urgent request of other men (9:18–19, 23–26). And women themselves seek Jesus out, actively and urgently, often at great personal risk, to find healing for themselves or others. A woman suffering long-term hemorrhages that have made her ritually unclean and thus untouchable (Lev 15:19–30) approaches Jesus from behind and "touches the fringe of his cloak" (9:20) in her desperate search for healing (9:21). And a Canaanite woman in the "district of Tyre and Sidon" makes a public nuisance of herself, "shouting" incessantly at Jesus on behalf of her demon-possessed daughter (15:22, 23) and adamantly refusing to take "no" for an answer (15:25, 27) in the face of Jesus' initial silence (15:23) and his repeated verbal rebuffs (15:24, 26).

But just as striking as the urgent appeals are the responses of Jesus. These responses are highly engaged and active. When Jesus arrives at the home of a synagogue official whose daughter has "just died" (9:18), he discovers that mourning rituals are already underway. So he first orders "the flute players and the crowd making a commotion" out of the house (9:23b-24), then physically evicts them (9:25a), before he "takes [the girl] by the hand" and raises her out of her "sleep" (9:25b; cf. 9:24). Jesus' responses break crucial boundaries. Jesus does not berate the hemorrhaging woman for violating social norms with her touch or for making him ritually unclean with her bleeding. Instead he accepts her touch and removes her uncleanness with the words, "Take heart, daughter, your faith has made you well" (9:22).

---

20. Similarly, when Jesus "lays his hands" on children (19:15), it seems reasonable to conclude that it is mothers who have "brought" their children to Jesus, although Matthew does not specify this (19:13).

21. But note the Markan parallel (1:29–34), where Simon, Andrew, James, and John "tell" Jesus about Simon's mother-in-law who is sick (1:29–30).

And Jesus' responses are highly unexpected. In a stunning scene of reversals, Jesus, who twice rebuffs the Canaanite woman—because his mission is for the "house of Israel" (cf. 15:24) and because the "children's food" should not be thrown to the "dogs" (15:26)—ultimately loses the battle of words and wits (15:27), acknowledges the "great faith" of the Canaanite woman (15:28a), grants her request (15:28b), and heals her daughter (15:28c). This scene is unprecedented and unparalleled within Matthew's narrative. No one else accomplishes what this Canaanite woman achieves: debating with Jesus once he has "pronounced" on an issue, winning the debate, and transforming Jesus' sense of mission and his ministry praxis (15:24; cf. 10:6).[22] Thus Jesus is not merely engaged in a healing ministry to women but finds himself transformed through this engagement.

Jesus likewise reaches out to women through his teaching ministry. To the rich young man who inquires about the "good deed" necessary for eternal life (19:16-22) Jesus commends "the commandments," including love of father and mother (19:19; cf. Exod 20:12; Deut 5:16). In teaching his disciples (5:1-2) Jesus radically sharpens the force of Mosaic Law (Exod 20:14; Deut 5:18), defining "adultery" in terms of "everyone who looks at a woman with lust" (5:28). And, apart from an exception for "unchastity" (5:32; 19:9), Jesus dismisses outright the Mosaic provision for divorce (5:31; 19:3, 7, 8; cf. Deut 24:1-4). For Jesus the very act of divorce is tantamount to adultery on all levels: for the divorced woman (5:32a); for the man who marries her (5:32b); and for the man who "divorces his wife . . . and marries another" (19:9). Here Jesus reaches behind the Mosaic divorce code—granted only as an "allowance" for "hardhearted" humans (19:8)—and invokes the Creator God, who "at the beginning 'made [human beings] male and female'" (19:4; cf. Gen 1:27) and established marriage as a union in which a man and a woman "become one flesh" (19:5-6a; cf. Gen 2:24). And Jesus concludes, "Therefore, *what God has joined together*, let no one separate" (19:6b, emphasis mine).

The unprecedented character of Jesus' sexual and marital ethics is transparent in the words of the men who encounter Jesus' teachings. The Pharisees ponder a world in which divorce might be legal "for any cause" (19:3). And Jesus' disciples respond to him in stunned disbelief: "If such is the case of a man with his wife, it is better not to marry" (19:10). Clearly Jesus' words transform the social status of women within family structures and, even more crucially, link that transformation to the express will of the Creator God from the beginning of time.

---

22. When Peter attempts a similar feat (16:22), he receives a sharp and instantaneous rebuke (16:23): "Get behind me, Satan!"

But while Jesus engages women actively in his healing ministry and transforms their social status through his proclamation, he does not call women into his circle of "disciples." Instead this circle comprises twelve men whom Jesus calls to "follow" him (cf. 4:18-22; 9:9) and whom he "sends out" in mission (cf. 10:1-4; 28:18-20). In this regard Matthew's story and Jesus' praxis clearly reflect the patriarchal character of first-century Palestinian society. But even here Matthew offers astonishing hints of a world where women and men serve equally as Jesus' disciples.

Jesus tells parables featuring women who exhibit the characteristics of the "kingdom of heaven" (13:33; 25:1-13). He cites real women—even "prostitutes" (21:31-32)—as positive examples of "faith" (9:22; 15:28) and faithful praxis (12:42; 21:31-32). He expands his circle of disciples exponentially (cf. 12:49) with his pronouncement that "Whoever does the will of my Father in heaven is my brother and sister and mother" (12:50). And Jesus portrays women, along with men, facing family divisions on his account (10:35b/c; cf. 10:35a/36), enduring the tribulations of the end times (24:19; cf. 24:17-18), and being "taken" at the Parousia of the Son of Man (24:41; cf. 24:40).

But perhaps the most striking portrait of women as "disciples" emerges from Matthew's depiction of the women who "follow" Jesus (27:55; cf. 20:20) and "serve" him (8:15; 27:55). When Jesus is well on his way to Jerusalem (20:17), "the mother of the sons of Zebedee" shows up in the traveling entourage (20:20). And following Jesus' crucifixion Matthew mentions "many women" in the crowd, who have "followed Jesus from Galilee" (27:55). And if women "follow" Jesus, they also "serve" him. When Jesus heals Peter's mother-in-law (8:14-15a), she "gets up and begins to serve him" (8:15b). And the women who "follow" Jesus from Galilee do so precisely in order to "serve" him (27:55; DJW). The significance of these descriptors is manifest. "Following Jesus" is the defining act by which people become "disciples" (4:20, 22; 9:9; cf.10:38; 16:24). And "serving" is the crucial modality of such discipleship. Just as Jesus has come "not to be served, but to serve" (20:28), so also must Jesus' disciples (20:26). And this "service" is ultimately the basis on which "all the nations" will be judged at the Parousia (25:31-46): "Lord, when was it that we saw you hungry or thirsty or a stranger or naked or sick or in prison, and did not [serve] you? (25:44; DJW). Thus while Matthew does not identify women formally as "disciples," his narrative rhetoric portrays them as disciples through their deeds.

Women, God, and the Passion/Resurrection of Jesus (26:1—28:20).

Matthew concludes his portrayal of women in a mode as sharply ironic as that with which it begins in 1:1–2:23. Here Matthew not only portrays women as faithful under duress but frequently juxtaposes these women ironically with male counterparts who fail their own fidelity tests.[23]

Jesus commends the woman who anoints his head with "very costly ointment" (26:7) and credits her with a "good service" (26:10), because she has "prepared [his] body for burial" (26:12). Jesus' disciples, by contrast, view only "waste" in the woman's gift (26:8–9). But Jesus rebukes them for their lack of insight (26:10–12) and pronounces high praise and unparalleled commendation for the woman's act (26:13): "Truly I tell you, wherever this good news is proclaimed in the whole world, what she has done will be told in remembrance of her."

The servant girls in Caiaphas' household (26:69, 71) exhibit no visible faith in "Jesus the Galilean/Nazarene." But their persistence in questioning Peter about his own association with Jesus serves ironically to highlight both their truthful proclamation that Peter belongs "with" Jesus (26:69, 71) and Peter's untruthful denials that he "knows" Jesus (26:70, 72).

Pilate's wife, whose portrait fills a single verse (27:19), nevertheless stands straight and tall by contrast to her husband (27:1–2, 11–26, 62–66).[24] She, like her counterparts, Joseph and the wise men, has a "dream" concerning Jesus (27:19d; cf. 1:20–21; 2:12, 13, 19–20, 22) to which she pays heed, "send[ing]" word to her husband" on Jesus' account (27:19b) and pleading for the life of "that innocent man" (27:19c). And although Matthew does not call her a "disciple," she has, in her words (27:19d), "suffered" many things on Jesus' account, just as Jesus' followers themselves will do (cf. 10:16–23; 24:9–22). By contrast Pilate, who knows both Jesus' innocence (27:23) and the evil motives of Jesus' enemies (27:18), pays no heed to his wife's appeal (27:19). Instead he relinquishes his judicial authority (27:17), proclaims his own "innocence" (27:24), and hands Jesus over for crucifixion (27:26).

The women who "follow" Jesus from Galilee and "serve" him throughout his ministry (27:55, DJW) are present at Jesus' cross (27:55–56) and tomb (27:61), in ironic contrast to Jesus' disciples. Judas "hands [Jesus] over" to the Jewish authorities (26:15, DJW; cf. 26:47–49), then "repents" of his "sin" (27:3–4), returns the "blood money" (27:5a; cf. 27:6), and takes his

---

23. But note 27:55–61, where Matthew pairs faithful women (27:55–56, 61) with a faithful man (27:57–60).

24. See Weaver, "'Thus You Will Know Them,'" 107–27.

own life (27:5b). The other disciples "desert" Jesus *en masse* in Gethsemane and "flee" the scene altogether (26:56b). Peter reappears, only to deny that he "knows" Jesus (26:70, 72, 74) and then to "weep bitterly" (26:75).

But perhaps most ironic is Matthew's portrait of the women who "[go] to see the tomb" on the first day of the week (28:1).[25] These women exhibit total command of their faculties in striking contrast to the Roman guards. The women maintain open eyes, open ears, and open hearts to the "great earthshaking event" (28:2, DJW) at the tomb and to the divine messenger who communicates its meaning (28:2–3, 5–7). The Roman guards, by contrast, are so "shaken by fear" (cf. 28:4a) that they fall into a "dead" faint, resembling the dead man they have been set to guard (cf. 28:4b).

And because the women's eyes, ears, and hearts are open, they become the crucial actors in the penultimate scene of Matthew's narrative. Not only do they witness the "great earthshaking event" (28:2, DJW) that reveals the empty tomb (28:2–3, 5–7). But they likewise encounter the Risen Jesus (cf. 28:8–10). And it is only through their obedience, first to the "angel of the Lord" (28:7; cf. 28:8) and then to the Risen Jesus (28:10; cf. 28:11), that word of Jesus' resurrection finally reaches Jesus' disciples and brings them "to the mountain to which Jesus [has] directed them" (28:16; cf. 28:11). The reunion of Jesus with his disciples (28:16–17) and the climactic and cosmic commission with which Jesus sends them out (28:16–20) are events made possible by the faithfulness of women, Jesus' first evangelists. Here, at the penultimate moment of his story, Matthew once again reveals through his narrative rhetoric the crucial role of women—even and precisely within a patriarchal world—for the life and the faith of the people of God.

Matthew's narrative concludes as surprisingly as it has begun. And women create the surprise. Let the reader understand.

---

25. See Weaver, "Matthew 28:1–10," 398–402.

12

Inheriting the Earth

Towards a Geotheology of Matthew's Narrative

INTRODUCTION

TO READ THE GOSPEL of Matthew as a narrative located in the real world and planted in the real soil of first-century Palestine is to encounter a striking geotheological claim unique within the Canonical Gospels. Jesus opens his ministry with an inaugural address, the Sermon on the Mount (5:1–7:29),[1] in which he establishes the character of "the kingdom of heaven" (5:3, 10, 19, 20; 7:21; 10:7; cf. 6:10, 33) that has "come near" (3:2; 4:17; 10:7) in his ministry of "teaching..., proclaiming..., and healing" (4:23; cf. 9:35; 11:1). Jesus begins this sermon, addressed to his disciples (5:1b-2) and overheard by the crowds (5:1a; 7:28–29), with a series of beatitudes (5:3–12), blessings pronounced on those whose character, actions, or personal circumstances align them with the salvific purposes of God, who will accordingly take action on their behalf.[2]

Within this series of beatitudes is one (5:5) which surely leaves both Jesus' disciples and Matthew's first readers in amazement: "Blessed are the meek, for they will inherit the earth."[3] While they surely recognize this

---

1. All biblical references refer to Matthew's Gospel unless otherwise identified.

2. On the debate over whether these "blessings" should be viewed as "reversals" or as "rewards," see Powell, "Matthew's Beatitudes," 460–79.

3. All biblical citations in English, except for those from Psalm 36, LXX, are taken from the New Revised Standard Version unless otherwise indicated. All English

saying as an almost-verbatim citation from their Jewish scriptures ("But the meek will inherit the land," Ps 36:11, LXX [Ps 37:11, MT]), they know from historical awareness and daily experience that it is not "the meek" but rather Rome, with its massive empire and its brutal functionaries, who rules the "earth" that they inhabit.

For Jesus' disciples Rome's hegemony includes the violent history of Herod, the half-Jewish client king serving the Romans, who massacred all the young children in Bethlehem (2:1–23) to exterminate his single rival, "the child . . . born king of the Jews" (2:2). For Jesus' disciples Rome's hegemony also includes the actions and/or reputations of Herod's sons: Archelaus, who rules Judea "in place of his father" and thereby strikes fear into simple peasants (2:22); and Herod the tetrarch, who rules Galilee and who has recently arrested John the Baptist (cf. 4:12) and will shortly execute him (14:1–12). Jesus' disciples likewise know the persistent humiliations of everyday life under Roman occupation. There are "taxes" levied by the emperor (17: 25; 22:17, 19; cf. 17:24, 25) and paid to Jewish "tax collectors" (5:46, 47; 9:10, 11; 10:3; 11:19; 18:17; 21:31, 32). Equally galling is the physical labor exacted by Roman soldiers, who have authority to "force" or "compel" hapless Jews to carry military gear or other burdens for one mile (5:41; 27:32). Most ominous of all, there is the threat of execution for any who denounce the Roman authorities (14:1–12; 17:9–13) or otherwise challenge the empire (2:1–23; 27:1–2, 11–37).

For Matthew's first readers, however, in late first-century Palestine (ca. 85 CE), the recent destruction of Jerusalem (70 CE) is central to Rome's hegemony. Within living memory Roman forces have "burned their [holy] city" (22:7; cf. 4:5; 27:53) and demolished their temple so completely that "not one stone [is] left . . . upon another" (24:2), "all [is] thrown down" (24:2), and the "house" of the Jewish people is "left to [them] desolate" (24:38). Roman soldiers have likewise "destroyed" the populace of Jerusalem (22:7) and put their leaders to "a miserable death" (21:41). Such is the power, reach, and brutality of Roman empire for Matthew's first readers.

There is thus no question within Matthew's narrative about Rome's hegemony in the first-century world. Accordingly, an urgent question emerges for Jesus' disciples, Matthew's first readers, and all subsequent readers: What does the Matthean Jesus mean with his claim that "the meek . . . will inherit the earth" (5:5)? And the sub-questions multiply. Who are these "meek"? What "earth" will they "inherit"? When and how will they gain this "inheritance"? What will this "inheritance" look like? And what do Jesus' words portend for the future of Rome and all successive world empires?

---

citations from Psalm 36, LXX, are my own.

The task of this essay is to examine the biblical intertext of Matthew 5:5, namely Psalm 36, LXX (Psalm 37, MT), and the immediate and wider Matthean contexts of this verse to discover narrative clues to Matthew's understanding of this beatitude. Part one examines Psalm 36, LXX, to assess the narrative rhetoric of this psalm as the theological basis for Jesus' saying. Part two examines Matthew 1:1–4:25, to identify the narrative backdrop to 5:5. Part three examines the framework and language of the beatitudes themselves (5:1–12) within their sermonic context (5:1–7:29), to identify structural and linguistic clues to the significance of 5:5. Part four examines 8:1–28:20 to follow Matthew's thematic of "inheritance" to its conclusions and to assess Matthew's narrative rhetoric vis-à-vis "inheriting the earth."

I. INHERITANCE OF THE LAND IN PSALM 36, LXX

When the Matthean Jesus pronounces a blessing on "the meek" who will "inherit the earth" (5:5), he is, as his own listeners and Matthew's first readers clearly recognize, citing a well-known Jewish Scripture. Matthew 5:5, "Blessed are the meek, for they will inherit the earth,"[4] reflects a near-verbatim citation of Psalm 36:11, LXX, "But the meek will inherit the land,"[5] and a clear allusion to the wider text of Psalm 36, LXX, with its five additional references to "dwelling in" (*kataskēnoō*: 36:3) or "inheriting" (*klēronomeō*: 36:9, 22, 29; *kataklēronomeō*: 36:34) the "land" (*tēn gēn*: 36:3; *gēn*: 36:9, 11, 22, 29, 34). Accordingly, the place to begin this study is with examination of Psalm 36, LXX, and analysis of its narrative rhetoric.

Psalm 36, LXX, derives from an "alphabetical acrostic" psalm in Hebrew.[6] The thematic of this psalm focuses on the contrast between God's faithful people and the evil ones. As Robert Alter notes, "This is emphatically a Wisdom psalm, expressing in a variety of more or less formulaic ways the idea that the wicked, however they may seem to prosper, will get their just deserts and the righteous will be duly rewarded."[7]

The Psalmist here depicts God's faithful people with a wide range of correlated terms. They are those "who wait on the Lord" (36:9), the "meek" (36:11), the "poor and destitute" (36:14), the "upright in heart" (36:14), the "blameless" (36:18), those "who bless him [= the Lord]" (36:22),[8] the "holy

---

4. *Makarioi hoi praeis, hoti autoi klēronomēsousin tēn gēn.*
5. *Hoi de praeis klēronomēsousin gēn.*
6. Alter, *Book of Psalms*, 129.
7. Ibid.
8. But note that Psalm 37:22, MT, speaks of the action of God and not that of humans: "*those blessed by the LORD*" (NRSV, emphasis mine).

ones" (36:28), and the "peaceful [people]" (36:37). But most prominently they are the "righteous" one(s) (36:12, 16, 17, 21, 25, 29, 30, 32, 39) and his/ their "seed" (36:25, 26).

Arrayed against God's righteous ones are those who oppose God and God's people. The psalmist depicts these antagonists in parallel but contrasting fashion to the righteous. These are the ones who "do evil" (36:1, 9, cf. 8), those who "practice lawlessness" (36:1) and the "unlawful" (36:28), those who "prosper in [their] way" (36:7), those who "carry out transgressions" (36:7) and the "transgressors" (36:38), the "enemies of the Lord" (36:20), those who "curse him [= the Lord]" (36:22),[9] and the "impious" (36:35) and their "seed" (36:28) or "remnants" (36:38). But most prominently they are the "sinner(s)" (36:10, 12, 14, 16, 17, 20, 21, 32, 34, 40).

The drama of this psalm lies in the hubris of the sinners and the threat which they pose to the righteous. As those who "prosper in [their] way" (36:7), the sinners have "great wealth" (36:16) compared to the "little" (36:16) of the righteous. Accordingly, they "glorify and exalt themselves" (36:20; cf. 36:35) and "raise themselves up like the cedars of Lebanon" (36:35). They are careless with others' resources, "borrowing" from others, but "not paying back" what they owe (36:21). And their evil extends to even more threatening actions. They "watch the righteous" (36:12) with sinister intent and "gnash their teeth against them" (36:12). They "observe the righteous intently" (36:32) and "seek to kill them" (36:32). They "judge" the righteous (36:33). And they "draw the sword" (36:14a) and "bend their bow" (36:14b) to "throw down the poor and destitute" (36:14c) and to "kill the upright in heart by violence" (36:14d). Faced with such self-aggrandizing and violent antagonists, the righteous have understandable cause for alarm.

The psalmist, however, counsels the righteous away from all alarmist responses and calls them instead to a life of goodness, compassion, and steadfast trust in the Lord. Negatively phrased this is a call to "not be provoked to anger/ jealousy" (36:1, 7, 8) and "not be driven to zealous action" (36:1) but rather to "cease from anger" (36:8), to "refrain from wrath" (36:8), and to "turn away from evil" (36:27; cf. 36:8). Positively phrased the call is to "practice kindness" (36:3), "have compassion" (36:21), "give" or "loan" to the needy (36:21; 36:26), "do acts of mercy" (36:26), "be a blessing" to others (36:26), "do good" (36:27), "communicate wisdom" (36:30a),[10] "speak

---

9. But note that Psalm 37:22, MT, speaks of the action of God and not that of humans: "those *cursed by him* [= *the LORD*] . . ." (NRSV; emphasis mine).

10. While *meletaō* usually connotes "practice," "devise," or "meditate," the clause *stoma dikaiou meletēsei sophian* (36:30a), with its reference to "the mouth of the righteous," connotes verbal communication as does its poetic parallel within the following clause, *kai hē glōssa autou lalēsei krisin* (36:30b), which unmistakably connotes verbal

justice" (36:30b), "maintain innocence" (36:37), and "observe uprightness" (36:37). Most crucial, however, to the lifestyle of the righteous is persistent God-directedness. The psalmist calls the righteous to "trust in the Lord" (36:3, 5, 40), "delight in the Lord" (36:4), "reveal [their] way to the Lord" (36:5), "submit [themselves] to the Lord" (36:7), "pray earnestly to the Lord" (36:7), live with "the law of [their] God in [their] heart[s]" (36:31), "wait for the Lord" (36: 34; cf. 36:9), and "keep [the Lord's] way" (36:34).

And while the sinners appear to present a life-threatening challenge to the righteous, equipped as they are with wealth at their disposal, evil in their hearts, and weapons in their hands, their actual power to effect their evil designs is far more ephemeral and far less potent than they or their counterparts imagine. They may threaten and intimidate, but the Lord gets the last laugh (36:13; cf. Ps 2:4): "But the Lord laughs at them, because the Lord foresees that their day is coming." And the psalmist then spells out the disaster awaiting these sinners. Without naming specific causes the psalmist announces that they will "wither quickly like grass" (36:2a), "fall away quickly like green plants" (36:2b), "perish" (36:20a), and "disappear like smoke" (36:20b). The psalmist names his own fervent desire that "their sword might enter their own heart" (36:15a) and that "their bows might break in pieces" (36:15b). And in passive phraseology, which clearly points to divine initiative, the psalmist declares that "the arms [of these sinners] will be broken" (36:17), that they "will be driven out" (36:28), and that they "will be utterly destroyed" (36:9, 22, 28, 34, 38a, 38b). In the near future ("in a little while," 36:10) the sinners will be gone. They will "no longer be in existence" (36:10a; cf. 36:36a) and "their place will not be found" (36:36b), even if one "searches" for it (36:10b; cf. 36:36b). Such is for the psalmist the sure but unthinkable fate of the sinners.

For the righteous, however, there is ultimate blessing, as God acts in power and compassion on their behalf. The Lord will "give [to the righteous] the desires of their heart" (36:4), "accomplish" that which they "reveal" and "entrust" to him (36:5), and "bring forth" their "justice" and "judgment" (36:6). The Lord will provide "an abundance of peace" (36:11) for the righteous and "keep them from shame in the time of evil" (cf. 36:19a), "fill them with food in the days of famine" (cf. 36:19b), and "never [leave] their children seeking bread" (cf. 36:25b). The Lord "supports the righteous" (36:17) vis-à-vis their adversaries and "supports their hands" (36:24) even when they fall. The Lord "knows the way of the blameless" (36:18), "keeps their footsteps straight" (36:23), and ensures that "their footsteps will not be moved" (36:31). Within the Psalmist's lifetime the Lord "has never

---

communication.

abandoned the righteous" (cf. 36:25); and the Lord "will never abandon them into the hands of the sinners" (36:33; cf. 36:28) nor "condemn them when they are judged" (36:33). Instead the Lord will "protect" his faithful ones "forever" (cf. 36:28), be "their defense in the time of tribulation" (cf. 36:39b), "help them" (36:40a), "deliver them" (36:40b), "rescue them from sinners" (36:40c), and "save them" (36:40d; cf. 36:39a).

But God's care for the righteous shows up most prominently in references to "the land" (*hē gē*: 36:3, 9, 11, 22, 29, 34), which God's people will "dwell in" (*kataskēnoō*: 36:3) or "inherit" (*klēronomeō*: 36:9, 11, 22, 29; *kataklēronomeō*: 36:34). This tangible, earth-bound theme, "inheritance of the land," runs like a vivid thread throughout the text of Psalm 36, LXX, and brings into ever-recurring focus the manner in which God will "save" God's people (36:39a) and resolve the conflict between the righteous and the sinners. This theme is tightly bound into the two-handed rhetoric of the psalm itself, since each reference to "inheritance of the land" stands in direct contrast to the fate of the sinners.[11] Accordingly, "inheritance of the land" is the central motif by which the psalmist expresses his theology here.

The outlines of this land-formulated theology are clear. First and fundamentally, the "land" belongs to God and is therefore God's to give as "inheritance." Just as it is God who works "the salvation of the righteous" (36:39) throughout this psalm, so it is likewise God who grants the righteous "inheritance of the land" (36:34, emphasis mine): "Wait on the Lord and keep his way; *and [the Lord] will exalt you to inherit the land [kai hypsōsei se tou kataklēronomēsai gēn]*."

Further, "inheriting the land" is a matter of profound ethical import for the Hebrew community, since it is precisely God-focused actions and God-focused lives which result in this inheritance. It is those who "trust in the Lord" (36:3), "wait on the Lord" (36:9, 34), "bless [the Lord]"[12] (36:22), and "keep [the Lord's] way" (36:34) who will "dwell in" the land (*kataskēnoō*: 36:3) or "inherit" it (*klēronomeō*: 36:9, 11, 22, 29, 34). And while the references to "the meek" (36:11) and "the righteous" (36:29) do not mention God, the rhetorical context of the psalm clearly establishes that they live similarly God-focused lives.

By contrast the sinners are not only, both by definition and by rhetorical function, excluded from "inheritance of the land"; but in the psalmist's ironic rhetoric these sinners will soon lose both their "place" (36:10, 36) and their very "existence" (cf. 36:10, 36) in the land which had once been theirs (36:10; cf. 36:36): "In a little while the sinners will no longer exist. You will

11. Thus 36:1-2/3, 9a/9b, 10/11, 22a/22b, 28b/29, 34a/34b.
12. But see n. 8 above.

seek their place, but you will not find it." Instead these sinners will "wither quickly like grass" (36:2a), "fall away quickly like green plants" (36:2b), "be driven out" (36:28) and "be utterly destroyed" (36:9, 22, 28, 34).

There is need, however, for the righteous to exercise patience. God's timeframe for action clearly lies in the future. In the present moment of the psalmist the sinners are still in their ascendancy. Otherwise the psalmist would have no need to decry them or offer courage to those whom they threaten. As the psalmist speaks, the sinners still make grandiose claims (cf. 36:20) and flex their military muscles (cf. 36:12, 14, 32), while God "laughs" at their pretensions and their threats (36:13; cf. Ps 2:4). Now is the time to "wait for the Lord" (36:9, 34), to "trust in the Lord" (36:3, 5, 40) and to await God's deliverance.

And deliverance will surely come. "In a little while" (36:10) and precisely as "the enemies of the Lord glorify and exalt themselves" (36:20), God will act. With the exception of 36:3, where the psalmist's present-tense imperative (*kataskēnou*) commands God's faithful to "dwell [and keep on dwelling] in the land," all language of "inheritance" lies in future tense verbs (*klēronomēsousin*: 36:9, 11, 22, 29; *hypsōsei . . . tou kataklēronomēsai*: 36:34): God *will exalt* God's faithful and they *will inherit the land* in a future time of God's own decision.

When this happens, it will be a permanent gift to God's people. As the psalmist reiterates, God's people will inherit and dwell in the land "forever" (36:18, 27; 29) and there God will protect them "forever" (36:28). In this "forever" world of the future God's faithful "will be shepherded [by God] on the bounty [of the land which they have inherited]" (36:3) and "will enjoy an abundance of peace" (36:11). Such is the ultimate outcome of God's laughter. Such is the life-sustaining faith of the psalmist. And such is the theological backdrop to Jesus' beatitude concerning "the meek" (Matt 5:5).

II. GEOGRAPHY AND THE NARRATIVE RHETORIC OF MATTHEW 1:1-4:25

If Matthew's Jesus evokes Psalm 36, LXX, with his claim concerning "the meek" (5:5), Matthew's wider narrative likewise reflects the rhetoric of Psalm 36, LXX, with its sharp conflict between the righteous and the sinners, its focus on land as a prominent medium for God's salvific actions, and its ironic narrative logic which turns apparent destinies on their heads by the will and through the power of God.[13]

---

13. On the fundamental irony underlying Matthew's narrative, see Weaver, "Power and Powerlessness," 179–96.

Matthew introduces this narrative rhetoric in 1:1—4:25. And the emphasis on two opposing character groups, the "righteous"[14] and their "evil" counterparts,[15] comes into focus early in the story. In 1:19 Matthew identifies Joseph as "a righteous man," as he ponders his response to the apparent unfaithfulness of his fiancée Mary and seeks to shield her from public shame. And after the birth of Mary's child, the one "born king of the Jews" (2:2), Matthew identifies Joseph's evil counterpart as he depicts King Herod (2:1-23), whose singular goal is to "search for the child, to destroy him" (2:13; cf. 2:20). From this angle the drama of chapter two unfolds as King Herod and Joseph take respective and opposing actions vis-à-vis "the child" (2:8, 13, 14, 16, 20, 21).

From an alternative perspective chapter two unfolds as the story of "worship vs. worship." Here "magi from the East" (2:1, DJW) appear in Jerusalem, announcing that they have "come to worship" the infant Jewish king (2:2). In response King Herod, whose paranoia is immense, whose cunning is great, and whose true intentions are murderous (2: 3-8, 13, 16-17, 20), informs the magi of his own plans to "worship" the child and inveigles them into his sinister plot (2:8). The magi depart for Bethlehem (2:9a), just as Herod has instructed (2:8). And a dangerous drama unfolds between Herod, who knows his true intentions, and the unsuspecting magi, who do not.

In chapter three the conflict shifts to the wilderness of Judea (3:1) and the Jordan River (3:5, 6), where John the Baptist is engaged in a ministry of proclamation and baptism (3:1-12. When Jesus shows up for baptism, John is about to refuse him (3:14) until Jesus announces (3:15; emphasis mine), "Let it be so now; for it is proper for us in this way *to fulfill all righteousness*." But when Pharisees and Sadducees appear (3:7a), John denounces them as a "brood of vipers (3:7b). And from here on the Pharisees[16] and Sadducees[17]—along with their elite Jewish colleagues the scribes,[18] the chief

---

14. Thus *ho dikaios/hoi dikaioi* (1:19; 5:45; 9:13; 10:41; 13:17, 43, 49; 23:29, 35; 25:37, 46; 27:19, 24), Matthew's prominent term for those who are faithful to God. By the same token Matthew designates God as doing "whatever is right" (*ho ean ē dikaion*: 20:4) and refers to "[God's] righteousness" (*tēn dikaiosynēn autou*: 6:33).

15. Thus *ponēros*, Matthew's prominent term for designating "evil" individuals or groups or for depicting their thoughts or actions (5:11, 39, 45; 6:23; 7:11, 17, 18; 9:4; 12:34, 35, 39, 45; 13:49; 15:19; 16:4; 18:32; 20:15; 22:10; 25:26. In corresponding fashion Matthew uses the term "the evil one" to refer to Satan (5:37; 6:13; 13:19, 38).

16. Thus *Pharisaioi*: 3:7; 5:20; 9:11, 14, 34; 12:2, 14, 24, 38; 15:1, 12; 16:1, 6, 11, 12; 19:3; 21:45; 22:15, 34, 41; 23:2, 13, 14, 15, 23, 25, 26, 27, 29; 27:62).

17. Thus *Saddoukaioi*: 3:7; 16:1, 6, 11, 12; 22:23, 34).

18. Thus *grammateis*: 2:4; 5:20; 7:29; 8:19; 9:3; 12:38; 13:52; 15:1; 16:21; 17:10; 20:18; 21:15; 23:2, 13, 14, 15, 23, 25, 27, 29, 34; 26:3, 57; 27:41. The close Matthean association of the terms "scribes" and "Pharisees" suggests that the "scribes" are in fact

priests,[19] and the elders of the people[20]—constitute the prominent face of human evil within Matthew's narrative.

In chapter four the conflict shifts to the wilderness of Judea (4:1; cf. 3:1), where Jesus engages in one-on-one debate with Satan (4:10), the ultimate "evil" opponent (5:37; 6:13; 13:19, 38), known as "the devil" (4:2, 5, 8, 11; cf. 13:39; 25:41) and experienced as "the tempter" (4:3). Here Satan challenges Jesus "Son of God" (4:3, 6; cf. 3:17), with three seductive messianic strategies: (1) turning stones into bread (4:3) to satisfy Jesus' own hunger (4:2) and perhaps that of the crowds as well (cf. 14:13–21; 15:32–39); (2) jumping from the pinnacle of the temple, the holiest building in the "holy city" (4:5–6; cf. 27:53), to gain protection from God's angels (4:6); and (3) "worshiping" Satan himself (4:9) in exchange for "all the kingdoms of the world and their [glory]" (4:8, DJW). Such is the gauntlet thrown down by Satan, the "evil one" (5:37; 6:13; 13:19, 38) in front of Jesus Messiah—God's "Beloved Son" (3:17) and God's ultimate "Righteous One" (cf. 3:15)—as he ponders his upcoming messianic ministry.

Matthew's narrative rhetoric, like that of the psalmist, clearly focuses on the conflict between the righteous ones and the evil ones. But the parallels go still further. In Matthew's narrative, as in Psalm 36, LXX, "land" (*gē*: 2:6, 20, 21; 4:15) and matters of geography play a prominent role within the unfolding story. The geographical footprint of 1:1–4:25 ranges widely across the first-century world. Before Jesus proclaims that "the meek . . . will inherit the earth" (5:5), Matthew's characters have already engaged in journeys of all types and distances across that "earth." Within "the land of Israel" (*gēn Israēl*: 2:20, 21; cf. 2:6) there is extensive travel throughout both Galilee (3:13; 4:12/15, 18, 23, 25) and Judea (2:1, 5, 6a, 6b, 22; 3:1, 5; 4:25; cf. 2:2). Action unfolds in cities, towns, and villages: Jerusalem (2:1, 3; 3:5; 4:25; cf. "the holy city": 4:6), Bethlehem of Judea (2:1, 5, 6, 8, 16), and Ramah (2:18)[21] in the Judean south; Nazareth (2:23; 4:13) and Capernaum (4:13) in the Galilean north. Action likewise unfolds in the wilderness of Judea (3:1, 3; 4:1), at the Jordan River (3:6, 13; cf. 3:16) and "all the region along the Jordan" (3:5), by the Sea of Galilee (4:18; cf. 4:13, 15),[22] and on a "very high mountain" (4:8). There are cross-border and long-distance journeys to

---

the "scribes of the Pharisees."

19. Thus *archiereis*: 2:4; 16:21; 20:18; 21:15, 23, 45; 26:3, 14, 47, 51, 57, 58, 59, 62, 63, 65; 27:1, 3, 6, 12, 20, 41, 62; 28:11.

20. Thus *presbyteroi*: 15:2; 16:21; 21:23; 26:3, 47, 57, 59; 27:1, 3, 12, 20, 41; 28:12.

21. Luz (*Matthew 1–7*, 143–44) notes that the Ramah of Matthew's citation (Jer 31:15) is a "village . . . north of Jerusalem."

22. Thus "Capernaum by the sea": 4:13; "Land of Zebulun, land of Naphtali, on the road by the sea": 4:15.

and from far-flung corners of the world: Babylon (1:11, 12, 17a, 17b) and "the [Persian] East" (2:1, 2, 9; cf. 2:12), Egypt in the south (2:13, 14, 15, 19), Syria in the north (4:24), and the Decapolis and "beyond the Jordan" (4:15, 25) in the near distance. At its farthest extent Matthew 1:1–4:25 reaches to "all the kingdoms of the world" (4:8; cf. 4:9), Satan's ultimate messianic offer to Jesus.

This wide-ranging geographical footprint provides a crucial clue to the understanding of Jesus' beatitude concerning "the meek." (5:5). On the one hand this geography marks the bitter oppression of God's people, sometimes faithful and sometimes faithless, and their loss of land and home. For first-century Jews "Babylon" is the universally recognized cipher for the epochal disaster in which their Jewish ancestors were forced from their "homes" (*hoi oikoi*) and their "land" (*hē gē*) of long-standing divine promise[23] by a "deportation to Babylon" (*tēs metoikesias Babylōnos*: 1:11, 12, 17a, 17b) which turned into a lengthy exile. "Egypt," the biblical cipher for 400 years of slavery and oppression for Hebrew "exiles" (*paroikon*) in a foreign land (Gen 15:13, LXX), points, within Matthew's narrative, to a powerless peasant couple who must "flee to Egypt" (2:13) as political refugees in order to escape a death threat issued by the king against their infant child (2:13–15).[24] And even when they return to their homeland under apparently safe conditions, since "those who were seeking the child's life are dead" (2:20), they do so still as powerless peasants whose travel destination is shaped by ongoing fear of the political dynasty in power (2:22): "But when [Joseph] heard that Archelaus was ruling over Judea in place of his father Herod, he was afraid to go there. And after being warned in a dream, he went away to the district of Galilee." Within Matthew's narrative rhetoric, geographical references clearly function to highlight the oppression, fear, and powerlessness of God's people, forced to live in exile from their homes and their land of promise.

But in Matthew's ironic *modus operandi*, these same geographical references ultimately serve to highlight God's providence and God's plans for the salvation of God's people. Babylon, in spite of its role within Jewish history as the national trauma *par excellence*, is now demoted by Matthew to a single "generation"—if a momentous one[25]—in a 42-generation list of

---

23. Thus Gen 12:1, 15:17–20, 17:1–8; Deut 1:21, 4:1, 21, 5:31, 6:10–12; Josh 1:1–2 et al.

24. On Matthew's narrative as the account of a "banished" (and ultimately "returning") messiah, see Beck, *Banished Messiah*.

25. In 1:17 Matthew summarizes his genealogy by way of its most crucial "generations": Abraham (1:17a; cf. 1:1, 2), David (1:17a/b; cf. 1:1, 6), the deportation to Babylon (1:17b/c; cf. 1:11, 12), and the Messiah (1:17c; cf. 1:1, 16).

fathers and sons marching down through Jewish history towards its climax in the birth of "Jesus ... who is called the Messiah" (1:16; cf. 1:1, 17, 18), the one whose very name highlights his God-given role to "save [God's] people from their sins" (1:21). Egypt, for its part, names not only the vulnerability and powerlessness of Joseph and his family but more importantly the place of refuge provided by God to protect Jesus "the child" (2:8, 9, 11, 13a, 13b, 14; cf. 2:20b),[26] and, accordingly, the place out of which God will ultimately "call [God's] son" in fulfillment of Jewish scripture ("Out of Egypt I have called my son" [2:15; cf. Hos 11:1, MT]).[27] Similarly, Galilee and Nazareth (2:22–23) reflect not simply forced alternatives to Judea and Bethlehem (2:1, 5, 6; cf. 2:8) but likewise the scripturally prophesied locations (2:23a; 4:14) which establish Jesus as a "Nazorean" (2:23)[28] and "Galilee of the Gentiles" (4:15; cf. Isa 9:1) as the primary locus for Jesus' upcoming messianic ministry.

The remaining geographical references within 1:1–4:25 focus crucially on the movement of individuals and crowds towards the emerging reign of God. Magi from the Persian distances travel to Jerusalem to worship the royal child whose "star [they] have seen in the East" (2:2). Huge crowds— "the people of Jerusalem, all Judea ... and all the region along the Jordan" (2:5)—follow John the Baptist to the Jordan and his baptismal ministry there (2:6). Jesus comes "from Galilee to the Jordan" (2:13, DJW) to seek baptism at John's hands (3:14–15) and to receive his messianic appointment as God's "Beloved Son" (3:16–17). And as Jesus travels "throughout all Galilee" (4:23, DJW), word about his ministry spreads "throughout all Syria" (4:24). Accordingly, "great crowds follow [Jesus] from Galilee, the Decapolis, Jerusalem, Judea, and from beyond the Jordan" (4:25). As Matthew clearly suggests with his narrative rhetoric, the reign of God draws the world, both far distant and nearby, into its sphere of influence through a powerful divine magnetic force that wills the "salvation of God's people from their sins" (cf. 1:21b).

Significantly, however, there is a clear and crucial limit to the geographical extent of Jesus' ministry activities. In the climactic messianic

---

26. Cf. Luz (*Matthew 1–7*, 146), who notes that "God's plan and God's hand stand over the destiny of Jesus. It is God's guidance alone which saves the child."

27. Hosea 11:1, LXX, widens the original Hebrew reference to "my son" into a historically motivated reference to "his children."

28. The "prophets" whom Matthew cites cannot be identified with clarity. But it appears most likely that Matthew here refers to Isaiah 11:1, MT; cf. Isa 53:2, MT), which speaks of the "shoot" that "shall come from the stump of Jesse." For a detailed discussion of the potential biblical sources for Matthew's citation, see Keener, *Gospel of Matthew*, 114–15.

temptation, Satan offers Jesus "all the kingdoms of the world and their [glory]" (4:8; DJW) in exchange for Jesus' "worship" (4:9). And Jesus firmly refuses this satanic offer of instant global "inheritance" (4:10): "Away with you Satan! for it is written, 'Worship the Lord your God, and serve only him.'" Jesus will carry out his messianic mission in the service of God alone and will receive nothing—whether bread, angelic protection, or all the kingdoms of the world—from the hands of Satan.

But perhaps the most crucial correspondence between Psalm 36, LXX, and the opening of Matthew's narrative lies in the ironic *modus operandi* with which Matthew portrays the ultimate outcomes of the conflicts between the righteous and the evil. Not only are prominent geographical symbols of oppression (Babylon and Egypt) transformed into instances of God's salvific will and providential care for God's people. But, by the same token, evil ones, whether human or beyond human, who appear to have all power and all resources at their disposal exhibit in the end true impotence vis-à-vis the genuine power of God and the faithfulness of God's agents on earth.

Herod the king, who has savvy instincts (2:4, 7-8, 16), political clout (2:3-6, 7-9a), military resources (2:16), and a clear strategic plan (2:13, 16, 20), is nevertheless incapable of achieving the singular goal he sets for himself. Instead, at every crucial juncture an angel of the Lord (2:13, 19; cf. 2:12, 22)—an opponent of whom Herod ironically has no awareness—intervenes and calls righteous ones into action in order to save the life of the child whom Herod wishes to destroy (2:13; cf. 2:8, 16, 20, 22). And even when Herod instigates a vicious massacre (2:16b), he clearly does not know that he still fails to achieve his singular goal. Ultimately, in sharp Matthean irony, Herod lies dead at the end of the story (2:15, 19, 20; cf. 2:22), while the once-endangered refugee child is alive and well in Nazareth (2:23).

The account of Satan and his threefold effort to seduce Jesus (4:1-11) exhibits parallel but heightened irony. Satan, whose cosmic[29] reach and worldwide power enables him to offer Jesus "all the kingdoms of the world and their [glory]" (4:8; DJW), is more than matched by power beyond his own. Here Satan, who "comes" to Jesus (4:3) and "tempts" him (cf. 4:3) with the most seductive and far-reaching messianic offers at his disposal (4:3, 6, 9), is in the end forced to "leave" (4:11a) at Jesus' own word of command (4:10), while God's angels now "come" and "serve" Jesus rather than "tempting" him (4:11b; cf. 4:3). Satan's power, cosmic as it may appear, is ultimately revealed to be impotent against the power of God and the faithfulness of God's agents on earth. And with this divine irony clearly in view Jesus' dis-

---

29. Here and throughout I use the word "cosmic" in intentional relation to its Greek root word, *kosmos*, or "world."

ciples and Matthew's readers now approach Jesus' claim that "the meek... will inherit the earth" (5:5).

III. "INHERITING THE EARTH" WITHIN ITS SERMONIC CONTEXT

Matthew frames Jesus' inaugural address (5:1—7:29) with contextual markers (5:1-2; 7:28-29) that set the stage for Jesus' words and point to their significance. Crucial to this scene, first of all, are the "crowds" (5:1), who have "followed [Jesus] from Galilee, the Decapolis, Jerusalem, Judea, and from beyond the Jordan" (4:25), as he travels "throughout all Galilee" (4:23, DJW) and as his reputation spreads "throughout all Syria" (4:24). It is on account of these crowds that Jesus "[goes] up the mountain" and "[sits] down" to teach (5:1a; cf. Luke 4:20). And when Jesus concludes his address (7:28a), the crowds are still there, clearly listening to Jesus and accordingly "astounded at his teaching" (7:28b).

But while the wide-ranging geographical impact of Jesus' ministry and the attendant "crowds" (4:25; 5:1) instigate Jesus' journey up the mountain, it is Jesus' "disciples" who approach him there (5:1b) and whom Jesus now "teaches" (5:2). These "disciples" are mission interns whom Jesus has "called" to "come after [him]" (4:19a, 21) and to become "fishers for people" (4:19b, DJW). In response they have "left" nets, boats, and family members behind in order to "follow" Jesus (4:20//22; cf. 19:27). And it is these committed "disciples" whom Jesus addresses directly (5:2),[30] while the "crowds" appear to receive Jesus' teaching from the sidelines (5:1; 7:28-29). Accordingly, Jesus' words in 5:3-12, including the promise that "the meek... will inherit the earth" (5:5), are words addressed pointedly to those who have "left everything and followed [Jesus]" (19:27).

But if people are crucial to this scene, so is "the mountain" itself (5:1). For first-century Jewish people this reference to Jesus "teaching" on "the mountain" clearly evokes Moses, Mount Sinai, and the revelation which Moses receives from God and relays in turn to the people waiting below.[31] Accordingly, for Jesus now to teach on "the mountain" is for Jesus, "Beloved Son" of God (3:17) and Jewish Messiah (1:1, 16, 17, 18), to reprise the epochal and people-forming Mosaic event in a heightened and messianic

---

30. Cf. Matthew 5:11, where Jesus pronounces a blessing in the 2nd person plural (*makarioi este*) on "you" who encounter verbal attacks and persecution "on account of me," clearly implying the commitment of a "disciple."

31. Thus Exod 19:1—34:35.

mode and to reveal the words of God to the people of God in a new place and for a new day (cf. 5:17-20, 21-48).

But, as Warren Carter notes, there is another crucial allusion in Matthew's topographical reference."[32] Satan has just taken Jesus to a "very high mountain" and offered him "all the kingdoms of the world" in exchange for Jesus' "worship" (4:8-9). And Jesus has rejected Satan's seductive offer with a firm scriptural commitment to "worship" and "serve" God alone (4:10; cf. Deut 6:13). Now, in pointed contrast to Satan and on a mountain of his own choice, Jesus "will manifest God's reign/empire"[33] in a move that makes a mockery of Satan's offer of easy "inheritance." And it is this repudiation of Satan and his cosmic enticement that is prominent throughout Jesus' manifesto of "God's reign/empire" (5:3—7:27), beginning with the beatitudes of 5:3-12.

Here and throughout his address Jesus draws a composite portrait of faithful discipleship, a portrait clearly evoking both the vocabulary and the themes of Psalm 36, LXX. Faithful disciples are the "poor in spirit" (5:3),[34] "those who mourn" (5:4), and "the meek" (5:5).[35] They are "the merciful" (5:7) and those who carry out "deeds of mercy" (6:2, 3, 4).[36] They are "the pure in heart" (5:8),[37] and "the peacemakers" (5:9),[38] "the good" (5:45) and those who do "good works" (5:16).[39] They refrain from "anger" (cf. 5:22),[40] "give" to the needy (5:42a),[41] and offer loans to those who wish to "borrow" (5:42b).[42] But above all they are "the righteous" (5:45),[43] that is, "those who hunger and thirst for righteousness" (5:6), those who exhibit righteousness that "exceeds" the highest standards (cf. 5:20), and those who "strive first for the kingdom of God and his righteousness" (6:33). And these righteous ones, like their forbears of Psalm 36, LXX, suffer on this account. Jesus depicts them as "those who are persecuted for righteousness' sake" (5:10; cf.

---

32. Carter, *Matthew and the Margins*, 129.
33. Ibid.
34. Cf. "the poor and destitute" (Ps 36:14, LXX).
35. Cf. "the meek" (Ps 36:11, LXX).
36. Cf. the one who "does mercy all day" (Ps 36:26, LXX).
37. Cf. "the upright in heart" (Ps 36:14, LXX; cf. Ps 36:37, LXX).
38. Cf. "the peaceful person" (Ps 36:37, LXX).
39. Cf. the psalmist's command to "do good" (Ps 36:27, LXX).
40. Cf. "cease from anger" (Ps 36:8, LXX).
41. Cf. the righteous one who "has compassion and gives" (Ps 36:21, LXX).
42. Cf. the righteous one who "does mercy all day and lends" (Ps 36:26, LXX).
43. Cf. "the righteous one(s)" (Ps 36:12, 16, 17, 21, 25, 29, 30, 32, 39, LXX).

5:11b, 44), those who are "reviled" (5:11a), and those who are "[slandered] falsely on my account" (5:11c, DJW).[44]

Jesus' words about persecution clearly demonstrate that the righteous face sturdy opposition from their antagonists. Not only do these opponents "persecute" (5:10, 11b, 44b), "revile" (5:11a), and "utter all kinds of evil" (5:11c) against the righteous. They likewise appear as "accuser" (5:25a), "judge" (5:25b),[45] and "[prison] guard" (5:25c). They are physically abusive (5:39), litigious (5:40), and militarily domineering (5:41). They are the "enemies" of the righteous (5:44a).[46] Most prominently they are the "evil" (5:39, 45a)[47] and the "unrighteous" (5:45b).[48] And in the face of such antagonists faithful disciples of Jesus have every apparent reason, just like their forbears, to respond in fear.[49]

But Jesus, like the psalmist, turns appearances on their head. With his beatitudes (5:3–12) Jesus reframes the collective circumstances of his disciples—both their faithfulness and their fears—into a life of present "blessing" (5:3a, 4a, 5a, 6a, 7a, 8a, 9a, 10a, 11) and "rejoicing" (5:12a) in light of future "reward" (5:12b; cf. 5:4b, 5b, 6b, 7b, 8b, 9b). And this "blessed" present and "rewarded" future are both framed and defined by the dynamic and inbreaking reality of God's reign, the "kingdom of heaven," which already belongs, if only in incipient form, to these disciples (5:3b, 10b). Just as God once cared for the righteous of Psalm 36, LXX, so God will now take strong and salvific action on behalf of Jesus' faithful ones, those who have "left" everything to "follow" him (4:20//22; 19:27). God will "comfort" them in their distress (cf. 5:4b), "fill" them with the righteousness that they crave as food and drink (cf. 5:6b), extend to them the "mercy" that they show to others (5:7b), gift them to "see" the unseeable God (5:8b; cf. Exod 33:20), and "name" them as God's own "children" (cf. 5:9b). And there is one more gift: Those who have "left" everything behind and "followed" Jesus at his call (4:20//22; cf. 19:27) will in God's own time "inherit the earth" itself (*klēronomēsousin tēn gēn*: 5:5b), the psalmist's promise of "land" (36:11, LXX) now cosmically expanded into "earth" within Jesus' messianic rhetoric.[50]

---

44. Cf. the psalmist's references to the sinister and violent actions taken against the righteous (Ps 36:12a, 12b, 14a, 14b, 14c, 14d, 32a, 32b, 33, LXX).

45. Cf. the psalmist's reference to the righteous who are "judged" (Ps 36:33, LXX).

46. Cf. "the enemies of the Lord" (Ps 36:20, LXX).

47. Cf. "those who do evil" (Ps 36:1, 9, LXX).

48. Cf. the psalmist's prominent references to "the sinner/sinners (Ps 36:10, 12, 14, 16, 17, 20, 21, 32, 34, 40, LXX).

49. Cf. 10:16–31, where Jesus challenges his disciples "not to fear" (10:26, 28, 31) those who "persecute" them (10:23).

50. Cf. Luz (*Matthew 1–7*, 236), who notes, "The earth, not only the land of Israel,

These salvific acts of God, phrased uniformly in future tense verbs, are clearly gifts of God's future, that eschatological age in which the "kingdom of heaven" has not only "come near" (*ēngiken*: 3:2; 4:17; 10:7) but is fully present (*elthetō hē basileia sou*: 6:10a), that age when "[God's] will [is] done on earth as it is in heaven" (*genēthētō to thelēma sou*: 6:10b). But, by the same token, these gifts of God are likewise gifts for the present world and the immediate future, framed as they are by Jesus' parallel references to "the kingdom of heaven" which is already, in incipient form, present reality and gift of God for the righteous (*autōn estin hē basileia tōn ouranōn*: 5:3, 10). God's reign over the human community is a dynamic reality, encompassing both present (5:3, 10) and future (6:10a/b) alike, beginning with the ministry of Jesus (3:2; 4:17; 10:7) and extending into God's ongoing future, the "age to come" (12:32).

Accordingly, God's promise of future "inheritance" points not only to the eschatological future and the "heaven" in which God will ultimately "reward" Jesus' disciples (5:12; cf. 19:27-30).[51] Instead this promise of "inheritance" likewise impinges on the present world, that world in which "the kingdom of heaven" has already "come near" (3:2; 4:17; 10:7) and already belongs, in incipient form, to the righteous (5:3, 10).[52] Jesus thus invites his listeners, and Matthew his readers, to search their own present world for tangible signs of the emerging "kingdom of heaven," and for proleptic pointers to their ultimate "inheritance."

One thing is clear. This "inheritance," by its very name, is a promise of divine gift and not a warrant for violent human initiative. God alone is "Lord of heaven and earth" (11:25). Thus God alone can grant such "inheritance." Accordingly, there will be no human battles fought and no human enemies slaughtered to gain this "inheritance." As David Garland notes, "The land does not come as a result of violent conquest but as a legacy, a gift."[53] And

---

will belong to those who are kind, for the traditional promise of the land had long been transposed into the cosmic realm." See also Carter (*Matthew and the Margins*, 133), who reads Jesus' words as a reference to "all of God's creation," citing 5:13, 5:18, and 6:10 as evidence. But note to the contrary Burge (*Jesus and the Land*, 35) and Raheb (*Faith*, 97), who restrict Jesus' reference to "Judea" and "Palestine" respectively.

51. Contra Witherington III (*Matthew*, 121), who notes that "Jesus did believe in an eschatological restoration of the land . . . but not before the eschaton."

52. Cf. Luz (*Matthew 1-7*, 236; emphasis mine), who notes that "the promise of the earth makes clear that the kingdom of heaven also comprises *a new 'this world.'*" Keener (*Gospel of Matthew*, 167; emphasis mine), acknowledges that "for Matthew and early Christianity as a whole the future kingdom *is in some sense present in Jesus*," but limits any concept of "inheritance" to "*a spiritual down payment* of these blessings in Christ in the present."

53. Garland, *Reading Matthew*, 56. Cf. Powell, "Matthew's Beatitudes," 467.

this gift of God reflects the radical reversal that characterizes Jesus' proclamation of the reign of God. As Gary Burge notes, "[There is] a scandal at the heart of Jesus' pronouncement," a "scandal" which emerges "[i]n a world where the powerful were ready to make bold political and military claims on the land [and] where the strong assumed that they had the right, thanks to their position or privilege, to take what was theirs."[54] Within this world of power and privilege "[t]he great reversal keenly felt throughout Jesus' ministry—*the last will be first!*—has now been applied to the land."[55]

Such is the mountaintop promise of Jesus to his disciples (5:5): a promise of earthly inheritance within the real world, a promise of God's salvific initiative on behalf of Jesus' disciples, a promise for the age to come which breaks directly into present reality, a promise cosmic in scope. But there is yet more, a cosmic calling. In his next breath (5:13-14) Jesus offers his disciples two parabolic images as cosmic as the promise itself: "You are the salt of the earth [*tēs gēs*: 5:13] ... You are the light of the world [*tou kosmou*: 5:14]." With these two short sayings Jesus instantaneously transforms his small cadre of mission interns on a mountain in Galilee into crucial agents of God's cosmic reign, persons whose everyday lives and everyday faithfulness have worldwide impact. Rome may still be the brutal and hegemonic empire of the day. But Jesus' disciples themselves are now agents of cosmic impact on behalf of God's reign. Their call is to "let [their] light shine before others" (5:16a), so that it "gives light to all in the [earthly] house" (5:15c) and so that their "good deeds" (5:16a) flavor the entire "earth" (5:13), enlighten the entire "world" (5:14) and inspire humankind to "glorify [the] Father in heaven" (5:16b), the one who alone is "Lord of heaven and earth" (11:25). Here then are cosmic promise and cosmic calling for those who follow Jesus as faithful disciples. Fulfillment of the promise and enactment of the calling still lie ahead within Matthew's narrative.

IV. DISCIPLE-MAKING AND "INHERITING THE EARTH"

Within his inaugural address the Matthean Jesus has evoked the words of Psalm 36, LXX, promising his disciples—among numerous other promises to God's righteous ones (5:3-12)—that "the meek ... will inherit the earth" (5:5) and calling them accordingly to "let [their] light shine before others" (5:16), since they themselves are "the light of the world" (5:14; cf. 5:13). To assess the significance of this promise and this calling and to search for

---

54. Burge, *Jesus and the Land*, 35.
55. Ibid.

their fulfillment within Matthew's remaining narrative requires attention to ongoing narrative clues concerning the mission of Jesus' disciples.

Fundamental here is the pointed correspondence which Matthew establishes between Jesus' mission and that of his disciples.[56] Once Jesus has proclaimed God's reign initially through word (5:1—7:29) and action (8:1—9:35), Jesus commissions his disciples for a ministry directly parallel to his own (9:35—11:1). Jesus gives his disciples the "authority" which empowers his own mission, namely, "to cast out [unclean spirits] and to [heal] every disease and every sickness" (10:1, DJW; cf. 4:23; 9:35). He calls his disciples to his own proclamation ("The kingdom of heaven has come near": 10:7; cf. 4:17) and to the deeds of mercy which characterize his own ministry ("[heal] the sick, raise the dead, cleanse the lepers, cast out demons": 10:8, DJW; cf. 4:23//9:35; 9:18-26; 8:1-4; 8:28-34). And he establishes for his disciples the same geographical restrictions that limit his own ministry. Jesus, who has rejected Satan's messianic offer of "all the kingdoms of the world and their [glory]" (4:8-10, DJW), knows his own calling to "the lost sheep of the house of Israel" (15:24); and it is this calling which he passes on to his disciples: : "Go nowhere among the Gentiles, and enter no town of the Samaritans, but go rather to the lost sheep of the house of Israel" (10:5b-6; cf. 15:24).

Accordingly, Jesus' own ministry unfolds predominantly within the geographical footprint of the Jewish community in Galilee: Nazareth (13:54; cf. 21:11; 26:71); Capernaum (4:13; 8:5; 11:23; 17:24; cf. 9:1); Chorazin (11:21); Bethsaida (11:21); Genessaret (14:34); Magadan (15:39) ; the "deserted places" (14:13, 15; 15:33); the "sea" (8:24, 26, 27, 32; 13:1; 14:25, 26; 15:29), and the "mountain" (5:1; 8:1; 14:23; 15:29; 17:1, 9). And it is here that Jesus' disciples likewise serve as mission interns both with Jesus (14:13-21; 15:29-39) and on his behalf (17:14-20).

But there are significant hints that Jesus' ministry, and accordingly that of his disciples as well, will ultimately reach far beyond Galilee and "the lost sheep of the house of Israel" (10:6; 15:24). When approached in his "own town" Capernaum (8:5; cf. 9:1) by a Roman centurion seeking healing for his paralyzed servant (8:5-6), Jesus not only heals the servant (cf. 8:13) but also commends the faith of the centurion in striking fashion (8:10-11a): "Truly I tell you, in no one in Israel have I found such faith. I tell you, many will come from east and west and will eat with Abraham and Isaac and Jacob in the kingdom of heaven." Jesus exorcises two demoniacs within the clearly Gentile "country of the Gadarenes" (8:28), where the local livelihood is raising swine (8:28-34). Jesus commends "the people of Nineveh,"

---

56. On this major motif, see Weaver, *Missionary Discourse*.

who "repented at the proclamation of Jonah (12:41), and "the queen of the South," who "came from the ends of the earth to listen to the wisdom of Solomon" (12:42). Jesus parabolically identifies the "field" in which the Son of Man "sows the good seed" (13:37) as "the world" in its entirety (*ho kosmos*: 13:38).[57] And it is precisely the Jesus who knows that his ministry is "only to the lost sheep of the house of Israel" (15:24) who finds himself so compelled by the noisy and persistent appeal of a "Canaanite" woman in the clearly Gentile "district of Tyre and Sidon" (15:21–27) that he commends her "faith" (15:28a,) and "heals" her daughter (cf. 15:28b).

But authoritative proclamation and compassionate outreach to the people of Galilee and scattered Gentiles beyond are merely step one of Jesus' mission, announced in 4:17 (emphasis mine): "From that time Jesus *began to proclaim . . .*": 4:17; cf. 4:18–22, 23–25; 5:1–7:29; 8:1–9:35). Jesus' ministry of proclamation and healing comes at a profound cost. Suffering and death follow inevitably for Jesus, as a direct result of his words and actions. Matthew introduces this theme in 12:9–14, where Jesus heals a man in a synagogue on the Sabbath and the Pharisees respond by "[going] out and [conspiring] against him, how to destroy him" (12:14). And once Matthew's narrative reaches its crucial mid-point (16:13–20), with Simon Peter's dramatic messianic confession (16:16), Jesus immediately turns himself (and the geography of the narrative as well) towards Jerusalem (16:21; 20:17; 21:1, 10; 23:37) and the upcoming suffering and death that he will encounter there (16:21; 17:22–23; 20:17–19; 26:1–2): "From that time on, Jesus *began to show his disciples that he must go to Jerusalem and undergo great suffering . . .*" (16:21, emphasis mine).

Nor is this suffering and death a mere mistake on the part of humans. Jesus assures Simon Peter that his journey to Jerusalem and his death there are in line with the will of God (cf. *ta tou theou*: 16:23). And the same God who has earlier confirmed Jesus' messianic ministry of proclamation and healing in a vivid display of divine power and approval (3:16–17) now confirms Jesus' divinely-willed (*dei*: 16:21) journey to Jerusalem and his upcoming suffering and death with a new display of divine glory (17:1–8) at the top of a "high mountain" (17:1). Accordingly, in an unmistakable allusion to his own upcoming passion—an allusion which ironically brings language of "inheritance" back into Matthew's narrative—Jesus tells his Jewish opponents, the chief priests, the elders of the people, and the Pharisees (21:23; cf. 21:45), the story of the vineyard owner who "sends his son" (21:37) to "collect his produce" (21:34) from the tenants of his vineyard. Instead the tenants immediately recognize the son as "heir" to his father's

---

57. On this point, see Riches, "Matthew's Missionary Strategy," 141.

vineyard (*houto estin ho klēronomos*: 21:38a) and conspire to kill him in order to "get his inheritance" (*schōmen tēn klēronomian autou*: 21:38b; cf. 21:39). And Jesus, whose triumphal messianic procession into Jerusalem proclaims him publicly as "Son of David (21:9, 14; cf. "king of Zion" [21:5// Zech 9:9]),[58] ironically experiences his messianic coronation as he is tried (26:57-68; 27:11-26), mocked (27:27-31), and crucified on a Roman cross (27:32-50) precisely as "Messiah" (26:63, 68; 27:17, 22), "King of the Jews" (27:11, 28-29, 37; cf. "King of Israel": 27:42) and "Son of God (26:63; 27:40, 43). Such is the earthly fate that overtakes Jesus, the "heir" to God's earthly "vineyard" and God's heavenly "kingdom." Jesus' "inheritance" comes at the ultimate cost.

And so will that of Jesus' disciples (5:5; cf. 19:27). Throughout his ministry Jesus speaks both directly and metaphorically of the future mission of his disciples. In parabolic words they will "go . . . to the lost sheep of the house of Israel" (10:6) and "call those who [have] been invited to the wedding banquet [of the king's son]" (22:3; cf. 22:2), a mission clearly focused on the Jewish people. But Jesus' disciples will likewise one day bear "witness" to kings, governors, and the Gentiles (10:18, DJW). And ultimately "this good news of the kingdom will be proclaimed throughout the [whole] world, as a [witness] to all the nations" (24:14a, DJW; cf. 26:13).

But this mission of Jesus' disciples, whether Galilean or worldwide, will progress in the very midst of their suffering and death, just as Jesus' own mission has done. Jesus' disciples will be "hated by all," both individuals and people groups alike (10:22; 24:9; cf. 24:10). They will be "persecuted/pursued" from town to town (10:23; 23:34), "handed over" to those in power (10:17, 19, 21; 24:9, 10), "flogged" in synagogues (10:17; 23:34), "dragged before governors and kings" (10:18), "tortured" (24:9), "mistreated" (22:6), "put to death" (10:21), "killed" (10:28; 22:6; 23:34; 24:9) and "crucified" (23:34; cf. 10:38), all "on account of [Jesus'] name" (10:22; 24:9; cf. 5:11) and the urgent and ultimately worldwide mission on which Jesus has "sent" them as "sheep in the midst of wolves" (10:16; cf. 22:3, 4; 23:34). If this is the disciples' journey toward "inheriting the earth" (5:5; cf. 19:27-30), it is a fearsome journey, in the footsteps of Jesus the crucified, towards an "inheritance" not for the faint of heart.

But the end is not suffering and death, neither for Jesus nor for his disciples. Just as God rescues the righteous of Psalm 36, LXX, so God now takes earth-shaking and epoch-changing action on behalf of God's faithful. At the very moment of Jesus' death, precisely when Jesus' opponents clearly consider their victory over Jesus accomplished (cf. 27:42-43) and

---

58. See n. 23 above.

their "inheritance" gained (cf. 21:38), God turns the tables on them definitively. In an act of unmistakable divine irony, pointing proleptically towards the imminent resurrection of Jesus, God "tears the curtain of the temple in two, from top to bottom" (cf. 27:51a), "shakes the earth" (cf. 27:51b), "splits the rocks" (cf. 27:51c), "opens the tombs" of "many saints" (cf. 27:52a), and "raises their bodies" (cf. 27:52b). Through God's initiative the earth itself offers a cosmic protest to the death of Jesus. And two days later God completes the divine two-step with a final "earth-shaking event" (cf. 28:2, DJW), as God "raises Jesus from the dead" (cf. 28:6, 7), and sends a divine messenger to reveal the empty tomb (28:2). Once again God gets the last laugh (Ps 36:13, LXX; cf. Ps 2:4).

In the final scene of Matthew's narrative (28:16–20), located strategically once again on a mountain in Galilee (28:16; cf. 4:8–10; 5:1–2), Jesus makes the all-crucial announcement to his disciples towards which Matthew's narrative rhetoric has been driving from its inception (28:18): "All authority in heaven and on earth has been given to me." The Risen Jesus, "Beloved Son" of God (3:17; 17:5), who during his earthly ministry firmly refused Satan's offer of "all the kingdoms of the world" (4:8–9), has now received from God his rightful and cosmic "inheritance" (21:38), far beyond what Satan has to offer. Accordingly, as John Riches notes, "Jesus is *cosmocrator*, even if his rule is recognized as yet only by the few who are his disciples and if his presence is assured only among them (18:20; 28:20)."[59]

But there is one thing more. Jesus' cosmic authority has a direct and immediate impact on his disciples as well. In the final and climactic words of Matthew's narrative (28:19–20), Jesus once again calls his disciples into mission on behalf of the kingdom of heaven (cf. 10:5–15). But this time the mission is worldwide in scope, enabled by Jesus' own cosmic authority (28:18; cf. 10:1), sustained by Jesus' enduring presence (28:20; cf. 1:23; 18:20), and no longer limited by ethnic, religious, or geographical boundaries (28:19–20, DJW; cf. 10:5–6): "Go therefore and make disciples of all [the] nations, baptizing them in the name of the Father and of the Son and of the Holy Spirit, and teaching them to obey everything that I have commanded you. And remember, I am with you always, to the end of the age."

Here, then, is the unbounded missionary mandate that will finally bring Jesus' disciples and their "witness" before governors, kings, and the Gentiles (cf. 10:18) and will ensure that "this good news of the kingdom will be proclaimed throughout the [whole] world, as a [witness] to all the nations" (24:14a, DJW; cf. 26:13). *And here, in the incipient but ever-unfolding reality of God's reign on earth, a reign that has already "come near" in Jesus*

---

59. Riches, "Matthew's Missionary Strategy," 141.

(3:2; 4:17; 10:7), *are the present form and emerging outlines of that "earthly inheritance" that Jesus has promised his faithful ones (5:5)*. Fuller and final "inheritance" lies ahead for Jesus' disciples "at the renewal of all things, when the Son of Man is seated on the throne of his glory" (19:28): thrones from which they will "judge the twelve tribes of Israel," families and fields exponentially multiplied, and eternal life itself. Then Jesus' disciples will "inherit [*klēronomēsate*] the kingdom prepared for [them] from the foundation of the world" (25:34). All that is future promise.

But in the meantime and in the present moment the "earth" which Jesus' disciples now begin to "inherit" in incipient form is "the whole world" (*holō tō kosmō*: 26:13; cf. *holē tē oikoumenē*: 24:14) in which they "proclaim the good news" of God's reign among humankind (10:7; cf. 24:14; 26:13) and "make disciples of all [the] nations" (28:19-20; DJW). To "inherit the earth" is, first of all and within the present age, to claim "the whole world" as the realm of God's reign and to baptize and teach "all the nations" into the ranks of Jesus' disciples.

Let Rome and all future world empires take good notice. They may flaunt their powers and intimidate God's righteous ones as they will (2:1-23; 14:1-12; 27:1-2, 11-37; cf. Ps 36, LXX). But it is the followers of Jesus Cosmocrator who even now "inherit the earth" (5:5), as they "make disciples of all the nations" (28:19) on behalf of God's cosmic and salvific reign among humankind (3:2; 4:17; 10:7). And this is "the good news of the kingdom" (24:14; 26:13).

Epilogue

An Advent Meditation from Bethlehem, Christmas 2000

The God Who Is "With Us"

IT WAS NOT AN especially pretty world, the world into which Jesus was born. The Palestine of Jesus' day was a world of grinding poverty for the masses, hard labor for a daily pittance, wealthy tax collectors who made their fortunes by extorting money from the impoverished, and brutal military occupiers whose preferred method of crowd control was crucifixion for all those who dared to rise up and resist the occupation. Nor was the town of Jesus' birth an especially peaceful place, and hardly the idyllic Bethlehem of our beloved Christmas carol, lying "still" under the "silent stars" in "deep and dreamless sleep." The Bethlehem into which Jesus was born was one which was soon to know the terrifying clank of military steel, the blood-curdling shrieks of terrified children ruthlessly slashed to death by Roman soldiers "just doing their job," and the heart-rending cries of anguished mothers inconsolable over the brutal massacre of their innocent infants.

Two thousand years later the picture looks strangely similar. The Palestine of Christmas 2000 is a world of massive unemployment and growing poverty. And the Bethlehem of Christmas 2000, with its sister cities Beit Jala and Beit Sahour, knows only too well the terrifying sounds and scenes of war: the menacing drone of helicopter gunships, operated by soldiers "just doing their duty" and raining down death and destruction from the skies; the rapid-fire report of machine guns aiming live ammunition at live human beings in deadly confrontations on the ground; the heavy and horrifying boom of tanks which send shells smashing through the stone walls of ordinary houses, fill children's beds with glass shards, and turn defenseless civilians into refugees without a home; the screaming of Palestinian children, too frightened to go to bed; and the voiced and unvoiced anguish of Palestinian parents, incapable of protecting their little ones from the ongoing terror and the ever-growing destruction all around them.

This is the world and this is the hometown of Jesus Emmanuel, "God with us." When God comes to be with God's people, it is not to an idyllic, fairy-tale world of beauty and peace and "dreamless sleep." There would in fact be no need for "God with us" in that "never never" world. The world that Jesus Emmanuel comes to is rather the real world that all of us know somewhere, somehow, at some time: the world of poverty, extortion, callous cruelty, unrelenting terror, and inconsolable grief. It is this world, and none other, into which God comes to be with us in the person of Jesus, the defenseless child and the crucified Messiah. The God who comes to be "with us" in Jesus, born in Bethlehem, is a God who walks our streets, experiences our daily struggles, shares our pain, weeps our tears, suffers our humiliations, and dies the most agonizing of human deaths at the hands of his enemies. This is our God, the one who "comforts those who mourn," claims "peacemakers" as "children of God," and grants inheritance in the kingdom of heaven to those who "hunger and thirst for justice." This is Jesus Emmanuel, God with us. And this is the "good news of the kingdom." Thanks be to God.

Bibliography

Abrams, M. H. *A Glossary of Literary Terms*. 3rd ed. New York: Holt, Rinehart and Winston, 1971.
Albright, W. F., and C. S. Mann. *Matthew*. AB. Garden City, NY: Doubleday, 1971.
Allen, Willoughby C. *A Critical and Exegetical Commentary on the Gospel according to S. Matthew*. ICC. 3rd ed. Edinburgh: T. & T. Clark, 1912.
Alter, Robert. *The Book of Psalms: A Translation with Commentary*. New York: Norton, 2007.
Anderson, Janice Capel. "Matthew: Gender and Reading." In *A Feminist Companion to Matthew*, edited by Amy Jill Levine and Marianne Blickenstaff, 25–51. Cleveland: Pilgrim, 2004.
Anderson, Megory, and Philip Culbertson. "The Inadequacy of the Christian Doctrine of Atonement in Light of Levitical Sin Offering." *AThR* 68, no. 4 (1986) 303–28.
Banks, Robert. *Jesus and the Law in the Synoptic Tradition*. Cambridge: Cambridge University Press, 1975.
Bauman, Elizabeth Hershberger. *Coals of Fire*. Scottdale, PA: Herald, 1954.
Beare, Francis Wright. *The Gospel according to Matthew*. San Francisco,: Harper & Row, 1981.
Beck, Robert R. *Banished Messiah: Violence and Nonviolence in Matthew's Story of Jesus*. Eugene, OR: Wipf and Stock, 2010.
Bellefontaine, Elizabeth. "Deuteronomy 21:18–21: Reviewing the Case of the Rebellious Son." *JSOT* 4, no. 13 (1979) 13–31.
Ber, Viktor. "The Social Dimension of Atonement in the Torah." *ExAud* 26 (2010) 110–24.
Boecker, Hans Jochen. *Law and the Administration of Justice in the Old Testament and Ancient East*. Minneapolis,: Augsburg, 1980.
Booth, Wayne. *A Rhetoric of Irony*. Chicago: University of Chicago Press, 1974.
Brown, Raymond E. *The Birth of the Messiah: A Commentary on the Infancy Narratives in Matthew and Luke*. Garden City, NY: Image, 1979.

———. *The Death of the Messiah: From Gethsemane to the Grave.* New York: Doubleday, 1994.

Burge, Gary M. *Jesus and the Land: The New Testament Challenge to "Holy Land" Theology.* Grand Rapids: Baker Academic, 2010.

Carlson, Richard P. "From Villain to Tragic Figure: The Characterization of Judas in Matthew." *CurTM* 37, no. 6 (2010) 472–78.

Carmichael, Calum M. *The Laws of Deuteronomy.* Ithaca, NY: Cornell University Press, 1974.

Carter, Warren. *Matthew and Empire: Initial Explorations.* Harrisburg, PA: Trinity, 2001.

———. *Matthew and the Margins: A Sociopolitical and Religious Reading.* Maryknoll, NY: Orbis, 2000.

Chevalier, Haakon. *The Ironic Tempter: Anatole France and His Time.* New York: Oxford University Press, 1932.

Clavier, Henri. "Matthieu 5:39 et la non-résistance." *RHPR* 37, no. 1 (1957) 44–57.

Craigie, Peter C. *The Book of Deuteronomy.* NICOT. Grand Rapids: Eerdmans, 1976.

Cunliffe-Jones, H. *Deuteronomy: Introduction and Commentary.* TBC. London: SCM, 1951.

Currie, Stuart D. "Matthew 5:39a—Resistance or Protest?" *HTR* 57, no. 2 (1964) 140–45.

Daube, David. *The New Testament and Rabbinic Judaism.* London: Athlone, 1956.

———. "The Old Testament in the New: A Jewish Perspective." In *Appeasement or Resistance and Other Essays on New Testament Judaism,* 1–38. Berkeley: University of California Press, 1987.

Davies, W. D., and Dale C. Allison. *A Critical and Exegetical Commentary on the Gospel according to Saint Matthew.* Vol. 1, *Introduction and Commentary on Matthew I–VIII.* Edinburgh: T. & T. Clark, 1988.

Dion, Paul-Eugène. "Tu feras disparaître le mal du milieu de toi." *RB* 87, no. 3 (1980) 321–49.

Donaldson, Terence. *Jesus on the Mountain: A Study in Matthean Theology.* JSNTSup 8. Sheffield: JSOT, 1985.

Dowsett, Rosemary M. "Matthew." In *The IVP Women's Bible Commentary,* edited by Catherine Clark Kroeger and Mary J. Evans, 517–41. Downers Grove, IL: InterVarsity, 2002.

Driver, S. R. *A Critical and Exegetical Commentary on Deuteronomy.* ICC. 3rd ed. Edinburgh: T. & T. Clark, 1902.

Duke, Paul D. *Irony in the Fourth Gospel.* Atlanta: Knox, 1985.

Fenton, J. C. *Saint Matthew.* PNTC. London: Penguin, 1963.

Filson, Floyd. *A Commentary on the Gospel according to St. Matthew.* London: A. & C. Black, 1960.

France, R.T. *The Gospel according to Matthew: An Introduction and Commentary.* TNTC. Grand Rapids: Eerdmans, 1985.

Friedlander, Gerald. *The Jewish Sources of the Sermon on the Mount.* New York: KTAV, 1969.

Gaechter, Paul. *Das Matthäus Evangelium.* Innsbruck: Tyrolia, 1963.

Garland, David E. *Reading Matthew: A Literary and Theological Commentary on the First Gospel.* New York: Crossroad, 1993.

Gibbs, Jeffrey A. "The Son of God and the Father's Wrath: Atonement and Salvation in Matthew's Gospel." *CTQ* 72, no. 3 (2008) 211–25.
Goldberg, Michael. *Jews and Christians, Getting Our Stories Straight: The Exodus and the Passion-Resurrection*. Nashville: Abingdon, 1985.
Grundmann, Walter. *Das Evangelium nach Matthäus*. THKNT 1. Berlin: Evangelische, 1968.
Guelich, Robert A. *The Sermon on the Mount: A Foundation for Understanding*. Waco, TX: Word, 1982.
Gundry, Robert H. *Matthew: A Commentary on His Handbook for a Mixed Church under Persecution*. Grand Rapids: Eerdmans, 1992.
———. *Matthew: A Commentary on His Literary and Theological Art*. Grand Rapids: Eerdmans, 1982.
Hare, Douglas R. A. *Matthew*. Int. Louisville: Knox, 1993.
Hayes, John H. "Atonement in the Book of Leviticus." *Int* 52, no. 1 (1998) 5–15.
Heil, John P. *The Death and Resurrection of Jesus: A Narrative-Critical Reading of Matthew 26–28*. Minneapolis: Augsburg Fortress, 1991.
Hengel, Martin. *Was Jesus a Revolutionist?* Translated by William Klassen. FBBS 28. Philadelphia: Fortress, 1971.
Hill, David. *The Gospel of Matthew*. NCB. London: Oliphants, 1972.
Horsley, Richard A. "Ethics and Exegesis: 'Love Your Enemies' and the Doctrine of Non-Violence." *JAAR* 54, no. 1 (1986) 3–31.
Howell, David B. *Matthew's Inclusive Story: a Study in the Narrative Rhetoric of the First Gospel*. JSNTSup 42. Sheffield: Sheffield Academic, 1990.
Judisch, Douglas McC. L. "Propitiation in the Language and Typology of the Old Testament." *CTQ* 48, nos. 2–3 (1984) 221–43.
"Kairos Document: A Word of Faith, Hope, and Love from the Heart of Palestinian Suffering." Kairos Palestine. 2009. http://kairospalestine.ps/index.php/about-us/kairos-palestine-document. Accessed January 31, 2017.
Kauffman, Christmas Carol. *Not Regina*. Scottdale, PA: Herald, 1954.
Keener, Craig S. *The Gospel of Matthew: A Socio-Rhetorical Commentary*. Grand Rapids: Eerdmans, 2009.
Kingsbury, Jack Dean. "The Developing Conflict between Jesus and the Jewish Leaders in Matthew's Gospel: A Literary-Critical Study." *CBQ* 49, no. 1 (1987) 57–73.
———. *Matthew As Story*. 2nd rev. and enlarged ed. Philadelphia: Fortress, 1988.
———. *Matthew: Structure, Christology, Kingdom*. Philadelphia: Fortress, 1975.
Kline, Meredith G. *Treaty of the Great King: The Covenant Structure of Deuteronomy— Studies and Commentary*. Grand Rapids: Eerdmans, 1963.
Klostermann, Erich. *Das Matthäus-Evangelium*. 2nd rev. ed. HNT. Tübingen: Mohr/Siebeck, 1927.
Lagrange, M.-J. *Évangile selon Saint Matthieu*. 7th ed. Paris: Lecoffre, 1948.
Lehman, Chester K. *Biblical Theology: New Testament*. Scottdale, PA: Herald, 1974.
———. *Biblical Theology: Old Testament*. Scottdale, PA: Herald, 1971.
Levine, Amy-Jill. "Matthew." In *The Women's Bible Commentary*, edited by Carol A. Newsom and Sharon H. Ringe, 252–62. Louisville: Westminster John Knox, 1992.
Levine, Amy-Jill, and Marianne Blickenstaff, eds. *A Feminist Companion to Matthew*. Cleveland: Pilgrim, 2004.
Levison, John R. "Responsible Initiative in Matthew 5:21–48." *ExpTim* 98, no. 7 (1987) 231–34.

Lienemann, W. *Gewalt und Gewaltlosigkeit: Studien zur abendländischen Vorgeschichte der Gegenwärtigen Wahrnehmung von Gewalt*. FBESG 36. Munich: Kaiser, 1982.
Lind, Millard. "Law in the Old Testament." In *The Bible and Law*, edited by Willard M. Swartley, 9–41. OP 3. Elkhart, IN: Institute of Mennonite Studies, 1982.
Lohfink, Gerhard. "Der ekklesiale Sitz im Leben der Aufforderung Jesu zum Gewaltverzicht (Mt 5,39b–42/Lk 6,29f)." *TQ* 162, no. 3 (1982) 236–53.
Long, Thomas G. *Matthew*. WBComp. Louisville: Westminster, 1997.
Lührmann, Dieter. "Liebet eure Feinde (Lk 6,27–36/Mt 5,39–48)." *ZTK* 69, no. 4 (1972) 412–38.
Luz, Ulrich. *Matthew 1–7: A Commentary*. Translated by Wilhelm C. Linss. Minneapolis: Fortress, 1989.
———. *Matthew 8–20: A Commentary*. Minneapolis: Augsburg Fortress, 2001.
———. *Matthew 21–28: A Commentary*. Minneapolis: Fortress, 2005.
Matera, Frank J. *Passion Narratives and Gospel Theologies: Interpreting the Synoptics through Their Passion Stories*. New York: Paulist, 1986.
Mayes, A. D. H. *Deuteronomy*. NCB. Greenwood, SC: Attic, 1979.
M'Neile, A. H. *The Gospel according to St. Matthew*. New York: St. Martin's, 1965.
Miller, Wendy J. *Jesus, Our Spiritual Director: A Pilgrimage through the Gospels*. Nashville: Upper Room, 2004.
Morris, Leon. *The Gospel according to Matthew*. Grand Rapids: Eerdmans, 1992.
Muecke, D. C. *The Compass of Irony*. London: Methuen, 1969.
Noth, Martin. *Exodus*. OTL. Philadelphia: Westminster, 1962.
Patrick, Dale. *Old Testament Law*. Atlanta: Knox, 1985.
Patte, Daniel. *The Gospel according to Matthew: A Structural Commentary on Matthew's Faith*. Philadelphia: Fortress, 1987.
Payne, David F. *Deuteronomy*. Philadelphia: Westminster, 1985.
Phillips, Anthony. *Ancient Israel's Criminal Law: A New Approach to the Decalogue*. Oxford: Blackwell, 1970.
———. *Deuteronomy*. Cambridge: Cambridge University Press, 1973.
Piper, John. *"Love Your Enemies": Jesus' Love Command in the Synoptic Gospels and in the Early Christian Paranesis*. SNTSMS 38. Cambridge: Cambridge University Press, 1979.
Powell, Mark Allan. "Matthew's Beatitudes: Reversals and Rewards of the Kingdom." *CBQ* 58, no. 3 (1996) 460–79.
Raheb, Mitri. *Faith in the Face of Empire: The Bible through Palestinian Eyes*. Maryknoll, NY: Orbis, 2014.
———. *I Am a Palestinian Christian*. Minneapolis: Fortress, 1995.
———. *Bethlehem Besieged: Stories of Hope in Times of Trouble*. Minneapolis: Fortress, 2004.
Rhoads, David, and Donald Michie. *Mark As Story: An Introduction to the Narrative of a Gospel*. Philadelphia: Fortress, 1982.
Rhoads, David, Joanna Dewey, and Donald Michie. *Mark As Story: An Introduction to the Narrative of a Gospel*. 2nd ed. Minneapolis: Fortress, 1999.
Riches, John. "Matthew's Missionary Strategy in Colonial Perspective." In *The Gospel of Matthew in Its Roman Imperial Context*, edited by John Riches and David C. Sim, 128–42. JSNTSup 276. New York: T. & T. Clark, 2005.
Schlatter, Adolf. *Der Evangelist Matthäus: Seine Sprache, sein Ziel, seine Selbständigkeit*. 5th ed. Stuttgart: Calwer, 1959.

Schniewind, Julius. *Das Evangelium nach Matthäus.* NTD 2. Göttingen: Vandenhoeck & Ruprecht, 1956.
Schottroff, Luise. "Non-Violence and the Love of One's Enemies." In *Essays on the Love Commandment*, translated by Reginald H. Fuller and Ilse Fuller, 9–39. Philadelphia: Fortress, 1978.
Schweizer, Eduard. *The Good News according to Matthew.* Translated by David E. Green. London: SPCK, 1976.
Senior, Donald. *The Passion of Jesus in the Gospel of Matthew.* Wilmington, DE: Glazier, 1985.
Stendahl, Krister. "Hate, Non-Retaliation and Love: 1QS x, 17–20 and Romans 12:19–21." *HTR* 55, no. 4 (1962) 343–55.
Strack, Hermann L., and Paul Billerbeck. *Kommentar zum Neuen Testament aus Talmud und Midrasch.* Vol. 1, *Das Evangelium nach Matthäus.* Munich: Beck, 1922.
Strecker, Georg. *The Sermon on the Mount: An Exegetical Commentary.* Nashville: Abingdon, 1988.
Strobel, A. "Macht und Gewalt in der Botschaft des Neuen Testaments." In *Macht und Gewalt: Leitlinien lutherischer Theologie zur politischen Ethik heute*, edited by Hermann Greifenstein, 71–112. Hamburg: Lutherisches, 1978.
Tannehill, Robert C. *The Sword of His Mouth: Forceful and Imaginative Language in Synoptic Sayings.* SemeiaSup 1. Missoula, MT: Scholars, 1975.
Theissen, Gerd. "Gewaltverzicht und Feindesliebe (Mt 5, 38–48/Lk 6, 27–38) und deren sozialgeschichtlicher Hintergrund." In *Studien zur Soziologie des Urchristentums*, 160–97. WUNT 19. Tübingen: Mohr/Siebeck, 1979.
Thompson, J. A. *Deuteronomy: An Introduction and Commentary.* TOTC. London: InterVarsity, 1974.
Van Braght, Thieleman J. *The bloody theater: or, Martyrs Mirror of the defenseless Christians who baptized only upon confession of faith, and who suffered and died for the testimony of Jesus, their Saviour, from the time of Christ to the year A.D. 1660.* Elkhart, IN: Mennonite, 1886.
von Rad, Gerhard. *Deuteronomy.* OTL. Philadelphia: Westminster, 1966.
Weaver, Dorothy Jean. "As Sheep in the Midst of Wolves: Mission and Peace in the Gospel of Matthew." In *Beautiful upon the Mountains: Biblical Essays on Mission, Peace, and the Reign of God*, edited by Mary H. Schertz and Ivan Friesen, 123–43. SPS. Scottdale, PA: Herald, 2003.
———. "Between Text and Sermon: John 18:1—19:42." *Int* 49, no. 4 (1995) 404, 406–8.
———. "Between Text and Sermon: Matthew 28:1–10." *Int* 46, no. 4 (1992) 398–402.
———. *Bread for the Enemy: A Peace & Justice Lectionary.* Orrville, OH: Mennonite Church Peace and Justice Committee, 2001.
———. "The Hard Sayings of Jesus in Real-World Context: Reading Matthew 5:38–48 within the Occupied Palestinian Territories. In *Matthew*, edited by Nicole Wilkinson Duran and James P. Grimshaw, 231–53. T@C. Minneapolis: Fortress, 2013.
———. "Inheriting the Earth: Towards a Geotheology of Matthew's Narrative." *JIBS* 2:1: 6–29 (2015) DOI: 10.7252/JOURNAL.02.2015S.02
———. "The Massacre of the Innocents." In *Christ for All People: Celebrating a World of Christian Art*, edited by Ron O'Grady, 54. Maryknoll, NY: Orbis, 2001.
———. *Matthew's Missionary Discourse: a Literary Critical Analysis.* JSNTSup 38. London: Bloomsbury Academic, 2015.

———. "On Imitating God and Outwitting Satan: Biblical Perspectives on Forgiveness and the Community of Faith." *MQR* 68, no. 2 (1994) 151–69.

———. "Power and Powerlessness: Matthew's Use of Irony in the Portrayal of Political Leaders." In *Treasures New and Old: Recent Contributions to Matthean Studies*, edited by David Bauer and Mark Allan Powell, 179–96. SymS 1. Atlanta: Scholars, 1996.

———. "Resistance and Nonresistance: New Testament Perspectives on Confronting the Powers." *HTS Teologiese Studies/Theological Studies* 61, nos. 1–2 (2005) 619–38.

———. "Rewriting the Messianic Script: Matthew's Account of the Birth of Jesus." *Int* 54, no. 4 (2000) 376–85.

———. "'Suffering Violence' and the Kingdom of Heaven (Mt 11:12): A Matthean Manual for Life in a Time of War." *HTS Teologiese Studies/Theological Studies* 67, no. 1 (2011). Art. #1011. 12 pp. http://dx.doi.org/:10.4102/hts. v67i1.1011.

———. "'They Did to Him Whatever They Pleased': The Exercise of Political Power within Matthew's Narrative." *HTS Teologiese Studies/Theological Studies* 65, no. 1 (2009). Art. #319. 13 pp. http://dx.doi.org/:10.4102/hts. v65i1.319

———. "'Thus You Will Know Them by Their Fruits': The Roman Characters of the Gospel of Matthew." In *The Gospel of Matthew in Its Roman Imperial Context*, edited by John Riches and David C. Sim, 107–24. JSNTSup 276. New York: T. & T. Clark, 2005.

———. "Transforming Nonresistance: From *Lex Talionis* to 'Do Not Resist the Evil One.'" In *The Love of Enemy and Nonretaliation in the New Testament*, edited by Willard M. Swartley, 32–71. SPS. Louisville: Westminster John Knox, 1992.

———. "'What Is That to Us? See to It Yourself' (Mt 27:4): Making Atonement and the Matthean Portrait of the Jewish Chief Priests." *HTS Teologiese Studies/Theological Studies* 70, no. 1 (2014). Art. #2703, 8 pages. http://dx.doi.org/10.4102/hts. v70i1.2703.

———. "'Wherever This Good News Is Proclaimed': Women and God in the Gospel of Matthew." *Int* 64, no. 4 (2010) 390–401.

Webster, Noah, and Philip B. Gove, eds. *Webster's Seventh New Collegiate Dictionary*. Springfield, IL: G. & C. Merriam, 1969.

Weinfeld, Moshe. *Deuteronomy and the Deuteronomic School*. Oxford: Clarendon, 1972.

Wigram, George V., et al. *The Englishman's Greek Concordance of the New Testament*. London: Bagster and Sons, 1903.

Wink, Walter. *Naming the Powers: The Language of Power in the New Testament*. Philadelphia: Fortress, 1984.

———. *Violence and Nonviolence in South Africa: Jesus' Third Way*. Philadelphia: New Society, 1987.

Witherington, Ben, III. *Matthew*. SHBC. Macon, GA: Smyth & Helwys, 2006.

Wright, G. Ernest. "Deuteronomy." *IB*. 2:417–18. New York: Abingdon-Cokesbury, 1951–57.

Author Index

Abrams, M. H., 29n14
Albright, W. F., 138n4, 139n10, 142n28, 144n35
Allen, Willoughby C., 138n4, 139n13, 142n28, 144n35
Allison, Dale C., 139n7, 139n11, 142, 143n32, 144n35, 145n43, 163n81, 165nn89–90, 166nn91–92, 167n93, 171n106, 172n109
Alter, Robert, 264
al-Zoughbi, Fadi, 187n24, 188, 189, 191, 193
Anderson, Janice Capel, 249n6
Anderson, Megory, 68n21
Ateek, Naim, 187n22
Awad, Alex, 186n19, 187, 189, 190, 194, 195

Banks, Robert, 138n4, 139n11, 144n35, 168n96
Bauer, David R., xviin7
Bauman, Elizabeth Hershberger, xiv
Beare, Francis Wright, 30n21, 31n25
Beck, Robert R., 271n24
Bellefontaine, Elizabeth, 156n69
Ber, Viktor, 68n21
Billerbeck, Paul, 145n39, 146n46, 168n96

Blickenstaff, Marianne, 248n2
Boecker, Hans Jochen, 144n38, 145n41, 153n54
Booth, Wayne, 29
Brown, Raymond E., 46nn10–11, 128n5, 255n17
Burge, Gary M., 277n50, 278

Carlson, Richard P., 80n58
Carmi, Nora, 186n17, 188, 190, 191, 192, 193, 197
Carmichael, Calum M., 153n56
Carter, Warren, 44, 46n7, 49n14, 54n27, 55n31, 56nn32–33, 63, 71n34, 75n41, 88n18, 96n47, 180, 182, 275, 277n50
Chevalier, Haakon, 27
Clavier, Henri, 138n4, 139n13, 141n26, 163n81, 165n87, 165n90
Craigie, Peter C., 142n28, 145n40, 155n67, 156n69, 157n75
Culbertson, Philip, 68n21
Cunliffe-Jones, H., 142n28
Currie, Stuart, 139, 139n8, 146n45

Daube, David, 145n39, 165n90, 166n90, 168n96, 168n97, 169n99, 171n106

Author Index

Davies, W. D., 139n7, 139n11, 142, 143n32, 144n35, 145n43, 163n81, 165nn89–90, 166nn91–92, 167n93, 171n106, 172n109
Dion, Paul-Eugène, 148n47, 154n61, 155n64, 156n71
Donaldson, Terence, 178
Dowsett, Rosemary M, 248n2
Driver, S. R., 157n75
Duaybis, Cedar, 186n21, 193, 194, 195
Duke, Paul D., 27, 28, 29n11, 29n15, 43
Duran, Nicole Wilkinson, xixn13

Fenton, J. C., 138, 139n13, 142n28, 144n35
Filson, Floyd V., 138n4, 139n10, 142n28, 144n35
France, R. T., 164n84, 165n89
Friedlander, Gerald, 138n4, 139n11, 141n23, 142n28, 144n35, 145n41, 168n96
Friesen, Ivan, xxn14

Gaechter, Paul, 138n4, 139nn11–12, 142n28, 144n35
Garland, David, 80, 81, 277–78
Ghandi, Mahatma, 191n35
Gibbs, Jeffrey A., 82n63
Goldberg, Michael, 42n38
Grimshaw, James P., xixn13
Grundmann, Walter, 139n7, 142n28, 144n35
Guelich, Robert A., 139n7, 143n32, 144n35, 146n45, 165n90, 166nn91–92, 167n93, 168n96
Gundry, Robert H., 45n5, 139n7, 142n28, 144n35, 145nn42–43, 165n89, 165n90, 166n91

Hare, Doughlas R. A., 80nn55–56, 81n61, 90n29, 95n43
Hayes, John H., 68nn21–22
Heil, John Paul, 58n35, 60n40, 60n42
Hengel, Martin, 141, 142n28
Hill, David, 139n7, 139n9, 142n28, 143n33, 144n35, 165n90, 166nn91–92, 172n109

Horsley, Richard A., 139n7, 140n16, 141, 143, 164n85, 165n90, 166nn91–92, 167n93
Howell, David B., 177

"Issa," 187, 188

Josephus, 168n96
Judisch, Douglas McC. L, 68n21

Kauffman, Christmas Carol, xiv
Keener, Craig S., 70n29, 71n34, 74n40, 272n28, 277n52
Khoury, Rana, 187n23, 188, 190, 191, 192, 193, 197
Khoury, Samia, 186n16, 187, 192, 193, 194n37
Kingsbury, Jack Dean, xiv, 68n23
Kline, Meredith G., 145n42, 157n75
Klostermann, Erich, 138n4, 139nn10–11, 142n28, 144n35

Lagrange, M.-J, 138n4, 139nn11–12, 142n28, 144n35
Levine, Amy Jill, 248n2, 250n13, 251n14
Levison, John R., 165n89, 167n94, 172n109
Lienemann, W., 141n26, 142n31, 170n103, 171n106, 172n109
Lohfink, Gerhard, 141n26, 142n30, 165n87, 165n90, 166nn91–93, 171n106, 172n109
Long, Thomas G., 73n38
Lührmann, Dieter, 141n26, 163n81
Luz, Ulrich, 46n9, 71n34, 73n36, 138n4, 139n12, 142n30, 143n32, 144n35, 165nn89–90, 166nn91–92, 167n93, 169n100, 170n103, 172n109, 270n21, 272n26, 276–77n50, 277n52

Mann, C. S., 138n4, 139n10, 142n28, 144n35
Matera, Frank J., 49n16, 58n38, 58n39
Mayes, A. D. H., 144n38, 145n39, 152n52, 154n59, 154nn61–62
M'Neile, Alan Hugh, 45n5, 47n12
"Mohammed," 175n2

Morris, Leon, 45n5, 50n17
Muecke, D. C., 28, 29, 45n6, 244n64, 249n7
Munayer, Salim, 189, 191n35, 192, 193, 194

Nassar, Amal, 192, 195, 197
Nassar, Daoud, 188n28, 190, 191, 192, 193, 194, 195
Nassar, Imad, 186n18, 192
Noor, Solomon J., 186n20, 187, 189, 190
Noth, Martin, 144n37, 145n40

O'Grady, Ron, xxin18

Patrick, Dale, 145n40, 148n47, 156n71, 157n75
Patte, Daniel, 31nn24-25, 34nn29-30, 37nn34-35, 42n38
Payne, David F., 145n42, 157n75
Phillips, Anthony, 144n36, 145n40, 152n52, 153n53, 154n61, 156n69, 157n75
Piper, John, 138n4, 139n13, 143, 143n32, 144n35
Powell, Mark Allan, xviin7, 262n2, 277n53

Raheb, Mitri, 187, 187n26, 188n27, 190, 191, 192, 196, 198, 223, 277n50
Riches, John, xviiin8, 280n57, 282

Schertz, Mary H., xxn14
Schlatter, Adolf, 139n7, 144n35, 164n86
Schniewind, Julius, 138n4, 139nn10-11, 142n28, 144n35
Schottroff, Luise, 141n26, 142, 169n100
Schweizer, Eduard, 139n7, 142n30, 144n35
Senior, Donald, 58n37
Sim, David C, xviiin8
Stendahl, Krister, 138n4, 139n10

Strack, Hermann L., 145n39, 146n46, 168n96
Strecker, Georg, 138n4, 139nn10-11, 142n30, 144n35, 145n39
Strobel, A., 141n26, 142n30, 172n109
Swartley, Willard M., xixn12

Tannehill, Robert C., 167n94, 168, 169n101, 171n105, 171n107, 172n109, 182n13
Theissen, Gerd, 140n14, 140n20, 141, 143n32, 161n80, 166n92, 170n103
Thompson, J. A., 142n28, 157n75

van Braght, Thieleman J., xiv
von Rad, Gerhard, 145n40

Weaver, Dorothy Jean, xvin5, 13n29, 14n33, 16n43, 21n52, 45n3, 46n7, 49n14, 54n26, 68n21, 69n25, 87n2, 87n5, 89n26, 95n44, 118n103, 129n6, 134n9, 135n15, 176n3, 181n11, 205n23, 207n24, 213n69, 215n70, 217n84, 219n91, 220n93, 223-24, 225n6, 226n16, 231n33, 232n36, 235n39, 237n44, 239n50, 243n61, 244nn65-66, 256n19, 260n24, 261n25, 268n13, 279n56
Weinfeld, Moshe, 154n59, 156n71, 157n73
Wink, Walter, 3, 4, 138n6, 140n15, 165n90, 166n91, 170n104, 172n108
Witherington, Ben, 71n34, 80n57, 81n61, 277n51
Wright, G. Ernest, 156n69

Zaru, Jean, 188n29, 190
Zoughbi, Zoughbi, 188n30, 189, 190, 194

Scripture Index

OLD TESTAMENT

Genesis

1:27	258
2:24	258
4:2–5	231
4:8–11	226, 231
12:1	271n23
15:13, LXX	271
15:17–20	271n23
17:1–8	271n23
38:1–26	252
38:1–30	250n12, 253
38:2	250n13
38:6	250n13
38:13–15, 21–22	128n3
38:24	128n3

Exodus

19:1—34:35	274n31
20:12	258
20:13	179
20:14	179, 258
21:17	230n27
21:22–25	143, 144, 145, 181n10
22:25–27	166, 180
23:20, LXX	203n14
26:31	74
26:31–33	71n34
26:31–34	71, 74
26:33	71n34
26:36	71n34
27:1–8	74
30:13	72n35, 73
33:1–6/12–23	110n94
33:3b	110n94
33:16a	110n94
33:20	276
40:23	70

Leviticus

4:13–21, 22–26, 27–31, 32–35	71n32
4:20, 26, 31, 35	68n24, 71n31
5:1–6, 7–10, 11–13, 14–16, 17–19	71n32
5:6, 10, 13, 16, 18	68n24, 71n31
5:7	72n35, 73
6:1–7, 24–30	71n32
6:7	68n24, 71n31
7:7–10	71n32
12:8	72n35, 73

Leviticus (continued)

14:2–3	70n29
15:19–30	257
15:31	68n22
16:2, 12, 15	71
16:2–34	71n33
16:16, 30, 34	68n24, 71n31
16:34	68n24, 71, 79
19:12	179
19:18	181, 181n9
19:22	68n24, 71n31
20:2	108n83
20:3	68n22, 157n73
20:9	230n27
20:10	252n16
24:5	70
24:5–9	70
24:8	70
24:9	70
24:14	108n83
24:16a–b	104n59
24:19–20	143, 144, 145, 181n10
24:20	145n43

Numbers

14:10b–25	110n94
15:25, 28	68n24, 71n31
16:41–50	110n94
19:13, 20	68n22
21:4–9	110n94
28:9–10	71

Deuteronomy

1:14, 18	158
1:21	271n23
1:28	148
4:1, 5, 6, 14	158
4:1, 21	271n23
4:10	157n74
4:24	149, 156
4:25–26	158n76
4:38	148
5:1, 27, 31, 32	158
5:5	157n74
5:9	149
5:9–10	149n49
5:10	149
5:16	258
5:17	179
5:18	179, 258
5:19	156
5:29	157n74
5:31	271n23
6:1	147, 148, 162
6:1, 3, 24, 25	158
6:1–3	146, 159
6:1–25	72
6:2	147
6:2, 13, 24	157n74
6:3	147, 148
6:5	158
6:10–12	271n23
6:13	275
6:14	148
6:15	149, 156
6:18	72, 157
7:1	148
7:1, 17	148
7:6	156, 162
7:9	149
7:9–10	149n49
7:10	149, 156
8:6	157n74
9:1	148
9:4, 5	148
9:19	157n74
10:12, 20	157n74
12:25, 28	157
12:30	148
13:1–5	154n59, 154n60
13:2–6, LXX	154n59, 154n60
13:4	157n74
13:5	154n58, 154n61, 155n63
13:5, LXX	157n74
13:6	148
13:6, LXX	154n58, 154n61, 155n63
13:6–11	154n59, 154n60, 154n61
13:7	148
13:7, LXX	148

Scripture Index 299

13:7–12, LXX	154n59, 154n60, 154n61	19:16, 18	150
13:8, LXX	148	19:16–21	146n45
13:8b	153n55	19:17	149, 150, 151, 167
13:9	156n70	19:18	146n45, 149, 151
13:9b, LXX	153n55	19:18, 19	150
13:10	108n83, 154n61, 155n66	19:18–20	146n44
13:10, LXX	156n70	19:19	150, 151, 152, 153n57, 154n61, 155n63, 164n84, 181n10
13:11	157n72		
13:11, LXX	154n61, 155n66	19:19b	153, 155, 156
13:12	157n73	19:20	150, 151, 153, 157, 157n73
13:12, LXX	157n72		
13:18	157	19:21	145n43, 150, 154n61, 155n65
13:19, LXX	157		
14:2	162	19:21, LXX	146n45
14:2, 21	156	19:21b	152
14:23	157n74	21:1–4, 6–8	71
17:2–7	154n59, 154n60	21:1–9	71, 80n58, 154n59, 154n60
17:5	154n61		
17:6	154n61, 155n66	21:4, 6	154n61
17:7	153n57, 154n61, 155n63, 156n70	21:5	71, 77
		21:5, 8	77
17:8–13	154n59, 154n60	21:6–7	106n62
17:12	154n58, 154n61, 155n63	21:8	71, 77
		21:9	72, 77, 154n58, 157
17:13	157n72, 157n73	21:18–21	154n59, 154n60
17:19	157n74	21:21	153n57, 154n61, 155n63, 155n66, 157n73
18:9	148		
18:15–22	154n59, 154n60, 154n61	21:21c	157n72
		21:33–45	80n58
18:20	154n61	22:13–21	154n59, 154n60
19:8–13	80n58	22:21	154n61, 155n63, 155n64, 155n66
19:11–13	80, 154n59, 154n60		
19:12	154n61	22:21, 24	153n57
19:13	154n58	22:22	154n58, 154n59, 154n60, 154n61, 155n63
19:13a	153n55		
19:15	104n57, 149, 150		
19:15, 16	150	22:22–24	252n16
19:15–21	xix, 143, 144, 145, 146, 146n45, 149, 150, 154n59, 154n60, 158, 162, 167, 181, 181n10, 181n11, 226n16, 229, 239n50	22:23–27	154n59, 154n60
		22:24	154n61, 155n66
		22:25	154n61
		23:21	179
		23:29–36	80n58
		24:1	179
19:16	146n45, 149, 151, 181n10	24:1–4	258

Deuteronomy (continued)

24:7	148n47, 153n57, 154n59, 154n60, 154n61, 155n63
24:10–13	180
24:10–13, 17	166
25:18	157n74
25:58	157n74
26:19	156
27:9	147, 148, 156
27:9–10	146, 159
27:9a	148
27:9b	148
27:10	148
27:25	80, 81
28:9	156
29:17, LXX	148
29:18	148
31:12, 13	157n74
31:28–29	158n76
32:35	189

Joshua

1:1–2	271n23
2:1	128n3, 250, 253
2:1–21	250n12
6:17	128n3
6:22, 25	253
6:22–25	250n12

Ruth

1:4	250
3:1–14	253
3:4, 7, 8	128n3
3:14	128n3, 253

2 Samuel

11:1–27	128n3, 252, 253
11:3	250n14, 251n14
12:7–12	204n19
12:10	250n14

1 Kings

10:1	251
21:1–16	193
21:17–24	204n19

2 Kings

22:24	180

2 Chronicles

9:1	251
24:20	231
24:20–21	227n19, 230, 233n37
24:20–22	108
24:21	230n29, 231

Psalms

2:1–3	121
2:4	xxii, 121, 185, 266, 268, 282
2:4–6	82
2:7	177
22	236
22:1a	236
26:6	106n62
26:14, LXX	275n37
27:22, MT	264n8
36, LXX	xxi, 262n3, 264, 267, 268, 270, 273, 275, 276, 278, 281, 283
36:1, 9, LXX	276n47
36:8, LXX	275n40
36:10, 12, 14, 16, 17, 20, 21, 32, 34, 40	276n48
36:11, LXX	xxi, 263, 264, 275n35, 276
36:12, 16, 17, 21, 25, 29, 30, 32, 39, LXX	275n43
36:12a, 12b, 14a, 14b, 14c, 14d, 32a, 32b, 33, LXX	276n44
36:13, LXX	282
36:14, LXX	275n34
36:20, LXX	276n46

36:21, LXX	275n41
36:26, LXX	275n36, 275n42
36:27, LXX	275n39
36:33, LXX	276n45
36:37, LXX	275n37, 275n38
37, MT	264
37:11, MT	263
37:22, MT	265n9
73:13	106n62
110:1	215
118:22	215
139:21–22	181n9

Isaiah

5:1–7	88n16, 102
7:14	256
7:14, LXX	127
8:23, LXX	135
9:1	272
9:1–2	177
9:2	82
11:1, MT	272n28
40:3, LXX	203
42:1, LXX	135
42:4, LXX	135
50:4–9	165n89
50:6	165n89
53:2, MT	272n28
56:7	69, 70, 72

Jeremiah

7:8–11a	77n47
7:11a	77
31:15	236, 256n18, 270n21

Ezekiel

34:1–10	110, 204n19

Hosea

6:6	82
11:1, LXX	272n27
11:1, MT	272

Amos

2:7–8	166, 180
4:1–3	204n19

Micah

5:2	32, 69n27
7:6	226, 226n10

Zechariah

9:9	281

Malachi

3:1, LXX	203, 203n14
3:22, LXX	204, 204n20
3:23, LXX	204
4:5	177

NEW TESTAMENT

Matthew

1:1	125, 126, 127, 131, 132, 136, 253, 254
1:1, 2	271n25
1:1, 2, 17	66, 177, 253
1:1, 2–16, 17	66, 178
1:1, 6	271n25
1:1, 6, 17	177
1:1, 16	271n25
1:1, 16, 17	66, 177, 253
1:1, 16, 17, 18	80, 87, 101n53, 254, 274
1:1, 16, 18	255
1:1, 17, 18	272
1:1—2:23	xix, 125, 131, 253, 257, 260

Matthew (continued)

Reference	Pages
1:1—4:25	264, 268, 269, 270, 271, 272
1:1—5:37	177
1:1-23	xvi
1:1-25	xix, 101n53, 125, 126, 129, 253
1:2	126
1:2, 17	253
1:2-6	253
1:2-16	126
1:2-16a	127
1:2-17	125, 131
1:3	127, 250n12, 250n13, 252, 253
1:3, 5, 6, 16	248n5, 250
1:5	127, 250, 250n12, 252, 253
1:5-25, 26-38, 39-56, 57-60	248n3
1:6	126, 127, 131, 250n14, 251, 252, 253
1:6, 17	131
1:6-11	253
1:7, 16	101
1:11, 12	271n25
1:11, 12, 17	177
1:11, 12, 17a, 17b	271
1:12-16	253
1:16	125, 126, 127, 253, 254, 255, 272
1:16, 17	131
1:16b	127
1:17	125, 126, 255, 271n25
1:17a	253, 271n25
1:17a-b	271n25
1:17b	253
1:17b-c	271n25
1:17c	253, 271n25
1:18	66, 127, 128, 128n4, 177, 249, 250, 252, 255
1:18, 20	128, 255
1:18—2:23	185
1:18—2:33	177
1:18-25	248n5, 251, 254
1:18b	254
1:18c	255
1:19	58, 128, 252, 252n16, 254, 255, 269n14
1:19a	255
1:19b	255
1:19c	255
1:20	34n28, 58, 126, 127, 128, 177, 250, 255
1:20, 24	58, 250n8
1:20-21	260
1:20a	255
1:20b	255
1:20c	255
1:20c-21	255
1:21	69, 71n31, 72, 79, 79n52, 83, 117, 131, 134, 136, 255, 272
1:21, 23, 25	250
1:21, 25	255
1:21b	255, 272
1:21c	255
1:22	67n16, 200, 200n7
1:22-23	131
1:23	127, 128, 249, 256, 257, 282
1:24	58
1:24-25a	255
1:24b-25a	127
1:25	128
1:25b	255
1:29-30	257n21
1:29-34	257n21
2:1	30, 31, 32, 58, 101, 129, 177, 178, 250
2:1, 2, 4	129
2:1, 2, 9	271
2:1, 3	31n24, 270
2:1, 3, 9	34, 88n20, 129
2:1, 5, 6	272
2:1, 5, 6, 8, 16	270
2:1, 5, 6a, 6b, 22	270
2:1, 9	132
2:1, DJW	269
2:1-2	31, 33
2:1-2, 7-8, 16	101
2:1-2a	30
2:1-6	75, 78
2:1-12	xix, 126, 131, 248n4, 256

Scripture Index 303

2:1–22	256
2:1–23	xix, 28, 30, 35, 45n3, 46, 86, 87, 87n2, 89, 91, 101, 111, 117, 126, 129, 129n8, 180, 183, 185, 224, 248n5, 251, 256, 263, 269, 283
2:1–52	248n3
2:2	31n24, 32, 33, 60, 76, 129, 129n7, 130, 131, 132, 178, 227, 232, 246, 250, 263, 269, 270, 272
2:2, 9, 10	129
2:2, 11	32, 60, 129, 132
2:2a	30
2:3	31, 33, 111, 130, 131, 232, 244
2:3, 22	130
2:3, TNIV	98
2:3–6	75
2:3–6, 7–9a	273
2:3–8	76
2:3–8, 13, 16–17, 20	269
2:3a, TNIV	98
2:3b	98
2:4	31, 32, 67n5, 67n6, 75, 76, 87n9, 87n10, 91n34, 91n35, 101n54, 101n55, 129n7, 177, 269n18, 270n19
2:4, 7	31, 111, 129
2:4, 7–8, 13, 16, 20	101n52
2:4, 7–8, 16	273
2:4–5	31
2:4–5, 7–9	244
2:4–6	80, 88, 101, 131
2:4–6, 7	129
2:4–8	232
2:4a	91
2:4b-6	91
2:5	200, 250, 272
2:5, 15, 17, 23	67n16
2:5–6	31, 75n42
2:5–6, 15, 17–18, 23	131
2:5–10, 11a	177
2:6	32, 80, 129, 129n7, 129n8, 131, 132, 135, 177, 178, 270
2:6, 20, 21	270
2:6b	69n27
2:7	31, 33, 91n34, 91n35, 99, 101, 227
2:7, 12, 13, 15, 16, 19, 22	30
2:7, 16	101n55
2:7–8	31, 227, 233
2:7–8, 13, 16–18, 20	31
2:7–8, 13, 20	244, 246
2:7–8, 16	31n24
2:7a	91
2:7b, 16c	91
2:8	31, 32, 33, 34, 91, 91n36, 99, 101n55, 114, 115, 132, 269, 272
2:8, 9, 11, 13, 14, 20, 21	32, 34, 129, 130
2:8, 9, 11, 13a, 13b, 14	272
2:8, 13, 14, 16, 20, 21	269
2:8, 16	111
2:8, 16, 20, 22	273
2:8–9, 16	130
2:9	31, 32, 91, 99
2:9–11	31, 99
2:9a	31
2:9b	31
2:11	32, 129
2:11, 13, 14, 18, 20, 21	250n9
2:11, 13, 14, 20, 21	256
2:11b	256
2:12	34, 58, 70n28, 99, 115, 233, 243, 271
2:12, 13, 19–20, 22	179, 260
2:12, 13, 22	112, 243
2:12, 13–14	245
2:12, 13–15, 19–22	130
2:12, 14, 21, 22	58
2:12, 22	58, 273
2:13	31, 33, 34, 34n28, 70n28, 99, 101, 112, 115, 116, 118, 227, 230, 243, 256, 269, 271, 273

Scripture Index

Matthew (*continued*)

2:13, 14	33, 129
2:13, 14, 15, 19	271
2:13, 16	232
2:13, 16, 20	273
2:13, 16–18, 20	132
2:13, 19	58, 273
2:13, 19–20, 22	58
2:13, 20	129, 130, 132, 178
2:13, 22	243
2:13, DJW	272
2:13–14, 19–21	252
2:13–15a, 20–21	256
2:13–15	252, 271
2:13–15, 19–23	224, 256
2:13–18	98
2:13–23	xxi, 119, 134, 242, 244, 256
2:13a	234
2:13a, 14	34
2:13b	34, 234
2:14–15	32
2:15	32, 33, 60, 129, 177, 178, 200, 272
2:15, 17, 23	200n7
2:15, 19, 20	34, 130, 179, 273
2:15–18	224
2:16	31, 31n25, 32, 33, 46, 47, 52n22, 88n23, 91, 91n36, 99, 111, 112, 114, 115, 117, 119, 130, 132, 225n8, 230, 230n28, 233, 252, 256n18, 273
2:16, 20	45n4
2:16–18	31, 132, 178, 179, 256n18
2:16a	98
2:16b	98, 102, 273
2:16c	108
2:17	256n18
2:17–18	115, 117, 252
2:18	236, 256n18, 270
2:19	34n28, 112, 116, 246
2:19, 20	112, 118
2:19, 20b	34
2:19–20	245
2:19–21, 22	245
2:19–23	112
2:20	31, 33, 34, 99, 101, 112, 116, 230, 269, 271
2:20, 21	33, 129, 270
2:20–11a	256
2:20a	34
2:20b	34, 272
2:21–23	116, 179
2:22	31n23, 34, 34n28, 129, 234n38, 242, 252, 263, 271, 273
2:22–23	34, 130, 252, 272
2:22a	34, 242n60
2:22a–b	256
2:22b	242n60
2:22b–23	34
2:23	32, 32n26, 118, 246, 251, 270, 272, 273
2:23a	272
2:36–38	248n3
2:111	32
3:1	203, 203n16, 269, 270
3:1, 3	270
3:1, 5	270
3:1–2	256
3:1—4:15	252
3:1–12	14, 269
3:1–17	177
3:1–23	112
3:1—25:46	257
3:2	79n55, 86n1, 203, 207, 217, 262, 277, 283
3:2, 7–10	80n55
3:2, 7–12	184
3:3	67n16, 184, 200n7, 203
3:5	203, 270
3:5, 6	269
3:5–6	204
3:6	79n52, 203
3:6, 7, 11	203n17
3:6, 7, 11, 13, 14, 16	203n15
3:6, 13	203, 270
3:7	67n3, 67n4, 75n41, 87n6, 87n7, 203,

Scripture Index 305

	204n22, 269n16, 269n17	4:8–9	6, 63, 275, 282
		4:8–10	282
3:7, 11	204n22	4:8–10, DJW	279
3:7–12	203	4:9	177, 270, 271, 273
3:7a	269	4:10	6, 270, 273, 275
3:7b	269	4:10–11	5n6
3:8	204, 204n22, 206	4:10–11a	177
3:9	126n2, 131, 177, 204	4:10a	63
3:9, DJW	66, 253	4:11	6
3:10, 12	184	4:11a	63, 273
3:10–12	204	4:11b	177, 273
3:11	203	4:12	14, 106n68, 183, 205, 224n3, 227, 246, 263
3:11–12	206		
3:11b	177	4:12–15, 18, 23, 25	270
3:11d	177	4:12–16	177
3:13	206, 270	4:12a	181
3:13, 14, 16	203n17	4:13	270, 270n22, 279
3:13–16a	177, 206	4:13, 15	270
3:13–17	246	4:14	67n16, 200n7, 272
3:14	269	4:15	135, 270, 270n22, 272
3:14–15	272		
3:15	58, 77, 77n48, 178, 269, 270	4:15, 25	271
		4:16	82
3:16	246, 270	4:17	46, 79n55, 177, 183, 207, 217, 262, 277, 279, 280, 283
3:16–17	6, 272, 280		
3:16b	177, 206		
3:16c	206	4:17, 23	86n1, 159
3:17	60, 63, 101n53, 104, 133, 135n13, 177, 178, 206, 215, 246, 270, 274, 282	4:17 et al.	63
		4:18	270
		4:18–22	160, 177, 259
		4:18–22, 23–25	280
3:17b	64	4:19	216, 217, 219
4:1	5, 177, 270	4:19a, 21	274
4:1—7:29	274	4:19b, DJW	274
4:1–11	62, 178, 273	4:20, 22	219, 259
4:1–42	248n4	4:20–22	274, 276
4:2	270	4:23	xxii, 67n8, 82, 184, 207, 208, 208n37, 218n87, 262, 279
4:2, 5, 8, 11	270		
4:2, 6, 9	273		
4:3	6, 11, 270, 273	4:23, 24	208n36
4:3, 5–6, 8–9	134	4:23, DJW	272, 274
4:3, 6	5, 60n40, 63, 133, 135n13, 177	4:23–25	177, 199n1
		4:24	8n13, 9n20, 12, 12n27, 12n28, 208, 208n34, 208n35, 208n38, 208n39, 210, 211n59, 271, 272, 274
4:4, 7, 10	6, 177		
4:5	67n9, 74, 79, 81, 263		
4:5–6	6, 74, 270		
4:6	270		
4:8	86n1, 179, 270, 271		
4:8, DJW	270, 273		

Matthew (continued)

4:25	112n95, 210n51, 210n52, 270, 272, 274
4:38–42	142
5:1	112n95, 160n79, 163, 207, 210n50, 274, 279
5:1–2	160, 258, 274, 282
5:1—7:27	207n29
5:1—7:29	158, 178, 262, 264, 279, 280
5:1–12	64, 264
5:1a	178, 262, 274
5:1b	274
5:1b–2	262
5:2	163, 274
5:2–12	275
5:3	179, 275
5:3, 10	162, 277
5:3, 10, 19, 20	86n1, 161, 262
5:3—7:27	275
5:3–12	178, 179, 262, 274, 276, 278
5:3a, 4a, 5a, 6a, 7a, 8a, 9a, 10a, 11	276
5:3b, 10b	276
5:4	162, 275
5:4b	276
5:4b, 5b, 6b, 7b, 8b, 9b	276
5:5	xxi, 162, 179, 262, 263, 264, 268, 270, 271, 274, 275, 278, 281, 283
5:5b	276
5:6	162, 179, 275
5:6b	276
5:7	162, 179, 210, 275
5:7b	276
5:8	162, 179, 275
5:8b	276
5:9	162, 179, 199, 199n2, 240, 240n55, 245, 246, 247, 275
5:10	58n36, 179, 183, 231, 245, 275
5:10, 11, 12	108n86
5:10, 11, 12, 44	218n88
5:10, 11, 44	225n9
5:10, 11b, 44b	276
5:10–11	118
5:10–12	180, 181
5:10–12, 38–42, 43–48	224n5
5:11	58, 160, 161, 164n84, 183, 218, 226n12, 226n13, 232, 245, 245n67, 274n30, 281
5:11, 39, 45	269n15
5:11, 44	161
5:11–12	165n88, 179, 221, 237
5:11a	276
5:11b, 44	276
5:11c	276
5:11c, DJW	276
5:12	67n15, 118, 162, 181, 183, 184, 201, 217n85, 224, 225n6, 225n8, 238, 245, 245n67, 277
5:12a	276
5:12b	183, 276
5:13	160, 217, 277n50, 278
5:13–14	278
5:13–16	178
5:14	160, 217, 278
5:15	217, 251
5:15c	278
5:16	193, 275, 278
5:16, 19	161
5:16, 45, 48	160, 162
5:16a	278
5:16b	278
5:17	67n12, 159, 160, 174, 178, 200n8, 207
5:17–20	159, 198
5:17–20, 21–48	275
5:18	67n12, 159, 277n50
5:19	67n13, 159
5:19a	160
5:19b	160
5:20	58, 67n3, 87n6, 87n10, 159, 160, 161,

Scripture Index 307

	162, 183, 269n16, 269n18, 275	5:38, 39a	146n45
5:20a	175	5:38, 40	226
5:21	179	5:38–39	226
5:21, 27, 33, 38, 43	208n32	5:38–39a	145, 146n45, 164n83
5:21–22, 27–28, 31–34, 38–39, 43–44	161n80	5:38–42	xix, 13n29, 137, 137n1, 141, 143, 144, 145, 146, 146n45, 146n46, 158, 160, 162, 179, 220n92, 239, 239n50
5:21–26	179		
5:21–26, 27–30, 31–32, 33–37, 38–42, 43–48	160, 178		
5:21–32	179	5:38–42, 43–48	179
5:21–37	181	5:38–48	xix, 137n2, 141, 175, 176, 177, 178, 179, 181n11, 183, 186, 242
5:21–48	160, 174		
5:22	161, 275		
5:22, 23, 24, 47	161		
5:22, 28, 32, 34, 39, 44	208	5:38–49	198
5:22–26	179	5:38a	162, 163
5:23, 24	72n35, 74, 79	5:38b	162, 164n84
5:23–24	68, 70, 72	5:39	xvii, 23, 48, 121, 138, 164, 181n10, 220, 239n49, 276
5:25	74, 161, 226, 228, 228n21, 228n24, 240n54		
		5:39, 40, 41, 42	220
5:25, 38, 39	225n7	5:39, 44	239
5:25a	276	5:39, 45a	276
5:25b	276	5:39, DJW	19
5:25c	276	5:39 DJW	4, 163, 218
5:27	179	5:39–39a	166n92
5:27–30	179	5:39–41	142
5:28	251, 258	5:39–42	143, 144
5:28–30	179	5:39a	138, 140n13, 146, 146n44, 161, 162, 163, 164n84, 169, 169n100, 171, 172, 173, 181, 239, 240
5:29	162		
5:30	162		
5:31	179, 208n32, 252, 258		
		5:39a, 44, 48	173
5:31, 32	250, 250n8	5:39a, DJW	175
5:32	179, 250, 258	5:39b	165n89, 167n93, 170, 179, 181
5:32a	258		
5:32b	258	5:39b, 40, 41, 42a, 42b	181
5:33	161n80, 179	5:39b–40	162
5:33–37	146n45, 179	5:39b-41	239
5:34	161	5:39b–42	162, 164n84, 164n85, 169, 170n103, 171, 171n106, 172, 172n109
5:34–37	179		
5:35	162		
5:36b–41	239n51		
5:37	139n11, 164n84, 269n15, 270		
		5:39c	165
5:38	137, 144, 145n43, 163, 181, 226, 226n16, 229	5:39c–42	165

Matthew (continued)

5:40	138, 163, 165, 166, 167n93, 170, 181, 218, 220, 276
5:40a	180
5:41	47, 64, 92, 138, 163, 165, 166, 166n92, 167n93, 170, 172n108, 181, 218, 220, 229, 263, 276
5:41–42	162
5:41a	180
5:42	138, 163, 170, 220, 239, 239n51
5:42a	165, 166, 180, 181, 275
5:42a–b	165, 166, 167n93
5:42b	165, 166, 180, 181, 275
5:43	173, 226n11, 240
5:43, 44	226n10
5:43–44	180
5:43–44, DJW	182
5:43–48	173, 179
5:43b	181
5:44	121, 161, 173, 218, 220, 240, 247
5:44a	173, 175, 276
5:44b	175
5:45	162, 164n84, 246, 269n14, 275
5:45, 48, DJW	240
5:45a	64, 183
5:45a, 48	183
5:45b	64, 183, 240, 276
5:45b–c	183
5:46	45n3, 50, 50n20, 89n26, 161, 162
5:46, 47	250, 263
5:46–47	183
5:47	161
5:48	162, 173, 188, 246
5:48a	183
5:389b–42	164n83
6:1	92n37
6:1, 2, 3, 4	210n46
6:1, 2, 5, 14, 15, 16, 18	161
6:1, 2, 5, 16	162
6:1, 4, 6, 8, 9, 14, 15, 18, 26, 32	160–161, 162
6:1, DJW	112
6:1—28:20	177, 183
6:2	92n38, 93
6:2, 3, 4	275
6:2, 5	67n8
6:2, 5, 16	110n93, 210n49
6:2a	112
6:2b, 5b, 16b	112
6:5	93
6:5, 16	92n37
6:5a	112
6:7	161
6:10	277n50
6:10, 13, 33	86n1
6:10, 33	161, 262
6:10a	277
6:10a–b	277
6:10b	243, 277
6:12, 14, 15	79n53, 209
6:13	7, 139n11, 164n84, 269n15, 270
6:16	93
6:16a	112
6:18	77
6:20	67n5
6:23	90n33, 269n15
6:25, 31	251
6:28	251
6:32	161
6:33	58, 269n14, 275
7:3, 4, 5	161
7:5	110n93
7:11	164n85
7:11, 17, 18	269n15
7:11, 21	162
7:12	67n12, 161, 200n8
7:17–18	64
7:20	44n1, 65
7:21	86n1, 161, 262
7:22	10n22
7:24	159, 160
7:24–27	159
7:26	159, 160

7:28	112, 160n79, 208, 210n50, 211n54, 213n67
7:28–29	160n79, 262, 274
7:28a	274
7:28b	274
7:29	53n25, 67n5, 67n17, 87n10, 110, 112, 161, 208, 269n18
8:1	112n95, 279
8:1–4	64n47, 68, 70, 279
8:1–4, 5–13, 14–15, 16–17, 28–34	218n87
8:1—9:35	279, 280
8:1—28:20	264
8:2	53n24, 133, 208
8:4	67n6, 70, 72n35
8:5	52, 70n29, 279
8:5, 8, 13	46n9
8:5, 13	88n22, 88n26
8:5–6	279
8:5–13	12, 45, 46, 52, 87n3, 91, 135n14
8:5–13 et al.	63
8:6	52, 64, 208, 208n39
8:6, 8	53, 60, 65
8:6, 8, 13	52
8:8–9	65
8:8a	53
8:8b	53
8:8c	53
8:9	46, 48, 53n25, 54, 88n23, 92, 209
8:9a	52, 53
8:9b	52, 53
8:10	52, 53, 135
8:10, 13	54, 60, 65
8:10–11a	279
8:10–13	135
8:11	53, 65, 135
8:11, 12	86n1
8:11–12	60n42
8:12	53, 136
8:13	53, 135, 279
8:13a	53
8:14	208, 249
8:14–15	251n15, 257
8:14–15a	259
8:15	251, 259
8:15b	259
8:16	9, 12n27, 208n34, 208n35
8:16, 28, 33	8n13, 208n38
8:16, 31	208n38
8:16–17	9n20
8:17	67n16, 200n7, 208, 208n36
8:18	112n95
8:19	67n5, 87n10, 269n18
8:22	216, 219
8:24, 26, 27, 32	279
8:25	82
8:26	209
8:27	209, 211n53
8:28	211n60, 279
8:28–34	9n15, 10, 212n63, 279
8:29	60n40, 133, 135n13, 207n25
8:31, 34	52n23
8:34	211n60, 212n63
9:1	279
9:1–8, 18–19, 20–22, 23–26, 27–31, 32–34	218n87
9:2	212
9:2, 5	82, 207
9:2, 5, 6	79n52, 79n53
9:2, 6	208n39
9:2, 22, 29	64
9:2–8	67n17
9:2–8, 9–13, 32–34	64n48
9:2–8, 10–13	114n97
9:2–8, 27–31	64n47
9:3	67n5, 87n10, 207, 212, 269n18
9:4	96, 164n84, 269n15
9:6	53n25, 212
9:8	53n25, 97, 112, 207, 211, 211n57
9:8, 33	210n50
9:9	47, 51, 160, 216, 219, 259
9:9, 10, 11, 12, 13	45n3, 89n26
9:9–13	50
9:10, 11	50n20, 263
9:10–11	211, 212

Matthew (continued)

9:10–13	67n17, 96, 96n48
9:11	97, 204n21, 250
9:11, 14, 34	67n3, 87n6, 269n16
9:12	50n20
9:13	50n20, 82, 110, 119, 207, 210, 269n14
9:14	114, 204, 211, 211n62
9:15	226, 236
9:18	208, 249, 257
9:18–19, 23–26	257
9:18–26	251n15, 279
9:20	208, 251, 257
9:21	257
9:21, 22	82
9:22	257, 259
9:23, 25	211
9:23b–24	257
9:24	211, 212, 257
9:25a	257
9:25b	257
9:26	211n59
9:27	133, 135n10, 210n45
9:27, 28	208n40
9:28	53n24, 133
9:31	211n59
9:32	8n13
9:32, 33	208n41
9:32, 33, 34	208n38
9:32–34	9n16, 96
9:33	112, 211, 211n53
9:33, 34	208n38
9:34	97, 209n43, 212, 219n91
9:35	xxii, 12n28, 67n8, 82, 86n1, 159, 184, 199n1, 207, 208, 208n36, 208n37, 216, 218n87, 262, 279
9:35—11:1	158n77, 199n1, 279
9:36	69n27, 80, 82, 110, 112n95, 119, 209
9:37, 38	217
9:38	184, 216
10	xiv
10:1	10, 12, 53n25, 209, 216, 218, 282
10:1, DJW	279
10:1–4	259
10:1–42	208n30
10:2	216n82
10:2–3	50
10:3	45n3, 89n26, 263
10:4	15, 57n34, 79n54, 227n20
10:5	217
10:5, 16	184, 200n5, 216n82
10:5–6	135
10:5–15	282
10:5a, 6	217
10:5b–6	279
10:5b–42	217n84
10:6	135, 206, 215, 216n83, 258, 279, 281
10:6, 23	220, 221
10:7	86n1, 217, 231, 242, 262, 277, 279, 283
10:7, 27	217
10:7–8, 12–13	184
10:8	209
10:8, DJW	279
10:8a	218
10:8b	184, 218
10:10	217
10:12	199
10:12, 13	217
10:13	199, 199n2, 218, 220
10:13b	185, 199
10:14	185, 217, 218, 220, 220n93, 221, 221n95
10:14b	185
10:15	210, 220n93
10:16	185, 219, 220, 221, 231n34, 234, 244, 281
10:16, DJW	226, 231
10:16–23	118, 260
10:16–31	276n49
10:16–39	182, 218, 224n5
10:16a	242
10:16b	185, 242

Scripture Index 311

10:17	67n8, 107, 107n79, 218, 220, 229, 262, 281
10:17, 19	106n68, 218
10:17, 19, 21	228n21, 281
10:17–18	225n8, 237
10:17–19, 21–33	222
10:17–19a, 21–22a, DJW	17
10:17–20	221
10:17a	185, 242
10:17a, 19a, 21a	185
10:17b	185
10:18	45n3, 49, 49n13, 49n15, 88n20, 88n21, 106n66, 108n81, 135, 217, 218, 228, 232, 281, 282
10:18, DJW	281
10:18a	185
10:19	215n77, 221, 237
10:19, 20	217n86
10:19–20	183n15, 240, 246
10:19a	185
10:19b–20	237
10:20	221
10:21	218, 219, 230, 281
10:21, DJW	227
10:21–22	225n7
10:21a	235
10:21b	185
10:22	5n8, 58, 218, 221, 226n11, 232, 235, 246, 281
10:22a	185
10:22b	185, 241n58
10:23	108n86, 185, 215n80, 218n88, 221, 221n94, 225n9, 242, 276n49, 281
10:23a	185, 225n6, 234, 234n39
10:23b	235n39
10:24–25	219
10:25	97, 218, 232, 237, 238
10:25, 28a, 31	237
10:25, DJW	226n14
10:25b	185
10:26	237
10:26, 28, 31	221, 276n49
10:26, 28a, 31	237
10:26a, 28a, 31a, DJW	185
10:27	217n86, 221, 237
10:27–30	281
10:27a	238
10:27a, DJW	185
10:27b	238
10:28	219n89, 230n28, 237, 238, 281
10:28a	185
10:29	246
10:29–31	237, 246
10:32	221, 238, 239n47
10:32–33	216
10:32a	185
10:33	239n47
10:34	199n2, 207, 226
10:34–35	219
10:34–36	207
10:34a–b	199
10:35	218, 226, 249, 250
10:35, 37	249, 250, 250n9
10:35, DJW	226
10:35a–36	259
10:35b–c	259
10:36	218, 219, 226n10
10:38	108n85, 212, 219, 219n90, 230, 230n31, 259, 281
10:38–42	248n3
10:39	43, 218, 219, 221, 230
10:39b	185
10:40	200n4, 206, 241
10:41	67n15, 217, 217n85, 269n14
10:41–42	221
10:42	217
11:1	159, 184, 199n1, 207, 213n67, 262
11:1–45	248n4
11:2	14n31, 106n69, 133, 135n11, 205, 228n24
11:2–5	181n12
11:2–6	5n10, 205

Matthew (continued)

11:2–7	211n62
11:2–19	224n3
11:3	133, 135, 203, 205
11:5	184, 208, 208n40, 208n41, 208n42
11:6	181n12, 239n49
11:7–15	177
11:8	88n20, 90
11:8a–b	90
11:9	204, 206
11:9, 13	67n15
11:10	184, 200, 203, 205
11:11	206, 246, 250
11:11, 12	86n1, 203n16
11:12	xx, 108, 109n88, 184, 205, 223, 224, 225n6, 244, 246
11:13	67n12, 200n7, 200n8, 203n13
11:14	204, 204n20
11:14b	184
11:16	211
11:16–19	212
11:18	204, 204n21, 205, 207
11:19	45n3, 50, 50n20, 89n26, 204n21, 207, 207n26, 211, 212, 250, 263
11:20	133, 211, 212
11:20, 21	79n55, 216n81
11:20, 21, 23	12n26, 207n27, 208n33, 213n68, 216n81
11:20–24	216n81
11:21	210, 216n81, 279
11:21, 23	133
11:22, 24	216n81
11:23	216n81, 279
11:25	277, 278
12:1–8	96, 97
12:1–8, 9–14	67n17, 208n31
12:1–8, 9–14, 22–37, 38–45	114n97
12:1–8, 9–14, 38–42	96n48
12:2, 4, 10, 12	67n14, 94n42
12:2, 10	75n43, 211
12:2, 14, 24, 38	67n3, 87n6, 269n16
12:3	135n10
12:3, 5	75n42
12:3–5	68, 70
12:4	67n9, 69, 70
12:4, 5	67n6
12:5	67n12, 71
12:5, 6	67n9
12:6	74, 79
12:7	82, 110, 119, 210
12:9	67n8
12:9–12	233
12:9–14	16, 87n4, 97, 102, 280
12:9–14, 22–32, 38–42	64n48
12:10	96, 208, 228
12:13	231, 233
12:14	67n18, 76n45, 100, 100n51, 102, 116, 212, 224n4, 227, 227n18, 230, 231, 235, 245, 280
12:15	12n27, 112n95, 208n34, 210n51, 210n52, 235
12:17	67n16, 200n7
12:18	52, 135
12:21	135
12:22	8n13, 208n40, 208n41
12:22, 24, 27, 28	208n38
12:22–24	9n16, 96
12:23	112, 133, 135n10, 210n50, 211, 211n55
12:24	97, 204n21, 209n43, 210n49, 212
12:24, 26, 27, 28	208n38
12:24, 27	219n91
12:25, 26	86n1
12:28	5n10, 8, 86n1, 207
12:29	9, 134
12:31	79n52
12:31, 32	79n53
12:32	277
12:34	210n49
12:34, 35, 39, 45	269n15
12:35	64, 164n84

Scripture Index 313

12:38	67n5, 87n10, 211, 269n18	13:54–58	251
12:38–42	96, 200n7	13:55	250n9
12:39	67n15, 200, 200n7, 200n9, 211	13:56	249
12:40	200n9	13:57	67n15, 201, 212
12:40, 41	200n7	13:58	118, 133, 207n27, 212
12:41	79n55, 200n7, 280	14:1	35, 88n20, 211n59
12:42	207n26, 251, 259, 280	14:1, 3	204
12:46, 47, 48, 49, 50	250n9	14:1–2	35, 36, 38, 118, 207, 207n28, 245
12:46–50	161, 251	14:1–2, 3–4	245
12:49	259	14:1–11	117
12:50	249, 259	14:1–12	xvi, 14, 14n32, 28, 35, 46, 87n3, 90, 90n28, 91, 95, 111, 112, 113, 117, 119, 121, 181, 205, 224n3, 244, 263, 283
13:1	279		
13:1–2	207		
13:1–12	45n3, 205n23		
13:1–35	207n29		
13:1–53	158n77	14:2	12n26, 35, 37, 38, 52, 133, 207n27, 208n33, 211, 213n68
13:2	210, 210n51		
13:10–17	248n3		
13:11	212	14:2, 8	203n16
13:11, 19, 24, 31, 33, 38, 41, 43, 44, 45, 47, 52	86n1	14:2–3, 8–11	231
		14:3	14n31, 35, 36, 37, 47, 106n65, 107n71, 205, 228, 228n22, 250n8
13:15	211, 212		
13:17	67n15, 200		
13:17, 43, 49	269n14		
13:19, 38	139n11, 164n84, 269n15, 270	14:3, 4, 6, 8, 11	111
		14:3, 4, 8	37
13:21	225n9, 226, 235n42	14:3, 5	238
13:33	251, 259	14:3, 6	35
13:35	12n27, 67n16, 200n7	14:3, 10	45n4, 106n69, 205, 228n24
13:36	207		
13:36–52	208n30	14:3–4	14, 56, 77, 77n48, 184
13:37	280		
13:38	280	14:3–4, 6–8, 11	251
13:39	270	14:3–5a	95
13:39, 40, 49	5n9	14:3–12	35, 36, 37, 38, 118
13:49	269n15	14:3a	35, 38
13:52	67n5, 269n18	14:3b	38
13:53	213n67	14:3b–4	35
13:54	67n8, 133, 207, 207n26, 207n27, 208, 209, 211, 211n54, 211n58, 279	14:4	36, 37, 38, 67n14, 94n42, 184, 204, 231, 238, 238n45, 250
		14:4b	38
13:54, 58	12n26, 208n33, 213n68	14:5	36, 38, 108n81, 204, 205, 230n28, 232, 245
13:54–56	211		

Matthew (continued)

14:5–12	77n48
14:5a	35, 37, 67n15
14:5a–b	37
14:5b	35, 95
14:5b–c	37
14:5c	37
14:6	90, 111, 249, 250, 251
14:6, 7, 8, 9, 11	111
14:6, 9b	95
14:6–7	95
14:6–7, 8b, 11a	95
14:6–8	37
14:6–11	232, 245
14:7	35, 37, 90, 111
14:8	36, 101, 116, 251
14:8, 9, 11	230
14:8, 11	35, 108n84, 205, 250n9
14:8–11	184, 230
14:8a, 11b	95
14:9	35, 36, 88n20, 90, 90n31, 111, 205, 232, 232n36, 245
14:9–10	37
14:9–11	37, 111, 251
14:9a	35, 37, 95, 113
14:9a–b	37
14:9b	35, 95, 113
14:9b–10	37
14:9b–11	35
14:9c	91
14:9c–11	37
14:10	36, 38, 46, 47, 88n23, 91, 108n84, 205, 225n8, 230
14:10–11	35, 236
14:11	36, 205
14:11a	101
14:11b	101
14:12	36, 117, 205
14:13	112n95, 210n50, 210n52, 235, 235n40
14:13, 15	279
14:13–21	209, 257, 270, 279
14:14	112n95, 208, 208n34, 209, 210n51, 218
14:16	218
14:19–21	218
14:21	251n15, 257
14:23	235n40, 279
14:25	209
14:25, 26	279
14:27, 30	59
14:28	209
14:28, 30	53n24
14:29	209
14:30	82
14:32	209
14:33	59, 133, 135n13
14:34	279
14:34–36	64n47
14:35	208n35, 210
14:36	52n23
14:57–58	104n58
15:1	67n5, 87n10, 269n18
15:1, 12	67n3, 87n6, 269n16
15:1–2	211, 212
15:1–9	64n48, 67n17, 96, 96n48, 114n97
15:1–20	208n31
15:2	67n7, 87n8, 97, 270n20
15:3, 6	67n13
15:4	230n27
15:4, 5, 6	250n9
15:5	70, 72n35
15:7	110n93
15:8–10	248n3
15:19	269n15
15:21–27	280
15:21–28	9, 135n14
15:21–28, 29–31	64n47
15:22	8n13, 133, 135n10, 208n38, 210n45, 250
15:22, 23	257
15:22, 25, 27	53n24, 60
15:22, 28	249, 250
15:23	257
15:24	69n27, 135, 200n4, 206, 215, 217, 241, 258, 279, 280

15:24, 26	135, 257		230n28, 241, 246, 269n18, 270n19, 270n20, 280
15:25, 27	257		
15:26	258		
15:27	258	16:21–22	6, 184
15:27, 28	215n80	16:21–23	15n41, 87n4, 179, 184, 224n4
15:28	60, 64, 135, 259		
15:28, 30	135	16:22	134, 241, 242n59, 258n22
15:28a	258, 280		
15:28b	258, 280	16:22–23	133
15:28c	258	16:23	6, 117, 184, 241, 258n22, 280
15:29	279		
15:29–31, 32–39	135n14	16:24	108n85, 212, 219, 219n90, 230, 230n31, 259
15:29–39	135n14, 279		
15:30	12, 208n34, 210n51		
15:30, 31	208, 208n40, 208n41, 208n42	16:24–26	224n5
		16:24a	232
15:31	112, 210n50, 211, 211n53	16:24b	232
		16:25	22, 218, 219, 221, 230, 241n58
15:31–28	9n17		
15:32	135, 209, 218	16:27	216, 221
15:32–39	135, 209, 257, 270	16:28	216
15:33	279	16:41–50	211
15:36–38	218	17:1	212, 280
15:38	251n15	17:1, 9	279
15:39	279	17:1–8	246, 280
16:1	96, 211	17:2	61n44, 246
16:1, 6, 11, 12	67n3, 67n4, 75n41, 87n6, 87n7, 269n16, 269n17	17:5	60, 101n53, 104, 133, 135n13, 206, 215, 246, 282
16:1–4	64n48, 96, 96n48, 114n97	17:5b	64
		17:6, DJW	59
16:3	110n93	17:7	59
16:4	212, 269n15	17:9	215n78
16:4, 14	67n15	17:9, 23	214n75
16:13–20	280	17:9–12a	231
16:14	203n16, 204, 211	17:9–13	118, 181, 224n3, 263
16:16	59, 133, 135n13, 280	17:10	67n5, 87n10, 269n18
16:16, 20	135n11	17:10, 11, 12	204n20
16:19, 28	86n1	17:10–13	14n32, 177, 204
16:20	133	17:11	204
16:21	67n5, 67n6, 67n7, 67n19, 75, 78, 87n8, 87n9, 87n10, 108n81, 109n88, 116, 117, 133, 181, 212, 212n65, 213, 214n75, 215n77, 215n78, 225n6,	17:12	109, 109n88, 184, 205, 206, 212, 225n6, 230
		17:12, 22–23	117, 225n6, 241n56
		17:12a	246
		17:12b	231, 246
		17:13	203n16

Matthew (continued)

17:14–20	9n18, 10, 10n22, 64n47, 279
17:15	53n24, 208, 208n35, 210n45
17:18	52n22, 208n38
17:19d	260
17:20–21	95
17:22	15, 57n34, 79n54, 106n68, 212n64, 227n20
17:22–23	116, 133, 181, 184, 280
17:23	67n19, 108n81, 212n65, 215n77, 215n78, 230n28, 246
17:24	279
17:24, 25	263
17:24–27	73, 77
17:25	49n13, 50, 89n27, 207, 263
17:25–26	45n3, 47, 89n26
17:40b, 42b	241n57
18:1, 3, 4, 23	86n1
18:1–4	179
18:1–8	248n3
18:1—19:1	158n77
18:1–35	208n30
18:7	210
18:11–15	45n3
18:15, 31	79n52
18:17	45n3, 50, 50n20, 89n26, 250, 263
18:20	282
18:21, 27, 32, 35	79n53
18:23–25	252
18:25	250n8
18:27	209
18:29, 32	52n23
18:32	269n15
18:33	210
19:1	213n67
19:2	112n95, 208n34, 210n51, 210n52
19:3	67n3, 67n14, 75n43, 87n6, 94n42, 96, 211, 252, 258, 269n16
19:3, 5, 8, 9, 10, 29	250n8
19:3, 7, 8	258
19:3, 7, 8, 9	250
19:3–9	96n48, 97, 208n31
19:4	75n42
19:5	250
19:5, 12, 19, 29	250n9
19:5–6a	258
19:6b	258
19:7, 8	252
19:8	258
19:9	250, 258
19:10	258
19:12	250
19:12, 14, 23, 24	86n1
19:13	251n15, 257n20
19:15	257n20
19:16–22	258
19:17	67n13
19:18	167
19:19	258
19:23a	96n47
19:25	208, 211n54
19:25–27	248n4
19:27	xxi, 160, 274, 276, 281
19:27–30	277
19:28	216, 221, 283
19:29	221, 249
20:1, 2, 4, 7, 8	88n16
20:1, 21	86n1
20:1–18	248n4
20:2	200n5
20:5–6	282
20:15	67n14, 94n42, 269n15
20:17	207, 213, 259
20:17–19	87n4, 181, 184, 225n6, 280
20:17–19, 22–23, 28	224n4
20:18	15, 57n34, 67n5, 67n6, 67n20, 75, 78, 79n54, 87n9, 87n10, 107, 212, 230, 269n18, 270n19
20:18, 19	106n68, 212n64, 227n20

Scripture Index 317

20:18-19	15n36, 89, 116, 117, 133	21:10	211n56
		21:11	112, 279
20:19	15, 47, 48, 49, 57n34, 78, 79n54, 107, 107n73, 107n79, 108n85, 212, 214n75, 215n78, 219, 228, 229, 230n30, 246	21:11, 46	67n15, 210n50, 211
		21:12	73, 74n39
		21:12, 14, 15, 23	67n9
		21:12-13	70, 72n35, 77, 97, 209
		21:13	67n9, 69, 72
		21:13a	70, 77
20:20	250n9, 259	21:13b	77
20:20, 21	250	21:14	12, 64n47, 74n39, 208n34, 208n40, 208n42, 210
20:20-21	251n15		
20:20-23	15n41		
20:20-28	62, 224n5	21:14-15, 46	112n96
20:22	212, 235	21:14-16	96
20:22, 23	219, 226, 241	21:14-16, 23-27	96n48, 114n97
20:22-23	226	21:15	52n22, 67n5, 70n28, 74n39, 75, 87n10, 133, 269n18
20:22a	242n59		
20:22b	242n59		
20:23	242n59	21:15, 23, 45	67n6, 74n39, 87n9, 270n19
20:24-28	179		
20:25	47, 49n15, 50, 53, 109, 119	21:15, 34, 41	67n3
		21:15-16	76, 211
20:25a	49, 49n13	21:16	75n42, 250, 251
20:25b	89	21:16, 42	75n42
20:25c	89	21:16a	70n28
20:26	259	21:19	209
20:26a	109	21:20	209
20:26b-28	109	21:23	67n7, 74n39, 75, 87n8, 113, 204n21, 209, 211, 270n20, 280
20:28	82, 207, 213, 216, 219, 226, 230, 259		
20:29	112n95, 210n51, 210n52	21:23, 24, 27	53n25, 97
		21:23—22:45	233
20:30	208n40	21:23-27	64n48, 67n17, 76, 96
20:30, 31	135n10, 210n45	21:23b	97
20:30, 31, 33	53n24	21:24, 27	209
20:30-31	133	21:24-25a	76, 94
20:34	209	21:25	113, 203n15, 204, 206
21:1, 10	213, 280		
21:1-4	248n3	21:25, 31, 32	205
21:4	67n16, 200n7	21:25, 32	64
21:5	135n12, 281	21:25b	94
21:5b	133	21:25b-26	94
21:8	210n51	21:25b-27a	76
21:9	112, 112n96, 133, 207, 210, 210n52	21:26	67n15, 94, 113, 204
		21:26, 46	94n40, 94n41
21:9, 14	281	21:27	94, 113
21:9, 15	135n10, 211		

Matthew (continued)

21:28	81, 88n16
21:28–31a	204
21:28–32	248n5
21:29, DJW	80n55
21:30	205
21:31, 32	45n3, 50n20, 89n26, 204n21, 250, 263
21:31, 43	60n42, 86n1
21:31–32	50, 204, 206, 250, 259
21:31b-32	204
21:32	80n55, 204, 212
21:32, 37–39	60n41
21:32a	184
21:33	87n13, 109, 212
21:33, 34, 35, 38, 40	87n12, 201n11
21:33, 39, 40, 41	88n15
21:33–36	181
21:33–37	219
21:33–44	94
21:33–46	16, 80, 87, 87n4, 89, 101, 121, 181, 184, 201, 227, 242
21:34	183, 201, 202, 231, 242, 280
21:34, 36	183, 200, 200n3, 201
21:34, 36, 37	202, 231n34, 234, 244n63
21:34–35	219
21:34–36	224
21:34–36a	184
21:35	107n78, 108, 108n82, 201, 229, 230, 231, 242
21:35, 36	202
21:35, 38, 39	108, 108n81, 230n28
21:35, 39	106n65, 228n22
21:36	201, 228n22, 229, 230, 230n28, 242
21:36–37	219
21:36a	202, 242
21:36b	202
21:37	200n4, 201, 202, 206, 212, 215, 241, 280
21:37, 38	59, 133, 135n13
21:38	78, 80, 82, 102, 105n60, 116, 118n102, 212, 233, 282
21:38, 39	67n19, 212n65, 227
21:38–39	76, 116, 202n12
21:38a	281
21:38b	281
21:39	116, 212, 227, 281
21:40	88n14, 201
21:41	81, 83, 109, 201, 201n11, 202, 263
21:41a	116
21:41b	116
21:42	75n42, 215
21:43	202
21:45	67n3, 74n39, 75, 76n44, 87n6, 94, 269n16, 280
21:45–46	113, 114, 245
21:46	106n65, 112, 116, 211, 212, 228n22
21:46a	94
21:46b	94
22:1–7	89
22:1–10	47n12, 121, 182
22:1–14	90, 224n5, 242
22:2	59, 86n1, 281
22:2, 42–45	133
22:2–3	60n41
22:2–4, 8–10	184
22:2–4a	218
22:3	100n51, 218, 281
22:3, 4	90n30, 184, 200n5, 216, 231n34, 234, 244n63, 281
22:3, 4, 8, 10	217
22:3, 9	217
22:3–4	231
22:3a	184
22:3a, 4	242
22:3b	242
22:4	90, 217n86
22:4b	218
22:5	218, 242
22:5–6	231
22:6	106n65, 107n74, 108, 108n81,

Scripture Index 319

		22:41–45	114
	185, 218, 219n89,	22:41–46	114n97
	228n22, 229,	22:42	135n11, 215
	230n28, 281	22:42, 43, 45	135n10
22:7	46, 47, 50, 51,	22:44	215
	64, 66n2, 81, 83,	22:46	114, 116, 233
	108, 202, 220n93,	22:46b	233
	231n32, 263	23:1	112n96
22:9	216n83	23:1–39	87n4, 121, 158n77,
22:10	164n84, 269n15		207n29
22:10, 11	90n31	23:2	109, 210n49
22:11, 12	90	23:2, 13, 14, 15, 23,	67n3
22:15	76n45, 96, 100,	25, 26, 27, 29	
	100n51, 101, 102,	23:2, 13, 14, 15, 23,	67n5
	116, 211, 233	25, 26, 27, 29, 34	
22:15, 34, 41	74n39, 87n6, 269n16	23:2, 13, 14, 15, 23,	269n16
22:15–18	51	25, 26, 27, 29	
22:15–22	45, 45n3, 47, 49n13,	23:2, 13, 14, 15, 23,	269n18
	62, 64, 89n26, 97	25, 26, 27, 29, 34	
22:15–22, 23–33,	64n48, 114n97	23:2, 13, 15, 23, 25,	87n6, 87n10
34–40		26, 27, 29	
22:15–22, 34–40	96n48	23:2–3a	88
22:16	74n39, 87n11, 208	23:3	119
22:17	67n14, 75n43, 94n42	23:3a	110
22:17, 19	50, 263	23:3b	110
22:17, 21	88n19	23:3c	110
22:18	96, 110n93	23:5	92n37, 93
22:19	51	23:5–7	119
22:19–21	50	23:5b	90
22:19–21a	63	23:6	90
22:20	51	23:6, 34	67n8
22:21a	51	23:6a	93
22:21b	63, 64, 89	23:6b	93
22:22	208, 211n53, 233	23:7a	93
22:23, 34	67n4, 74n39, 75n41,	23:7b	93
	87n7, 269n17	23:8, 10	133, 135n11
22:23–28	75n43, 250	23:9–13	182
22:24, 25, 28	250n8	23:9a, 10	185
22:24–28	211, 252	23:13	86n1
22:31	75n42	23:13, 14, 15, 23, 25,	110n93
22:33	112, 208, 210n50,	27, 29	
	211n54	23:13, 15, 23, 25, 27,	210n48
22:34	233	29	
22:34–36	75n43	23:13–36	64
22:35	96, 211	23:16, 17, 21, 35	67n9
22:35–36	97, 233	23:16, 18	75n43, 210
22:36	67n12	23:16–17	74
22:36, 38, 40	67n13	23:16–22	74
22:40	67n12, 200n8		

Matthew (continued)

23:17	74
23:18, 19	72n35
23:18, 19, 20	72n35
23:18, 19, 20, 35	74, 79
23:18–20	70
23:18–20, 35	72
23:20–22	235
23:21	69, 71, 74, 79
23:23	67n12, 110, 119, 210
23:23–24	75n43
23:25	231
23:26–31	248n3
23:27	93
23:27, 28	92n37
23:28	93
23:29	201
23:29, 30, 31	183, 184
23:29, 30, 31, 37	67n15
23:29, 35	269n14
23:29–31	181
23:29–31, 35	118
23:29–39	224n5
23:30	109n89, 201, 229
23:30, 44	215n80
23:31	108, 201
23:31, 35	230
23:34	67n15, 107, 107n79, 108n85, 108n86, 200n5, 217, 217n85, 218, 218n88, 219, 222, 225n9, 229, 230n30, 234, 281
23:34, 37	108n81, 118, 184, 216n82, 219n89, 230n28, 244n63
23:34, DJW	242
23:34–36	180, 181, 182
23:34a	184
23:34b	185
23:35	73n36, 108, 109n90, 111, 201, 203n13, 224, 226, 230, 230n29, 231
23:37	60n41, 67n15, 67n19, 108n82, 185, 200, 200n3, 200n6, 201, 202, 212, 217n85, 219, 224, 230, 231n34, 280
23:37–38	47n12
23:38	51, 66n2, 67n9, 74, 83, 220n93, 231n32
23:39	207, 215n80
24:1	67n9, 74, 74n39, 220n93
24:1–2	47n12, 66n2, 79, 82, 89, 202
24:1—25:46	208n30
24:1—26:1	158n77
24:1–31	224n5
24:2	51, 74, 81, 83, 220n93, 263
24:3	5n9, 135
24:3, 6, 13, 14	230
24:3, 27, 37, 39	xxi
24:3, 30	135
24:4–29	231
24:5, 23	133
24:6	5n8, 230, 237
24:6, 7	225
24:6–8	237
24:7	86n1, 231
24:9	58, 106n68, 108n81, 219n89, 230n28, 232, 235, 281
24:9, 10	218, 219, 226n11, 281
24:9, 14	115n99
24:9, 21, 29	226
24:9–10	239
24:9–14	17, 118
24:9–22	260
24:9a	185, 235
24:9b	235
24:9b, 10	185
24:10	228n21, 235, 281
24:13	5n8, 185, 221, 235, 241n58, 246
24:14	xxii, 86n1, 115n100, 135, 217, 221, 221n94, 237, 283
24:14a	239
24:14a, DJW	281, 282
24:14b	239

Scripture Index 321

24:15	67n16, 200n7, 231	26:2, 15, 16, 21, 23, 24, 25, 45, 46, 48	57n34, 106n68, 227n20
24:15–16	235	26:2, 15, 16, 21, 23, 24, 45, 46, 48	79n54
24:15–22	242, 252	26:2, 17, 18, 19	67n10, 72n35
24:16	231, 252	26:2, 21, 24, 45, 46	212n64
24:17–18	259	26:3	75, 76
24:17–20	231	26:3, 14, 47, 51, 57, 58, 59, 62, 63, 65	67n6, 87n9, 270n19
24:19	210n47, 250, 251, 252, 259	26:3, 47	54
24:20	252	26:3, 47, 57	75
24:20–21	235	26:3, 47, 57, 59	67n7, 87n8, 270n20
24:21, 29	224, 231	26:3, 51, 57, 58, 62, 63, 65	54
24:22	231	26:3, 57	67n5, 74, 75, 76, 87n10, 269n18
24:23, 26b	242	26:3, 58, 69	74
24:24a	243	26:3–4, 57–59	101n54
24:24b	243	26:3–4, 59, 65–66	55
24:24c	243	26:3–5	77, 116, 118
24:26a	243	26:3–5, 14–16	116, 245
24:30	216	26:3–5, 14–16, 47–66	103
24:38	263	26:4	55n29, 67n19, 73n37, 76, 77, 94, 100, 100n51, 102, 103, 108n81, 116, 212, 227, 227n18, 230n28, 232
24:40	259		
24:41	251, 259		
24:42, 43, 46	215n80		
25:1, 7, 11	249		
25:1, 34	86n1	26:4, 48, 50, 55, 57	106n65, 228n22
25:1–13	249n5, 251, 259	26:4, 55	117
25:2	133	26:4, 59	102
25:5b	94	26:4a	72
25:7	251	26:5	67n11, 76, 94n41, 96n46, 211, 232
25:9–10	251	26:5a	94
25:10, 19, 27	215n80	26:6–13	251
25:26	269n15	26:7	236, 251, 260
25:31	215n80, 216	26:8–9	251, 260
25:31–46	64, 216, 259	26:10	251
25:32	82, 216	26:10–12	260
25:34	162, 283	26:12	212, 236, 260
25:34, 40	133	26:12, 13	239n48
25:37, 46	269n14	26:13	217, 260, 281, 282, 283
25:41	5n6, 270	26:13a	248n1
25:44, DJW	259	26:14, 57, 59	54n28
25:59	228	26:14–16	xviii, 77, 79, 92, 102, 103, 116, 233
26:1	213n67		
26:1–2	116, 181, 184, 225n6, 280		
26:1—27:54	121		
26:1—28:20	224n4, 260		
26:2	15, 78, 108n85, 117, 212, 219, 230n30		

Matthew (continued)

26:15, 16	79
26:15, 16, 48	15n38, 106
26:15, 16, DJW	55n29
26:15, DJW	260
26:15a	233
26:15b	73, 233
26:15c	233
26:16	233
26:17	67n10
26:18	79n52
26:21–25	15n35
26:24	210
26:26	213
26:27–28	69
26:28	68, 71n31, 71n33, 72, 79, 79n53, 82, 83, 84, 213, 226, 230
26:28a	70
26:28b	68, 70
26:29	86n1
26:31	82, 212, 218
26:31, 33	235n42
26:32	215n77
26:33, 35	235n42
26:34	239n47
26:36	103
26:36–46	15n41
26:37	236
26:38	212n66, 213, 236
26:38, 40, 41	236n43
26:38, DJW	236
26:39	236
26:39, 42	6, 82, 212, 213, 226
26:39, 42, 44	219
26:39a, 42a	241
26:39b, 42b	241
26:40	7n11
26:40, 41	236
26:40, 43, 45	236n43, 243n62
26:40b-41	243
26:41	213
26:41, alt	6, 7
26:43	7n11
26:44	82, 213, 241
26:45	7n11, 15
26:46	15n35, 213
26:46–56	213
26:47	39n37, 55n29, 74, 107n72, 228
26:47, 55	184, 260
26:47–49	117, 121
26:47–56	103
26:47b	214, 214n72
26:48	55n29, 214
26:48, 50, 57	214
26:49, 50	55n29, 107n70, 213, 214, 228
26:50	184
26:50a	74, 134, 184, 213, 240n53, 243n62
26:51	184, 214
26:51–52	184, 189, 213, 247
26:52	16
26:52–54	240n53
26:52a	240n53
26:52b	46, 46n11, 52n23, 88n24, 134, 184, 213
26:53	214, 241
26:53–54	15n41, 184
26:54	67n9, 74, 74n39, 106n64, 212, 228
26:55	241
26:55–56	103
26:55a	103
26:55b	7, 67n16, 117, 200, 235n41, 235n42, 242n59, 243n62
26:56	261
26:56b	75, 104, 106n67, 134, 214, 228, 228n23
26:57	75
26:57, 62, 63, 65	55n29
26:57–64	117
26:57–66	101, 281
26:57–68	74
26:58	67n20, 74, 75, 76, 77, 104, 108n81, 111, 117, 214, 230, 233
26:59	213n71, 239n48
26:59, 60	100, 104
26:59–60	245
26:59–61	104n58
26:59a–60a	76, 77, 104, 228
26:60	214n75
26:60–61, 63a	

Scripture Index   323

26:60b	104n58	27:1, 7	73n37, 76, 100
26:60c–63a	104, 104n58	27:1, 11, 20, 26, 27	40
26:61	67n9, 74, 81	27:1, 20	55
26:62	213n71, 214, 226n13	27:1–2	38, 88, 103, 105, 116, 118
26:62, 63, 68	213n70	27:1–2, 11–26, 62–66	260
26:63	20n44, 20n50, 55n30, 117, 133, 134, 135n13, 213, 238, 239n48, 281	27:1–2, 11–27	91
		27:1–2, 11–37	89, 263, 283
		27:1–2, 11–38, 54, 62–66	38
26:63, 65–68	55	27:1–2, 11–54	64, 244
26:63, 68	135n11, 281	27:1–2, 11–54, 57–66	53
26:63–64	59, 231	27:1–2, 12, 20	42
26:63–65	76	27:1–2, 15–26	102
26:63b	104	27:1–2, 20	116
26:64	134, 214, 238n46	27:1–2, 62–66	75
26:64a	104	27:1–2,11–38, 54, 62–66	xvi, 28
26:64b	104	27:1—28:15	38
26:65	104, 228	27:1–66	45, 45n3, 46
26:65–66	55n29, 75, 77, 78, 117, 231	27:2	39, 40, 49, 54, 55n29, 57n34, 78, 106, 107n71, 108n81, 214, 228, 228n23
26:66	67n20, 107, 213, 230, 246		
26:66b	104	27:2, 3, 4, 18	214n72
26:67	78, 107n75, 107n76, 107n77, 165n89, 180, 214, 225n8, 229, 238	27:2, 3, 4, 18, 26	227n20
		27:2, 4, 26	106n68
		27:2, 11, 14, 15, 21, 23, 27	88n21
26:67–68	55n29, 117, 118	27:2, 18	15n39, 49, 79n54
26:68	20n44, 78, 107, 107n77, 118, 228, 229	27:2, 18, 26	40
		27:2, 31	40, 106n67, 214, 228
		27:2–66	49
26:69, 71	260	27:3	73, 213, 230
26:69–75	7, 239n47, 242n59, 243n62	27:3, 4	15n38, 57n34, 79n54
		27:3–4	227, 260
26:70, 72	239n47, 260	27:3–4, 19, 23	111
26:70, 72, 74	261	27:3–4, 41–46	119
26:71	279	27:3–4a	76, 105, 110
26:74	239n47	27:3–4a, 5	79
26:75	261	27:3–5	73n37
27:1	39, 40, 55n29, 57n34, 67n20, 74, 75, 76, 100n51, 108n81, 212, 213, 214, 230	27:3–10	xviii, 69, 94, 233
		27:3a	79
		27:3b	79, 110
		27:3c	80
27:1, 3, 6, 12, 20, 41, 62	67n6, 87n9, 270n19	27:4	71, 77, 83, 106n63, 109n91, 230n26, 232
27:1, 3, 12, 20, 41	67n7, 75, 87n8, 270n20	27:4, 6	72
		27:4a	69, 80
27:1, 3, 20	54	27:4b	79, 80, 105

Matthew (continued)

27:5	100n51
27:5, 40, 51	67n9
27:5a	94, 260
27:5b	261
27:6	67n14, 70, 71, 73n37, 76, 77, 83, 84, 94, 94n42, 100n51, 227, 260
27:6, 24, 25	109n91
27:6, 41, 62	54n28
27:6-7	76
27:6b	81
27:7	100n51
27:7-8	95
27:7-10	77
27:9	200n7
27:9, 35	67n16
27:11	20n47, 40, 49, 55n30, 57, 134, 213, 214
27:11, 13, 29, 40, 41	213n70
27:11, 13-14	39-40
27:11, 14, 15, 21	39
27:11, 14, 15, 21, 27	49
27:11, 17, 22	133
27:11, 28-29, 37	281
27:11, 29, 37	135n12
27:11, 37	48
27:11-14	184
27:11-14, 17, 22	55
27:11-15	227n19
27:11-26	103, 281
27:11-26a	117
27:11-37	87n3
27:11a	40, 50
27:11b	40
27:11b, 13-14	50
27:12	134, 213, 228
27:12, 13	40, 50
27:12, 14	54, 239n48
27:12, 14a	214n75
27:12-13	39, 75
27:12-14	54, 245
27:13	40, 54, 213n71, 226n13, 228
27:13, 14b	214
27:13, 17, 22, 24, 58, 62, 65	49
27:13, 17, 22, 24, 62, 65	39
27:14	54, 134
27:15	41, 54, 56, 57n34, 67n11, 93, 105, 113
27:15, 16	228
27:15, 17	39
27:15, 17, 21	105
27:15, 17, 21, 26	50
27:15-16	50
27:15-18	117
27:15-18, 19, 21-23	55
27:15-26	111
27:15b	95
27:16	41, 56n33, 106
27:16, 17a, 20a, 21	105
27:17	40, 41, 56, 260
27:17, 21	54
27:17, 21-23	54
27:17, 22	20n44, 40, 48, 55n30, 135n11, 281
27:17, 62	76
27:17-18, 20-24a	55
27:17-20, 21a-b, 22a-b, 23a-b	41
27:17a	93
27:18	41, 55n31, 56, 56n33, 57n34, 95, 105, 113, 227, 232n35, 233, 260
27:18, 19	57
27:18, 19, 23	54, 64, 232
27:18, 19, 23, 24-26	119
27:19	39, 40, 41, 42, 45, 49, 50, 55, 56, 59, 65, 102, 105, 232n35, 243n61, 248n5, 250, 250n8, 251, 260
27:19, 23	105
27:19, 24	269n14
27:19, DJW	55, 55n31, 56, 56n33
27:19a	51
27:19a, 23a	113
27:19b	96n47, 260
27:19b, DJW	95
27:19c	260
27:19d	260

Scripture Index 325

27:20	39, 40, 50, 54, 55, 55n31, 67n18, 92, 97, 102, 105, 111, 114, 214, 227, 230	27:26, 35	246
		27:26–38	48
		27:26a	41, 47, 50, 91, 106
		27:26b	42, 48, 50, 57, 91
27:20, 21	39	27:26b-31	117
27:20, 22, 23	39	27:26c	106
27:20, 41–43	81	27:27	40, 46, 48, 59, 88n23, 88n25, 214, 229
27:20–23	69n26, 113, 117, 245		
27:20–23, 24–25	60n41	27:27–29	59
27:20–23, 25	113	27:27–31	40, 107, 233, 281
27:20b, 22–23	105	27:27–31, 35	225n8
27:21	39, 41	27:27–38, 51–54	47
27:22	40, 213n69	27:27–53	59
27:22, 23	39, 55n31	27:27–54	45
27:22, 23, 25	246	27:27–66	46
27:22, 23, 26, 31	40	27:27a	50
27:22, 23, 26, 31, 35	78, 214n73	27:27b	49
27:22, 23, 26, 31, 35, 38	108n85, 230n30	27:28	40, 48, 90n29, 229
		27:28, 31	40, 48, 107, 214, 229
27:22, 23, 26, 31, 35, 38, 44	50	27:28–29	107, 233
27:22–23	95	27:28–30	118
27:23	40, 41, 55n31, 56, 56n33, 57, 96, 98, 106n63, 227, 232n35, 260	27:28–31	20n47
		27:29	40, 48, 90, 214, 229
		27:29, 31	40, 48, 78, 228
		27:29, 31, 41	107n73, 214
27:23a	96, 97, 98	27:29, 37	40, 214
27:23b	41, 98, 98n49	27:29, 41–43	118
27:23b–24a	98	27:29, 42	118
27:24	40, 41, 55n31, 56n33, 64, 69n26, 113, 227, 260	27:29–30	233
		27:29a	90n29
		27:29b	90n29
27:24, 25	230	27:29c	90n29, 107
27:24–25	113	27:30	40, 48, 59, 107n75, 107n77, 214, 229
27:24–26	55, 64, 116, 117		
27:24a	56, 96, 98, 105, 106, 232	27:31	40, 59, 107, 214, 229
		27:31, 35	59
27:24b	54, 56, 106, 232	27:31b–38	40, 119
27:24b–26	98	27:32	47, 92, 166n92, 180, 218, 229, 230, 263
27:24c	56		
27:24d	56	27:32, 38, 44	214n73
27:25a	56	27:32, 40, 42	108n85, 230n31
27:25b	57	27:32–38	118
27:26	15n40, 40, 47, 50n18, 56n33, 57n34, 59, 78, 79n54, 96, 105, 107n80, 214, 229, 232, 245, 260	27:32–50	281
		27:34	134, 214, 214n74
		27:35	40, 47, 214, 229
		27:36	214
		27:36, 51–54	48
27:26, 31–38	47	27:36, 54	47

Matthew (continued)

27:37	20n47, 40, 48, 55n30
27:37, 40, 42, 43	133
27:38	57, 78
27:39	214, 228, 229, 243
27:39–40	134
27:40	74, 81, 228, 241
27:40, 42	241
27:40, 42–43	6, 184
27:40, 43	20n50, 60n40, 281
27:40, 43, 54	117
27:40, 54	135n13
27:40a	110
27:40a, 42a	241n57
27:41	67n5, 75, 78, 87n10, 228, 269n18
27:42	20n48, 64, 135, 241, 243, 281
27:42, 44	243
27:42–43	78, 107, 228, 281
27:42a	110, 134
27:42b	110
27:42b–43	134
27:43	59, 118
27:43b	110
27:44	108n85, 214, 226n12, 243
27:45	236
27:46	110, 214
27:46, 50	134
27:48	214n74
27:50	6, 134, 213, 214, 236
27:50b	184
27:51	59, 71, 71n34, 74, 79, 82
27:51–53	246
27:51–54	21, 45, 64, 134
27:51a	81, 82, 282
27:51b	282
27:51c	282
27:52	59
27:52a	282
27:52b	282
27:53	74, 263, 270
27:53, 64	215n77
27:54	20n50, 46, 46n9, 48, 59, 65, 88n22, 88n26, 133
27:55	251, 252, 259
27:55, DJW	259, 260
27:55–56	251n15, 252, 257, 259, 260
27:55–56, 61	260n23
27:55–61	260n23
27:56	250n9
27:57	76
27:57–58	49
27:57–59	57, 77
27:57–60	260n23
27:58	49, 57
27:59	102, 215
27:60	61
27:61	260
27:62	49, 67n3, 75, 76, 87n6, 88, 269n16
27:62—28:20	185
27:62–64	39, 42, 60
27:62–66	45, 47, 49, 55, 60, 64, 75, 78, 113, 215, 227n19, 245
27:63	39, 40, 42, 49, 53, 215n77, 228
27:63, 64	246
27:63–64	60, 62
27:64	45n5, 49, 60, 61, 215, 229, 245, 247
27:64, 65, 66	57, 60–61, 61
27:64, 66	60
27:64–65	57
27:65	45n5, 60, 75
27:65, 66	47, 60
27:66	57, 61, 118, 215
27:67	229
27:69, 71	251
28:1	252, 261
28:1–4	118
28:1–6	247
28:1–10	134
28:1–10, 16–20	118, 119
28:1–11	102
28:1–11a	251n15
28:1–15	28, 38
28:1–20	121, 253

Scripture Index 327

28:2	118, 215, 282	28:14	39, 49, 55, 57, 62, 88n21, 113, 245
28:2, DJW	261, 282	28:14, DJW	98
28:2–3, 5–7	261	28:14a–c	102
28:2–4	64, 65	28:14b	39n37, 102
28:2–4, 11–15	60	28:15	61, 102
28:2a, DJW	61	28:15a	62, 100
28:2b	61	28:15b	62, 68, 100, 115, 116
28:3	61	28:16	217n84, 282
28:4	47, 60, 61, 61n45, 118, 215	28:16–17	209, 261
28:4a	261	28:16–20	62, 101n53, 199n1, 261, 282
28:4b	261	28:18	xxi, 53n25, 209, 215, 247, 282
28:5	108n85, 230n30	28:18–20	259
28:5, 8, 10	59	28:18b	63, 64
28:5–6	99	28:19	101n53, 116, 135, 216n83, 217, 222, 283
28:5–7	42, 61, 61n45	28:19–20	xxi, 63, 115, 221n94, 282
28:5a	61n45	28:19–20, DJW	282, 283
28:6	50, 215	28:20	5n9, 67, 215, 217, 221, 247, 282
28:6, 7	215n77, 247, 282	28:20b	83
28:7	261	28:63, 68	55n30
28:7, 8–10, 16–20	247	36:1	265
28:8	261	36:1, 7, 8	265
28:8–10	61, 261	36:1, 8, 9	265
28:10	261	36:1–3, 9a–b, 10–11, 22a–b, 28b–29, 34a–b	267n11
28:11	47, 55, 60, 61, 67n6, 75, 87n9, 99, 114, 261, 270n19	36:2a	266, 268
28:11–12	54	36:2b	266, 268
28:11–15	xvi, 45, 46, 47, 49, 53, 61, 64, 65, 75, 77, 78, 81, 86, 87, 87n5, 92, 99, 101, 115, 118, 119, 134, 215, 245	36:3	264, 265, 267, 268
		36:3, 5, 40	266, 268
		36:3, 9, 11, 22, 29, 34	267
28:12	61, 67n7, 73, 73n37, 75, 76, 77, 87n8, 88n23, 100, 100n51, 101n54, 270n20	36:4	266
		36:5	266
28:12–13	55, 60	36:6	266
28:12–13a	100	36:7	265, 266
28:12–14	42, 101	36:8	265
28:12–15	102, 114	36:9	264, 266
28:12–15a	115	36:9, 11, 22, 29	267, 268
28:12a	61	36:9, 11, 22, 29, 34	264, 267
28:12b	92, 102	36:9, 22, 28, 34	268
28:13	45n5, 61, 62	36:9, 22, 28, 34, 38a, 38b	266
28:13–14	215	36:9, 34	267, 268
28:13b	100, 102	36:10	266, 267, 268

Matthew (continued)

36:10, 12, 14, 16, 17, 20, 21, 32, 34, 40	265
36:10, 36	267
36:10a	266
36:10b	266
36:11	264, 266, 267, 268
36:12	265
36:12, 14, 32	268
36:12, 16, 17, 21, 25, 29, 30, 32, 39	265
36:13	266, 268
36:14	264
36:14a	265
36:14b	265
36:14c	265
36:14d	265
36:15a	266
36:15b	266
36:16	265
36:17	266
36:18	264, 266
36:18, 27, 29	268
36:19a	266
36:19b	266
36:20	265, 268
36:20a	266
36:20b	266
36:21	265
36:22	264, 265, 267
36:23	266
36:24	266
36:25	267
36:25, 26	265
36:25b	266
36:26	265
36:27	265
36:28	265, 266, 267, 268
36:29	267
36:30a	265
36:30b	265n10, 266
36:31	266
36:32	265
36:33	265, 267
36:34	266, 267, 268
36:35	265
36:36	267
36:36a	266
36:36b	266
36:37	265, 266
36:38	265
36:39	267
36:39a	267
36:39b	267
36:40a	267
36:40b	267
36:40c	267
36:40d	267
38:14	45n5

Mark

1:2–8	14
1:10–11	6
1:12–13	5
1:14	14
1:23–28	9n14
1:27	9
1:32	8n13, 12n27
1:32–34	9n20
1:34	10, 12n28
1:39	9n20
1:40–45 parr.	12
2:1–12 parr.	12
3:1–6	16
3:1–6 parr.	12
3:10	12n27
3:11–12	9n20, 10
3:13–15	10n21
3:15	10
3:19	15
3:27	9
5:1–20	9, 9n15
5:15, 16, 18	8n13
5:21–24, 35–43 parr.	12
5:25–34 parr.	12
5:30	12, 12n25
6:2, 5, 14	12n26
6:7	10
6:7–13	10n21
6:13	10, 12
6:14–29	14, 14n32, 90n28
6:17	14n31
6:17–18	14

6:44	257	15:26	20n47
6:56	12n27	15:29–30, 32	6
7:11	70	15:32	20n45, 20n48
7:24–30	9, 9n17	15:33 parr.	21
7:31–37	12	15:37	6
8:9	257	15:38	257
8:22–26	12	15:38 parr.	21
8:31–32	6	15:39	20n50
8:31–33	15n41		
8:33	6		
8:35	22		

Luke

9:14–29	9n18, 10, 10n22
9:31	15
9:38	10n22
10:6	5n4
10:33	15, 15n36
10:35–40	15n41
10:46–52 parr.	12
11:15–19	16
12:1–9	109n92
12:1–12	16
13:7	5n8
13:9–13	17
13:13	5n8
13:19	5n4
14:10, 11, 44	15n38
14:18–21	15n35
14:32–42	15n41
14:36	6
14:37	7n11
14:38	6, 7
14:40	7n11
14:41	7n11, 15
14:42	15n35
14:50	7
14:51–52	7
14:61	20n44, 20n49
14:65	165n89
14:66–72	7
15:1, 10	15n39
15:2	20n47
15:7	138
15:9	20n47
15:12	20n47
15:15	15n40
15:16–20	20n47
15:17, 20	90n29
15:21	166n92

1:5	30n20
2:1–2	30n20
3:1–18	14
3:10–20	14
3:19	14
3:19–20	14n31
3:21–22	6
4:1–2	5
4:3	6
4:3, 9	5
4:4, 8, 12	6
4:5–7	6
4:9–11	6
4:12–13	5n6
4:13	6
4:14	12
4:16–21	5n10
4:18–19	11
4:20	274
4:33–37	9n14
4:36	9
4:40	12n28
4:41	9n20, 10
5:17	12
6:6–11	16
6:18	9n20
6:19	12, 12n25
6:27–36	137n2, 141
7:11–17	12
7:18–19	14n31
7:21	9n20
8:1–3	9n19
8:26–39	9n15
8:36	8n13
8:46	12, 12n25
9:1	10, 12

Mark (continued)

9:1–6	10n21
9:6	12
9:7–9	14, 14n32
9:24	22
9:37–43	9n18, 10n22
9:37–43a	10
9:44	15
9:49	10n22
10:1–20	10n21
10:13	12n26
10:17	10
10:18	5, 5n6
10:19a	10
10:19b	10
10:20	10
11:4	7
11:14–15	9n16
11:20	5n10, 8
11:21–22	9, 11n23
11:21–22, alt	9
11:22	11
12:11	17
12:50	15n41
13:10–17	12
13:16	8, 12
13:31–33	15n41, 16
13:32	8
14:1–6	12
15:23, 27, 30	90n32
17:11–19	12
18:32	15, 15n36
19:37	12n26
19:45–48	16
20:9–20	16
20:20	15n39
21:9	5n8
21:12–19	17
22:4, 6, 48	15n38
22:4, 52	74n40
22:21–23	15n35
22:31–32	7
22:35, 37	6
22:38–46	15n41
22:40, 46	6, 7
22:42	6
22:45–46	7n11
22:48	15n35
22:49–51	16
22:50–51	12
22:54–62	7
22:67	20n44
22:70	20n50
23:3	20n47
23:19, 25	138
23:25	15n40
23:34	17
23:35	20n45, 20n46
23:37	20n47
23:38	20n47
23:39	20n44
23:42	20n47
23:46	6
24:7	15
24:20	15n39
24:26	21
24:49	12

John

1:29, 36	72n35
3:14	21
6:15	6
6:64, 71	15
8:5	108n82, 252n16
8:28	21
8:39, 42	183
9:1–41	12
10:17–18	15n41
10:21	8n13
11:1–44	12
11:45–57	16
12:23–24	21
12:23–25, 27–33	21
12:25	22
12:27	6, 15n41
12:31	5n6
12:31–32	21
12:33	21n51
12:34	21
13:2	15n38
13:11	15
13:21–30	15n35
15:21	17
16:33b	21
18:2, 5	15n38
18:10–11	16
18:11	15n41

Scripture Index 331

18:22	165n89
18:30	15n39
18:30, 35	15n36
18:33	20n47
18:35	15n39
18:36	16
18:36–37	20n47
18:39	20n47
19:1–15	20n47
19:3	165n89
19:7	20n50
19:10, 16	15n37
19:11	15n36, 15n37
19:16	15n40
19:19–22	20n47
19:30	6
19:31	72n35
21:20	15n35

Acts

1:8	12
2:22	12n26
2:33	21n51
3:8	13
3:12–13	15n39
3:12–16	13
4:8–10, 30	13
4:30	13
5:3	7
5:5, 10	7
5:12–16	10, 13
5:17–40	18
5:31	21n51
5:41	18
7:58–59	108n82
7:60	18
8:3	17
8:4–8	10
8:6–8	13
8:13	13
9:32–35	13
10:38	8, 11, 12
12:4	17
16:16–19	10
19:11	13
19:11, DJW	13
19:11–12	10, 13
19:40	138

21:8–10	17
21:11	17, 18
21:13	19
22:4	17
26:17–18	5n6
27:1	17
28:7–10	13

Romans

12:19	189
16:20	5n6

1 Corinthians

1:23–24	19
1:25	19
4:11–13	18
5:5	5
7:5	8
10:13, NIV, alt	8
11:23	15n42
12:7, 9	13
12:10	11
15:20–28	5n7

2 Corinthians

4:8–11, alt	18
11:14–15	5n5
12:12	13

Galatians

3:5	13
6:1	8

Ephesians

1:20–23	5n7
6:10–17	11
6:11	5n5
6:11, 13	11
6:12	11
6:13	11
6:14	11
6:15	11
6:16	11
6:17	11

Philippians

2:5–11	19
2:8	19
2:9	19, 21n51
2:10	19

Colossians

2:13–15, alt.	20

1 Thessalonians

1:9–10	5n7
3:5	8

2 Thessalonians

2:9–10	5n5

1 Timothy

6:9	7

Hebrews

2:14	5, 5n6
2:14–15	20
4:15, alt	7
9:26	5n9

James

1:12	8
1:14–15	7n12
4:7	xvii, 4, 5n6, 23

1 Peter

2:23	17
4:19	5n4
5:8	4, 5
5:8–9	4

1 John

3:9	5n6
4:1	11
4:2	11

Revelation

3:14	5n4
5:5	22
5:6	22
5:9–10	22
7:9–17	22
7:14	22
11:15b	4
11:15b, alt	23
12: 10, 12	5
12:7–12	5n6
12:9, 10	5n5
12:9, 13	5
12:10	22
12:10–12	22
12:11	22
12:12	5
17:3, 4	90n29
18:12, 16	90n29
20:1–3, 7–10	5n6
20:3, 7–8	5n5

APOCRYPHA

2 Macc

10:3	70

Josephus, Antiquities

4.8	168n96

TALMUD

Mishnah Baba Qamma

8.6	166n90, 168n96

www.ingramcontent.com/pod-product-compliance
Lightning Source LLC
Chambersburg PA
CBHW071151300426
44113CB00009B/1166